DAWN H. CURRIE

WITHDRAWN

'Girl Talk:
Adolescent Magazines and Their
Readers

UNIVERSITY OF TORONTO PRESS
Toronto Buffalo London

© University of Toronto Press Incorporated 1999
Toronto Buffalo London
Printed in Canada

ISBN 0-8020-4415-8 (cloth)
ISBN 0-8020-8217-3 (paper)

Printed on acid-free paper

Canadian Cataloguing in Publication Data

Currie, Dawn, 1948–
  Girl talk

  Includes bibliographical references and index.
  ISBN 0-8020-4415-8 (bound)
  ISBN 0-8020-8217-3 (pbk.)

  1. Youth's periodicals – United States.   2. Teenage girls – Books and
  reading.   3. Women's periodicals, American.   4. Sex role in mass media.
  5. Gender identity.   I. Title.

  PN4878.C87 1999   051'.0835'2   C98-932362-5

University of Toronto Press acknowledges the financial assistance to its publishing
program of the Canada Council for the Arts and the Ontario Arts Council.

This book has been pubished with the help of a grant from the Humanities and Social
Sciences Federation of Canada, using funds provided by the Social Sciences and
Humanities Research Council of Canada.

To Joan, Faye, Sara, and our mother – the most important women in my life

Contents

viii   Contents

Acknowledgments

Girl Talk took much longer to complete than I had initially planned. As a consequence, I find it difficult to remember everyone who helped along the way. I want to thank my friend and colleague, Valerie Raoul, who convinced me that adolescent magazines are, indeed, a legitimate venue for serious scholarly investigation. Without her encouragement I would not have applied for the Social Science and Humanities Research funding which made this project possible. The financial support of SSHRCC allowed me to involve a number of undergraduate and graduate students in the fieldwork. I am indebted to my research assistants, each of whom contributed to the completion of *Girl Talk*. Over the years they included Raewyn Bassett, Kerri-Lynn Bates, Shelley Budgeon, Jennifer Fenton, Susan Juby, Ann MacLean, Alissa Sacks, Jonna Semke, Nariko Takayanagi, and Sarah Wright. I also thank two of my previous graduate students who were hired on the project, Lisa Parsons and Rebecca Raby, as well as Theresa Harding and Larissa Petrillo for their library assistance in the final stages. Along the way, a number of friends and colleagues showed interest in my work by sharing relevant magazines, news items, and articles from everyday cultural venues that reminded me of the social significance of the research. I hope that these friends and colleagues will be gratified to learn how helpful their expressions of interest have been. At the institutional level, in addition to the support of SSHRCC for the fieldwork, my term as a UBC Scholar at the Centre for Research in Women's Studies and Gender Relations gave me time to pursue theoretical aspects of the work. I also acknowledge the financial assistance of the Canada Council for the Arts and the Ontario Arts Council which made publication of the manuscript with University of Toronto Press possible. Finally, I acknowledge the invisible labour of others that makes all academic publishing possible, including that of anonymous reviewers and the staff at University of Toronto Press. In my case, I am particularly grateful to Virgil Duff, for his support of this project, and Beverley Beetham Endersby, for her fastidious editorial work, and Anne Forte, for ushering this project through the final stages of production. Last but not least, I especially thank Brian for his intellectual stimulation and moral support over the many years of the project.

GIRL TALK:
ADOLESCENT MAGAZINES AND THEIR READERS

'Girls Doing Girl Things': A Study of Girls Becoming Women

I read *Seventeen* magazine and like that's mostly how I got to do *all* my make-up, just from looking at magazines, looking at models, and seeing how they're doing it. Like I'd sit for two hours doing my make-up for something to do. It was fun. (Seventeen-year-old Margaret describing how she started using make-up)

I guess it was kind of fun [wearing make-up]. I was into the 'girls' scene,' like you know, in Grade 7 you got your girlfriends and the guys are kind of there [laughs] and it's girls doing girl things, and make-up just happened to be one of those girl things. It was fun. It was fun wearing eyeliner and mascara. (Nineteen-year-old Pauline remembering when she started wearing make-up)

This book is about the activities of Margaret and Pauline: it explores young women's development of gendered identities, and the place of fashion and beauty magazines in this process. 'Gendering' as a concept draws attention to de Beauvoir's dictum that 'one is not born, but rather becomes a woman' (1961: 9). The implication of her claim is that our core identities are social projects, not biological destiny. As commonplace as this claim appears today, before the emergence of feminist studies little attention was paid to the fact that being women or men is a product of how we orient ourselves in the everyday social world. In Western cultures gendered identity influences our expectations about ourselves, others, and women's place on the stage of world history. While de Beauvoir challenged us to think about gender as a cultural construct and, therefore, as an arena of political struggle, we are only just beginning to unravel the complexities of the relationship between patriarchal culture and our embodiment as 'women.' *Girl Talk* is a contribution to feminist theory and politics, which take this complexity as their problematic.

Emphasizing the cultural rather than biological dictates of womanhood, early sex-role theories which dominated feminist sociology took the position that women, as readers of social texts such as magazines and television, internalize messages which are presented as 'scripts' of femininity. While virtually all cultures include different scripts for women and men, from the nineteenth century until the 'liberation' of women in the 1970s, Western cultures mandated femininity as the pursuit of physical beauty, in opposition to intellectual development. By internalizing this gender script, women place limitations upon themselves, often unconsciously (Waters 1986). However mundane the activity of applying make-up appears to be, it engages women in the everyday reconstitution of their gendered identity. This engagement naturalizes cultural prescriptions of femininity, and therefore obscures patriarchal relations of domination and subordination on the basis of gender, but also race and class.[1]

Ferguson (1983) describes the gender scripts in women's magazines as constructing a 'cult of femininity.' So persistent is their promotion of traditional femininity that Reed (1986) calls women's magazines a 'huge propaganda machine.' Along these lines, Wolf (1991) associates contemporary images in women's magazines with a backlash against women's liberation (see also Faludi 1991). She argues that women's magazines, which have proliferated during the past century, perpetuate a 'beauty myth.' By 'myth' she means the belief that every woman can achieve idealized femininity through the proper regimes of dress, diet, exercise, skin care, and surgery – preoccupations which deflect women from the political goal of women's liberation. As commonsensical as this line of reasoning may appear to be, social scientists have not been able to causally link activities like magazine reading to participation in the beauty rituals described by Mararget and Pauline. One purpose of this book is to explore why this may be the case.

As recent gender theorists note, identities can never be contained in any one moment or place, although they can be made to appear at what Probyn (1993: 167) calls 'certain intersections.' As constructs, gendered identities are constantly being re-enacted through practices that express a continual process of becoming as well as being. Against sex-role theory, this position is based on the active negotiation of gendered identity: women make conscious decisions to wear (or not wear) make-up, thoughtfully choose the wardrobes through which they make their public presence, and so on. Going further, Butler (1990a: x) draws on the instability and negotiation of gender identity as an opportunity to denaturalize and resignify bodily categories through what she calls 'parodic practices'; practices which parody the *idea* of the natural and the original (p. 31). Against the view of gender construction as constitutive constraint, she argues that the normative scripts of gender produce not only dominant definitions, but also unthinkable, abject, unlivable bodies (1993: xi). By 'unlivable' she does not mean merely the opposite of what has come be thought of as 'normal' gender: this position simply replaces traditional femininity with versions of its masculine counterpart. While such an inversion has been endorsed among some sections of the feminist movement, its successful promotion in popular films – such as *Aliens* and *Sheena* – about 'liberated' women testify to its failure to disrupt gender categories. Butler wants us to go beyond such inversion in order to explore the potential for new modes of identity. Because she draws on performance theory, some commentators accuse her of viewing gender as something which we consciously adopt at will. For them, the notion of performance implies that the activites of Margaret and Pauline should be considered experiments in gender 'play' rather than re-enactments of women's subordination (see Pleasance 1991).

Clearly, these competing positions are important, because they direct us to entirely different politics surrounding cosmetics and fashion. One purpose of *Girl Talk* is to engage in current controversies surrounding women's everyday gender practices, although I hardly claim to resolve them once and for all. However, I draw attention to the fact that although the everyday practices of femininity are played out on women's bodies, and thus are central to theorizing about identity, they are also about much more than is often included in 'gender theory.' Specifically, our participation in beauty rituals is an economic as well as cultural phenomenon because it engages us in commodity consumption. As a consequence, gendered identities cannot be studied apart from the huge 'culture industry' that provides many of our everyday understandings of 'gender.' From this perspective the growing interest in cultural studies promises to offer fresh insights into the relationship between magazine reading, gender identity, and women's social status. As we shall see, however, it is my conviction that consumption as an economic activity is depoliticized in much current theorizing in cultural studies. I have in mind Fiske's (1989a: 14) celebration of shopping as the 'crisis of consumerism,' where 'the art and tricks of the weak can inflict most damage on, and exert most power over, the strategic interests of the powerful.' By 'tricks' he means the ways in which consumers can, and often will, employ the meanings of commodified culture as well as material commodities to create new, subversive meanings. Fiske claims that 'in the same way that language need not be used to maintain the social relations that produced it, so too commodities need not be used to support the economic system of capitalism.' Consumption offers a means of controlling to some extent the context of everyday life, given that conscious meaning in most people's lives now comes from what they consume rather than what they produce (pp. 24, 25). Thus, Fiske maintains that, until the revolution comes, the Left does not help its cause by discounting or ignoring the 'art of making do,' the everyday practices by which people in subordinated social formations win tricks against the system. At the very least, such tricks are tactical victories that maintain the morale of the subordinate, and may well produce real gains in their cultural and social experience (p. 32). While I do not intend to overstate Fiske's position, it is important because it reappears in feminist writing about the pleasures which commodity consumption brings to many women's lives. Iris Young, for example, views the female pastime of shopping as a pleasurable opportunity for women to bond:

Many a lunch hour is spent with women in twos and threes circulating through Filene's Basement, picking hangers off the racks and together entering the mirror-walled common dressing room. There they chat to one another about their lives and self-images as they try on outfits ... Women take care of one another in the dressing room, often knowing when to be critical and discouraging and when to encourage a risky choice or an added expense. Women buy often enough on these expeditions, but often they walk out of the store after an hour of dressing up with no parcels at all; the pleasure was in the choosing, trying, and talking, a mundane shared fantasy. (1990: 184)

While I am sympathetic to attempts to restore dignity to the everyday practices that, in the past, have been equated with false consciousness by elite academics, I am reluctant to elevate these activities to guerrilla warfare in a new politics of consumption. At a time when even the Left has embraced the celebration of consumption as a form of resistance by the subordinated, it seems appropriate to explore the popular pleasures of consumption as a serious arena of critical feminist analysis.

The surge of interest in 'leisure' and 'consumption' as new sites of struggle and resistance coincides with the emergence of feminist cultural studies. While it is not entirely clear just what *feminist* cultural studies entails (see Franklin, Lury, and Stacey 1991; Walters 1995), one theme is the redemption of women-centred media such as soap operas, romance fiction, and fashion magazines as venues of female pleasure and resistance (see Mattelart 1986; Brown 1990). This redemption challenges a tradition of feminist critique, especially by Marxist feminists, that links these commercial media to women's oppression. Within this tradition, resistance to patriarchal capitalism necessarily implies a rejection of patriarchal culture. Within cultural studies, commentators suggest that the pleasures rather than evils of cultural consumption are central to the formulation of feminist cultural politics. This reformulation of current cultural politics requires that feminists break with the paternalism of an outdated position which maintains that women are passive victims of deceptive messages of mass media and it totally disregards the pleasures that these venues provide. Ang (1985), like others, advances this position by arguing that fantasy and fiction do not function in the place of, but instead beside, other dimensions of life: fantasy is a source of pleasure because it puts 'reality' in parenthesis (p. 135). Unlike Marxists, Ang suggests that the pleasures of ideological representation do not necessarily correspond to their 'function.' While I agree with her complaint that the tendency to draw distinctions between feminism and the consumption of mass culture sets up a feminist politics of 'them' and 'us,' I also agree with McRobbie's observation (1991b: 7) that the issue of pleasure, connected with consumerism, was 'drawn into a political vocabulary as feminists and gay men attempted to theorize those experiences which they enjoyed, even though orthodox left opinion seemed to disapprove. In both cases consumer goods had a role to play in the insistence that "guilty pleasure" could be used as part of a process of self- and collective empowerment.' In other words, one of the problems is that this position, which advances consumption as political resistance, is rooted in a specific set of practices: those of middle-aged activists/academics. I have in mind Winship's (1987: xiii)[2] guilt-ridden confession of being a closet reader of women's magazines, a position which informs her research interests: 'Whether feminist friends voiced it or not I felt they were thinking that if I really had to do research ... I should do it on something more important politically: "Surely we all know women's magazines demean women and solely benefit capitalist profits. What more is there to say?"' (p. xiii).

My research on women's magazines began with many of the concerns shared by critics and supporters of commercial media for women. Like Wilson, Winship, and others who confess to the unfeminist pastime of at least occasional magazine reading, I find fashion and beauty magazines a pleasurable venue and an escape from my otherwise neglectful approach to everyday appearance. However, I am also old enough to have experienced a brief respite from the beauty mandate; however brief, the women's movement of the 1960s and 1970s challenged patriarchal proscriptions which characterize the fashion and beauty industry. Given that there has been a documented resurgence of the beauty standard since about the middle of the 1980s, I am curious about claims that women themselves are 'returning' to these proscriptions. My everyday encounter with this resurgence has not been through reading magazines, however, but rather insistence by young female students that the sexualized representations and expressions of femininity in contemporary magazines embody a new wave of women's emancipation. Without trying to induce a moral panic, like Barker (1992) I am interested in asking how the existence of multibillion-dollar industries promoting fashion and beauty links young women's desires to cultural representations of femininity. In a purely journalistic vein, Barker links the success of the $40-billion diet industry to advertising; because of its glamorized images of thin, young women – many of whom themselves confess to years of struggle with anorexia and bulimia (see *People* 17 Feb. 1992: 92) – she claims that advertising capitalizes on young girls' lack of confidence. More provocative, however, is her observation that 'despite all the progress made by feminism, the women who should be their role models do the same thing.' As she notes, 'young girls aren't putting up pictures of Roberta Bondar or Barbara McDougall in their lockers. Most of them don't even know who these women are. Their role models are Madonna and Cindy Crawford, or the cast of *Beverly Hills 90210* ... What has the women's movement really accomplished when an 11-year-old girl watches Cindy Crawford on the new Pepsi commercial and decides that, instead of being a dentist, she wants to be a model?' (1992). While it might be claimed that Barker thinks too little of young women or too much of feminism, in my opinion there is truth in her claim that feminism has paid insufficient attention to the experiences and desires of young women. I am also disturbed that so few college women consider themselves to be feminist.[3] Perhaps out of guilt as much as curiosity, I began to research the ways in which fashion and beauty magazines, as a popular reading medium for young women, present messages of feminism and femininity (which I once believed to be oppositional). Through funding from the Social Sciences and Humanities Research Council of Canada I was able to extend this activity into a two-part study which explores the contents of adolescent fashion magazines popular in North America and interviews girls between the ages of ten and seventeen years about their reading of these magazines. By locating magazine reading in the context of school culture, the girls' activities provide a glimpse of the everyday 'doing' of gender. *Girl Talk* is an account of this research.

While many of the comments by Barker are substantiated by the current study – for example, a number of girls in my sample *did* want to be like Madonna – the more questions I asked, the more that were raised; the further the research progressed, the more it questioned the tenets of sociological inquiry. In the final analysis, I hope that the work discussed in this book sheds light on complexities surrounding both the status of women's magazines in the lives of young women, and sociological inquiry into everyday practices surrounding identity formation. In order to engage in popular debate, I have written for an audience that may have little background in cultural theory; however, in order to engage scholars in the field of women's studies, I address methodological and epistemological issues concerning the social-scientific study of women's lives. In order to consider the latter, we need to begin by reframing political controversies as analytical debate.

From the Polemics of Debate to Social-Science Research

Girl Talk: Adolescent Magazines and Their Readers explores the current tension between an analysis of magazines as 'the purveyor of pernicious ideology to be condemned' and their analysis as a venue of woman-centred pleasure to be embraced (see Ballaster et al. 1991: 4). In order to do so, disagreement over the moral position of feminism on magazine consumption needs to be reframed as analytical debate. For sake of clarity, I characterize analytical debate as situated in one of two theoretical traditions which dominate feminist thought on the matter. Based on the humanism of traditional sociological inquiry, within the first tradition feminists continue to find women's magazines problematic because they claim that these texts work to reconstitute women's oppression. For liberal feminists, women's magazines are among the texts through which women learn to conform to patriarchal definitions and standards of femininity. While liberal feminists seldom connect problematic images to the conditions and relations of their production, Marxist feminists argue that commercial culture necessarily expresses the interests of the dominant economic class. Hansen and Reed (1986) trace this latter position in North America to a series of articles appearing in publications by the Socialist Workers' Party during 1954. Carried into feminist debate in the early years of second-wave feminism, this line of argumentation draws on dominant sociological views of power, agency, and the nature of social life. On the other hand, feminists working to reclaim women's magazines as a legitimate arena of women's fantasy and pleasure follow more recent theories of cultural representation, within which meanings are polysemic, unstable, and subject to subversive appropriation. In this view, women are not simply 'dupes' of capitalism; they actively negotiate meanings in their everyday lives, often in opposition to patriarchy and capitalism. The simple act of taking pleasure through a female-centred venue itself resists patriarchal prescriptions of a self-abnegating and passive femininity. This position often draws on Foucauldian notions of power, and post-structuralist views of human subjects and the discursively constructed nature of both Self and 'the social.'

Characterized in this way, analytical debates surrounding women's magazines re-enact Stuart Hall's (1980) paradigms of cultural studies: one which concerns itself with the production and reception of texts as sociological phenomena, and one in which the text is primarily an effect of the relation between text and reader. Along these lines debates also re-enact disciplinary boundary-marking and hostility which Angela McRobbie finds 'disappointingly commonplace' over the past few years. Within this boundary-marking, 'cultural studies has been characterized as excessively concerned with texts and meanings and has been seen by many sociologists as lacking in methodological rigour. Sociology in turn is often regarded in cultural studies as being interested in questions which cannot be contained within the existing language of 1970s Marxist/feminist theory. Cultural studies flaunts its wild style while sociology prides itself on its material steadfastness' (1996: 30). In order to transcend this impasse, McRobbie argues for a research mode which prioritizes multiple levels of experience, including the ongoing relations which connect everyday life with cultural forms. Such research must foreground how difference, subjectivity, and pleasure fit into the landscape of everyday social relations. As phenomena not ordinarily included in sociological study, they push the social sciences into terrain historically occupied by the arts and literary criticism. This foray challenges the material steadfastness of conventional sociological inquiry. According to Michèle Barrett, one result has been the eclipse of sociology as we (currently) know it:

academically, the social sciences have lost purchase within feminism and the rising star lies with the arts, humanities and philosophy. Within this general shift we can see a marked interest in analyzing processes of symbolization and representation – the field of 'culture' – and attempts to develop a better understanding of subjectivity, the psyche and the self. The type of feminist sociology that has a wider audience, for example, has shifted away from a determinist model of 'social structure' (be it capitalism, or patriarchy, or a gender-segmented labour market or whatever) and deals with questions of culture, sexuality or political agency – obvious counterbalances to an emphasis on social structure. (1992: 204)

While Barrett goes on to note that the implications of this new emphasis are not yet clear, she maintains that it will not be enough to simply shift attention from one direction to another, or to apply the critical tools of one discipline to another's traditional subject matter. In the final analysis both the subject matter of sociology and its methods of inquiry need to be critically rethought.

Girl Talk engages in the kind of rethinking of sociology which both McRobbie and Barrett suggest are required for research that can account for the everyday, experienced worlds of women. As we shall see, I do not simply question what sociology can learn from the humanities, but also what literary and cultural critics might take from sociology.[4] Also considering the ways in which cultural studies can, potentially, move feminism beyond social-structuralist accounts of human agency, Lury (1995: 41) warns of an emerging cultural essentialism. By this she means the tendency for culture to become a totalizing explanatory force which is all-powerful and elusive. While much feminist discourse no longer attempts to evoke a falsely universalizing 'woman' who stands outside cultural representation, a focus on 'feminine identity' as a cultural construct works to displace embodied women with hypothetical Subjects who exist entirely within feminist discourse. This problem is taken up throughout *Girl Talk*, where it is analysed as an effect of conflating the cultural and the social dimensions of human life. In the current study, conflation of the cultural and social occurs when cultural critics and sociologists alike read social life off texts. As we shall see in chapter 1, feminists often make claims about the everyday effects of cultural representations through academic readings of magazine texts. In doing so they treat systems of signification (such as language, texts, and discourse) as reflections of 'society' as our 'real' object of interest. While literary critics draw attention to these systems as constitutive of social life, they only make matters worse if they replace an investigation of the social with the study of cultural objects. Clearly, what keeps sociologists and post-structuralist literary critics apart is disagreement over the 'reality' of social life. Thus the epistemological dilemma to be worked through is whether we can draw upon post-structural insight into the textual nature of social life without extending it to the textual nature of research. As sociologists interested in culture, can we continue to maintain a clear distinction between the cultural and the social, between cultural production and sociological 'knowledge'?

Because this question arose as a practical rather than theoretical dilemma in the current research, it is taken up later in this book. Here it seems necessary to point out that, although exploring the power of social texts through literary theories of signification, throughout *Girl Talk* I maintain a distinction between 'the cultural' and 'the social.' While the former refers to the products and practices which engage us in meaning-making, the latter refers to the everyday organization of people and resources necessary for meaning-making to be possible. The former is an easily observable aspect of everyday life; the latter occurs at a level and in a manner typically hidden from everyday consciousness. One conceptual tool that helps sociologists to explore the interconnectedness of these two distinct realms is 'discourse.' Throughout this book, 'discourse' refers to the everyday spoken, written, and bodily texts which comprise a shared system of meaning because they have as their reference a common object of analysis. Discourses frame a certain mode of thinking and being by deploying a system of (relatively) stable and coherent concepts (see Smart 1985: 39). A discourse both defines and is used by a socially constituted group of speakers because it provides the semantic, aesthetic, and ideological terms of reference which make a social world possible. It provides what is discussed in chapter 4 as a 'frame of intelligibility,' or way of knowing. In a narrow sense, many writers treat the written texts of fashion and beauty magazines as discourse. However, in this study we are not interested in magazines as isolated cultural objects: we want to know how the meanings in fashion and beauty magazines are taken up by readers. From this perspective, women's magazines are texts that form the basis for a discourse which includes in its frame of intelligibility embodied expressions of femininity. Approached in this way, discourse includes more than the magazine texts themselves, because it includes the ways in which magazines are read and their meanings are taken up as everyday practice. In our study of reading magazines, discourse includes the embodied 'doing' of femininity.[5] Thus *Girl Talk* draws on Smith's (1988, 1990a) notion of women's magazines as texts which mediate the everyday discourses of femininity; our study of 'discourse' treats the text as process rather than a 'thing' in itself.

As *social* texts, women's magazines organize our ways of thinking about femininity and acting as 'women'; they encode an 'ensemble of rules according to which the true and the false are separated and specific effects of power attached to the true' (Gordon 1980: 132). This is not to say that readers of women's magazines slavishly follow magazine prescriptions. Rather, it draws attention to the fact that whatever our personal commitment to femininity may be, it will be read (by self and others) against the dominant (and sometimes contradictory) categories which claim to express the 'truth' of womanhood. This Foucauldian approach thus takes us beyond debates about whether texts, such as women's magazines, *reflect* a truth about the social world which the researcher can access entirely from the text. It directs us to the study of how certain texts, such as women's magazines, claim to speak to the 'Truth' of our being. As social texts, magazines make particular constructions of what it means 'to be a woman' possible by providing the logic and the 'rules' about what can be said and done (and therefore what is left unspoken and undone). Social texts mediate a cultural realm inhabited by hypothetical feminine Subjects and a realm of embodied women as magazine readers: in other words, as texts women's magazines orchestrate the relationship between the cultural and the lived aspects of 'being a woman.' Whether or not this orchestration is successful is another matter. In the final analysis, the nature of the interconnectedness of the cultural and the social as everyday practice is an empirical and not theoretical question. It also reminds us that textual representations can never fully capture social life as lived relations. Experience always exceeds accounts provided by social texts such as women's magazines (or women's studies textbooks) which confront readers as already accomplished systems of meaning. This already accomplished system of meaning offers an objectified account of social life, what Smith (1987) refers to as 'objectified knowledge.' In this context the term 'objectified' does not refer to these representations as material objects, to 'magazines' as cultural artefacts. Rather, it points to the social relations of their production. Readers are not engaged in the production of the classifications and labels employed in their magazines, even though readers' participation is discursively evoked. In fact, very few of us actively engage in the production of those accounts of the social world which confront us as official, or 'Truthful' representations of social life; magazine accounts are no different. My original intention was to include an analysis of the material production as well as cultural consumption of adolescent magazines, because the production of women's magazines highlights an economic aspect of social life missing from much commentary on fashion and beauty. Regrettably, this exploration is an entirely separate project awaiting future research. The current study by necessity limits analysis of adolescent magazines to their reading, although the concluding chapter identifies the economic production of women's magazines as a latent subtext of their sociological decoding.

Referring to social texts as objectified knowledge does not mean that as readers we simply accept as self-evident the 'truth value' of objective accounts of social life. Rather, the problematic of this study is how magazine texts come to have truth value for many, but not all, readers. As we shall see, readers draw upon experiential knowledge of the social world during meaning-making; experiential knowledge comes through our everyday doing of social life. As Smith (1981, 1987) and others have noted, because women inhabit a world which is defined, labelled, and classified according to men's and not women's interests, their lived experiences may call official accounts of 'what it means to be a woman' into question. Smith (1981, 1987) refers to this disjuncture between women's experiential knowledge and official accounts of social life as a 'fault line' inviting feminist rewriting of the social. Consciousness-raising among women in the 1960s and 1970s is an expression of this disjuncture. Because consciousness-raising helped to redefine the social world from a distinctly women's standpoint, experience is typically privileged as a source of feminist knowledge. This is not to say that women's experiences rather than texts speak to the 'truth' of women's lives, however. While lived experience can be a 'raw' source of knowledge about social life, our understanding of experience is always, necessarily, culturally mediated. Experience is given meaning through the labels and classifications available to the knower, although the process through which dominant meanings are able to provide satisfactory accounts is never seamless or uncontested. By taking the everyday struggle over meaning as the research problematic, a sociological investigation of women's magazines differs from purely textual study. While we require textual analysis when we use the text as our point of entry into the world of femininity, our investigation transcends the immediacy of the text as a self-contained, available system of signification. It extends to those processes through which textual definitions and labels are, or are not, taken up by readers. Our study of magazines thus takes us into the everyday world of reading femininity. While I am tempted to say that this manner of working is what makes a sociological account of social texts 'better' than a purely textual study, let me simply say that it raises episte-mological issues that are forestalled by the study of cultural artefacts.

For sure, ethical dilemmas accompany the engagement of embodied rather than discursive Subjects in our research. The ways in which these ethical con-siderations shaped the current study are discussed in chapter 3. Here I am con-cerned with methodological issues surrounding the textual treatment of women's experiences as data. What I mean is that sociological research itself entails the creation of texts – written field notes, interview transcripts, question-naire data, and so on – which become the basis of knowledge claims. Not too long ago, sociologists would not be willing to admit that they 'read' rather than simply 'measure' the social world. Such an admission draws attention to the subjective rather than objective activities of the social scientist. Nor would soci-ologists until recently consider in their wildest dreams that they actually 'write' the social; in other words, that sociologists create rather than discover what we have come to think about as 'the social' (see Game 1991). For better or for worse, anti-humanist critiques have forced us to think about these matters. Cer-tainly, I could not evade them in a sociological study of the cultural realm. For this reason, *Girl Talk* can also be read for what it tells us about our own prac-tices as researchers.

In the final analysis, while I found literary theory and ways of working both engaging and useful, *Girl Talk* remains an identifiably sociological text. The most obvious sociological characteristic of this study is its inclusion of the embodied Subjects of magazine discourse. A central tenet of the current research is that many of the knowledge claims made in the name of cultural studies are based on researcher readings of social texts. By reading texts such as women's magazines against post-structural or psychoanalytical theories of sub-jectivity, writers evoke what I refer to as hypothetical Subjects. If I had made margin notes while reading much of this work, they would have been very sim-ilar to those by Beverley Skeggs:

... women were said to respond ... to being positioned as: convinced, troubled, creative, divisive, delighted, distracted, etc. ... I went through one book writing 'for example?' all over it and I pondered over how such wild universalistic speculations (do all women have the same psychic make-up regardless of difference, of nation, of class?) had gained space and validity. And, more importantly, why should we take this work seriously? It made me ask, are feminist cultural theories just a matter of speculation? Can anybody do it? (1995: 1)

As we shall see in in chapter 4, there are considerable differences between researcher and everyday readings of social texts. Given that I am committed to a politics of culture, as well as cultural theory, differences between academic and everyday reading became part of my sociological problematic. These differences draw attention to the implications of the power working through social texts as knowledge.

Foucault draws attention to the way that all power operates through, and is implicated in, systems of knowledge. Importantly, he refers to both objectified, official knowledge and subjugated knowledges, those knowledges which may inform daily life, even though they fail to achieve truth status by being deemed 'personal,' non-scientific, irrational, and so on. Thus power does not reside solely in institutions above individuals, acting against them, but circulates throughout the social body (1980: 96). Power acts through regimes of truth embodied in social texts which make specific discourses and their effects possible. Foucault thus argues that power, through discourse, is productive – it 'produces' social life. Power does not repress authentic human nature; rather, it produces identities and human subjects. One of the most relevant themes of Foucault's work for feminists centres around the way in which power as knowledge operates through human bodies to produce embodied women as sex(ed) and gendered 'subjects.' Various writers draw on the 'modes of objectification' which Foucault identified as transforming human beings into subjects (1980: 208). These three modes include: the modes of inquiry, which base truth claims by giving themselves the status of science; the disciplinary powers and techniques of normalization by which subjects are divided internally and from one another; and techniques of self, or the ways in which a human being turns her- or himself into a subject. These modes identify new mechanisms of power that are implicated in enlightenment thinking, producing oppressions which have been ignored by Marxism. Although Foucault did not discuss gender among these new oppressions,[6] feminists identify points of convergence between feminism and Foucauldian analyses:

Both [feminism and Foucault] identify the body as the site of power, that is, as the locus of domination through which docility is accomplished and subjectivity constituted. Both point to the local and intimate operations of power rather than focusing exclusively on the supreme power of the state. Both bring to the fore the crucial role of discourse in its capacity to produce and sustain hegemonic power and emphasize the challenges contained within marginalized and/or unrecognized discourses. And both criticize the ways in which Western humanism has privileged the experience of the Western masculine elite as it proclaims universals about truth, freedom, and human nature. (Diamond and Quinby 1988: x)

In short, the convergence between feminism and Foucault arises from shared observations that knowledge has bodily effects. From this insight feminists have brought to light those knowledges through which bodily practices produce a modality of embodiment that is peculiarly feminine (Bartky 1988: 64). As a social text that mediates discourses surrounding femininity, women's magazines are part of the process of signification through which the female body, as signifier, is invested with characteristics which are culturally read as 'feminine.' This signification requires 'body work' on the part of women, because not all, or any, female body is deemed, a priori, as signalling the aesthetic requirements of 'femininity.' As Smith (1988) and others note, an underlying assumption of magazine messages is that feminine beauty requires active intervention and the proper management of bodily processes. By bringing the work required to achieve (or approximate) femininity into view, feminists have found affinity with Foucault's (1980) analysis of the 'micro-mechanisms' of power. Foucault rejects the notion that 'the mechanisms of power have been accompanied by ideological productions'; instead, 'we must ... base our analysis of power on the study of techniques and tactics of domination' (p. 102). He calls this new type of power 'disciplinary power' that operates through the hegemony of norms, political technologies, and the shaping of the body. The ultimate effect of disciplinary power is a normalization that produces 'useful and docile subjects through a refashioning of minds and souls' (Best and Kellner 1991: 47). Emphasizing the bodily effects of normalization, Foucault draws attention to a new mode of 'bio-power.'[7]

Despite Foucault's treatment of the body as undifferentiated or as lacking gender,[8] his notion of bio-power has inspired Foucauldian analyses of sexual difference. The importance of sexual difference in feminist theory makes the body central to analyses of women's oppression because women's inferiority to men is typically legitimated by references to biology: 'firstly, women's bodies are marked as inferior by being compared with men's bodies, according to male standards and, secondly, biological functions are conflated with social characteristics' (McNay 1992: 17). In theorizing this difference, social-constructionist approaches favoured for the sociological study of gender bypass the corporeal reality of the body by taking it as given. That is to say, gender is distinguished from sex in order to separate the natural and the cultural experiences of existence. Foucault offers a way to place the sexualized body at the centre of feminist analyses without recourse to essentialism. Beginning from Foucault's identification of the body as both the principal instrument and effect of modern disciplinary power, feminists have demonstrated that this power is always gendered. They have done so by drawing attention to the ways in which female bodies are physically transformed into 'useful and docile' feminine ones. Although serving patriarchal interests, this transformation occurs through the labour of women themselves. Thus a Foucaldian framework identifies the physical body as both an instrument and a medium of patriarchal power. For Bordo (1988) this power crystallizes in anorexia nervosa, which clearly illustrates the gendered nature of bio-power. It also illustrates how social practices change women's experiences of their lived bodies. These practices are identified as dieting, exercising, and beauty and fashion rituals. They change women's experiences of their bodies by requiring bodily objectification; by separating sense of Self from Self-embodiment, women experience their bodies as something alien, something in need of control and constant management. Thus disciplinary power constructs a feminine body not only with regard to its appearance, size, and shape, but also with regard to its gesture, movement, and manner of Self-expression (Bartky 1988).

For Bartky (1988: 81), the disciplinary project of femininity as the production of the ideal body is a peculiarly modern phenomenon accompanying the emergence of industrial societies: 'Women are no longer required to be chaste or modest, to restrict their sphere of activity to the home, or even to realize their properly feminine destiny in maternity: normative femininity is coming more and more to be centred on woman's body – not its duties and obligations or even its capacity to bear children, but its sexuality, more precisely, its presumed heterosexuality and its appearance' (p. 81). As Smith does (1988, 1990a), Bartky points out that disciplining of the female body occurs within a context which encourages a pervasive sense of bodily deficiency. Smith links the dissatisfaction that women express about their bodies to fashion and beauty magazines: discontent with the body is not just a happening of culture, it arises in the relation between text and she who finds in texts images reflecting upon the imperfections of her body (1990a: 185). This relation can be observed most directly in photospreads which mirror a feminine Self that cannot be achieved by very many (if any) women. For example, the typical fashion model who graces the pages of women's magazines is 5'8" in height and 115 pounds in weight. The average North American reader is more likely to be 5'3" in height and 144 pounds in weight. Only the thinnest 5 per cent of women in the general population fall into the same weight category as fashion models (Sheinin 1990: 1). What the gap between the cultural Ideal and experienced Self creates is desire; a desire by women to be thinner, more beautiful, more accomplished in their femininity. This discursive construction of desire accounts for the seeming paradox of women as self-policing subjects, committed to relentless self-surveillance of make-up, hair, wardrobe, caloric intake. Because women's magazines instruct readers in this self-surveillance, Smith directs attention to these texts as implicated in the operation of Foucault's micro-mechanisms of modern bio-power. Specifically, beauty and fashion magazines orchestrate women's desires and everyday bodily practices with the cosmetic and fashion industries, which benefit from women's relentless self-regulation. By linking magazine discourse to the interests of powerful industries, beauty and fashion magazines make the economic interests behind women's subordination to patriarchal ideals readily transparent.

The current study entails a rethinking of sociological notions of power along these lines. Sawicki (1991: 21) identifies three ways in which a Foucauldian notion of power differs from the traditional, humanist conceptualizations which characterize much Marxist feminist writings until the 1980s. Overall, Foucault claims that power is exercised rather than possessed; it is primarily productive rather than repressive; and it is analysed as coming from the 'bottom up,' rather than 'top down.'[9] Within cultural studies these tenets have been used to explore how power operates to create 'women' as gendered subjects, through the micropolitics of identity formation. We have already seen above that an emphasis on the productive nature of power, and its exercise 'from below,' has led a number of postmodern writers to characterize cultural consumption as the empowerment of individual women. While *Girl Talk* likewise draws on a Foucauldian notion of power, which pays attention to the agency and creativity of reading, it also testifies to the fact that some forms of knowledge are more powerful in their effects than are others. Specifically, we will see that the knowledge promoted by magazine discourse is more compelling for many young readers than is the insight provided by individual instances of personal knowledge. In this study, disjunctures between experiential and objectified knowledge encouraged readers to call into question conceptions of Self rather than discursive constructions. Clearly, a Foucauldian notion of power will not tell us why. As Smith (1990b) notes, however fruitful Foucault's configuration of power/knowledge, 'both "power" and "knowledge" are mystified; they capture a sense of something significant about contemporary society that they are incapable of explicating. Power has no ontology, no form of existence' (p. 70). The task of sociology is to provide an ontology of textual power. By 'ontology' I mean answers to the sociological questions (Who? Where? When?) which tell us what power looks like through an observation of its everyday operation.

The Structure of This Study

In answering the question of why power, as knowledge, operates in certain ways, *Girl Talk* develops what Hennessy (1993) calls '*critical* cultural studies.' She contrasts critical cultural studies with attempts to merely update literary study into textual study. Critical cultural studies has as its goal inquiry into the processes whereby reading and writing in their broadest sense continually remake social relations in their everyday context. This inquiry brings to light not only the textual organization of knowledge, but its effect through the formation of subjectivities. In order to develop such a critical approach to cultural studies, the exploration of Subject-ivity provided here rewrites Marxist feminism in the light of contemporary questions about subjectivity, power, and the cultural construction of the social. It therefore offers a feminist sociology informed by issues and perspectives until recently associated with the humanities or the interdisciplinary field of 'cultural studies.'

In order to locate the current study in this way, chapter 1 reviews the kinds of debates, both theoretical and political, on the subject of women's magazines among feminist researchers and cultural critics. Readers familiar with research on women's magazines and the debates that they have generated may want to skip this discussion. I argue in chapter 1 that the paucity of research on the adolescent magazine as a distinctive cultural genre arises, in part, from a belief that such magazines represent simply an 'younger' version of the more general genre of women's magazines. In order to develop a critical analysis of social texts such as adolescent and women's magazines, chapter 2 reframes the debates raised in chapter 1 in terms of sociological issues concerning power, agency, and the cultural construction of the social. Working from a Marxist feminist perspective means that I focus discussion around theories of ideology that dominated the sociology of gender throughout the 1980s. In the conclusion to chapter 2, I identify the specific questions which became the subject of the current research.

Chapter 3 describes the research design and methodologies employed in *Girl Talk* as an investigation grounded in empirical rather than theoretical research. Following Skeggs (1995), chapter 3 makes transparent the 'who, where, when, and why' of the current study. As we shall see, the current study employs both methods of conventional sociology and literary ways of working with texts. The way in which these methodologies together enable us to study the text as 'process' rather than as 'specimen' is described in detail in chapter 4. As process, this current study draws on Smith's (1988, 1990a) notion of femininity as textually mediated discourse. Drawing on theories of subjectivity, but preserving the presence of embodied readers, the research problematizes Subject-ivity as an effect of magazine reading. The texts chosen for analysis in chapter 4 are advertisements. This choice reflects the prominence of advertising in women's magazines, but also the extent to which they are the basis for academic debate. In this chapter we begin to identify differences between researcher readings and everyday readings of social texts. This difference directs us to an investigation of the types of texts favoured by girls participating in this study. As shown in chapter 5, despite the emphasis which cultural critics give to the glossy pictorials characteristic of advertising texts, the girls in this study prefer to read written texts, especially advice columns, quizzes, and 'real life' stories. For the most part, this preference reflects the claim by readers that these texts address the reality of teenage life and offer readers 'something useful.' Chapter 6 thus takes up the task of exploring how (most but not all) readers come to construct a sense of Self and of the social world of adolescence from magazine texts.

Treating social texts as processes rather than specimens for analysis, however, requires us to go further than analysis of texts and the immediate context of their reading. It requires us to locate teenzine reading within the everyday world of reading, studied here as school culture. Chapter 7 thus explores how school culture reinforces the appeal of contradictory magazine messages to look good, know more about boys' opinions and behaviours, and 'be yourself.' In this chapter we see that the contradictory nature of magazine messages often resonates with lived experiences of being a girl in a patriarchal culture. While other writers have argued that contradiction is an important site at which to study reader agency as a potential moment for resistance, in this study contradictions often led to the 'undoing' of the Subject. 'Undoing' refers to Self-doubt and anxiety; it testifies to the unstable nature of Subject-ivity. As we shall see, undoing can arise through comparison reading which results in girls questioning themselves rather than cultural constructions. In chapter 7 we see that teenzines, when read in the context of school culture, can contribute to both the 'doing' and 'undoing' of the Subject. However, by locating this process within school culture, we are also able to explore why some girls – a minority in this study – actively reject magazine messages. Chapter 8 thus explores those cases where reading does not contribute to the undoing of the Subject. However, this chapter also differentiates between sceptical readers, who reject specific texts because of representational failures, and readers who reject adolescent magazines as a genre. This distinction is important because sceptical readers do not reject magazines; they only wish that editors or advertisers would 'try a little harder.' Unlike critical readers who reject commercial magazines, sceptical readers accept them as a potential source of knowledge about Self and the social world of adolescence. This chapter allows us to see why more girls are likely to be sceptical readers than rejecters of commercial media. In doing so, it directs attention to the social rather than discursive relations which ensure the continued popularity of fashion and beauty magazines among young girls. Thus, comparison reading also illustrates why we cannot extrapolate from adult to adolescent reading of commercial cutlure.

The concluding chapter revisits issues raised throughout *Girl Talk* about doing feminist sociology as cultural practice. In light of Barrett's claim that 'the social sciences have lost purchase within feminism and the rising star lies with the arts, humanities and philosophy' (1992: 204), the conclusion addresses questions about the ways in which literary theory and methods can enhance sociological study. The purpose of this exploration is to identify the disappearance of the social within work that replaces socio-structural determinism with a new form of cultural determinism. In conclusion I draw on insights from post-structuralism to describe ways of working with social texts from a materialist epistemology.

In the final analysis, *Girl Talk* is about more than adolescent magazines and their readers; it is also a sociology of knowledge. It is a study of the ways in which institutional knowledge is produced and consumed in everyday contexts, and it implicates feminist scholarship in this process. It is perhaps unavoidable that a foray into cultural studies will follow this path, given that it raises questions about the nature of 'Truth' and the construction of ourselves. This book thus intends to show how feminist sociology is necessarily political in that it engages practitioners in the struggle over meaning. As Barrett (1982) maintains, the contemporary women's liberation movement emerged as a struggle over what it means to be 'woman.' How can we, as feminists, take responsibility for reformulating ourselves through new meanings of gender, of being women and men, if we cannot understand how current meanings are produced and circulated through the powerful institutions of which we are a part?

1

Just Looking: Exploring Our Point of Entry

As noted in the introduction, women's magazines are the point of entry into *Girl Talk*. One reason that we begin by looking at the content of these texts is because women's magazines are encountered by women as an already accomplished system of meaning. While the ways in which they are subsequently read will determine how this codified system of meaning is taken up, these texts are 'raw data' that both everyday readers and researchers 'work up.' We thus begin by examining the content of women's magazines as documented by previous researchers and media commentators. What might we see when we turn back the glossy covers of women's magazines? Why has the content of women's magazines, so readily dismissed by 'serious' journalism, been the subject of acrimonious debate among feminists?

As Earnshaw (1984: 411) notes, until the emergence of feminist scholarship women's magazines attracted very little attention from academics or governments, despite the fact that they are one of the most widely read sectors of the press. For example, although over 26 per cent of all adult women in Britain read *Women's Own*, this publication has never been subjected to the level of investigation which surrounds texts such as *The Times*, read by a mere 1.9 per cent of the population. Clearly, there is a misogynist dimension to this neglect, evidenced by the racist reference to women's magazines as 'journalism for squaws' (cited in Winship 1987; also see Randall 1991). This dismissal reflects the historical association of women with the private and domestic; femininity is the absent 'other' against which our notions of the public and the social are constructed. The femininity in women's magazines stands in contradistinction to the unacknowledged masculinity of war, political events, and financial dealings discussed in magazines such as *The Times*. While the latter texts are typically considered to be 'ungendered,' media such as domestic magazines, television soap operas, romance fiction, and certain film genres bear the identity of the feminine.

The task of feminist cultural study is to demystify these types of associations and, in doing so, challenge their currency in both popular and academic discourse.

The most obvious way to explore women's magazines as texts is through studying their content. Given their historical neglect by social scientists,[1] the first stage in the process of demystification is critical examination of magazine messages that have given rise to debate which divides feminists along the lines of opposing or supporting women's magazines. What might we find when we open the inviting cover of a magazine which promises to entertain and inform us, to address our specific concerns 'as women'? Feminists interested in answering this question provide a wealth of research documenting the content of women's magazines. From the 1960s until more recently, it was claimed that content analysis provided a systematic and objective account of the substance and themes of cultural texts (see Berelson 1952; Budd, Thorp, and Donohew 1967); given its scientific credentials, it was adopted by pioneers of feminist social science to substantiate complaints that the mass media are biased against women (see Reinharz 1992).[2]

Blowing the Cover: Exploring the Content of Women's Magazines

Whereas the American Socialist Workers' Party was equating fashion and cosmetics with the exploitation of women during 1954, publication of *The Feminine Mystique* in 1963 proved to be a more significant impetus for academic research[3] and writing on women's magazines. In her (now controversial)[3] association of representations in women's magazines and 'the problem with no name,' Friedan drew attention to media proscriptions for (white) women in Middle America.[4] Her choice of magazines reflects their prominence in women's lives: White (1970: 216) claims that, during the 1950s, five out of six women read at least one magazine weekly. What they saw was the representation of women as wives and mothers rather than as 'persons.' According to Friedan, these representations influence the way in which women are viewed by society, mandating a 'single, overprotective, life-restricting, future-denying' role (p. 125) for women by tying their identities to heterosexual romance, marriage, and motherhood. Through advertising in particular, these magazines create an image of women as fulfilled and happy in domestic roles. Friedan asked, 'What happens when women try to live according to an image that makes them deny their minds? What happens when women grow up in an image that makes them deny the reality of the changing world?' (p. 38). Through interviews with women whose lives approximated magazine images,[5] Friedan brought to light a deep sense of dissatisfaction among American women. She concluded that American housewives were being manipulated into finding their sense of 'identity, purpose, creativity, the self-realization, even the sexual joy they lack – by buying things' (p. 208).

The advertisements, feature articles, and stories in women's magazines provided a wealth of information about the cultural representation of women for feminist researchers of the 1960s and 1970s. Early research by social scientists treated these texts as definitions through which women come to understand themselves, their relationships, and their needs. The term 'gender' was used to differentiate these cultural proscriptions from the biological dimensions of being men or women (see Oakley 1981). The notion of 'sex roles,' which dominated feminist sociology in Canada throughout the 1970s, provided an analytical framework by referring to the behaviours, values, and attitudes which a culture prescribes as appropriate for men and women (see Andersen 1988; Weinreich 1978). Commentators on sex-role depictions in commercial media typically referred to the ways in which these media 'teach' girls to be women: 'Watching lots of television leads children and adolescents to believe in traditional sex roles: Boys should work, girls should not. The same sex-role stereotypes are found in the media designed especially for women. They teach that women should direct their hearts toward hearth and home' (Tuchman 1979: 37; also see Waelti-Walters 1979; Reed and Coleman 1981).

Within sex-role theory, therefore, the effects of commercial media lie in reader identification. Based on this assumption, feminist cultural politics concerned itself, initially, with the images of women circulating in various mass media. As a consequence of the conviction that women's magazines both express and naturalize gender inequality, until the 1980s content analysis was the preferred method of charting the magazine world of women, particularly in North America. Through content analysis, representations of the dominant goals and values surrounding normative femininity have been systematically documented by sociologists and researchers from marketing and communication studies. Given their prominence, advertisements received extensive attention, not as descriptions of products, but rather as proscriptions of femininity. Early research suggested that the descriptive facts of women's magazines are rather straightforward. Researchers denounced the misrepresentation of women in mass media, whether visual or written, as 'negative,' 'limited,' somewhat 'distorted,' and as reinforcing traditional norms and values for women (Courtney and Lockeretz 1970; Franzwa 1975; Tuchman 1979; Tuchman, Daniels, and Benet 1978; Wagner and Banos 1973). They declared women's magazines a patriarchal prison that creates false images of women based on male fantasies and interests rather than flesh-and-blood human beings (Komisar 1971: 211). Through a narrow range of representations, as readers women are addressed as a universal group sharing specifically female interests.

As a vehicle for the socialization of women into this group, Marjorie Fergu-son (1983: 39) documents how the messages of femininity in women's maga-zines separate and differentiate women from men, giving the impression that a common essence transcends women's differences from one another. At its most obvious level, this belief system perpetuates a natural law of classification based on biological differences and the sexual division of labour. At a more sophisticated level, it provides charters or codes that legitimize attitudes, beliefs, behaviours, and institutions within a female world. Its effect is to rein-force the symbols and rituals that bind a female subculture to itself, and link it to the wider world. Drawing on the work of French sociologist Emile Durkheim, Ferguson describes the practices advocated by these magazines in terms of a 'cult of femininity': 'The direct parallels are these: the oracles that carry the messages sacred to the cult of femininity are women's magazines; the high priestesses who select and shape the cult's interdictions and benedictions are women's magazine editors; the rites, rituals, sacrifices and obligations that they exhort are to be performed periodically by the cult's adherents. All pay homage to the cult's totem – the totem of Woman herself' (p. 5).

Through content analysis of features, problem pages, beauty articles, and fic-tion, Ferguson (1983) identifies five themes that dominate the cult of femininity in the pre-feminist period, from 1949 to 1974. The most repeated messages of the cult were: the importance of getting and keeping a man; the necessity of maintaining a happy family; the promotion of self-help, or emphasis on how women overcame misfortune and achieved perfection; the working wife as a bad wife; and how to be more beautiful (also see Peirce 1985). Ferguson notes a turning point in how the cult of femininity is presented between 1975 and 1978, a period which corresponds to significant social changes for women. Editorial style became noticeably less authoritative, and the stern moralizing, sexual ambiguity, and lofty detachment of an earlier era were replaced by a more direct, no-nonsense approach (p. 92). More importance was attached to fea-tures, and on these pages the range of topics broadened. However, while a theme of female self-determination became a new editorial norm, it did not pre-clude the goal of getting a man as both central and necessary to women's self-fulfilment, so that maintaining a family was still very much in the foreground. Even though magazines during the 'feminist era' of 1979–80 portrayed a wider range of roles for women than previously, the roles of wife and mother outnum-bered all the rest (p. 109). While the most important shift in values of the cult of femininity has been towards self-realization, self-determination, and indepen-dence for women, these new values are overshadowed by the ever-present goal of getting and keeping a man (see also Ho 1984).

The consolidation of feminist scholarship during recent decades has resulted in a daunting array of research literature on the content of women's magazines. In the final analysis, the themes identified by researchers are repetitive and persistent (see McCracken 1993; Ballaster et al. 1991; Winship 1987; Stanger 1986; Ferguson 1983; McDowell 1977; Ortiz and Ortiz 1989; Kaiser 1979). For sake of expediency, the following discussion highlights three dominant themes[6] and the debates which these themes generated. The most persistent messages of women's magazines have been documented as 'the domestication of women' (Oakley 1974), the perpetuation of oppressive beauty standards, and the absence of visible-minority women. Overall, these messages about 'being women' bind the sexes together in an unequal relationship at the emotional as well as economic level (Gledhill 1994). Given their importance for the current study, the research on adolescent magazines is discussed in a separate section.

A Woman's Work Is Never Done: Femininity as Domesticity

Reflected in Ferguson's analysis, a key debate, which gained momentum in the 1980s, concerns the ways in which magazine imagery encourages women to think of themselves primarily as wives and mothers. Women's magazines position women in the domestic sphere, and remind working women that they must not neglect their domestic obligations. First identified by Friedan, this theme has persisted despite the fact that women have been increasingly drawn into waged employment since the late 1960s, a process which Friedan (initially) equated with the 'liberation of women.' In an often optimistic attempt to chart the progress of women's liberation in the mass media, researchers documented what promised to be the progressive movement of women from the domestic to the public realm in magazine representations. Given the strength and visibility of the women's liberation movement in the early 1970s, it may be a sign of the times that, despite the persistence of media stereotypes of women, some researchers maintained that things were looking (relatively) good for women (see Wagner and Banos 1973; Belkaoui and Belkaoui 1976; Culley and Bennett 1976; Kerin, Lundstom, and Sciglimpaglia 1979; Weinberger, Petroshius, and Weston 1979). Geise (1979) found that the themes of 'love, marriage, and family' were making room for the notion that careers could be equally important for women. Overall, studies showed that the proportion of women portrayed as working outside the home had increased over time, with greater (although small) numbers of women shown in middle-level or upper-level managerial positions. It was projected that this trend would continue into the 1980s. Saunders and Stead (1986) based their projection on a study of women's clothing in magazine ads: they found that, between 1963 and 1983, models were increasingly dressed in business suits (see also Sullivan and O'Connor 1988). Optimism about changing representations of women seemed to be further supported by a flood of new titles available by the mid-1980s in both North America (see McCracken 1993) and Britain (see Winship 1987).[7] Reflected in titles such as *Working Woman*, *Options*, and *New Woman*, a specialized audience was being identified by magazine producers as more and more women entered the paid labour force. The question for researchers was whether the promises implied by the new titles were carried into magazine content; for the large part, this did not prove to be the case. In *Working Woman*, Glazer (1980) finds that the 'new woman' was portrayed as either a 'sociological male' or a 'superwoman.' While *Working Woman* was well attuned to the conflicts surrounding women's new roles – in fact, one could argue that the publishers capitalized on these conflicts – rather than discuss how the double day of paid and unpaid labour is socially created, the magazine encouraged readers to understand conflicts as 'personal problems.' In a sample of seven women's magazines published between 1975 and 1982, Henry (1984) similarly reports that, although one-third of the editorial articles discussed problems for women arising from the necessity to combine job and family, very few articles actually offered solutions or realistic alternatives. Instead, balancing work and family become the image of the new 'superwoman,' perpetuating new oppressive ideals for middle-class women. Viewing women's magazines as moral guides, Keller (1992) explores how they construct social reality for women by failing to show alternative ways of dealing with domestic conflicts, such as asking husbands to share housework or criticizing the patriarchal social structure. This editorial construction resonated with messages from advertisers. By affirming housework as work, advertisers perpetuate women's dedication to domestic life (Fox 1990). This traditional ideology appears in the emotional as well as physical labour of housewives (Cancian and Gordon 1988). Corresponding to changes associated with women's liberation, the new magazines encouraged women to develop and express both their interests and their anger, sending messages which support equality in marriage; however, these new norms were placed within the context of women's continued responsibility for maintaining a loving marriage (p. 337).

In Britain, Winship (1978, 1987) documents a similar trend in the popular *Women's Own*. While contemporary editors were becoming much more willing to acknowledge that married life was not always wedded bliss, the institution of marriage was never questioned, only women's behaviour within it (1987: 85). Agony columns advised women to 'be practical and work out how the home can be successfully run in the new circumstances' of women's waged labour (p. 87). The two most common ways for editors to impart this message were through personal testimonials of successful couples and practical tips on what

'you' the reader 'can achieve too' (p. 88). Winship (1987) concluded that
women's magazines act as a survival guide for women living in a patriarchal
society: the ideal femininity that magazines advise readers to aspire towards is
constructed around a mythical woman who exists outside powerful sociocultural structures and constraints.

Despite extensive scrutiny and criticism by feminists from the 1960s onwards,
messages in women's magazines seem to testify that, for women, 'nothing ever
changes' (Barthel 1988: 11). While research in the early 1970s was optimistic
that commercial media were reflecting changes associated with women's liberation, this optimism soon waned. Examining the content of women's magazines
during the height of women's liberation, Busby (1975: 122) concludes that 'sex
roles in the mass media are traditional and do not yet reflect the impact of the
recent women's movement,' while Gerbner (1978) claims that things were getting worse for women, in part because of a backlash against women's liberation.
This theme of backlash became prominent during the 1990s.

Into the 1990s, the primacy of domestic roles for women in their magazines
coincides with public debate about the importance of family for women. Does
the domestic content of women's magazines act to reinforce marriage and
motherhood, or does it re-evaluate, in a positive way, important areas of
women's lives which have been historically neglected and devalued by masculinist assessments of the social? This is an important debate: it implies that the
feminist critique of motherhood and domesticity which gained currency in the
1970s, and which informed much feminist writing on women's magazines,
adopts and thus perpetuates devaluation of a femininity which resonates with
contemporary women. It also illustrates how the tradition which I have credited
to Friedan's inspiration went far beyond her own rethinking of women's liberation in the 1980s. In *The Second Stage* (1982), Friedan questioned the double
burden of working wives and the accompanying feminist aspiration that women
can, through their own heroic effort, 'have it all': 'after nearly twenty years of
the women's movement, it becomes clear that most women are still saddled
with the work they used to do in the family (serving the physical needs of children, men, home) in addition to their hard new "male" jobs, at a price of fatigue
and stress only superwomen can endure. Or they are facing economic misery in
divorce and the loss of whatever power they had through that "female" family
role – devalued and sometimes even replaced by other women who got into the
men's world and sometimes took away their husbands' (p. 83). According to
Friedan, women of the 1980s needed to recognize the *limits* rather than the
potential of women's power, and the possibilities of transcending those limits
through a new kind of power. This new power can be realized only when
women reject the false polarization between sexual equality and family.

This type of thinking, which reflects Friedan's liberal humanism, appeals to a new generation of women beleaguered by images of 'superwoman.' Feminist critiques of domesticity appear to suggest that pursuits which many women enjoy are a sign of their 'false consciousness.' Along these lines, some writers disavow a necessary connection between traditional femininity, associated with the past generation of women, and women's current pursuit of domestic arts. For example, Winship (1991) argues that, although the trade press of the earlier years yoked women's magazines to traditional femininity, the new 'centre of interest' magazines are situated in a context in which the dominant ideology of femininity has been disrupted by alternative meanings, including those of feminism. She argues that these alternative discourses allow the reader to criticize and critically reflect upon domestic themes in a way which was not possible for an earlier generation of women. Furthermore, the range of roles and activities for women in contemporary magazines is extensive. 'Their readers, it appears, hold down a job, look after children, run a household *and* find time to do all this domestic activity: a driven lifestyle unrelieved by real time off. But does an emphasis in these magazines mean readers *are* into practical home-making in a big way?' (p. 146). Winship speculates 'not.' What is raised in these magazines is wish-fulfilment. She concludes that 'craft and practical home-making is "the impossible" because it too "serves so many different (symbolic) functions, supplies so many diverse needs." Bringing it out of the closet in the late 1980s is neither an actual return to, nor symbolic hankering for, the good/bad old days of the 1950s. But it does mark tensions around femininity and women's relation to mass consumption' (p. 148). Although a critic of the mass media, Winship implies that women enjoy their magazines for 'what they are.' Within this context, women's reading pleasures are redefined, primarily through a position which distinguishes the realm of fantasy from 'the real,' the content of images from their form. In drawing attention to the glossy coloured pages devoted to advertising, beauty and fashion, cookery, and home, Winship maintains that 'we frequently luxuriate in the advertising without ever a thought of the product ... I've gained enormous pleasure from [ads, even though] I have no intention of buying the product. Indeed I am hard put even to remember what it is the image is advertising. We recognize and relish the vocabulary of dreams in which ads deal; we become involved in the fictions they create; but we know full well that those commodities will not elicit the promised fictions' (1987: 55–6).

From these kinds of arguments, the commonsense claim was advanced that we need to separate pleasure from commitment to the text, because we can enjoy browsing without necessarily buying everything on offer. To acknowledge the reading pleasure which women's magazines afford is not necessarily to abandon political commitment to women's liberation (see for example, Ang 1988).

However appealing, this analysis stands in contrast to a less favourable view of women's magazines advanced by writers who describe a renewed emphasis on recipes, patterns, and household tips as constructing a 'new traditionalism.' Deborah Leslie (1995) describes the new traditionalism as a theme, created by advertising agencies, that ageing Baby Boomers are rediscovering fulfilment through home and family life. In an appeal to advertisers, *Good Housekeeping*, for example, maintains: 'A new kind of woman with deep-rooted values is changing the way we live ... To us, it's a woman who has found her identity in herself, her home, her family. She is the contemporary woman whose values are rooted in tradition' (cited in Leslie 1995: 354). Leslie maintains that these campaigns are based on advertising research[8] revealing anxiety among women about family and femininity. Their main target is middle-class white women over the age of thirty-five who are experiencing the tensions about work and family life which have been raised to public awareness, but not resolved, by the feminist movement. The message constructed by such a discourse, of course, is that we inhabit a post-feminist era. According to *Good Housekeeping*, the new traditionalist woman 'started a revolution with some not-so revolutionary ideals. She was searching for something to believe in and look what she found. Her husband, her children, herself' (p. 355). Drawing on *Good Housekeeping's* survey findings, the prestigious *Wall Street Journal* announced that traditional values are flourishing, that the family is becoming much stronger, and that working mothers are more optimistic and confident about what they can achieve for their families (p. 356).

While these types of debates are not resolved by the current research, the ways in which they have been framed are central to the analysis presented in *Girl Talk*. Specifically, these debates establish a new feminist distinction between 'fantasy' and what is considered to be the 'reality' of women's lives, a distinction we will return to later. This distinction is important because it provides a position from which to reconsider women's reading pleasures and the purported harmfulness of women's magazines.

Getting and Keeping a Man: Femininity as Beautification

Banner (1983: 3) claims that, more than any other factor, the pursuit of beauty and its attendant features of fashion and dress bind women together into a femininity that transcends class, region, and ethnicity, and constitutes a key element in a specifically female experience of life (also see Brownmiller 1984). While the pursuit of beauty has been subject to feminist critique since the nineteenth century (see Donovan 1985), more recent complaints include the overt sexualization of women through the contemporary beauty standards perpetuated by women's magazines (see Posner 1982; Soley and Reid 1988; Duquin 1989; Wolf 1991). The most notorious example is *Cosmopolitan*. First published in 1886, *Cosmopolitan* was transformed in the 1970s under editorship of Helen Gurley Brown, author of the best-seller *Sex and the Single Girl*. Extending her celebration of singleness and women's sexual pleasure to the magazine forum, the new *Cosmo* was an immediate and huge success (Winship 1987: 106). With its emphasis on (hetero)sexuality,[9] *Cosmo*, Winship maintains, provided a venue for young, middle-class women, who found it an attractive alternative to the moralizing of 'women's libbers.' What *Cosmo* extolled was not 'anger and discontent but an optimistic *joie de vivre* about what women in 1972 could enjoy and achieve. The magazine enthused that women could successfully combine "independence" and more traditional aspects of femininity; brains and beauty could be a winning combination' (p. 110).

The 'Cosmo Girl' has been the subject of much analysis and debate (see Faust 1980; Peirce 1985; Michels 1985; Valverde 1985; McMahon 1990). Significantly, she has provided fertile ground for assessment of the construction of women's sexual desire. Commentators generally share Peirce's (1985: 5) view that *Cosmopolitan*, in claiming to speak to a new generation of liberated women, promotes 'entrepreneurial femininity' as a developed skill that helps every woman get what she wants, in part through manipulation of her sexuality and physical appearance. Thus *The New York Times* declared that Brown's *Cosmopolitan* offered 'half a feminist message' to women who would otherwise have none (cited in McMahon 1990: 382). Peirce calls *Cosmopolitan* a 'woman's owner's manual,' a magazine that instructs the reader how to use her feminine assets to make it in a man's world. In the final analysis, however, *Cosmopolitan* continues to reinforce traditional role expectations in most areas of women's lives: like more conventional magazines, *Cosmopolitan* does not demand any great changes in men or society, but merely encourages women to take more responsibility for, and to make more effort towards, achieving their goals.

Given the rapid transformation of social attitudes towards sexual relations, and towards women's sexuality, increasingly explicit sexuality was not confined to 'specialty' magazines like *Cosmo*. Beauty and sexual objectification have been shown to be dominant themes in a broad range of contemporary women's magazines. Overall, research suggests that the sexual objectification of women, already present before women's liberation, has increased as the portrayal of women in domestic/reproductive roles has declined (Belkaoui and Belkaoui 1976; Wagner and Banos 1973; Kerin, Lundstom, and Sciglimpaglia 1979; Sexton and Haberman 1974; Pingree et al. 1976; Ferguson, Kreshel, and Tinkham 1990; Soley and Reid 1988). Including store-window displays in her study, Posner (1982: 39) claims that advertising has evolved from seemingly innocuous displays of sex-role stereotyping as submission to the more explicitly sexual but also brutal images characteristic of contemporary pornography.[10] Given these types of findings, it is (perhaps) surprising that the heterosexism of women's magazines has received little condemnation for being the unstated principle of heteropatriarchy which demands a sexuality organized around men's desire. Instead, negative features of sexual objectification remain the focus of debate.

While the documented sexualization of women in magazine portrayals gives credence to Posner's parallel between advertising and pornography, one of the liveliest areas of debate concerns a new 'body fashion' which links beauty, sexual desire, and thinness (Bartky 1988). The context of these debates is the 'epidemic' of eating disorders that was beginning to be documented during the 1970s. While medical professionals and traditional social scientists attempted to incorporate these new disorders within existing medical models, feminists identified anorexia (and later bulimia) as 'socio-somatic' diseases, thereby linking eating disorders to the cultural representation of women (Currie 1988: 206). Rather than perpetuate the view of anorexia as aberrant behaviour, feminists pointed to research showing that dieting for cosmetic (rather than health) reasons is widespread among women. For example, a Canadian Health Promotion Survey found that 70 per cent of women want to diet and lose weight (Brown 1993), while in the United States *Psychology Today* claims that 62 per cent of women between the ages of thirteen and nineteen are unhappy with their weight (Garner 1997). More striking, perhaps, is the finding that a significant proportion of women (15 per cent) would give up more than five years of their lives to achieve a 'normal' weight. Cash and Henry (1995) claim that this type of thinking among women has been growing over time (also see Schwartz, Thompson, and Johnson 1985; Boskind-White 1985).

Drawing on film theory, feminists suggested that the feelings of inadequacy which underlie women's cultural pursuit of beauty are testimony of women's internalization of 'the male gaze' (see Berger 1972; Mulvey 1975, 1989).[11] Most obvious in media indulging male spectatorship (particularly pornography), this gaze constructs a way of looking at women which reduces women to objects valued for their aesthetic qualities only. John Berger (1972), who first drew attention to this way of seeing, argued that looking is not the neutral activity which we often assume it to be: looking carries with it relations of power, access, and control. In patriarchal cultures the male gaze is a form of male control over women: 'Men look at women. Women watch themselves being looked at. This determines not only most relations between men and women but also the relations of women to themselves. The surveyor of women in herself is male: the surveyed female. Thus, she turns herself into an object of vision: a sight' (pp. 46, 47). This notion of the male gaze has been influential in feminist cultural studies (see Mulvey 1975, 1989; Devereaux 1990; Kaplan 1983; Betterton 1987; Doane 1981, 1982). Associating it with the representation of women in fashion and beauty magazines, the male gaze seems to explain women's 'relentless pursuit of thinness' (Bartky 1982; Chapkis 1986). When women assume the Subject position in relation to the male viewer, the effect is to estrange them from their bodies which become experienced from the outside, as 'spectacle': 'On the one hand, I am it and I am scarcely allowed to be anything else; on the other hand I must exist perpetually at a distance from a permanent posture of disapproval. Thus, insofar as the fashion–beauty system shapes one of the introjected subjects for whom I exist as an object, I sense myself as deficient ... All the projections of the fashion–beauty complex have this in common: they are images of what I am not. For me, attention to the ordinary standards of hygiene is not enough; I am unacceptable as I am' (Bartky 1982: 136).

By encouraging women to believe that they are unacceptable as they are, media representations set a standard to which women strive. Writers thus causally linked magazine representations to the prevalence of eating disorders among women. They noted that from the mid-1960s onwards, the sex goddesses of the 1950s and early 1960s were displaced by women who embody an androgynous femininity that resonates with women's liberation. The reproductive femininity of buxom stars like Elizabeth Taylor and Sophia Loren has been deemed excessive; the slender body, by contrast, signals freedom from reproductive destiny and women's entry into the public arena dominated by male standards. Models like Jean Shrimpton and Twiggy, who made their debut during the 1960s, symbolize this new femininity of slimness in fashion magazines (see Bordo 1990; DeLibero 1994). Kate Moss, a contemporary model who often appears in *Seventeen* and *YM*, has been described, like her predecessor Twiggy, as an 'idealized anorexic.' Bartky (1988: 64) describes the contemporary beauty standard as taut, small-breasted, narrow-hipped, and embodying a slimness bordering on emaciation; it is a silhouette more appropriate to an adolescent boy or newly pubescent girl than to an adult woman. While every historical epoch constructs criteria against which to adjudicate female beauty, the problem today is that the market availability of a vast array of beauty and 'fitness' products, including body surgery, implies that beauty can/should be every woman's 'calling' (see Duquin 1989; Dull and West 1991). Similar to their focus on domesticity, the emphasis on beauty and self-improvement links women's magazines to the position that these media are an obstacle to women's liberation, a theme which made Wolf's *The Beauty Myth* (1991) a best-seller.

The Beauty Myth is an ambitious attempt to link the beauty messages of women's magazines to the current anti-feminist backlash. According to author Naomi Wolf, the beauty myth tells a story: 'The quality called "beauty" objectively and universally exists. Women must want to embody it and men must want to possess women who embody it. This embodiment is an imperative for women and not for men, a situation which is necessary and natural because it is biological, sexual, and evolutionary: Strong men battle for beautiful women ...' (1991: 12). Wolf sets as her task documentation of the ways in which this myth is not true: 'beauty,' like the gold standard, is a currency system. Like any economy it is determined by politics and their embodiment in dominant values. Women's magazines deserve special attention because they democratize the beauty standard, making it seem to be available to all women through their participation in a multibillion-dollar beauty industry. In the same way that advertisers in the past have capitalized on women's 'guilt over hidden household dirt,' they now focus on the never-ending pursuit of beauty. Once the housewife market began to fall after the second wave of feminism, the beauty myth arose to take the place of the 'feminine mystique,' a strategy which enables advertisers to escape the economic fallout of the women's revolution (p. 66). At the same time, it assures magazine editors that their readers would not 'liberate themselves out of their interest in women's magazines' (p. 63). Within Wolf's framework, women's magazines contain very little to redeem them.

Overall, magazine research and the debate which this research has generated among feminists helped to restate the feminist slogan that 'the personal [appearance] is political.' Debates spilled over into notions of how feminists *should* dress, a position criticized by Elizabeth Wilson in a series of works (1985, 1990, 1992). For some time, women who did not actively reject standards of feminine dress were deemed complicit in the conspiracy to enslave women in the unending pursuit of beauty. During the 1970s, it was a truism that feminists could be identified by their unadorned bodies and drab (but comfortable) attire: in retrospect, it is perhaps not surprising that many women would reject the moralism implicit in the notion that they are victims of femininity (see *Esquire* Feb. 1994:47). For example Jane Reed, editor of *Woman*, complained to readers that 'hard-liner feminists have made us feel guilty for enjoying dressing up, putting on make-up, looking after our families, doing housework' (21 August 1982: quoted in Coward 1985: 157). These sentiments even appeared in the columns of the feminist periodical *Spare Rib*: 'Recently I have been the target of a lot of criticism from women ... because they do not like the way that I dress and wear my hair (i.e. Mohican, Bondage, etc.). They tell me that I am ignoring its racist and sexist overtones, that it is not "feminist," and that I am allowing myself to be exploited by the fashion market ... Is not the whole point of feminism to help a woman to realise her right to control her own life and make decisions for herself?' (quoted in Wilson 1985: 236). These examples illustrate the way in which feminist critique historically has underestimated the extent to which women's roles and identities can be sources of pleasure for women. One response has been the reframing of feminist debate in order to account for both women's pleasure and the potential for this pleasure to act as the vehicle for social change.

Elizabeth Wilson (1985; see also Barrett 1982) interprets the current reframing not simply as a rejection of the moralism of earlier feminism, but as evidence of the ambivalence which feminism historically has shown towards pleasure. Fashion has been seen as capitulation to capitalist consumption, and yet at the same time it has been acknowledged as one of the few legitimate avenues of women's creative self-expression. Wilson (1985) wants feminists to emphasize the latter. In fact, she argues that 'it important to recognize that men have been as much implicated in fashion, as much "fashion victims" as women; we must also recognize that to discuss fashion as simply a feminist moral problem is to miss the richness of its cultural and political meanings. The political subordination of women is an inappropriate point of departure if, as I believe, the most important thing about fashion is *not* that it oppresses women' (p. 13; emphasis in original). Wilson maintains that feminists can use and play with fashion as not simply a new aesthetic, but a vehicle to seed a new cultural order (p. 245). Her position reflects a re-evaluation, by academic feminists across a number of disciplines, of the feminine culture promoted by women's magazines.

The context for this rethinking includes the phenomenal success of Madonna and the emergence of 'attitude dressing.' Madonna linked fashion to exhibitionism and aggressive sexuality, connecting fashion revolt with rebellion. The (early) 'Madonna look,' known as 'flash-trash,' encouraged thrift-shop, downscale fashion, for a style that almost any teenage girl could afford to emulate. Madonna fashion made it appear possible that teenage girls could reject traditional fashion through its parody: the Madonna look included underwear as outerwear, loose T-shirts, cheap jewellery, and crucifixes (which mocked her upbringing in Catholic schools). In short, Madonna fashion appears to allow girls to produce their own identity, make their own fashion statements, and reject traditional codes (Kellner 1995: ch. 8; see hooks 1992, ch. 10). Importantly, the ambiguity of Madonna's self-representation gave rise to an academic industry of 'Madonna-ology' (Schwichtenberg 1993). For some, Madonna signals that fashion is a vehicle for fantasy; as performance art, it speaks dread as well as desire; above all, fashion is fun. Writers like Wilson (1990) argue that 'clothing is a necessary condition of subjectivity ... in articulating the body it simultaneously articulates the psyche' (p. 229). This position allows Wilson to suggest that the tenets of postmodernism, with its emphasis on the playful, arbitrary, and chosen aspects of personal identity, make dress an important contribution to feminist critique. Rather than naturalizing the arbitrary, fashion play denaturalizes supposedly natural identities and thus has the potential to draw attention to radical alternatives.

As in the case of domesticity, the issue of pleasure through dress and fashionable appearance is central to *Girl Talk*. However, the current study questions whether the treatment of women as active agents necessarily frees them from the power of mass media. As noted in the introduction, the equation of agency with pleasure allows commentators to claim women's participation in commodity consumption as grounds for feminist resistance to patriarchy. The current study challenges these types of claims, drawing on accounts by adolescent girls rather than by middle-aged academics of 'doing' femininity. As we shall see, there are important differences between how young girls and academics 'read' women's fashion, as well as the ways in which fashion is experienced as everyday practice by adolescents rather than adult women.

Missing in Action: Femininity as Whiteness

In the same way that feminists identified femininity as an absent marker for masculinity, writers are more recently beginning to identify absent subjects who make contemporary beauty standards possible. These writers draw attention to women conspicuous for their lack of representation in women's magazines: obese women, visibly ageing women, women with disabilities, visible-minority women, and working-class women (Nett 1991; Culley and Bennett 1976; Duquin 1989; MacGregor 1989). Content analysis reveals a remarkable similarity in the women portrayed in women's magazines: the women inhabiting magazine texts are young, beautiful, and white. For example, Duquin (1989) found that only 3 per cent of all ads in thirteen U.S. women's magazines depicted visible-minority women. Examining Canadian print media, MacGregor (1989) reports that the representation of visible-minority women increased from 0.2 per cent to only 1.5 per cent between 1954 and 1984. The few existing depictions contain negative stereotypes of visible-minority women as decorative/idle, dancers, or poor/idle. On the other hand, McMahon (1990: 383) draws attention to the use of 'ethnic models' as an exotic 'other' that acts to emphasize rather than displace the dominant ideal of white beauty. Her observation resonates with a trend during the 1990s for ad agencies to promote 'ethnic beauty.' While this promotion has given a number of minority women supermodel status – Coco Mitchell, Naomi Sims, China Machado, and Fatou Ndoye – the traditional standards of beauty have not been dramatically altered.[12]

McMahon also draws attention to the class-specific nature of women's magazines, which otherwise have been characterized as promoting a false sense of women belonging to a common group based on biological sex. Against the claim of promoting a community of women, she maintains that the entrepreneurial femininity of *Cosmopolitan* 'offers a mix of the Cinderella myth and Horatio Alger story for working-class women ... The text offers the fantasy of revenge for class and gender subordination through images of women's sexuality used to control men on their own turf. The middle-class man is represented as an enemy; the middle-class woman as privileged rival' (1985: 394). Unlike previous writers, McMahon is optimistic that the contradictory nature of this discursive resolution to working-class women's subordination offers a subversive potential: the working-class reader may well suspect that she deserves better (p. 393).

Against this view, however, Maureen Honey (1984) argues that the values and ideas espoused in media for working-class women encourages them to tolerate exploitation in the workplace and isolation in the home. Honey is interested in confessional magazines because historically they have been marketed for working-class women; in fact, research shows that middle-class women have a negative evaluation of confessional literature and avoid magazines like *True Confessions* (Gerbner 1958; Butler-Flora 1971; McCallum 1975). Honey links their exclusive appeal to the strategies which these magazines provide for recognition and self-worth: as with other fantasies marketed for women, confessional stories allow readers to exorcise feelings of inferiority produced by unequal access to power in society by glorifying female selflessness (1984: 316). However, while affording some relief from the pain of victimization and powerlessness, the confessional formula ultimately cannot serve the interests of its readers. The standards of self-sacrifice in confessional narratives are so high that failure is guaranteed. Honey's analysis of the confessions suggests that many wage-earning women look to their roles as wives and mothers for primary meaning in their lives rather than to achievement in the public arena (p. 317). While Honey criticizes the notion that these magazines are solely an instrument of oppression, she concludes that confessional magazines encourage women to accept their lot.

Also interested in classed-based readership, Valverde (1985) notes that, like all commodities, women's magazines are geared towards specific markets that typically correspond to socio-economic status. While market segmentation has resulted in a seemingly rich variety in magazine choices, within magazine discourse differences among women are presented as differences in 'lifestyle.' It is not simply that the heroines of the articles, fiction, and ads of women's magazines do not have a class: the point is that magazines all pretend that class does not exist while trumpeting the values of consumer capitalism (p. 18). The effect is that women's magazines constitute an image of 'real women' as necessarily white and middle-class. For example, being poor might be covered as an 'issue' that is reported by 'sensitive' editorial writers; being middle-class is not an issue at all. Similarly, being non-white is an issue, and one may read an article about a Black woman to find out what her life is like; but being white is not an issue (p. 18).

Together, these types of critiques provide further support for the claim that women's magazines present a distorted picture of social reality, and of women as social actors. While market segmentation has given rise to specialty magazines for women based on their difference from the white, middle-class norms identified above, it does not appear that new venues significantly challenge the association of female readers with traditional femininity. For example, although the emergence of a visible Black magazine audience in the United States during the 1970s gave rise to *Essence*, publisher Jonathan Blount promised advertisers that its readers would buy products: he described the new *Essence* reader as 'the young inquisitive, acquisitive black woman' (quoted in Ballaster et al. 1991: 224). Ballaster and colleagues (1991) report that, although *Essence* breaks new ground for women's magazines through the inclusion of articles on political issues and Black history, these messages conflict with the magazine's attractive images of consumerism. For example, while purportedly advancing Black pride and confidence, *Essence* contains a considerable number of advertisements for hair products – dyes, relaxers, shampoos, wigs, and gels – which encourage readers to pursue white ideals of beauty (also see Bordo 1991). Further, although using Black models, the images of Black consumerism frequently echo the stereotypical and degrading portrayals of women found in established magazines (p. 228). The authors conclude that, while *Essence* offers women more political messages than do other women's magazines, the contradictory system it creates with these negative images misdirects readers (p. 229). However unintentional, the advertisers in *Essence* cultivate feelings of inadequacy and insecurity in readers about their racialized bodies (Bordo 1991: 121). In the final analysis, racialized difference, like sexual difference, is transformed by commercial interests into a specialty consumer group.

Through her notion of the cult of femininity, Ferguson (1983: 7) argues that women's magazines provide readers with a 'sense of sharing and belonging ... as members of a broad social group, the female sex.' More noticeable now than when she made this claim is the way in which the 'woman' addressed by women's magazines is an exclusionary construction: the femininity of women's magazines has been, and remains, an identity of white, heterosexual women who are valued primarily for youth, beauty, and domestic virtue. While this construction is based on the otherness of older, non-white, non-heterosexual women, the absence of representations of these women renders the racism and heterosexism of this construction invisible, hence unquestioned. As Valverde (1985) notes, difference is considered only in terms of the identity of 'other': if race is included in the editorial pages of established magazines, for example, it is discussed through an examination of the lives of Black women. In this way, the racism of women's magazines reflects and reconstructs the racism of the more general consumer culture; by failing to question this construction, feminist research faces the danger of also reflecting and reconstructing racism in debates on 'what it means to be a woman.'

While white feminists have drawn attention to women's magazines as a venue of oppression, it should not be surprising that fashion and beauty magazines seldom appear as a matter of inquiry for Black feminist writers. Angela Davis (1981: 7), for example, argued that the ideology of femininity, with the benefits it brought white women, never included Black women who were slaves. However, this does not mean that this ideology did not affect Black women. bell hooks (1981: 48) argues that the ideology of 'true womanhood' had an intensely demoralizing effect on enslaved women who assimilated white American values. Many chose to wear dresses in the fields rather than trousers and, after emancipation, Black women's groups sought to change their negative images by stressing behaviour that emulated the white 'lady' (p. 55). Patricia Hill Collins (1990) argues that the issue of beauty – particularly skin colour, facial features, and hair texture – is a concrete example of how dominant cultural representations continue to devalue African-American women. Specifically, the blue eyes and blonde hair of white women could not be considered beautiful without their contrast to the classical African features (p. 79). As 'Other,' African-American women experience the pain of never being able to live up to externally defined standards of beauty applied by white men, white women, Black men, and also, potentially, by Black women themselves.

Given the exclusionary nature of the women addressed by women's magazines, it seems appropriate to identify them as 'specialty' magazines venerating the women idealized in patriarchal, racist culture: young, white, heterosexual women. One important question which arises, then, is how these magazines have the power to define 'womanhood' as a universal, seemingly acultural ideal. Clearly, women's magazines are about racialization as much as they are about gendering the female body. However, as we shall see, this does not mean that visible-minority women do not read, or do not take pleasure from, magazines promoting Caucasian standards of femininity. One goal of the current study is to explore why this may be so.

The Girl as Mother to the Woman: Adolescent Magazines

Given the importance of gender identity during adolescence, and the focus upon gendered socialization in feminist commentary on print media, the lack of research on adolescent magazines is curious. As yet, very few systematic and comprehensive analyses of adolescent magazines have been conducted. In my view, this situation reflects both the general neglect among women's studies scholars of young women, and the assumption that these texts simply represent an 'earlier form of socialization' (Ferguson 1983: 34). From a sociological perspective, print media addressing adolescent readers is an interesting phenomenon. In both Britain and North America, the proliferation of this specialty media after the Second World War coincides with the discovery of the young as consumers (Abrams 1959).

Adolescent Girls and the Magazine Market

While they never sustained circulation figures comparable to those of women's magazines, specialty publications for young, unmarried women appeared during the late nineteenth century. Drotner (1983) traces the proliferation of girls' magazines in Britain after the First World War to the transformation of girls' education. She notes that, although a number of recreational periodicals aimed at young female readers have existed since at least the 1860s, none of these was directed specifically at schoolgirls as a group for the simple reason that girls did not experience a shared school culture. Throughout the nineteenth century, the lives of working-class and middle-class girls were sharply divergent; the middle-class concept of childhood was accepted as valid for working-class children as well only after the turn of the century (p. 35). Class distinctions were blurred by the Education Act in 1918, which raised the general school-leaving age to fourteen, prohibited part-time work for all pupils, and increased the opportunities for poor but 'able' children to receive free secondary training (p. 36). With the spread of education, by the 1930s reading was the most popular pastime for girls (taking second place with boys). Examining the school weeklies' published for this new audience, Drotner maintains that fictional narratives served to obscure the class differences which continued to characterize girls' educational experiences despite the rhetoric of educational meritocracy. She suggests that the independence, physical mobility, and power attributed to the weeklies' heroines vicariously fulfilled readers' needs for independence while obscuring the real impossibility of having these needs met (p. 45).

The weeklies described by Drotner (1983) ceased publication in 1940, allegedly because of paper shortages. While the content of weeklies such as *School*

Friend, Schoolgirls' Own, and *Schoolgirls' Weekly* provided action-based stories throughout the decades of their existence, Drotner draws attention to the motion-picture industry as an influence which was to foreshadow the appearance of the adolescent magazines in the middle of the twentieth century. During the 1920s, cinema-going established itself as a stable Saturday treat for working-class children in Britain. By the 1930s fiction for girls included cinema stories of schoolgirl–turned–film star, and star biographies were almost indistinguishable from these fictional accounts. An earlier preoccupation with schoolgirl independence through adventure was challenged by a romance with 'stars' (p. 43).

While the history of adolescent magazines is yet to be written, the emergence of a distinctly adolescent magazine follows trends that have been documented in women's periodicals more generally. Like adult women's publications, British magazines for girls established in the late nineteenth century gave advice on matters of social etiquette, not fashion and beauty (Dancyger 1978). As a genre, women's magazines emerged at a time when the moral hierarchy of Church, Monarch, and State was challenged by the rise of individualism. This challenge opened a gap between meaning and personal motivation, filled, in part, by emergent cultural industries that had, as their appeal, an explication of the morality of the new bourgeois order. The personalized nature of women's magazines reinforced the individualism of this new order. This textual strategy has been credited to Edward Bok, appointed editor of *Ladies' Home Journal* in 1889. In an attempt to identify what women liked and disliked in magazine reading, Bok surveyed readers. His survey revealed that young women needed a confidante to fill a role their mothers were no longer taking. Under the pseudonym 'Ruth Ashmore,' Edward Bok devised the original advice column for female readers (Mott 1957; Peterson 1964; Wood 1971). Initially, this advice concerned 'personal' problems for women striving to achieve the femininity espoused by their magazines. From their inception, magazines for girls adopted this personal form of address, integrating their textual messages into the intimacy of readers' lives.

With the spread of consumerism and the emergence of a bourgeois class requiring guidance about appropriate dress as well as manners, the conditions were laid for fashion advice as necessary for the accomplishment of ideal womanhood. It was not until after the Second World War, however, that the potential for a specifically teenage fashion market was fully realized. *Mayfair,* published from 1946 until 1950, is cited as the first British 'teenzine,' the term used to refer to fashion and beauty magazine for specifically adolescent readers.[13] *Seventeen,* established in 1944 in North America, remains in print, making it the 'queen' of teenage titles. Up until this time, magazine fashion had been too up-market and too mature for teenage girls. By the 1960s, however, the notion of 'teenagers' emerged as one effect of the postwar baby boom. As Braithwaite and Barrel (1979) note, the category 'teenager' emphasized the social, and not physiological, status of adolescents.[14] Throughout the 1960s and 1970s, magazines for adolescent females helped to develop the teenage fashion market. For example, Honey Boutiques opened in Britain during the mid-1960s to exploit the success of *Honey* magazine. In 1961, *19* was launched in an attempt to take advantage of the success of *Honey*, as were *Petticoat* (1966) and *Look Now* (1972), although *Honey* continued to dominate the market (Braithwaite and Barrel 1979: 40–2, 58, 59). A Young Spending Survey, published by IPC Magazines in October 1970, estimated the total net income of women aged fifteen to twenty-four to be £925 million. Claimed as the most comprehensive market survey yet conducted among this group of women, it itemized the spending of young women.

In the United States, *Mademoiselle* emerged in 1935, targeting readers aged eighteen to twenty-five, although it also had a sizeable following among younger readers. *Mademoiselle* was the first periodical to provide fashion coverage exclusively for younger women (Ford 1969; White 1970). Focusing on the college campus, and employing college women as temporary editors throughout the summer months, the magazine continues to serve collegiate and young careerists (White 1970; Taft 1982). In 1944, *Seventeen* emerged as a magazine orienting girls aged thirteen to nineteen towards a traditionally feminine domestic role. Now edited as a fashion magazine, *Seventeen* publicizes itself as the place 'where the girl becomes the woman' (quoted in Barthel 1988: 37). Advertisers are reported to see *Seventeen* as a bridge between traditional pre-teen titles and adult women's magazines such as *Cosmopolitan* and *Glamour* (Donaton 1990). After the Second World War, *Junior Bazaar* emerged as a serious competitor to *Mademoiselle* and *Seventeen*, merging with *Harper's Bazaar* in 1948. Throughout the 1950s and 1960s, a series of fashion magazines for young women were launched, including *Young Miss* (1955) for girls aged nine to fourteen, *Ingenue* (1959) for those thirteen to nineteen, *Teen* (1960), and *Elegant-Teen* (1963) for younger Black readers (Ford 1969; White 1970; Wolseley 1971). However, a period of recession saw the failure of many of the U.S. magazines: those that survived underwent an editorial transformation which tied them more closely to advertisers as the primary source of revenue. At the time of the current study, *Teen*, *Seventeen*, and *YM* dominated the Canadian teenzine market, with *Sassy* positioning itself as an 'alternative' magazine. Like the majority of fashion and beauty magazines for adult women, teenzines 'service' white, middle-class girls.

Magazines for adolescent girls by no means lack readers. At time of initiating my research, *Seventeen* boasted an annual circulation of 1,940,601 paying readers, and *YM* 1,701,615 (*Advertising Age* 21 Feb. 1994: 25). In a survey of Canadian adolescents, Baker (1985) found that girls were much more likely than boys to read magazines: 67 per cent of the girls in her study indicated that reading was among the leisure activities which they enjoyed. The most frequently mentioned reading material of girls was romantic novels and teenzines. Without trying to impute a causal relation, it is interesting to note that 75 per cent of the girls expected to be married by the age of thirty, and most of these girls described marriage in very romantic terms: sitting in front of a fireplace, talking to a loving husband after the children have been put to bed (pp. 116, 188). What this finding clearly indicates is that, whatever the 'cause,' women's attachment to the values of domesticity and heterosexual romance has already begun before their adult reading of women's magazines. Available research links these romantic visions to teenzine content.

Inside Teenzines

Adolescent magazines are only just becoming an object of scholarly investigation. Historically commentators have treated these magazines as a specialty segment of the more general genre of women's magazines. Content analysis of teenzines both confirms this view, and points to unique characteristics of media for adolescent women. For example, Evans and colleagues (1991) analyse the content of three market-leading North American magazines for adolescent girls distributed during 1988. Taken together, fashion topics were the dominant subject across all magazines, accounting for about 35 per cent of total content, followed in emphasis by feature articles, beauty, entertainment, and special recurring columns (p. 104). They list the dominant identity-related themes of feature articles as interpersonal relations, self-esteem, education and career, special problems, and ideology. The largest category of identity themes – interpersonal relations – was dominated by articles about dating and heterosexuality, followed by discussions of relations with peers and family. These writers conclude that, although ostensibly governed by the theme of self-improvement, similar to most women's magazines, these publications approach this topic largely through fashion and physical beautification, giving only modest attention to normative problems in primarily female–male relations. They note that the theme of physical beautification extends into related areas of health and nutrition. They conclude that, except for the matter of heterosexual adjustment (especially issues of sexuality), themes that are emphasized in psychological research on adolescent females are not given a high profile in teenzines. They claim that writers for these magazines appear to assume that their target population is largely uninterested or unable to process material which moves beyond concrete, here-and-now issues in order to consider problems of future orientation, longer-term consequences of behaviour, and issues associated with transition to adult roles. Discussion of political issues, of personal development through intellectual and aesthetic pursuits or sports, or of women's independent professional development was absent, or these themes were subtly derided (p. 112). Evans and colleagues conclude that contemporary magazines for girls support 'traditional' socialization for women.

While little longitudinal research is available, what does exist shows that contemporary content differs from earlier proscriptions for young girls. In a review of issues of *Seventeen* published from 1962–3 to 1972, Ramsdell and Gaier (1974) report that there was an increased emphasis on individual identity for teenage readers. When comparing the adolescents of 1962 to their counterparts in the 1970s, the authors summarize the key difference in terms of the adolescent's questioning of what life is actually like rather than what it should be like, and of what is meaningful for the individual. Unlike teenagers of the 1970s, the adolescents of 1962 were 'on the whole not deeply involved in ideology, nor ... prepared to do much individual thinking on value issues of generality' (p. 589). A more recent study by Kate Peirce (1990) also documents the changing construction of 'the adolescent' and notions of 'adolescent femininity.'

Beginning from similar questions about the socialization of teenage girls, Peirce (1990) analyses editorial copy in *Seventeen* for 1961, 1972, and 1985. These dates are significant in that they allow a comparison of materials published before the emergence of postwar feminism, during the height of public awareness of feminist issues, and during the current 'post-feminist' period. Her analysis supports many of the findings of Evans and colleagues (1991) in that, across these publication periods, the topic of physical beauty makes up about 50 per cent of all editorial copy. Together, the traditionally feminine subjects of beauty, fashion, and domestic crafts dominate magazine content for all three periods. Although feminist messages of self-reliance and independence increased somewhat – from 7.5 per cent in 1961 to 16.6 per cent during 1972 – they pale beside the amount of space devoted to traditional topics. Furthermore, by 1985 self-development topics returned to their pre-feminist figures (p. 498). Peirce concludes that the dominant message of *Seventeen* is that a teenage girl should be concerned with improving her appearance, finding a man, and learning how to take care of the house. As did Evans and colleagues, Peirce concludes that *Seventeen* perpetuates a traditional ideology of womanhood.

In Britain, Angela McRobbie (1991a) compares adolescent magazines published in the 1970s and 1980s. Rejecting the quantitative approach of content analysis, she is interested in how magazine texts work to make teenzines 'fun' to read. Employing a semiological analysis, McRobbie identifies the codes of teenzine discourse which act as the discursive mechanisms (visual and narrative) through which the meaning of adolescent femininity is constructed. McRobbie identifies four codes in popular adolescent magazines of the 1970s: romance, personal and/or domestic life, fashion and beauty, and pop music, (pp. 93, 94). During the 1980s, the romance code was being displaced by a new realism highlighting the problems and difficulties of heterosexual relationships. Pop music, and fashion and beauty, remain important. McRobbie concludes (p. 146) that contemporary teenzines concentrate on their readers as potentially sophisticated and discerning young consumers. From this perspective, there is little to differentiate this magazine genre from its adult counterpart.

Given the paucity of research on adolescent magazines, one of the first tasks of the current study was to develop a systematic characterization of teenzine content. While the method for this characterization is discussed in chapter 3, this chapter is an appropriate point at which to sketch out the major descriptive findings. These findings are based on the content analysis of the four leading teenzines in Canada at the time of the current study – *Teen, Seventeen, Young and Modern (YM),* and *Sassy.* Given their popularity among teenage readers, these titles have received the most academic attention.[15] This attention corresponds to reading preferences for the girls in this study. While these preferences are the analytical problematic of the current study, and thus are discussed at greater length in later chapters, commentary from readers is included here to bring together texts and their readers. Later we will see that *Girl Talk* highlights the necessity to read magazine texts against girls' accounts of them.

Similar to women's magazines, teenzines comprise a diversity of textual formats, differentiated in this study as advertising texts, which are the major source of glossy pictorials; editorial texts in the form of feature articles and regular columns; texts attributed to readers, as in the case of letters as well as poems or, less frequently, commentary and stories; and fiction. As we shall see in later chapters, texts (purportedly) written by readers are one of the main attractions of teenzines for girls in the study:

I like the poetry section. It's called 'Stuff You Wrote' and it's just poems and stuff that other people wrote and some of them are really good. (Fifteen-year-old Chelsea)[16]

I just read it [*YM*] 'cause, uhm, all these little, the little short stories, like all the letters that they write in and all that kind of stuff.
[Interviewer:] Why is that interesting?
Uhm, just 'cause it's people writing in. It's not just, you know, a bunch of fiction. (Sixteen-year-old Lindsay)

Like they have issues in *YM*, but the have two sides to things sometimes. Like when they have controversial stuff, like if there's a question sometimes they'll have one article, like someone agreeing with it, and someone disagreeing. I found it more tells you to do what you *feel* rather than to '*don't* do it' ... It also has like what guys think of certain things – like they do a lot of interviewing so it's not just the *editor,* usually it's a lot of people's opinions. (Seventeen-year-old Roshni)

However, despite the appeal of texts written by readers rather than editors, these texts comprise a very small proportion of magazine content. For example, texts attributed to readers account for 7.7 per cent of all units of analysis coded in *YM*, which contains the greatest proportion of text attributed to readers, and 2.6 per cent in *Seventeen* which contains the least (Currie 1992). Given that over 90 per cent of written texts appear as regular editorial columns, feature articles, and advice pages, the content of these texts was systematically enumerated for subject matter. Together, these three types of texts constitute the bulk of written texts in teenzines. As we see below, content analysis of the four magazines in this study yields themes similar to those identified by previous research; our task is to understand why the content of teenzines appeals to young readers and, ultimately, why teenzines are such a pervasive force in the life of many adolescent girls.

Feature articles are important in attracting readership; many of the girls claim that they decide to read (or buy) a magazine on the basis of its feature article or story:

Usually I just take it a page at a time. I don't really go to any section in particular first *unless* something's on the cover. You know, it says something that I'm interested in at the time, like you know, it says inside 'on page whatever,' then I'll go to it [first]. (Seventeen-year-old Roshni)

I usually flip through and – [pause] – go to the one the front page, you know how it will like have a special thing that it's talking about. Usually, with the clothes and stuff they'll have like a big section with different kinds of clothes and stuff like that – I don't go to that. I go to whatever's the *main* part of the magazine. (Seventeen-year-old Victoria)

What I usually do when I'm reading a magazine is I'll go for the cover story first, 'cause that's usually why I picked up the magazine, is the cover. I'll read that if it interests me. Like I'll get halfway through it and if it's good I'll keep reading or whatever, and then I'll just flip through and see if [there's] anything else. If there's like, *good* fashions, I'll check those out as well. (Seventeen-year-old Jamie)

Table 1.1 summarizes the subject matter of feature articles. Here we can see that, although more than twenty categories of subject matter were developed during coding, the content of editorial texts covers a narrow range of topics: fashion/ beauty, heterosexual romance, and celebrities account for at least half of the topics of all texts except those in *Sassy*. These topics have a tendency to be linked. For example, fashion is linked to celebrities when the lives of runway models are featured, as well as to heterosexual romance when male pop stars talk about their preferences in girlfriends. While the success stories of mega models naturalize the association of women with beauty, interviews with young, handsome male celebrities that highlight their romantic preferences naturalizes heterosexuality. This process is reinforced when these themes are linked to the less frequent, apparently 'alternative' themes, such as female success. While *Teen* quite often features female success by interviewing women athletes, *Seventeen* is much more likely to link female success to beauty through the story of an 'ordinary' reader who became a supermodel. Other important pairings include the body with sexuality and personal testimonials with social issues. Chapter 7 explores in detail how framing topics in these ways invites reader identification while naturalizing the constructed world of adolescence. Overall, however, the most striking association found in editorial texts is their link to advertising. This textual strategy reflects what Earnshaw (1984: 418) calls the 'advertising editorial' and McCracken (1993: 54) an 'advertorial.' Both terms refer to the blurring of boundaries between advertising text and editorial matter through a merging of the visual and verbal styles in which editorial and advertisements are presented. Although stories about celebrities and movie stars are seldom considered to be advertorials, they are ultimately connected to marketing of fashion and cosmetics, as well as music CDs, movies, and videos. In the final analysis, although appearing in editorial texts the topics of beautification and entertainment are linked to the promotion of commodities in ways that naturalize these associations. This theme is taken up in chapter 5.

The second type of editorial text appears as regular columns. Unlike in feature articles, the topic of a regular column is fixed from month to month and is attributed to the same author. Regular columns give magazine content a predictability which many readers enjoy:

I always flip through the whole thing before I read anything. I'd probably read, like my horoscope and look through the questions, and if an article interested me on someone I knew, I'd probably read that. I know the layout of *YM*, so I usually *know* what to turn to. I usually look at the 'Say Anythings,' like because they're really funny, and my horoscope first. (Fifteen-year-old Kirsten)

Table 1.1: Subjects of Feature Articles in Four Adolescent Magazines[1]

Category	% of features with theme[2]			
	Teen	YM	Seventeen	Sassy
Beauty & Fashion				
1 Beauty	25.0	16.0	27.3	6.7
2 Fashion	17.3	25.2	39.0	29.3
Relationships				
3 Romance, guys	11.5	19.9	15.6	6.7
4 Peer relationships	6.4	0.8	2.6	2.7
5 Family relationships	1.9	4.6	7.8	1.3
Success Topics				
6 Stardom, celebrities	12.2	25.2	7.8	10.7
7 Female success stories	3.8	5.3	6.5	9.3
Self				
8 Self-discovery	8.3	0.0	1.3	0.0
9 Psychological well-being	5.1	0.8	1.3	1.3
10 Body, health	3.8	6.1	1.3	5.3
11 Sexuality	0.6	3.8	1.3	2.7
12 Work, career	0.6	0.8	3.9	6.7
13 Education, college	0.6	0.0	2.6	1.3
Social Issues				
14 Social issues	6.4	7.4	6.4	24.0
15 Personal testimonial	5.8	8.4	5.2	13.3
Entertainment				
16 Reviews of books, movies, music	3.8	3.8	0.0	0.0
Miscellaneous				
17 Sports	–	–	2.6	2.7
18 Recipes	–	–	1.3	–
19 Shopping	–	–	–	2.7
20 Other	3.8	–	–	6.7
Base *N*	156	131	77	75

1 Features taken from all issues published between June 1993 and May 1994
2 Each feature can have more than one theme.

YM has this thing in it – 'Say Anything' – and it's about all these embarrassing moments and everything and I really like it and so it's just something that I get all the time, like, every month. (Fifteen-year-old Tiffany)

Let's see, I look at the horoscope first, then check out who's wearing what, where, in the ads – I don't really read a *lot* in the ads, like the make-up ads – and then I go through the ones they have in every issue – like the 'Ask Jane,' the beauty tip section, that kind of thing [laughs] – and *then* I go to the Contents and see what the theme article is and see if it interests me. (Thirteen-year-old Stephanie)

Table 1.2 summarizes the topics coded for regular columns. Similar to the editorial content of features, fashion/beauty, heterosexual romance, and stardom account for most of the themes in these texts. In addition to these topics, about one-third of the regular columns of *Seventeen* and almost 40 per cent of those in *Sassy* contain articles about physical health or the body and social issues. Again *Sassy* is notable in that regular columns give no attention to romance, and contain considerably more commentary than either *YM* or *Seventeen* on books, movies, and music. Overall, the style of regular columns is very similar, if not identical to, feature material. In fact, it was often difficult to decide which texts were regular versus featured text without cross-checking for recurrence in other monthly issues.

The third type of editorial text is found on advice pages, taking a question-and-answer format. We will see later that advice is among the most frequently mentioned readings:

Well, there's 'Your Body' and questions and stuff about body parts and everything, and some of them are about guys and things like that. (Fifteen-year-old Chelsea)

And it has questions. Like you can ask about your body. There's questions, like everyday questions you can ask to this model that answers them. They just seem to relate more to me, like age-wise and everything. (Fifteen-year-old Kirsten)

Although most advice appears in regular columns, it was enumerated as a separate category of text to allow coding of individual question/answer pairs. In table 1.3 topics were coded according to the questions posed, which act as a framework for the answer, a discursive technique discussed in chapter 7. As shown in table 1.3, the topics discussed on advice pages cover three main themes: boys, the body, and beauty. Together, these categories account for at least half of the topics discussed. Interestingly, *Seventeen* contains the smallest proportion of these topics in advice columns, a finding discussed later. As well,

Table 1.2: Subjects of Regular Columns in Four Adolescent Magazines[1]

	% of regular columns with theme[2]			
Category	Teen	YM	Seventeen	Sassy
Beauty & Fashion				
1 Beauty	20.8	16.2	9.3	6.6
2 Fashion	8.3	6.6	5.2	6.6
Relationships				
3 Romance, guys	29.2	25.7	19.2	0.0
4 Peer relationships	1.0	2.2	1.0	1.2
5 Family relationships	0.0	2.2	1.0	0.0
Success Topics				
6 Stardom, celebrities	1.0	10.3	9.3	7.8
7 Female success stories	20.8	0.0	1.0	0.0
Self				
8 Self-discovery/assessment	1.0	8.1	2.4	5.4
9 Psychological well-being	1.0	0.7	1.7	1.2
10 Physical health, information on body	3.1	2.9	13.1	21.6
11 Sexuality (psychological and physical)	3.1	0.7	2.4	3.6
12 Work, career	0.0	9.6	1.0	0.6
13 Education, college	0.0	0.7	3.8	0.0
Social Issues				
14 Social issues	4.2	4.4	21.0	16.8
15 Personal testimonial	0.0	0.0	1.4	1.2
Entertainment				
16 Reviews of books, movies, music	0.0	2.2	2.1	20.4
Miscellaneous				
17 Horoscope, numerology	11.5	14.7	4.1	4.8
18 Sports	7.3	0.0	3.1	1.2
19 Recipes	–	–	3.4	–
20 Other	1.0	7.4	8.2	5.4
Base *N*	96	136	291	167

1 Regular columns from all issues published between June 1993 and May 1994
2 Each regular column can have more than one theme.

Table 1.3: Types of Questions on Advice Pages in Four Adolescent Magazines[1]

Category	% of questions with theme[2]			
	Teen	YM	Seventeen	Sassy
1 Boys, relationships with boys	18.2	36.7	31.3	31.7
2 Body, health	12.3	25.8	20.9	25.6
3 Beauty	48.6	10.8	0.0	14.6
4 Friendship	9.1	6.7	7.0	6.7
5 Family relationships	5.0	8.3	15.1	7.9
6 Psychological problems	3.2	3.3	7.0	7.9
7 Miscellaneous	3.5	8.3	18.6	5.5
Base N	361	107	82	159
No. of ques/answer pairs per issue	32.8	10.7	6.8	14.5

1 Questions taken from all issues published between June 1993 and May 1994
2 Each question/answer pair can have more than one theme.

Seventeen contains the greatest proportion of questions about family relationships; most of these questions are about parents. Also, *Seventeen* contains the greatest number of miscellaneous topics, which include questions about teenage rights (such as to birth control or abortion) and social issues (such as being raped by a family friend). Given their popularity among the readers in this study, advice texts are discussed in greater length in chapter 7.

In summary, the written texts of teenzines included in this study cover a narrow range of topics: fashion and beauty, heterosexual romance, and stardom are the dominant topic themes of editorial texts. Although teenzines include a smaller amount of factual discussion of the female body, these texts attract the attention of young readers. These findings suggest that adolescent magazines are very much like their adult counterpart, because they advance the traditional concerns of femininity. Because these themes have been documented by previous researchers, these findings are not novel and, in fact, may not appear to be significant. However, our analysis is just beginning. To say that the content of teenzines mirrors that of women's magazines is not to say that these texts play an identical role in the life of adolescent girls. In this study, textual similarity is seen to belie the common origin of these magazines as commercial texts. What remains to be demonstrated is the significance of these texts in the everyday lives of young readers. As we shall see, this significance cannot be 'read off the text.' While the identification of content helps us, as researchers, to gain familiarity with teenzine texts as the 'object' of investigation, it does not answer questions about how texts work or why so many girls enjoy them. Unlike cul-

tural critics who 'read' the social effect of teenzines off their content, here enumeration of content is for the singular purpose of establishing researcher
familiarity with these magazines. In order to discover what these topics mean to
their adolescent readers, and to assess their significance in the lives of teenage
girls, we need to move beyond simply an enumeration of magazine content.

Conclusion

If we look at the content of women's magazines, the evidence seems incontro-
vertible: the representation of women within women's magazines associates
femininity with the sphere of domesticity and heterosexual romance; it emphasizes youth and the physical beauty of whiteness; and it underrepresents the
diverse identities and concerns of women as a social category. These themes
appear to also describe magazines produced specifically for adolescent girls,
although very little research has been conducted on this venue. These three
themes are historically persistent, despite dramatic changes in the social and
economic position of women, and extensive criticism of the mass media by
feminist commentators. Like the woman of yesteryear, today's liberated female
continues to be shown as not only conforming to, but embracing, traditional
standards of feminine beauty and patriarchal sexuality (see Lingard 1993).
Based on these types of findings, Ballaster and colleagues (1991: 169) conclude
that, although women's magazines have undergone a variety of transformations
since their first appearance in the seventeenth century, they exhibit remarkable
continuity in terms of their address to readers and social function (p. 169). From
their inception, women's magazines have posited female subjectivity as a problem and themselves as an answer: they offer female readers a guide to living as
women in a patriarchal (racist) culture. It now seems so self-evident to claim
that women's magazines perpetuate stereotypical representations of femininity
that Jaddou and Williams (1981) describe content analysis as merely 'restate-
ment of the obvious.'

   Although I endorse many of the criticisms which Jaddou and Williams (and
others) raise against content analysis, it seems to me that this approach has
played an important role in raising analytical interest in the cultural representation of women. As we shall see, this claim may be more correct for the North
American than the British context, where qualitative and ethnographic methods
dominate sociological research on women's media. In either context, however,
before the 1970s little attention was paid to the reconstitution of gender relations through the mass media. One reason for this lack of interest is the pervasive naturalization of gender, which was not considered a sociological
phenomenon until the emergence of feminist sociology and, later, women's

studies. One exception is Erving Goffman (1979), who anticipated the eventual shift away from the study of content to textual form. He was among the first to question why the cultural representations of advertisements, which treat grown women as children, do not seem strange to readers, and hence call their construction into question. His answer directed researchers to 'gender displays': the reason that advertisements do not look strange to us is because they gain meaning from the stock of commonsense expressions of gender norms that people use to make sense of everyday life. We explore this process in the remainder of this study. For the moment we note that researchers following Goffman have systematically documented the appearance of gender displays in everyday cultural texts (see Belknap and Leonard 1991; Massé and Rosenblum 1988). Although I agree that much of this research is repetitive, in my view the charting of gender through content analysis was a necessary stage for the incorporation of feminist cultural debate within the social sciences. In effect, it opened the door within sociology for contemporary approaches to the theoretical study of social texts. We can already see that, while debate about the cultural representation of women begins from the (manifest) content of mass media such as women's magazines, it does not stop there: feminist objections to this imagery are the result of belief in the power of cultural representation.

Looking at debates which surround the content of women's magazines, two opposing approaches to social texts have been identified. On one side, feminists argue that women's magazines are a medium of cultural representation that helps to reproduce the dominant order through the construction of identities which resonate with the patriarchal subordination of women. In this approach women's magazines are treated as scripts which reproduce gender identities as relations of domination and subordination through a male gaze which disciplines women and is responsible for a backlash against women's liberation. From this perspective there is little to redeem women's magazines. On the other side of the debate, however, women's magazines are more recently described as women-centred texts which provide resources for women's playful self-expression and utopian fantasies. In this approach, women's magazines are a vehicle of female pleasure and are not to be mistaken for reality: Winship (1981: 55) maintains that feminist critiques often overlook the fact that women's magazines are 'first and foremost fantasies for pleasure rather than practical action, and that they are recognized as such by the viewer.' Underlying the opposition of these two claims are opposing views of power. In the first approach, texts are seen as all powerful and as determining, in effect, the responses of readers. In the second approach, by way of contrast, readers remain very much in control of textual meanings and their consumption. When framed in this way debates on women's magazines appear to be at an impasse, reflected in feminist disagreement over these texts as vehicles of oppression as opposed to pleasure (see Walters 1995). Magazines are either celebrated or condemned; there seems to be little middle ground. Ballaster and colleagues (1991: 4) blame this impasse on the duality of women's magazines: women's magazines are a commodity in themselves and a medium for the sale of commodities, but simultaneously a set of images referring to an imaginary world. Rather than advance one side of this dual nature, Ballaster and colleagues explore the relations between these two levels and functions (discussed in chapter 2). In doing so they view women's magazines as bridging the economic and the cultural.

While I agree with Ballaster et al. that the current impasse will not be resolved as long as women's magazines are treated as simply cultural objects, for me the impasse reflects the analytical conflation of the cultural and the social. What I mean is that researchers, whether from the social sciences or literary studies, tend to read the social off the textual. In this chapter we have seen, for example, that, although feminists disagree on the precise nature of the effect of magazine reading, both sides tend to support their position through analysis of magazine texts alone: both sides read the social effects of women's magazines from the text itself. I refer to this manner of reading as 'researcher reading' of women's magazines. In the next chapter we explore how feminists have theorized the power of women's magazines and the agency of readers through researcher readings of social texts. The review presented in chapter 2 is premised on the post-structuralist position that all meaning is intertextual: academic texts exist in dialogue with other bodies of writing. Chapter 2 thus makes visible the otherwise absent discourse that gives *Girl Talk* unique meaning.

2

Materialist Feminism: The Ideology of Women's Magazines

Chapter 1 directed our attention to debates about the role which cultural imagery plays in women's lives and the stand which feminism should take on women's magazines. As framed in the current research, these debates are based on differing assumptions about power, agency, and the cultural construction of the social. Discussion of these issues moves us from descriptions of images to explanations of how images work. Only the latter analysis will help us understand the social significance (rather than content) of women's magazines, allowing us to resolve the political debates which this content has raised. While debates concerning the 'value' of women's magazines are (too) frequently dismissed as a battle for moral position, political positions resonate with theoretical traditions within feminist theory and women's studies.

The first tradition discussed in this chapter frames neo-Marxist debates on the status of culture and agency of human subjects. Beginning with this approach reflects my personal starting point within materialist feminism; it makes visible the frame of reference from which *Girl Talk* was written. In this chapter we explore shifts in Marxist feminist analyses of culture, beginning with the work of the influential Centre for Contemporary Cultural Studies. Within a sociological discourse, women's magazines are one of many processes through which bodies become 'gendered.' Other processes include, for example, role modelling and symbolic interaction, which typically would not be analysed as social texts; while these types of processes are ignored in this chapter, we acknowlege their importance later.

As we saw chapter 1, sex-role theory provided one way for feminist sociologists to conceptually link the content and the effects of cultural representation. Sex-role theory is implicit in writing which treats women's magazines as scripts of femininity: women are said to learn femininity through identification with cultural representations. Within liberal feminism these representations are problematic because they offer stereotypical depictions of women. By 'stereotype,' feminists generally mean 'a one-sided, exaggerated and normally prejudicial view of a group of people' (Abercrombie, Hill, and Turner 1988: 242). The term 'stereotype' thus implies that texts are capable of providing a 'truer' picture of the world. Furthermore, because the stereotypes of women in magazines are restrictive, they are seen to distort the true interests of women, to repress women's 'authenticity.' Liberal critics demand that social roles prescribed on the basis of biological identity be replaced by representations of 'real' women, women as they actually are or can be. Advocates of this position support the notion of androgyny: the combined presence of socially valued feminine and masculine characteristics in individuals, regardless of their biological sex (Kaplan and Sedney 1980). They claim that this principle overcomes the forced dualism of prescribed femininity and masculinity, providing instead unity and totality.[1]

While Marxist feminists do not disagree that women's magazines are among the social texts through which gendered identities are reproduced, for them the liberal critique does not go far enough: specifically, it advocates a reform of imagery rather than change in those processes through which imagery is produced. For Marxist feminists reform neglects questions about power, not simply as men's vested interests in the domestication of women, but also as economic interests which are served when femininity gives primacy to home and hearth and constructs women as consumers. These writers point out that, while individual men may benefit from the domestic service of their wives, women's commitment to domesticity also serves powerful economic interests. For example, traditional femininity has been used to render women an available source of cheap labour (see Armstrong and Armstrong 1984; Connelly 1978). Thus, when Marxist feminists study women's magazines as social texts, they do so primarily to link the cultural representation of women to powerful interests beyond the text, embedded in social formations which are the primary beneficiaries of commercial cultural production. Thus Marxist feminists do not expect the text to reflect the reality of women's lives.[2] Despite this important difference between liberal and Marxist feminism, however, in many ways they share an analytical agenda: within sociology,[3] liberals and Marxists alike analyse magazines primarily as a vehicle through which women acquire gender and sexual identity. However unintentional, this emphasis often results in teleological arguments characteristic of social-reproduction theory more generally, a problem we return to in the conclusion of this chapter.

The analytical term favoured by Marxist analysis of the reconstitution of the gendered social order, and which appears almost universally in feminist discussion of mass media until more recently, is 'ideology.' While ideology is one of the most debated concepts in social science, in feminist debate it typically refers to the way in which ideas, beliefs, and systems of meaning serve to sustain relations of domination (see Thompson 1984). To view images as ideological is not only to expose them as stereotypical constructions, but to also draw attention to the interests that they serve by restricting and fixing the meanings of social life. Reference to the ideological nature of women's magazine images links their existence and their effects to patriarchal economic interests. Because these messages advance powerful interests which lie beyond the text, the images and messages of women's magazines are viewed as symptomatic of their material production; in doing so, writers reject the treatment of women's magazines as simply texts. For example, Ballaster and colleagues (1991) note that, in Britain, about £60 million was spent to purchase women's magazines in 1985. During the past few decades, publishing giants have become multinationals with a vested interest in constructing their readers as consumers of their magazines, as well as the many products promoted between magazine covers. They thus link the content of women's magazines to financial interests outside the text and use this link to account for the form of women's magazines. One advantage of theories of ideology therefore is the identification of women's magazines not as simply *social* texts, because they participate in popular discourse, but as *commercial* texts, because they are produced in the service of capitalist production. This is an important distinction which we retain for the remainder of *Girl Talk*.

However useful they are in directing attention to the economic interests of women's print media, a second limitation of Marxist theories of ideology is their treatment of reading Subjects. As does the tradition initiated by Friedan, many theorists of ideology give the impression that women are manipulated by mass media and led to believe that consumption is a panacea for their oppression. As Johnson (1993) notes, this approach implies the existence of an 'authentic' womanhood which is repressed or denied through magazine messages about 'femininity' and the proper role of women: 'women' become 'an always-already-constituted group, a group whose shared characteristics are assumed to be somehow pre-existing the forms in which women are addressed by mass culture' (p. 32). As Ang (1988) and Tasker (1991) point out, such a view implies that only the academic, privileged through a 'non-ideological' reading of the text, knows the true interests of women. As well as promoting academic elitism, however, ethnographic research can disappoint these theoreticians because actual readers do not always behave as predicted. Elizabeth Frazer's (1987) ethnography of young teenzine readers caused her to question whether actual readers ever behave the way theoretical accounts of ideology predict. She found, for example, that her readers' reflexivity and reflectiveness undercut the effects of ideological appeals. The feminist tradition of ethnographic research which challenges notions of ideology commonly employed by Marxist sociologists is discussed in the conclusion of this chapter. Here we note that both theoretical problems inherent in the notion of ideology and empirical research call for approaches giving greater attention to the polysemic and unstable nature of cultural representation.

Commercial Text as Ideology: Centre for Contemporary Cultural Studies

While the works of Raymond Williams, E.P. Thompson, and Stuart Hall have been central to the emergence of 'cultural studies' in Britain, analyses of the representation of women begin with the work of graduate students at the Centre for Contemporary Cultural Studies (CCCS) in Birmingham during the 1970s.[4] Founded in the mid-1960s as an interdisciplinary project, the CCCS was interested in 'history from below': the everyday struggle of individuals to make their lives through cultural and material resources bequeathed by history. Stuart Hall (1982), who was to become director, describes the encounter between Marxism and British cultural studies as a critique of reductionism and economism, problems which were seen to be extrinsic and not intrinsic to Marxism.[5] He refers specifically to the dominant model of base and superstructure, 'through which sophisticated and vulgar Marxism alike had tried to think the relationships between society, economy and culture' (pp. 279–80). Storey (1993: 44) characterizes British cultural studies by its emphasis on human agency through the active rather than passive consumption of culture. This approach explicitly rejects the view, perpetuated by the Frankfurt School, of mass culture imposed 'from above' in favour of the study of culture transformed through its consumption. The Birmingham school thus distinguished mass culture from 'popular culture,' the latter referring to the meanings and practices which people actively make from their use of products of the culture industry (Williams 1976: 199).

As Johnson (1993: 30, 31) notes, the study of youth culture figured prominently in the work of the Birmingham Centre. Here the notion of popular culture as resistance emerged in response to widespread worry that the visible consumption by postwar youth testified to their 'Americanization' through manipulation by new industries directed at them (see Strinati 1995). Instead, the use of commodities such as clothing and music by particular groups of young people to construct distinctive subcultures was analysed as 'resistance through rituals.' As McRobbie (1980) notes, these studies of popular culture drew primarily on all-male subjects: gender issues were incorporated only through feminist critique of work which marginalized young women and failed to address how girls are positioned within youth subculture.

Within this context, the Women's Studies Group (WSG) put the representation of women on the agenda of the Media Conference held in 1974 (see Editorial Group 1978). Although the WSG was relatively short-lived, the original members went on to make significant contributions to feminist cultural studies: for example, the group included Charlotte Brunsdon, Dorothy Hobson, Angela McRobbie, Christine Weedon, and Janice Winship. At the time of its formation, the WSG identified as its problematic the articulation of sex/gender with class. This focus reflects that fact that, while feminist analyses of domestic labour were beginning to be taken up by orthodox Marxists – a theme dominant in Canadian Marxist feminism – sexuality and class continued to be separated through neglect of the specificities of sex and gender (Editorial Group 1978: 13). It is interesting that, looking back, McRobbie (1991a) claims: 'If I had to go back and consider this problem now, I would go about it in a very different fashion. I would not harbour such a monolithic notion of class, and instead I would investigate how relations of power and powerlessness permeated the girls' lives – in the context of school, authority, language, job opportunities, the family, the community and sexuality' (p. 65). As we shall see, the 'relations of power and powerlessness' evoked by McRobbie resonate with Smith's (1987) 'relations of ruling,' discussed in chapter 5.

The work of the WSG during the 1970s reflects what Stuart Hall (1982), then director, calls a 'rediscovery of ideology.' That rediscovery was influenced by readings of Althusser and, later, Gramsci, which drew attention to 'reproduction' as a necessary process through which a social formation reconstitutes the conditions of its existence over time. This focus on social reproduction is important because it directed analytical attention of Marxists away from economic production.[6] Althusser's impact is evident in attempts to theorize subjectivity through his interpretation of ideology. Specifically, Althusser rejected a mechanical interpretation of the superstructure as merely a 'reflection' of the economic base, preferring instead the notion of 'social formation' as comprising three interrelated practices: the economic, the political, and the ideological. Rather than interpret the superstructure as a passive reflection of the economic infrastructure, Althusser viewed the superstructure as necessary to the existence of the base. His formulation therefore allows for the 'relative autonomy' of the superstructure, which is determined by the economic base only 'in the last instance.' While the economic therefore remains a determinant, it does so through a 'structure of dominance.' This determination is designated as 'overdetermination': the structured articulation of a number of contradictions and determinations at any one historical conjuncture. Overdetermination accounts for the way in which ideology is rendered invisible: ideology comes from so many different sources that it seems like common sense.

Following from this, two themes in Althusser have had a major influence on cultural studies. Unlike earlier interpretations of ideology as expressing the relationship between human actors and the conditions of their existence, Althusser saw ideology as an *imaginary* relation: 'In ideology men [*sic*] ... express, not relations between them and their conditions of existence, but the ways they live the relation between them and the conditions of existence: this presupposes both a real relation and an "imaginary," "lived" relation' (1969: 233). Importantly, although Althusser defined ideology as generated from logical structures of the mode of production, ideology works through human subjects. In other words, it is through ideology that human actors *live* their relations to the conditions of existence. However, although Althusser thus posited an active Subject, he argued that our subjectivity or sense of ourselves as free, rational agents is actually an effect of bourgeois ideology. From Lacan, Althusser posited subjectivity as misrecognition, related to the way in which ideologies were seen to work: 'I shall then suggest that ideology "acts" or "functions" in such a way that it "recruits" subjects among the individuals (it recruits them all), or "transforms" the individuals into subjects (it transforms them all) by that very precise operation which I have called interpellation or hailing, and which can be imagined along the lines of the most commonplace everyday police (or other) hailing: "Hey, you there!"' (pp. 162–3). The problem is that the individual, in taking up the position of the Subject in ideology, assumes that she or he is the author of the ideology which constructs her or his subjectivity. Althusser calls the mistaken obviousness that 'you' and 'I' are self-constructing Subjects 'the elementary ideological effect' (p. 161). While he thus retains belief in a stable, coherent Subject (capable of being hailed), Althusser claims that this Subject is inauthentic, a problem discussed at greater length below.

Followers of Althusser interpreted ideology as existing to smooth over or dispel contradictions in lived experience. Ideology accomplishes this effect by offering seemingly true, but patently false, resolutions to problems of existence. A major caveat to this assertion is that only 'scientific knowledge' – such as Althusserian Marxism – can see through the veil of ideology to the 'real' conditions of existence. In part, this caveat is based on ideology as a total and closed system: it sets only problems which it can answer (and then, of course, 'falsely'). The task of Althusserian critical practice is to deconstruct ideological accounts of the social through symptomatic reading, which will reveal the underlying problematic. Althusser describes symptomatic reading as the key to Marx's method of identifying those processes which, although absent from dominant discourse, are necessary to the social formation. Owing to their invisibility – hence lack of discursive articulation – these absences generate contradictions in lived experience which ideologies attempt to smooth over. The contribution of feminists adopting this method includes identification of processes of patriarchal domination: while gender ideology represents the unpaid domestic labour of women as natural, for Marxist feminists it is part of the necessary social formation of capitalist relations of production. By positing a natural (*cum* biological) basis for the sexual division of domestic labour, patriarchal ideologies smooth over the difficulties which women experience in their daily lives. Furthermore, these ideologies provide women a way to live in patriarchal culture by relegating the contradictions of their oppression to the realm of individual, personal problems. Given the discussion in chapter 1, it is easy to see why feminists at the CCCS identified women's magazines as a primary source of gender ideology which acts in this way to reproduce women's oppression.

Janice Winship (1978) posed one of the first sustained challenges to the liberal feminist interpretation of women's magazines as simply an example of the patronizing abuse and trivialization of women's 'real' position in society. Instead, Winship identified the images of women's magazines as ideological constructions which work at both a conscious and an unconscious level to smooth over the experiential contradictions of women's lives. These contradictions arise through women's position both 'inside and outside' capitalist relations of production. Drawing on Althusser, she documents how these contradictions are managed through magazine representations which offer women a portrayal not of the system of real relations which govern their existence, but of *imaginary* relations. She thus views femininity as not merely passive acceptance by women of patriarchal domination, but *active subordination* (p. 135: emphasis in original). In an examination of *Woman*, Winship works through the contradictions of the ideology of femininity and the magazine's means of representing them (pp. 140, 141). She concludes that, although real-life problems spill over into magazines – particularly in advice columns – the oppressive aspects of traditional femininity are represented as 'individual' particular problems so that women's shared oppression will not be recognized by readers. Thus, the contradictions of femininity which women experience and seek advice about cannot be challenged from within femininity, which is what the magazine as a whole endorses (p. 152).

Along similar lines, Angela McRobbie (1978) challenged the absence of girls across an entire range of disciplines claiming to deal with youth. Drawing on the work of Hall and Jefferson (1976), she examines the culture of working-class girls aged fourteen to sixteen years. The purpose of her study is to explore their 'peculiar and distinctive way of life' and 'the meanings, values and ideas embodied in institutions, in social relations, in systems of beliefs in mores and customs, in the uses of objects and material life' (p. 96). Reflecting her membership in the WSG, McRobbie linked this culture to the material position occupied by these girls as a result of their gender, age, and class, and to their likely future roles. Among the influences on these girls were official ideologies of youth, espoused in adolescent magazines such as *Jackie* and through school policies. In the former, McRobbie shows how adolescence, as an ideological construct, is given meaning and made comprehensible through those topics included in the *Jackie* repertoire – 'problems,' 'romance,' 'jealousy,' and so on. She find that girls who are the subjects of this discourse operate within these categories (p. 99).[7] She questions how the girls are 'interpellated' as class subjects, and how the effects of their positioning find expression in their identity.

To answer these types of questions, McRobbie looks at the material position of the girls, specifically their economic dependence upon parents and their attendance at school. Here she draws attention to a tension that emerges between identity as articulated through working-class family life and as operating through the school. While family life presents a consistent set of values, expectations, and assumptions about the girls' future role as wives and mothers, the dynamics of schooling present the girls with contradictory expectations owing to their class location. Simply put, although both working-class and middle-class girls are pushed in the direction of the home, middle-class girls are coached in different aspirations. While schooling for working-class girls emphasizes an adaptable, pliable, and docile labour source with only marginal skills, middle-class girls are (at least) somewhat more encouraged to think of themselves as having an identity independent of their future domestic roles (p. 102). Probably her most novel and influential finding, however, is the way in which the girls in her study combat the class-based and oppressive features of the school. Specifically, the girls introduce their 'femaleness,' via their sexuality, into the classroom: they reject the official ideology for girls in the school (neatness, diligence, appliance, femininity, passivity, etc.) and replace it with a *more* feminine, more sexual code. The girls took great pleasure in wearing make-up to school and spent vast amounts of time discussing romantic relations with boys, a theme elaborated in a later publication of this work (McRobbie 1991a; also see Lesko 1988). The problem is that this culture – which for our purposes is propagated by teenzines – projected the girls more clearly towards traditional femininity through a future of marriage and family, despite the fact that the girls were well aware of the potentially oppressive dimensions of these institutions. McRobbie concludes that the culture of femininity espoused by working-class girls is a response to the material limitations imposed on them as a result of their class position and, more generally, of their sexual oppression as women.

Hegemony and Counter-Hegemony: Ideology Revisited

As influential as the Althusserian Marxism of the CCCS was in rethinking the relationships among society, economy, and culture, Althusser himself was aware of some of the ambiguities and difficulties of his work. In 'Essays in Self-Criticism' (published in English in 1976), Althusser corrected the notion of ideology as 'pure error': 'Ideologies are not pure illusions (Error), but bodies of representations existing in institutions and practices: they figure in the super-structure, and are rooted in the class struggle' (p. 155). While this reworking clearly posits ideological reproduction as a much less monolithic process than many followers imply, conflict is still defined in terms of class relations. One result is that many feminist writers have found it more useful to rework theories of ideology through Gramscian revision. Drawing on Gramsci's notion of civil society, the realm of private citizenship and individual consent to the dominant social order was identified as an arena of political struggle. Although Althusserian Marxism tended to imply a rather unproblematic reproduction of the social order, Gramsci himself had stressed the contested nature of consent. Returning to Gramsci's work, three themes have been identified by feminist writers that are seen to address the more obvious problems of Althusserian Marxism: rejection of a distinction between 'scientific' and socially constructed knowledge, the importance of struggles in the cultural realm, and Gramsci's formulation of the relationship between politics and civil society.

The central theme of Gramsci's writings, found in Marx's early work, is the question of the relationship between human subjectivity as thoughts, feelings, and desires to the 'objective' conditions of existence. In addressing this question, Gramsci rejects the notion – common in Marxism of then and now – that 'scientific truth' (such as that produced by scientific socialism) can be set against socially constructed knowledge, such as religion, which Marxists designate as ideological and therefore 'false.' Clearly this view (not held by Marx but, Gramsci claims, by Engels) implies a universe independent of its human creators. The context for this claim was the notion, held by Italian Communists of Gramsci's time, that the purpose of a socialist revolution is to destroy the institutions of political power by force in order to set up new institutions acting in the name of the proletariat. For Gramsci, this approach to social transformation depends too much on the creation of an intellectual vanguard who can provide the proletariat with knowledge about their social position, a position about which this vanguard has no experience. In Gramsci's view, all the concepts through which our knowledge of the world is organized are related primarily, not to 'things,' but to relations among the users of those concepts (Kolakowski 1978: 230). While Gramsci endorsed the notion that these relations may not be immediately apprehended, he made it the task of 'organic' intellectuals to lead the subordinated classes to revolutionary consciousness. Clearly, Gramsci is rejecting the approach which claims that it is the task of theoreticians to provide either politicians or 'the people' with a practical plan of action based on 'scientific' or 'objective' analysis of the social. In fact he maintained that political action, and awareness of that action, its direction, and its purpose, are not separable phenomena but aspects of a single unity, making it difficult to speak of 'primacy' (Kolakowski 1978: 233). An organic intellectual provides leadership, not by describing social life from outside according to scientific laws and formulations, but through the language of lived culture, in a way which expresses the experiences and feelings of the subordinated classes. Because political processes express class (and, we would add, gendered and racialized) consciousness, social transformation entails a cultural project. For this reason, Gramsci also rejected the theoretical separation of the economic 'base,' as determinant of history, from a 'superstructure,' as cultural representation of the interests which underlie history. According to Kolakowski, Gramsci thought it 'absurd ... that the "superstructure" was a world of mere appearances or a "less real" side of life than productive relations' (p. 231).

While Gramsci saw consciousness as rooted in economic reality, he did not view the relationship between economics and politics, as the concrete expression of consciousness, in a reductionist way. For Gramsci, civil society acts as mediator: between the coercive realm of economic production and the state lies an area of social life which is experienced as the realm of the private citizen and of individual consent. While Marxists tend to emphasize the coercive nature of capitalist domination, Gramsci points out that, in practice, secure states rule more through consensual politics that by brute force. However, consent cannot be taken for granted, guaranteed through the simple circulation of dominant ideas as culture. Gramsci emphasizes that consent is under constant threat of being undone, and is maintained only through processes of negotiation and incorporation: that is, dominant culture is not imposed on the masses from above, but is the consequence of struggle. While Gramsci allows for resistance on the part of the underclasses against their subordination, successful incorporation into the values and meanings of bourgeois culture means that the underclasses actively participate in maintenance of the dominant order. For Gramsci, this relation between the political and civil society, played out through culture, is a process fraught with contradictions and struggle.

By emphasizing the active nature of hegemonic rule, Gramsci appears to solve a central problem of Althusserian Marxism: 'its monolithic and vertical concept of how the dominant ideological apparatuses function does not conceive of them as being subject to class contradictions ... The most concrete effect of this approach is that its field of observation marginalizes the resistance practices of the dominated classes against the dominant ideology, as well as it marginalizes the internal incoherencies which characterize the operation of those ideological apparatuses' (Mattelart and Siegelaub 1979: 29). Gramsci's concept of hegemony emphasized culture as a site of struggle between the forces which would incorporate groups into a dominant system of meaning and forces of resistance arising within subordinate groups. Analytically, the shift away from Althusser and towards Gramsci replaces notions of dominant ideology and interpellation with those of hegemony and negotiation. Within cultural studies (and often in contrast to sociology), the latter became more important. For our purposes, the notion of hegemony is important because it draws attention to the role of the cultural industries in negotiation of 'the social,' problematizing relationships between the cultural and the social realms of life. Hegemony as struggle for consent implies that there are everyday levels of political involvement and success unrecognized by orthodox Marxism. Furthermore, it affords political status to ordinary texts otherwise devalued by traditional scholarship. This allows McRobbie (1991a), for example, to locate *Jackie* within the political struggle to win young women's consent to patriarchal domination: '*Jackie* exists within a large, powerful, privately owned publishing apparatus which produces a vast range of newspapers, magazines and comics. It is on this level of the magazine that teenage girls are subjected to an explicit attempt to win consent to the dominant order – in terms of femininity, leisure and consumption, i.e. at the level of culture' (p. 87). Furthermore, *Jackie* occupies the sphere of the personal or private, what Gramsci calls 'civil society.' As a result, while there are visibly coercive elements to the other spheres which teenage girls inhabit – for example, the family, school, or community organizations – in their leisure pursuits girls (appear to) have the freedom to do as they please.

The appeal of Gramsci also coincides with a discernible move away from discussion of 'mass culture' to notions of 'popular culture.' While the term 'mass culture' retains the negative connotations assigned by the Frankfurt school, popular culture is seen to 'consist not simply of an imposed mass culture that is coincident with dominant ideology, nor simply of spontaneously oppositional cultures, but rather is an area of negotiation between the two within which – in different particular types of popular culture – dominant, subordinate and oppositional culture and ideological values and elements are "mixed" in different permutations' (Bennett 1986: xv–xvi). Here Bennett alludes to a key process in neo-Gramscian theory: articulation, meaning both 'to express' and to 'bring together.' Popular culture, as the ways in which audiences 'use' mass culture to create everyday, sometimes oppositional, meaning, is said to be marked by disarticulation–articulation (Mouffe 1979; see also Hennessy 1993). While Bennett highlights class conflict, scholarship in popular culture includes feminist explorations of conflicts surrounding gender, race, generation, sexual preference, and other marks of difference which, traditionally, have fallen outside the purview of Marxism (see O'Brien 1984). As Roman and Christian-Smith note (1988: 3), 'if one takes a Gramscian position on the relationship of popular culture to hegemony, then popular cultural forms matter for feminist materialist struggle because they are involved in securing and producing the consent of women and men to particular hegemonic meanings for gender ... and sexual difference.' From this perspective, Gramscian theories draw positive attention to the struggles of feminism as a counter-ideological force attempting to realign women's political commitments (see Jaddou and Williams 1981). Thus, the Gramscian notion of struggle within popular culture not only emphasizes the agency of individual readers/viewers, but equates cultural consumption with the making of history. Everyday activities like reading fashion magazines are associated with the political rather than the private realm, elevating their status within academic inquiry. For materialist feminists it became possible to raise issues of women's pleasures of consumption, without dismissing the role of women's magazines in perpetuating women's oppression. Along these lines, Ballaster and colleagues (1991) argue that their pleasurable qualities enable magazines to maintain their hegemony in women's lives. Exploring how women's magazines ensure reading pleasure, they found that readers were both selective and loyal in their choice and use of magazines. Self-identity, specifically as married or single, is closely related to choice of magazine. Despite individual preference, however, the authors note similarity in magazine definitions and understandings of what it means to be female (p. 129). This discursive similarity does not mean that readers have been simply duped by the appearance of variety and choice. The authors emphasize that their 'discussions with readers show that they *are* conscious of the magazines as bearers of particular discourses of femininity (domesticity, glamour, maternity) and that the magazines' primary address to specific groups of women is through their use of commodity display' (p. 130). Their readers' comments show clear consciousness of reading. In fact, the complaint of stereotypes was commonly articulated by the young readers, with one reader, for example, commenting that, even if it were possible to attain the 'ideal' self imagined by the text, it would not render the 'happiness' these representations presuppose (p. 131). The authors read these types of comments as evidence that the magazines *do* elicit a duality of ideology and pleasure; the task set for researchers is to forge an understanding of the significance of women's magazines which moves debates beyond the current impasse of magazines as *either* oppressive *or* pleasurable, either bad or good.

Against writers who celebrate women's pleasure as necessarily progressive, Ballaster and colleagues (1991) reject the principle which underlies this position, that pleasure can be 'pure' or 'authentic.' Instead, they point out that all pleasure is socially constructed: 'the construction and maintenance of any social order entails the construction and maintenance of certain pleasures that secure consent and participation in that order. That any cultural form is both pleasurable *and* ideological is, then, neither surprising nor worrying – what else could pleasure be? and how else could ideology work?' (p. 162).

That women's magazines engage in the social construction of pleasure does not mean that these magazines acknowledge or reveal this construction. Rather, by addressing women as a naturally occurring, homogeneous group, they presume that women's pleasures are similarly ahistorical, naturally occurring, and homogeneous. However, although women's pleasure is represented as homogeneous and unified by the dominant editorial voice of the magazine, it is in heterogeneity and contradiction that the readers derive their pleasure (p. 162). Thus Ballaster and colleagues are not alarmed that readers must make their way through overtly contradictory, if not incoherent, messages about what it means 'to be a woman.' Anything can coexist with anything on the pages of the magazine (and does). The transparency of these contradictions within the text does not embarrass editors, writers, or readers, because they resonate with the contradictory experiences of lived femininity in a patriarchal culture. In order that hegemony be maintained, contradictions do not have to be disguised, smoothed over, or explained away, as earlier writers implied. Furthermore, their existence in textual form gives readers the opportunity to freely consume or reject individual, contradictory messages. This claim leads the authors to a central purpose of their study: to view magazines in their role as a commodity instead of an arena for textual criticism by academics (p. 4). Ballaster and colleagues link pleasure to, not simply the contents, but also the commodity form of women's magazines. In terms of content, women's magazines privilege emotional, sexual, and personal issues as areas of women's priorities and concern, placing women at the centre of all experience. In doing so, the magazine reverses the conventional gender hierarchy so that masculinity functions as the 'other,' the 'not feminine.' This reversal re-presents the female domestic sphere, with its powerlessness and dependence, as a realm of power, value, and self-fulfilment (p. 175). Through consumption, magazines offer readers the pleasures of participation and belonging, as well as those of change and personal improvement. The authors describe this type of pleasure in terms of the safety provided by magazines: at the same time that magazines draw readers into a private sphere of feminine domesticity, the dangers and confusions of the world outside the text are peripheral to the magazine's vision, understood as both threat and unreality (p. 165).

In conclusion, Ballaster and colleagues note that, although women's magazines have undergone important transformations since they first appeared in the late seventeenth century, these magazines retain remarkable continuity in terms of their address to readers and their social function. However pleasurable, magazine reading cannot be seen as 'innocent' of power relations, separated from the ideological function of commercial media in women's lives. From their inception, women's magazines have posited female subjectivity as a 'problem,' and themselves as the answer, offering their female readers a guide to living, a means of understanding their experiences as women. However, as a result of their claim to represent rather than direct or influence women, magazines reproduce those very contradictions and paradoxes that they ostensibly resolve. While the authors are clear that they do not lay the blame for women's oppression at the door of women's magazines, they argue that these texts depoliticize 'woman' as a potentially political category:

> Women are repeatedly told that their problems can only be dealt with through individual, rather than collective, responsibility. Agony columns, readers' letters, single articles, do, of course, insist on the commonality of women's experience ... Ultimately, however, women are informed that they must 'help themselves' and thus, implicitly, that their problems are their responsibility and may be of their own making. In other words, women's magazines are so structured, ideologically and formally, that they cannot offer political resolutions to what they consistently define as 'personal' problems. (p. 174)

For this reason, Ballaster et al. maintain that, although women's magazines offer readers a privileged space, or world, within which to construct and explore the feminine Self, these magazines must be understood as a cultural form produced and published, primarily, for profit (p. 176).

Exploring the Pleasures of Ideological Consumption

Women's pleasures of consumption were to become increasingly central to feminist analyses during the 1980s. Viewing women's magazines as vehicles of pleasure and a site of discursive struggle, analysts turned to semiotics and, subsequently, psychoanalytic theory in order to study social texts as venues where meaning is contested rather than imposed. As Gledhill (1994) notes, neo-Marxist aesthetics of the 1970s began to question three assumptions which shored up the implied opposition between ideology and reality, stereotypes and 'real' women, truth and fantasy: 'first, that feminist understanding of the real world can be promoted by appeal to experiences that it is assumed all women share; second, that language and form are transparent, acting as vehicles for the accurate reflection of reality; and third, that representation of reality should be the major goal of art and entertainment' (p. 111). This challenge emerged initially in film theory, which raised questions about how meaning works and at what level ideological effects could be located. Breaking ground with the humanist literary (and sociological) tradition, this challenge directed attention to structural semiotics. As a 'science' of signs, semiotics tells us how texts construct meaning, rather than simply documenting what texts appear to say (to the researcher). Importantly, semiotics assumes that meaning is not reflected, but rather produced. It thus links reading pleasure to the workings of ideology through the text, providing a useful way to explore how commercial texts, such as women's magazines, can be simultaneously 'harmful' and 'pleasurable.'

Problematizing the reading Subject as the source of meaning, the issue of women's pleasure and desire in popular culture was initially raised outside sociology. In a study of romance narratives, Tania Modelski (1982) points out that women writing about feminine narratives historically have tended to adopt one of three positions towards women's consumption of mass culture: 'dismissiveness; hostility – tending unfortunately to be aimed at the consumers of the narratives; or, most frequently, a flippant kind of mockery' (p. 14). In order to move beyond the elitism implicit in these positions, Modelski proposed a 'feminist reading of women's readings.' This reading does not condemn the novels or the women who read them; rather, it draws attention to the conditions which make romantic fantasies both pleasurable and necessary in women's lives. Thus, Modelski was among the first to point out that the readers of fantasies and the feminist reader have something in common: both are motivated by dissatisfaction with the reality of women's lives under patriarchy. She challenged feminists 'to stop merely opposing soap operas and to start incorporating them, and other mass-produced fantasies, into our study of women' (p. 114).

Such a study was undertaken by Rosalind Coward. *Female Desires* is about women's pleasures: about things that women enjoy; about things that women are said to enjoy; and about things that women 'are meant to enjoy and don't' (p. 13). Significantly, the pleasures which Coward explores are the feminine pleasures from her everyday life – food, cooking, clothes, novels, soap operas, and so on. Thus she does not approach women's pleasures as a distant critic, 'but as someone examining myself, examining my own life under a microscope' (p. 14). She reads these everyday cultural objects as working to construct female desire as universal and unchangeable, arising from the female condition. Coward identifies how this meaning is signified through images common in women's magazines: advertisements for thin thighs, fashion, ideal homes, food, pornography, and so on. Although her readings gain a commonsense appeal through Coward's claim that her essays 'are not the result of painstaking academic research,' they reflect the influence of Roland Barthes' *Mythologies*.[8] Contrary to Marxist thinking of the time, Barthes maintained that realism, paradoxically, produces ideology in the form of 'myths.' His work thus signals a radical departure from the demand for realism as the necessary 'corrective' to ideological representations of social life.

Drawing on structural semiotics, Barthes (1968, 1972) explores how ideology works in the social texts of everyday objects such as magazine covers, boxing matches, steak and chips, and Citroën cars. Emphasizing the form of cultural representations over simply their content, *Mythologies* explores how 'denotation,' as primary signification, and 'connotation,' as secondary signification, operate to produce a realism based on partial, ideologically motivated representations of the everyday world. Barthes likened this effect of signification to myth making. Here 'myth' refers to a specific relation between denotation and connotation: 'the first system [denotation] becomes the plane of expression or signifier of the second system [connotation] ... The signifiers of connotation ... are made up of the signs (signifiers and signifieds) united of the denoted system' (Barthes 1969: 89–91).[9] For Barthes (1972), myths are attempts to fix connotative meanings on signifiers which are otherwise capable of a full range of meanings. A myth is not simply a mistaken concept or idea, but rather a distinct mode of signification. Drawing on Saussure's schema of Signified/ signifier = sign, Barthes' mode is based on the relationship between what he calls 'first order' and 'second order' signification. First-order signification refers to a message constructed through a chain of cause and effects that have as their referent social and political processes in their full historical and political meaning. Social scientists typically think about this level of meaning as that which corresponds to historical 'fact.' Myths are based on these historical and political facts, but arise through second-order signification. Second-order signification does not simply transfer meaning from the first to second order, however: that relationship would imply that the relation between the two orders is one of content. Instead, Barthes identifies the relation between the first and second orders as one of form. Specifically, the sign of the first order becomes an emptied signifier available to be reused in the second-order system. Whether language, photography, or everyday objects, the materials of mythological speech are emptied of historical and political significance and reduced to pure signifying function. That is, meaning as established by the first order is removed from its context so that movement from first- to second-order signification is like a revolving door because 'the turnstile stops at a certain point' (Barthes 1972: 123). Barthes argues that the function of mythology is not to hide but to reconstitute chains of cause and effect that, although presented as everyday facticity, are entirely motivated. Myths correspond to what Marxist

sociologists analyse as ideology: Barthes locates the study of ideology in everyday cultural objects whose taken-for-grantedness helps to reconstitute the naturalness of the dominant social order.

Mythologies work in popular culture as 'what goes without saying' by transforming history into nature. The work of the critical reader of everyday culture
is to 'decipher myth' through a reading that focuses on the mythical signifier as
'an inextricable whole made of meaning and form.' The reader must penetrate
the myth in order to recognize it as a semiological system of values, not facts
(1972: 127–9). Importantly, Barthes drew attention to the way in which photography renders ideological processes of representation seamless. Through photography, perfect representation is possible, making photographic imagery appear as
flawless objectivity: the signifier seems to exactly reproduce its signified
(Barthes 1977). Photography thus facilitates the naturalization of ideological
representations. A relevant example comes from Michels's (1985) deciphering
of the cover of *Cosmopolitan* in order to show how femininity becomes culturally coded as sexuality. Michels argues that *Cosmo* Girl is instructive because her
imagery confronts women everywhere, on and off the actual magazine; it constructs a myth of the perfect woman as utterly sexual, ideally young, festively
idle, and physically flawless. He shows how this myth is semiotically constructed
in *Cosmo* magazine, but notes that this myth is sustained through so many other
cultural signs which denote this specific meaning of 'woman' that *Cosmo* Girl is
imagined as a reality prior to her signification (p. 201).

Probably the most extensive system of cultural signs that promotes the
mythology of Woman through the realism of photography can be found in
advertising. Barthel (1992: 137) claims that typical readers spend an average of
twenty-five to thirty minutes daily looking at magazines, during which time
they would be exposed to sixty-five to seventy advertisements. About thirty-
five of these will be seriously scanned. In addition, the average television
viewer sees ninety-five to a hundred commercials daily, seriously watching
about sixty of them. Due to this ubiquity, advertisements have been extensively
analysed as semiotic systems. One of the most influential of these studies is
Decoding Advertisements (1978). In this work Judith Williamson links the
semiotic form of advertisements to psychoanalytic theory in order to identify
how advertising attempts to construct an ideological Subject. Her interest in
advertising is particularly relevant to the current study: 'As a teenager, reading
both Karl Marx and "Honey" magazines, I couldn't reconcile what I knew with
what I felt. This is the root of ideology, I believe. I knew I was being
"exploited," but it was a fact that I was attracted. Feelings (ideology), lag
behind knowledge (science). We can learn from their clash' (p. 9). Williamson
argues that the influence of ads stems, in part, from their existence in more than

any single medium: their ubiquity gives them a sort of independent reality. That seeming reality is a result of the structure of ads, which transforms the language of objects into that of people, and vice versa. Because ads provide a structure in which we and advertised goods are interchangeable, they are selling us to ourselves. In order to understand how this occurs, Williamson analyses 'advertising-work.'[10] Her analysis draws on structural semiotics to explain the basic meaning of ads; Althusser to explain how advertisements address readers; and Lacan to explain how readers are constructed, ideologically, as Subjects.

Using structural semiotics, Williamson explores ads as referent systems which gain meaning from connotation as much as denotation. Her analysis shows how products, as signifiers, are made to convey much more than what they concretely denote. She uses as an example an ad which juxtaposes the picture of a bottle of Chanel perfume with a photograph of the face of the well-known actress Catherine Deneuve. In this case, the face of Deneuve stands for much more than the model herself; as signifier Deneuve conjures up the values of glamour and beauty, as what is actually signified by her photograph. When the bottle of perfume is equated with the values signified by Deneuve, Chanel perfume takes on the characteristics of beauty and glamour. Through transference, which is structured in the layout of the ad, the resulting meaning is much more than simply a product, in this case a bottle of fragrance as one of many toiletries used by women. Significantly, virtually no written text is needed: the associations which make this type of meaning possible come from a common stock of cultural knowledge. Because the system is based on seemingly logical connections and associations (such as the general association of women with beauty and glamour), over time the connection between Chanel and glamour takes on a commonsense inevitability that gives it the status in some 'real' or 'natural' order. Overall, advertising work is about giving products seemingly natural value-meaning: 'So the product and the "real" or human world become linked in the ad, apparently naturally, and the product may and does "take over" the reality on which it was, at first, dependent for its meaning. As product merges with the sign, its "correlative" originally used to translate it to us, one absorbs the other and the product becomes the sign itself' (p. 35). In this way the commodity itself, in real life, becomes a signifier of human values – prestige, glamour, beauty, femininity, and so on. But advertising work is more than making associations between simply elements on the page, because meaning also requires a reading Subject: the types of exchanges described above depend upon our cooperation. Drawing upon Althusser, Williamson argues that

to investigate the dynamics of these relationships [of signifiers and signifieds] we must enter the space between signifer and signified, between what means and what it means.

This space is that of the individual as subject: he or she is not a simple receiver but a creator of meaning. But the receiver is only a creator of meaning because he/she *has been called upon to be so*. As an advertisement speaks to us, we simultaneously create that speech (it means *to us*), and are created by it *as its creators* (it assumes that it means to us). Thus we are constituted as 'active receivers' by the ad. (p. 41; emphasis in original)

Advertising work thus requires mechanisms to appellate the reader. Simple examples would be the positioning of the photograph of Catherine Deneuve in such a way that she makes eye contact with the reader, or the inclusion of textual reference in the ad to 'people like *you*.' By decoding several genres of ads, Williamson identifies the discursive procedures which facilitate the appellation of readers by advertisements. She then takes us from semiology to psychology in order to argue that the interchangeability of ourselves and empty signifiers in the ad – such as the simple word 'you'[11] – is facilitated by the viewing subject's desire for coherence and meaning in him- or herself. Her argument is based on Lacan's notion of the mirror stage, a notion which has been influential in feminist cultural studies (for fuller accounts, see Grosz 1990; Lorraine 1990; Wright 1984).

Unlike Freud, Lacan grounds difference in the Symbolic order of language rather than biology. Wright claims that 'Lacan's Freudian revolution is the systematic claim that the unconscious is more than the source of primal instincts linked at random to ideas and images. Lacan rejects this randomness. Conscious and unconscious are asymmetrically co-present: the inner structure maps the outer conceptualizations. This mapping is above all governed by linguistic practice' (1984: 107). Because the psyche is structured by language, Wright argues, it can be viewed as text. Locating the psyche in language also means that Lacan rejects the interpretation of Freud which posits a stable and fixed ego. Instead, Lacan stresses that there can be no Subject except in (self-)representation; however, no representation can adequately capture 'what we are.' Through a structural reading of Lacan,[12] Williamson explains how the Subject created by advertising work invites identification by offering us an image of ourselves that we may aspire to but never achieve (p. 64). In conclusion, Williamson identifies advertising as an ideological apparatus, a signifying system within the Imaginary which is able to *re*-present to the Subject her or his place in the Imaginary: 'in the ad, the sign never *is* the referent, the picture is not what it represents – but this is not acknowledged by desire. The function of this in the ad is to make up a fundamental imbalance: between one sign and another; between the signified other and the self. It is precisely desire that traverses this space and makes up a lack' (p. 65). In the final analysis, things in an ad signify us, the absent; they refer to what is not there, the spectator. In ads, this play of absence/presence produces a symbolic world that positions the Subject. We are positioned both in the ad, by filling the absence, and in relation to the ad, by deciphering it. The activity of deciphering the ad allows for the ideological illusion of freedom. However, unlike other writers, Williamson maintains that this interpretation is *consumed* rather than *produced* – we do not produce a genuine meaning but consume a predetermined 'solution' since the process is bounded by the ad itself (p. 75). Much of *Decoding Advertisements* is about the technical structure of ads which bound meaning.

In summary, Williamson grounds Althusser's notion of interpellation in systems of signification constructed around commodity consumption. Drawing on Lévi-Strauss, she describes advertisements as an interface between Nature and Culture: ads 'cook' Nature, transforming it into Culture, but ads also re-present Culture as natural. Unfortunately, as Leiss, Kline, and Jhally (1985) note, this use of Lévi-Strauss obscures the specificity of advertising as a historically and culturally unique form of signification. What is missing from Williamson is a connection between advertising work and the social context within which advertising is both produced and consumed. A number of writers since have thus attempted to extend her work by linking the specific semiotic form of advertising, as a process of signification, to commodity production. In doing so, commercial texts are analysed as semiotic systems which dis/re-articulate everyday meanings. One such analysis appears in *Reading Ads Socially* (1992).

Reading Ads Socially did not begin as simply a study of advertisements; as author Robert Goldman notes, it began as 'a project which aimed at bringing critical theory down to earth by grounding it in the relations and texts of daily life' (1992: 8). Significantly, Goldman's insight came from reading fashion magazines: 'One day, by chance, I picked up a fashion magazine and turned to a perfume advertisement. In a sudden flash of recognition I thought I saw revealed in that perfume ad the structural inner workings of the commodity form. Here was the ideal social text for charting the relationship between the commodity form and ideology' (p. 8). As Williamson did, Goldman begins from the premise that, because ads are so pervasive and our reading of them so routine, we tend to take the social assumptions which make them possible for granted: we do not ordinarily recognize advertising as a sphere of ideology. Also like Williamson, Goldman is more interested in the form than in the content of ads: he sees in this form the 'social grammar of hegemony.' In short, advertisements are commodity-signs: they join together a named material entity (a good or service) as a signifier with a meaningful image as a signified (bringing together, for example, Chanel perfume and 'glamour'). As commodity-signs, advertisements embody the logic of twentieth-century capitalism. According to Baudrillard (1981), corporate capital reorganizes consumption practices to convert economic exchange value into sign value, and vice versa. Not only are commodities joined to signs, but commodities get produced as signs, and signs become produced as commodities, through advertising. Commodity-signs are organized by, and into, a code which governs the interplay of signifiers and exchange value. From this Goldman argues that 'the frames and codes of advertisements are the starting point for interpretation, not the outcome: meaning is always negotiated in the semiotic process, never simply imposed inexorably from above by an omnipotent author through an absolute code' (1992: 2).

By 'frames,' Goldman means the semiotic context within which exchanges of meaning can take place: as a system of signification, advertisements compose connections between the meanings of products and images. To study the logic of ads is to study their frames of meaning, a task taken up throughout *Reading Ads Socially*. This task is informed by the way in which advertising, as part of the culture industry, constitutes an apparatus for reframing meanings in order to add value to products. Ads arrange, organize, and steer meanings into signs that can be inscribed on products. In this way, advertising comprises a system of commodity-sign production designed to enhance the exchange value of commodities. This system has as its internal structure the joining of signifiers to signifieds driven by the logic of the commodity form – the goal of profit. As exercises in framing exchanges of meaning, advertisements commodify semiotics for the purpose of building a currency of sign values (pp. 5, 6). The purpose of Goldman's project is to decode[13] the structure of commodity semiotics in order to reveal a pure form of commodity logic. This decoding occurs in relation to how industry's marketing and advertising practices shape an encoding process designed to prompt the most efficient articulation of commodity-signs by viewers. This efficiency is increased through market-segmentation, one of the most important changes in the marketing of commercial culture during the past few decades. Improved marketing tools (based on the tenets of social-science research) allow advertisers to pinpoint potential consumers, who then become the audience to whom ads are addressed.

Along these lines, Goldman decodes advertisements which target women: ads for pantyhose, cosmetics, and weight-control products. Reading ads published between 1977 to 1990, he maintains that they present a narrative about women's liberation in terms of women's 'increased social power as a function of voluntary self-fetishization. While these ads continue to position women as commodity selves posed for an absent male spectator-owner, they hail female subjects with the flattering ideological rhetoric that appropriately outfitted women can be confidentially in charge of their lives and their relations with men ... ads can be read as commodity narratives about the relationship between envy, desire and power' (p. 10). One of the strengths of Goldman's work is his identification of the changing form of commodity semiotics. Of relevance here is his identification of the way in which feminism has been reframed through the commodity form, a process which has turned the political discourse of feminism into 'commodity feminism,' a discourse of style (see also Goldman, Heath, and Smith 1991). He concludes that

since the 1960s there has been a gradual loosening of capitalist hegemony from the moorings of dominant class interests – supplanted by the purer, more structural, logic of market shares and market segments ... Although bourgeois homilies still punctuate our mass-mediated discourses, the climate of relativism and cynicism fostered by the practices of the culture industry cuts away from the credibility of bourgeois narratives. Class-based capitalist hegemony as a unified dominant ideology has now given way to a form of fractured hegemony grounded in the privatized discourse of commodified desire. (p. 14)

Goldman thus links the changing nature of the advertising form to both the economic imperatives which underlie its production and the characteristics of consumers who are targeted by specific ads. He argues that, due to the saturation of both the public and the private realm by advertising, viewers have become alienated interpretive labourers (p. 173). Their resistance to advertising forms and techniques results in the ongoing transformation of the form of advertising.[14]

   While Goldman limits his decoding to specific, select ads,[15] Ellen Mc-Cracken (1993) deploys semiotics in order to decode the genre of women's magazines, connecting these texts to commodity production. The purpose of *Decoding Women's Magazines* is to offer an oppositional reading through a negative hermeneutics that calls into question the textual strategies that conflate commodities and desire (p. 301). She draws on theories of signification to join 'close textual readings of the visual and verbal systems of magazines' to an analysis of women's magazines as a multimillion-dollar industry. Drawing on the neo-Gramscian notion of ideology as a site of struggle for discursive power, McCracken departs from the interpretation of ideology as simply forcing distorted images and meanings upon readers: 'Readers are not force-fed a constellation of negative images that naturalize male dominance; rather, women's magazines exert a cultural leadership to shape consensus in which highly pleasurable codes work to naturalize social relations of power. This ostensibly common agreement about what constitutes the feminine is only achieved through a discursive struggle in which words, photos, and sometimes olfactory signs wage a semiotic battle ...' (p. 3). Understanding women's magazines as business enterprises as well as cultural texts reveals the crucial role of advertising in shaping the content of this struggle. In her analysis, McCracken looks for, among other things, structures of meaning that disguise one level of content with another. She thus directs attention to the covert advertising which results from structural relationships between editorial and advertising texts within each magazine issue. Drawing attention to the blurring of boundaries between purchased advertising and editorial content, McCracken brings into view the extent of covert advertising through 'advertorials': she thus presents a convincing case for treating women's magazines in their entirety as advertisements. Importantly, advertorials are not instances of disguise, but rather a system of mutually sustaining techniques and themes. Analysis of these techniques and themes directs us to look beyond the surface appearance of the content of magazine representations, as cultural texts, to subtexts which connect this content to the commercial interests which magazines represent as commodity signs. This type of analysis

> directs our attention to factors such as a company's ownership of various products, some of which receive covert promotions while others are advertised directly; agreements between advertisers and editors ...; and a magazine's current advertising 'health,' including factors such as ad volume and revenue per issue, an important element in publishers' decisions to use certain forms of covert advertising. Together, analysis of the ideology and infrastructure of covert advertising can reveal it as an *economically motivated system* of mutually sustaining techniques and themes. (p. 41; emphasis added)

Again it is important to emphasize that McCracken does not subscribe to a determinist notion of ideology. Readers may, or may not, interiorize ideological messages: the point of analysing ideology is to demarcate the various illusionary strategies at work (p. 69). These strategies are part of the struggle within the field of representation to fix competing definitions of reality. While this struggle is waged at both ends of the communication process, encoders and decoders do not hold equal power. The producers of magazines as encoders are able to control signification through cultural leadership to a greater extent than are readers as, simply, decoders of messages. Thus, according to McCracken, the power of ideology is the power to signify events in a certain way (pp. 69, 70).

Rather than adopt a position which examines only the negative work of ideology in the text, McCracken highlights the positive, utopian elements through which ideological texts appeal to consumers. This utopia is linked to the 'complex strategy of rhetorical persuasion in which substantial incentives are offered for ideological adherence' (p. 71). This appeal, and the impulses which commercial media both utilize and strive to manage, works through fantasy and pleasure offered by the text. In the final analysis, however, McCracken argues that this fantasy and pleasure must ultimately serve certain ideological functions. Hegemony is achieved (uncoercively) in cultural forms like women's magazines because readers experience them as an arena of freedom, free choice, and free time (p. 72). Overall, McCracken argues that, through the combination of these two methods of inquiry, semiotics and sociology, researchers can transcend surface appearances and first impressions, in order to link ideology to semiotic codes which offer utopian fantasies to women.

In her exploration of various specialty magazines, McCracken examines *Seventeen* as a vehicle for the socialization of young women into a lifelong habit of consumption. She begins by pointing out the huge revenues which this publication garners for its parent corporation.[16] *Seventeen* sustains these profits through the revenue of advertisers who want teenage consumers. Along these lines, McCracken draws attention to the ways in which various texts in *Seventeen*, however pleasurable, exacerbate feelings of anxiety about physical appearance and suggest that increased consumption is the remedy. For example, by using the technique of answer and question, advice columns encourage readers to think that their peers have written to the magazine with particular problems. If a reader has not yet thought about herself in the ways outlined in editorial answers, she should begin to do so if she wishes to be beautiful and share the concerns of her peers (p. 138). Because problems focus on physical appearance, such advice columns uphold the interests of the magazine's primary advertisers – cosmetics and apparel companies.

Through this type of analysis, McCracken argues that the pleasure which women's magazines provide is a key to the cultural leadership which they exercise:

Compelling, but necessarily transitory pleasures work to win credibility for these master narratives, thereby securing the publishers' and advertisers' commercial goals. Indeed, commodified desire is an important semiotic tool whereby encoders of magazine texts strive to anchor a preferred social ... in the grand tale that they construct about reality. The commodity base of the pleasure must be so pervasive that it appears to be an essential characteristic of contemporary feminine desire. The smaller narrative segments – from individual ads and parts thereof, to fashion features, advice columns, and voyeuristic documentary fiction – combine to build a master tale that aims to win readers to this consensual view about reality. (p. 299)

Importantly, McCracken maintains that social reality always threatens this discursive struggle to construct consensus because as it acts as 'an existential corrective' (p. 3). In the struggle for hegemony, however, readers and publishers are not equal: readers have little input into the monthly representations that make claims about their lives, notwithstanding publishers' attempts to secure the target audience's receptivity of their texts. In the final analysis the publishing industry, through serving the financial interests of advertised industries, demarcates the grounds upon which struggle over what it means 'to be a woman.' The immense circulation and profits of these publications suggest that the master narratives they construct succeed quite well in channelling women's desires into consumerism.

The Limitations of Ideology Critique

As we have seen in this chapter, theories of ideology have a long and lively history within cultural studies and feminist sociology. Within the latter field, debates surrounding ideology resonate with those in sociological theory more generally.[17] Reflecting the influence of Althusserian Marxism, one important debate concerns the tendency to attribute ideology a material status. As Gledhill (1994) notes, 'the power of ideology lies in the fact that it operates not just as ideas in the head, but in the cultural assumptions that shape the way we do things. In this sense ideology is "materialized" in the habitual activities of everyday life. Ideologies are systematized in the institutional practices of home, school, church, and media, and in the professional and representational practices of journalism, fiction, film, television, advertising' (p. 113). For Barrett (1980), the insistence that ideology is material arises from an unsuccessful attempt to resolve the classic paradox of Marxism, that being may determine consciousness, but revolutionary transformation of the conditions of being will depend upon raising the level of class-consciousness (p. 89). One problem for her is that, if ideology is transformed into a material force, crucial questions concerning the relationship of ideological processes to historical conditions of the production and reproduction of material life remain unexamined: if meanings are declared material, the term 'material ceases to be intelligible' (p. 90; see also Eagleton 1980). The kinds of criticisms she raises against much of the then contemporary work on ideology foreshadows the eclipse of Althusserian Marxism generally in academic circles.

Within sociology, Anthony Giddens (1983: 65) criticizes Marxist theories of ideology because of the way in which they have become framed within theories of social reproduction.[18] As we have seen, feminists emphasize the role ideological texts play in the acquisition of gendered (and racialized)[19] identities and incorporation into the patriarchal order. Thus these theories are committed to the thesis, criticized by Giddens, that social integration, hence reproduction, depends upon the 'internalization' of common values. Giddens argues that this thesis obscures the knowledgeability of actors: the taken-for-granted cannot be equated with the accepted-as-legitimate. The internalization thesis implies an inherent connection among motives, norms, and legitimation in the activities of everyday life. In contrast, Giddens points out that social life contains many types of practices that are sustained in and through the knowledgeability of social actors but which they do not reproduce as a matter of normative commitment. Important to our study, he notes that some of the most potent forms of ideological mobilization do not rest on shared beliefs, but, rather, in the *form* of their social organization.

In the final analysis, the turn away from ideology in cultural studies was predicated on both theoretical and empirical grounds. Objections to the theoretical expediency of 'ideology' as an analytic concept are linked to, at least in part, the rising popularity of postmodernism and post-structural analyses of texts – especially in the North American context. Three criticisms of theories of ideology gained audience during the 1980s, many of them appearing in feminist culture studies. The first complaint is that both Marxist accounts of ideology and their feminist variants have tended to be functionalist, hence teleological. For example, many feminist accounts of cultural representation resort to the self-evident claim that patriarchal ideology directly benefits – hence serves to perpetuate – the interests of capital and/or the collective interests of men. As Walters (1995: 35) notes, one result is 'an almost conspiratorial notion of mass media.' Barrett (1980: 93) traces this problem to the tendency to emphasize the reproduction of patriarchal relations through gender beliefs, rituals, and practices. This view of women's subordination is premised on the 'top down' operation of power; power as acting against, or being exercised over, women. While this notion of power is readily apparent in liberal feminist theories of the passive socialization of women (and men) into sex roles through scripts (such as those identified in women's magazines), ironically it paradoxically reappears in a Marxist feminism which consciously positioned itself against liberal feminism.

The second problem is that ideology sets up a dichotomy between ideological and scientific representations, hence between 'false' and 'true' knowledge. While the former are seen to necessarily provide only a distorted view of the social world, the latter claim the status of knowledge of a reality outside or beyond (mistaken) discussion about it. Part of the objection here lies with the Althusserian notion of misrecognition: this notion allowed claims made by women and other marginalized groups based on their (untheorized) experiences of oppression to be discounted. Appeals to Science, especially when espoused by feminists, seemed to imply that only academic feminists can see through the veil of patriarchal ideology, creating a new form of 'us' and 'them.' Women who did not feel oppressed were seen to exhibit 'false consciousness,' and their reading pleasures dismissed. Against these orthodoxies which were prevalent throughout the 1970s and into the 1980s, Ang (1988) insists that academics cannot set themselves up as the guardians of Truth about women's oppression and liberation (see also Kaluzynska 1980). This elitist position implies that we need to make 'them' – the feminine Subjects of feminist discourse – more like 'us' – the feminist experts (see Ang 1988: 183).[20] In retrospect, these types of problems should not be surprising. Interest among Marxist scholars in cultural questions expressed through theories of ideology emerged in a context of asking why the working class does not behave in ways which behoove the revolutionary Subject of Marxism. As a consequence, it could be argued that, from their inception, Marxist cultural analyses posited *effects* of mass culture which they then claimed to scientifically 'discover' through analysis of social texts. The limitations of this way of working become apparent when researchers study social texts within the everyday realm of their consumption, the third problem, discussed in the following section.

From Text to Reader: Feminist 'Ethnography'[21]

Outside the WSG, the Media Group at Birmingham pursued research on media in the context of their reading. While market researchers have generated an extensive literature assessing the 'effects' of advertising on audiences, analyses of the reception of social texts are, relatively speaking, a minor theme within sociological studies of women's magazines. One stimulus for this focus is lively debate in film theory, much of it appearing in the influential *Screen* (see Moores 1993). Bringing together semiological and sociological concerns, Hall (1980)[22] explores the 'encoding/decoding' of television messages as ideological production. On the one side, encoding stresses the structural requirement for TV news production to offer hegemonic meanings; on the other side, decoding emphasizes the ways in which 'preferred readings' constrain and close down the otherwise wide range of available meanings in any text. While personal, therefore diverse, readings of mass media are always possible, Hall (1973: 15) insisted that perception is rarely individual, emphasizing instead the 'structure of dominance' in cultural representations. The issue of decoding was taken up by Brunsdon and Morley in a study of television audiences of the BBC's *Nationwide* (Brunsdon and Morley 1978; Morley 1980) which marks a turning point for cultural theory. Probably the most influential (and controversial) finding of this research was the conclusion that any viewer's decodings of TV texts cannot be reduced to his or her socio-economic location. While that location limits the array of codes and discourses available, interviews with television viewers suggested that groups occupying roughly the same class position offered differing responses to the same text.

The work of Morley and others played an important role in moving the examination of textual forms towards the study of audience engagement with texts (see Moores 1993). Studies of audience conversations about television provided the basis for what came to be called 'reception theory,' or 'active audience theory.' This research uses a combination of interviews, participant observation, and conversation analysis to determine how audiences respond to social texts. For this reason, it offers the potential for more adequate theorization of the reading Subject. However, although Morley (1981: 56) concluded from his audience research that we need to investigate 'the ways in which structural factors are articulated through discursive practices,' the new focus on the agency of readers led to claims that audiences hold far greater power over the mass media than has been acknowledged, and to an emphasis on how media 'empower' viewers.[23] Feminist research on audiences similarly emerged as a challenge to the tendency, apparent in Althusserian theory, to treat readers as cultural dupes. Ethnographic research on women's media began to document considerable differences between researchers' descriptions of how femininity is constructed in magazines, as well as other texts, and how readers identify (or not) with these representations. Feminists turning their attention to the world of readers (see McRobbie 1991a; Radway 1984/91; Gray 1987; Frazer 1987; Roman and Christian-Smith 1988) began to question many of the assumptions perpetuated by neo-Marxist theories of ideology.

One of the most widely cited challenges comes from Janice Radway's ethnographic research on romance readers in 'Smithton,' U.S.A. Radway (1984/91) was interested in the fact that women are not coerced or duped into reading romances, but consciously choose texts as objects of their attention. Exploring her respondents' assessments of what they enjoy, she found what feminists might consider to be an interesting dilemma: the ideal romance narrative is one in which an intelligent and independent woman is overwhelmed – after a period of mistrust fostered by cruelty at the hands of men – by an intelligent, tender, and caring man. In explaining the appeal of such seemingly 'regressive' narratives, Radway claims that 'the story permits the reader to identify with the heroine at the moment of her greatest success, that is, when she secures the attention and recognition of her culture's most powerful and essential representative, a man. The happy ending is, at this level, a sign of a woman's attainment of legitimacy and personhood in a culture that locates both for her in the roles of lover, wife, and mother' (1984/91: 84). Explaining the expressed desire for the heroine to be nurtured in ways traditionally expected only of women towards others, Radway draws on Chodorow (1978) to conclude that romantic fantasy is a form of regression in which the reader is transported to a time when 'she was the center of a profoundly nurturant individual's attention.' In a critique of writers who reclaim women's reading pleasures as a positive force, Radway argues that 'it is the constant impulse and duty to mother others that is responsible for the sense of depletion that sends some women to romantic fiction.' Because the relief is transient and temporary, if the reader herself is not materially nurtured by others, romance reading will suggest itself as a reasonable compensatory solution. Thus, the short-lived therapeutic value of romantic fantasy is made both possible and necessary by a culture that creates needs in women that it cannot fulfil (pp. 84, 85).[24] While this type of finding may not seem much different from earlier ideological critique, a potential departure rests in her more positive assessments of the effects of romance reading in readers' lives. Contrary to critics of romance novels who see women's consumption only in terms of the financial benefits for the publishing industry, Radway claims that, by engaging in the selection and rejection of texts, readers are actively taking emotional benefits for themselves: 'they at least partly reclaim the patriarchal form of the romance for their own use. By selecting only those stories that will reinforce their feelings of self-worth and supply the replenishment they need, they counter the force of a system that functions generally by making enormous demands upon women for which it refuses to pay' (p. 184). Clearly, this type of claim does not regard women as 'duped' into passive complicity with patriarchy. Furthermore, readers openly admitted that the universe of romance fiction bears little resemblance to the world they know, although they were more likely to claim that the *reactions* and *feelings* of the heroine resembled their own. Radway also points to the fact that reading requires women to claim time for themselves and their pleasures away from the demands of family and domestic duties. 'Not only is [reading] a relaxing relief from the tension produced by daily problems and responsibilities, but it creates a time or space within which a woman can be entirely on her own, preoccupied with her personal needs, desires, pleasure' (p. 61). Significantly, this preoccupation felt threatening for many of the male partners in readers' lives.

In the final analysis, although Radway identifies the potential benefits (as well as dangers) of romance reading, she is reluctant to draw definitive conclusions about just how feminists should view romance fiction. In part, this reluctance reflects the complexity[25] of romance reading, which can lead researchers to different conclusions, depending on whether the text or the act of reading is the focus of inquiry. If research focuses on the narrative fantasy of the texts, one can conclude that 'the romance's narrative structure embodies a simple recapitulation and recommendation of patriarchy and its constituent social practices and ideologies.' In contrast, focus on reading suggests that 'romance reading is oppositional because it allows women to refuse momentarily their self-abnegating role' (p. 210). Thus romance reading contains an element of utopian protest, but it also encourages readers to decode male indifference and male violence as expressions of love. For our purposes, Radway's work is important because it distinguishes between the text (as inhabiting the 'cultural' realm) and its reading (as a social phenomenon).

A less qualified support of patriarchal romance emerges in Ien Ang's (1985, 1990) analysis of television soap operas. Ang (1988: 186) accuses Radway of reducing pleasure to 'an ideological function.' Against this view she argues that we must see pleasure as something that can 'empower' women and not as something which always works 'against their own "real" interests' (p. 188). In her study of soap operas, Ang solicited written commentary from Dutch viewers of the American program *Dallas*. She received forty-two letters from both admirers and critics of *Dallas*, which she used to identify 'the mechanisms by which pleasure is aroused' (p. 2). It is potentially relevant that Ang identifies herself as a regular viewer of soaps as a source of pleasure: 'The admission of the reality of this pleasure ... formed the starting point for this study – I wanted in the first place to understand this pleasure, without having to pass judgment on whether *Dallas* is good or bad, from a political, social or aesthetic view. Quite the contrary; in my opinion it is important to emphasize how difficult it is to make such judgments – and hence to try to formulate the terms for a progressive cultural politics – when pleasure is at stake' (p. 12). Instead of trying to answer what she considers the mistaken question about 'the effects' of pleasure, she turns instead to the mechanisms of pleasure; how is it produced and how does it work?

From her analysis of viewers' letters, Ang argues that the pleasures and displeasures of *Dallas* are determined by whether the letter-writer found the program to be 'real' (good) or 'unrealistic' (bad). Ang does not assess this realism in terms of its correspondence to either the material reality of women's lives or the ability of the filmatic representation to present itself as real. Instead, she argues that *Dallas* is best understood in terms of its 'emotional realism.' Thus she makes a distinction between what the text denotes in terms of the literal content of the program, and what it connotes through associations and implications: 'It is striking; the same things, people, relations and situations which are regarded at the denotative level as unrealistic, and unreal, are at the connotative level apparently not seen at all as unreal, but in fact as "recognizable." Clearly, in the connotative reading process the denotative level of the text is put in brackets' (p. 42). Given the way that the emotional responses evoked at the denotative level oscillate between bliss and misery, Ang argues that the text creates a 'tragic structure of feeling.' She locates this structure of feeling in the combination of melodramatic elements and the narrative structure of soap operas. This structure of feeling finds expression by tapping into the bottled-up emotions of viewers who readily admitted that they often enjoyed a good cry as they follow the tragedies of the players. Ang does not identify this pleasurable release as escapism; instead, she claims that it is not a denial of reality as much as it represents a playing with it. This playing is a game 'that enables one to place the limits of the fictional and the real under discussion, to make them fluid. And in that game an imaginary participation in the fictional world is experienced as pleasurable' (p. 49). In order to engage in this type of play, it is necessary that viewers possess the cultural capital to take up a reading informed by the 'melodramatic imagination.' This imagination enables viewers to see beyond the suffering of grand classical tragedy, to ordinary day-to-day existence which includes its own victories and defeats, agony and ecstasies, unclouded by ideological interpretations. Ang claims that this cultural capital is a competence linked to women's existence under patriarchy, where they are routinely connected to, hence able to empathize with, the emotional trauma of everyday life. For those who see the world in these terms, 'the pleasure of *Dallas* ... is not a compensation for the presumed drabness of daily life, nor a *flight* from it, but a *dimension* of it' (p. 83; emphasis in original).

Because the melodramatic imagination is the consequence of a reading formation, not all viewers will read *Dallas* in this way. In accounting for differences among the responses to *Dallas* by viewers, Ang argues that an ideological component works by interpellating individuals into one of three reading positions: fans, ironical viewers, and those who hate the program. Those who hate the program express their response in terms of what she calls the common 'ideology of mass culture': the claim that mass culture, as a commodity, initiates an endless circulation of degraded culture, benefiting only the profits of producers. Ang finds this response one-sided and superficial because it makes the search for more detailed and personal explanations superfluous. This is not to say that it is wrong to dislike *Dallas*, only that these statements of rejection are often made without thinking, and thus reflect the confidence of uncritical thought. As Ang points out, it is possible to subscribe to the ideology of mass culture and still enjoy *Dallas*. This enjoyment is reflected in the position of ironical viewers, who resolve the program's contradictions through 'mockery and irony' (p. 97). While both haters and ironical viewers subscribe to the ideology of mass culture as 'bad,' ironical viewers have pleasure without guilt. She claims that haters suffer conflicting feelings if, in spite of their evaluation of the program as 'degraded,' they cannot escape its seduction (p. 101). To explain the third position, fans of *Dallas*, Ang describes a much more complex process.

Fans of *Dallas* also find it necessary to locate their pleasure in relation to the ideology of mass culture. They do so in one of three ways: they internalize the ideology of mass media and remain closet viewers; they negotiate with the ideology, acknowledging that, while the program is bad, it has redeeming virtues; or they use 'surface irony' to defend their pleasure. Surface irony condemns the characters as bad, but demonstrates intimate knowledge of the details of the program and an involvement in its narrative complexities. Similar to Hobson's (1982: 110) viewers of the soap opera *Crossroads*, there was a tendency for fans of *Dallas* to feel guilty and apologetic that they like something which is treated in such a derogatory way by critics. Ang sympathizes with the way in which fans of soap opera are forced to defend their position in the face of inhospitable definitions of mass culture as degraded, and therefore harmful.

In the final analysis, Ang inverts the earlier proposition that enjoyment of mass consumption stems from uncritical thought because the consumer is 'duped' by dominant ideology (see also Polan 1988). Instead, she argues that respondents who simply dismiss *Dallas* as a 'form of degraded culture' are, in effect, duped by dominant ideologies of mass culture. From this inverted position, Ang maintains that feminism must break with the paternalism of the ideology of mass culture in which women are seen as the passive victims of deceptive messages, their pleasure totally derided (pp. 118, 119). For too long, pleasure has been interpreted as an obstruction to the goals of women's liberation. While cultural representations of women can still be condemned for being reactionary, to experience pleasure from them is an entirely different issue. Pleasure arises because fantasy and fiction do not 'function in the place of, but beside, other dimensions of life' so that our pleasure 'need not imply that we are also bound to take up these positions and solutions in our relations to our loved ones and friends, our work, our political ideals, and so on' (p. 135): 'Fiction and fantasy, then, function by making life in the present pleasurable, or at least livable, but this does not by any means exclude radical political activity or consciousness. It does not follow that feminists must not persevere in trying to produce new fantasies and fight for a place for them ... It does, however, mean that, where cultural consumption is concerned, no fixed standard exists for gauging the "progressiveness" of a fantasy. The personal may be political, but the personal and the political do not always go hand in hand' (pp. 135, 136). The types of inversions made by Ang have been subject to considerable critique (see Polan 1988); suffice it to say that Ang's legitimation of readers' pleasures helped to bring into doubt the feminist appeal to 'ideology' as a self-evident explanation of why women are 'complicit' in the reproduction of a patriarchal order. For the large part, ideology was seen to predict a particular relationship between readers and texts, between reading and behaviour, that was not always found when researchers turned from textual analysis to the study of embodied readers. A final important example for the current study comes from the work of Elizabeth Frazer.

Frazer (1987) explores the acquisition of feminine gender and sexual identity through research with girls who read *Jackie*. As did many studies on adult readers, Frazer found that, on the whole, adolescent readers of *Jackie* did not coincide with the hypothetical reader constructed through textual critique. As a consequence, she rejects the notion of 'ideology,' claiming that 'it predicts a certain sort of relationship between readers and the texts which are said to be bearers of ideological meaning and is taken as an explanation of people's beliefs or behaviour. A more or less passive reader is implied: my data shows [*sic*] that, on the contrary, readers take a critical stand vis a vis texts' (p. 407). This critical stand meant that her readers were freer of the text than much theory would imply. Thus Frazer concludes that 'the kinds of meanings which are encoded in texts and which we might want to call ideological, fail to get a grip on readers in the way the notion of ideology generally suggests. Ideology is undercut, that is, by these readers' reflexivity and reflectiveness' (p. 419). Frazer argues that the concept of ideology is too monolithic and 'predicts that people will be more, or differently, affected by "ideology" than evidence actually shows they are' (p. 410). She disputes that there is one valid and unitary meaning of a text and proposes that 'we care to check whether, even if we grant that there is one meaning, it does have this, or an ideological effect on the reader' (p. 411).

In place of ideology, Frazer proposes the notion of 'discourse register' as an institutionalized, situationally specific, culturally familiar, public way of talking. Discourse registers both constrain and enable what is sayable in any particular situation. Thus, Frazer implies that data collected through dialogue with readers may tell us more about the structure of the research situation than about actual reading itself; this issue is taken up in chapter 4. Her work interests us here because it reflects the general move within cultural studies away from 'ideology' to 'discourse analysis' and postmodern cultural critique. As we have seen, for Foucault there is no disinterested (that is, non-ideological) knowledge, because knowledge and power are inextricably linked. Many writers adopt the notion of discourse in order to avoid the Marxist tendency to counterpoise itself as scientific truth against bourgeois ideology as politically motivated, hence necessarily 'false,' knowledge.

From Discursive to Empirical Subjects

As both postmodern critics of ideology and ethnographic researchers point out, meaning is much more complex and unstable than theories of ideology imply. The problem is that sociologists have historically tended to believe that the meaning, hence significance, of women's magazines is immanent and readily apprehended from a study of the text. Through content analysis in particular, sociologists imply that different readers of the same texts will come to more or less the same reading as the researcher. In their early formulations, both Marxists and structural linguists posited stability in meaning through reader identification. In discourse, for example, stability was seen to arise through identification with the empty signifier 'I.' Because this identification provides a (mistaken) sense of coherence, the Subject remains the apparent guarantor of meaning. By drawing on Lacan, post-structuralists posit meaning through difference: 'self' is the unconscious product of distance between 'I' and 'you' or 'they' and so on. One result, therefore, is much greater play in meaning. Within this perspective, unconscious motives and processes are the 'real' guarantors of meaning. Drawing upon post-structuralist theories of meaning making, literary critics maintain that much of what social scientists claim to 'discover' through scientific analysis of texts (as in the case of content analyses) is, in fact, the researcher's own misconstructions based on a desire for coherent and stable meaning (see Game 1991; also Sumner 1979). If cultural critics begin from the premise that women's magazines are 'bad' because they misrepresent women and their interests, they will necessarily read images of idealized femininity in this way. However, if starting with a different assumption – for example, that women's magazines offer utopian fantasies of both women and commodities – pleasurable readings of idealized femininity can be 'liberated' from the text. Because meaning is a subjective and not entirely objective process, the analyst should not assume that only one meaning for any text exists, however obvious, nor that all readers will arrive at the same reading of any text. These types of debates raise serious challenges for the sociological study of social texts that became the central problematic of *Girl Talk*. As we see in subsequent chapters, this problematic directs us to everyday reading rather than researcher reading of the text. For the moment we attend to criticisms which suggest that, regardless of the polysemic nature of cultural representation, ideology could never work in the ways which structuralists maintain.

As noted in this chapter, while proponents of ideology begin from the study of social texts, their power is seen to lie outside, or beyond, the text itself. Specifically, power is located in social formations which are deemed the beneficiaries of the social order that these texts purportedly reproduce. To thus view women's magazines as ideological is an important move because it contextualizes cultural representations by placing them, analytically, within the social world which produced them. Such a move exposes cultural naturalizations as historical and political, questioning the interests served by representations of women as homemakers and sexual objects. Clearly, such questioning is central to a critical cultural studies which aims to make visible the links between consciousness and self-determination, between women's knowledge of the social world and the powerful social arrangements which benefit from women's subordination. As we have seen, however, the inexplicable problem is that ethnographic research indicates that researched subjects do not always behave in the ways that theories of ideology would lead us to predict. Empirical research has found that embodied readers of women's culture are more discerning, more critical, and more reflexive than theories of ideology typically allow. Furthermore, even accounts that acknowledge the semiotic pleasures of texts that contain demoralizing representations of women tend to describe these pleasures as 'misplaced.' In the final analysis, where theories of ideology fail us for the current study is in their treatment of women's agency as readers. As they did with power (but distinct from the study of power), the tendency has been for Marxist theoreticians to attribute human agency to capitalism rather than its Subjects. In other words, the problem is not simply that sociologists tend to treat the 'text' as 'mirrors' of the social, as much as they treat embodied Subjects as 'mirrors' of capitalist ideology. In this way, the readers constructed through 'ideology critique' (as this approach has become known) are simply bearers of dominant ideas and values. By reading Subjects off the text, sociologists have reduced Marx's analysis of ideology to a new form of textual idealism. As we shall see, while the current study does not reject the analytical usefulness of 'ideology,' it develops a materialist manner of working with texts. This manner of working, described in chapters 3 and 4, requires the study of meaning making as everyday practice – in our case a practice which brings together social texts and embodied readers in the everyday context of teenzine reading.

The current study likewise shows that readers do not behave in ways that theoreticians might prefer. The ways in which teenage readers, rather than middle-aged researchers, understand cultural representations of femininity is the topic of chapter 4; here I maintain that, empirical research aside, readers could never behave in ways suggested by theories of ideology outlined above. No matter how much emphasis is given to culture as a site of struggle and to readers as active Subjects, theories of ideology which emphasize the ideational qualities of commercial texts are typically functionalist, hence teological, constructions based on circular logic (see Sumner 1979; Barrett 1993).[26] This theme, with all its attendant problems, is not limited to feminist analyses of culture. For example, it is prevalent in much sociology of leisure (see Firth 1981).[27] Explaining the content of women's magazines, feminists have argued that these contents are restricting and demeaning. For the large part, women are represented in magazines as subservient to men and as finding fulfilment through patriarchal proscriptions of womanhood. In this way, women's magazines are claimed to represent patriarchy but to misrepresent women's actual lives and women's full human potential, expressed more authentically through the feminism of the women's liberation movement. Through the notion of 'mis'representation, reality is thus posited out-side the text, and evoked as a measure of the adequacy of cultural representation. In effect, however, what is argued is that misrepresentations are problematic because they help to perpetuate the status quo, which thus must be what is actually represented. The only way around this analytical dilemma is to posit an authentic meaning of womanhood which is outside the text, but which cannot be known by everyone, because ideology prevents women from recognizing the truth of patriarchy and the nature of their own interests. The key here is 'most' and not 'all' women, because feminists, for example, can see 'non-ideologically.' Feminists can see non-ideologically because they bring to their reading true understanding of women's lives outside cultural representations. Overall, it is the experience of women outside the text, and which remains unrepresented/able in patriarchy, that can call the construction of ideology into question. Once again, only some and not all women, as readers, draw upon this experience to call patriarchal proscriptions into question.

This ability of experience to call ideology into question brings with it constant struggle over ideological reconstitution that is threatened by an authenticity which lies outside ideology. To repeat, experience exists outside (but not inde-pendent of) social texts which signify reality. However, as a source of meaning, we cannot always see experience as such because ideology creates a Subject position from which we make sense of experience. According to Althusser, we see ourselves in ideology, but our seeing amounts to misrecognition, because we mistake the ideological Subject as a Subject of our own doing. The problem is, of course, that for Althusser a Subject must already exist. Consider Althusser's appealing, but simplistic, reference to ideology as hailing 'Hey you.' Clearly, the existence of a Subject is premised by Althusser's notion of interpellation. Barrett (1993: 174) draws attention to the problems inherent in this disembodied way of theorizing. Importantly, she draws attention to the gender implications of Althusserian presuppositions. In contrast to Althusser's claim (1971: 163) that, through a verbal call or whistle on the street, 'the one hailed always recognizes that it is really him who is being hailed,' Barrett points out that being whistled at on the street is likely to deny women their sense of personal identity. As in the case of reality, the authentic feminist researcher-as-Subject, unlike the feminine Subject theorized from the text, must already exist for these types of theories to work. In other words, theories which read the social from the textual cannot ade-quately consider how texts position readers, whether as researchers or everyday readers. This dilemma is a serious challenge for any theoretical work committed to the notion that dominant ideas, expressed as ideology, play a role in the recon-stitution of the social order. How this dilemma is worked out in the current study unfolds in the remainder of *Girl Talk*.

3

Materialism Revisited: Doing *Girl Talk*

Historically, sociologists distinguish between social texts – such as women's magazines – and their reading Subjects. Because texts (like discourses) are typically seen as vehicles of meaning which express ideas, they are treated as 'things' in themselves. This is not to say that sociologists do not look for the effects which texts may have on their readers (or vice versa): huge literatures, on pornography and television violence, for example, attempt to establish causal relations between social texts and human behaviour.[1] Rather, it is safe to say that texts, as objects of sociological investigation, occupy an 'ontological category apart from their human creators. This categorization reflects more general sociological distinctions between culture and society, between the Subjects and objects of sociological analysis, distinctions which give rise to a series of analytical conundrums which inform the history of sociological debate since its inception. The most vexatious of these distinctions is expressed through debates surrounding 'agency versus structure': when they are formulated in this way, sociology has not been able to answer the kinds of questions raised by *Girl Talk* very well. Specifically, what role does culture play in the everyday reconstitution of gender subordination and resistance to the same? Michèle Barrett (1992: 215) predicts that it will likely be a long time before the far-reaching influence and effects of materialist dichotomies such as structure/culture and base/superstructure have been recognized, let alone worked through. As noted in the introduction to *Girl Talk*, she links the analytical difficulties which follow from these dichotomies as giving rise to the current interest among sociologists in the literary methods employed in cultural studies. However, Mariana Valverde (1991: 173) notes, debates about literary methods in social research as yet fail to identify the specificities of social as opposed to literary ways of reading texts or, more generally, of analysing systems of signifiers sociologically. For her there are important differences in literary modes of reading which seek to uncover the internal workings of discourses, and social analysis which has as its concern the formation and reformulation of social subjectivities. She also notes that, despite the many advances in social theory which follow both structural and post-structural theories of subjectivity, much social-science research is today still trapped in the dilemma of structure versus agency. This dilemma plays itself out in two dominant frameworks in sociology:

The first [is] the old humanist framework grounding social action in a subjectivity that was taken as formed prior to discursive struggles: this humanism came in both material-ist (mainly Marxist) and idealist varieties. This humanism emphasized agency – of the working class, in Marxist humanism, or of great thinkers, in idealist humanism – seeing discourse as the result and not the origin of human action. The second model relie[s] on Althusser's 'subject of ideology,' who did not exist prior to being interpellated by the ruling ideology and who [is] thus a mere creature of discourse. These two models (pre-sented here in an oversimplified fashion, needless to say) can in retrospect be seen as undialectical opposites ... (p. 182)

One way in which the tension between these two frameworks has been analyti-cally resolved is to portray social subjectivity as composed of internalized ruling ideology side by side with an impulse to resist, without problematizing linkages between these two elements. This type of move has given rise to what Valverde calls a 'new humanism': 'scholars writing about women are increasingly reluc-tant to portray them as victims of structural oppressions, and are attempting instead to document the by-ways of women's everyday, unheroic resistance ... the new humanism, often linked to the political struggles of oppressed groups, is cer-tainly a vibrant force in the theoretical landscape. Its main limitation, however, is that while it can and does acknowledge subjectivity and agency, it is generally unable to theorize it' (p. 181). In order to transcend this impasse, Valverde argues, sociologists need to consider the potential usefulness of post-structuralist theories of subjectivity. While these theories may currently tell us more about how *not* to think of subjectivity than about positive guidelines to social research, post-structuralism advances the (structuralist) insight that subjects are not the authors of social meaning, but avoids the (structuralist) tendency to see subjectivity as singular and as fully determined rather than determining: 'Through recognition of the multiplicity and ambiguity of social discourse, it [post-structuralism] can begin to understand how social subjects can start to exercise some agency if only by using one discourse against another. The ambiguity of post-structuralist sub-jectivity can, in addition, correct a fallacy often committed by neohumanist fem-inist and labour historians, namely assuming that the exercise of agency on the part of oppressed groups is always evidence of resistance' (p. 183).

Treating fashion and beauty magazines as social texts which attempt to frame women's subjectivities in specific ways (that is, to link their female readers' sense of Self and feminine identities with commodity consumption), *Girl Talk* draws on both structuralist and post-structuralist insights in order to explore the kinds of issues which Valverde raises. In doing so I do not claim to transcend the kinds of analytical dilemmas and theoretical disputes which continue to haunt sociology. Rather, I claim only to take advantage of the kinds of openings made possible by current debate among social scientists over the relevance of literary theory in order to explore how feminist sociology can contribute to the development of what Hennessy (1993: 11) calls *critical* cultural studies. Critical cultural studies emphasizes the relationship between power and knowledge, particularly the ways the disciplining of knowledge is implicated in the formation of social subjects. Critical cultural studies aims to make visible and put into crisis the structural links between the disciplining of knowledge and larger social arrangements. The remainder of this chapter recounts how *Girl Talk* develops such a critical cultural studies. It accounts for *Girl Talk* by making transparent the basis for which its claims are advanced. The conclusion takes up the issue of feminist sociology more generally again, in light of research findings presented in the following chapters.

The presentation which follows is not meant to suggest that theory was the basis from which the current project proceeded; while this interpretation might easily arise from the presentation which an accounting of research typically requires, in my experience (of this and other projects) the relationship between theory and research is never linear. While the framing of the project certainly reflects my theoretical commitment to materialist feminism, the conceptual framework drew on early interviews and discussions with young women and girls. Specifically, my interest in women's magazines emerged through dialogue with students while teaching 'An Introduction to Women's Studies'; early group discussion and interviews with adolescent girls directly informed how I thought about both the 'objects' and the 'subjects' of the current study. The study unfolded through what can best be described as 'dialogue' between my readings of adolescent magazines and girls' talk about these magazines, within a context of feminist writing on the topic. As difficult as it may be to provide a suitable (*ex post facto*) representation of the current project, the account provided here is an attempt to avoid the impression, often given, that exploratory and qualitative research is entirely 'creative,' 'intuitive,' or somehow uninformed by a systematic assessment of data (see Skeggs 1995). I provide a detailed account of the project in order to make the study accountable, demystify interpretative and qualitative ways of doing feminist research, and invite critical response productive of new questions. However pleasurable the reading of accounts of 'sociology on the ground' might be, very often I am required to speculate about the mundane aspects of doing research: under what conditions was the research conducted, how did these conditions shape the research agenda, who is speaking and who is missing from the story, how representative are the data, and so on.[2] While these questions seem to be avoided when 'empirical research' (traditionally the domain of the social scientist) is replaced with 'interpretative reading' (by the cultural critic), in my opinion they are merely forestalled. Reading itself, the foundation of all academic work, is shaped by its historical and political context: similar to the scientific practice of observing and recording 'data,' reading is never a neutral activity. If cultural critique (of any sort) is to be more than an ideological account,[3] no matter how compelling the products of our efforts they must be represented as a process which itself demands careful critique, analysis, and reconsideration. In advancing a similar position, Skeggs identifies the kinds of questions which adequate accounts of feminist research must address:

- why was the area of study chosen, what institutional, economic and socio-political factors underpinned the choice?
- which frameworks of established knowledge were used, referred to, challenged, ignored and why?
- which methods were chosen for study and why? Why were other approaches not used?
- how did the initial questions and research relate to the final product? (1995: 4)

The remainder of this chapter attempts to answer these types of questions.

Working with Texts

As noted in the introduction, early discussions with young female university students sparked my interest in the current project. My initial concerns were framed around issues of female identity: the ways in which young women come to understand and express themselves specifically as 'women' (rather than, for example, as simply 'persons'), and how this understanding is (or is not) mediated by the everyday meanings provided by commercial culture, including those which challenge dominant definitions of 'being a woman.' Classroom discussion of these issues typically deployed women's magazines as an everyday reference for shared definitions of femininity. As occurs in academic debate, attitudes among the class towards the 'merits' of these texts were mixed; more importantly, the students' attitudes were rooted in strong emotional commitment. The young women either deplored or lauded fashion and beauty magazines; few were noncommittal. The most heated debates about make-up and fashion were framed in terms of 'self-expression,' and students on both sides appealed to a notion of 'women's true interests.' What became obvious in these debates was the way in which women's magazines mediate our everyday thinking about ourselves as women and about societal attitudes towards womanhood: whether one accepts or rejects the traditional femininity of magazine culture, these discursive constructions of 'woman' remain a shared point of reference for debate. Thus women's magazines and their reading offer a point of entry to a study of women's identities as contested terrain.

At this point I began to read magazines familiar to these university women – *Glamour, Seventeen, Mademoiselle, Cosmopolitan*, and so on. In the main, this reading was new territory; unlike many other researchers, I did not read very many of these magazines as a teenager or young woman, although they certainly were available during the 1950s and 1960s, when I negotiated the transition from thinking about myself as being simply a person to thinking about my life as a woman. This transition coincided with major changes in my expectations and goals in life – towards something 'realistic,' I was told. Only as a sociologist, many years later and as a second career, did I begin to think about my life as social process rather than personal choice. Within this context and as an adult reader, I found that there was an obviousness to women's magazines which made them at first appear innocuous. This quality of 'obviousness' became a point of analytical interest. Why do cultural images invested with such specific (and limited) meanings for their referent, 'women,' appear to merely restate something obvious, and unchanging, about the social world? How do young women come to understand these images in relation to their everyday experiences of *being* women?

Cultural debate has begun to question the way in which such texts are implicated in the formation of social subjects; we have seen in chapter 2 that within postmodern discourse, emphasis has been given to the 'productive' nature of this relation. However, as McRobbie (1991b) notes, celebration of the pleasures of creative self-expression through the consumption of social texts such as women's magazines can lead to 'an extrapolation of cultural objects out of the context of their materiality'; for some writers they have been 'prised away from their place in history and from their role in social relations, and have been posited instead in a kind of vacuum of aesthetic pleasure and personal style' (p. 3). For McRobbie, all consumption takes place not so much in the sphere of pure leisure as in the sphere of necessary reproduction – a term missing from current vocabulary of much cultural studies. Once the notion of consumption as reproduction is replaced with the view of consumption as an act of opposition or expression of identity (see Fiske 1989a, 1989b), the sphere of leisure as an everyday avenue for the reconstitution of subordination is hidden. Along these lines, I find three problems with the uncritical celebration of Subjects constituted through the creative appropriation of commercial texts. First, as McRobbie complains, by equating consumption with leisure this approach obscures consumption as reproductive labour (see Bella 1988). Second, the celebration of consumption, especially as an expression of identity or an act of resistance, fails to acknowledge that women's wages – hence ability to participate in consumption as resistance – remain, overall, at a fraction of men's. While some writers have suggested that resistance arises from the consumption of meanings rather than products, or that pleasure arises from the *fantasy* rather than actuality of consumption, I find these moves depoliticizing because they erase the material importance of class differences in the lived experiences of women. Finally, consumption as pure pleasure fails to acknowledge that the mandate of women's fashion can reinforce feelings of inadequacy for some women. For example, a recurring advertising theme for a national weight-loss program is framed as a promise to 'make shopping fun again.' As we shall see, even young readers who were drawn to the pleasures of magazine reading often claimed that magazine representations contribute to anxiety about personal appearance. These types of themes did not emerge, however, if investigation remained at the level of magazine reading: in this study, the effects of magazine reading became apparent only when girls openly discussed their everyday experiences of school culture. For these reasons, I find the postmodern celebration of consumption not only masculinist and class-biased, but the product of research which separates the consumption of culture from the full range of social experiences which shape our lives as women. As such, it cannot be the basis for a critical cultural studies.

My interest in consumption – in this case, as the reading of adolescent fashion magazines – is based on the view that, however pleasurable, cultural consumption is implicated in the reproduction of relations of domination and subordination through the construction of gendered subjectivities. Thus, although this study is about fashion and beauty magazines and the way these texts engage readers in understanding themselves as women, it is about much more than texts, images, and representations because it leads to questions about the nature of everyday relations which sustain these understandings. In the final analysis, understanding social relationships is necessary for understanding the ways in which power works as a vehicle of both subordination and resistance. Only a critical analysis of relationships between audiences and commodities, between the consumption of culture and its production, can help us to understand how sociocultural differences – such as those constructed around gender, race, age, and sexual orientation – continue to be categories not simply of identity, but of inequality. Social relationships are thus the necessary focus of a materialist feminist analysis as the basis for a critical cultural studies.

Advancing a materialist approach, *Girl Talk* draws on, but transforms, Marxist feminism in order to theorize relationships between cultural meanings of womanhood, the material conditions of their production, and the re/production of gendered subjectivities as the study of social power. This type of analysis leads us to economic as well as 'cultural' questions. While I certainly take to heart the kinds of critiques which have been raised against the 'science' of sociology as well as humanist feminism, my worry is that the post-structural dispersal of both the subjects and objects of sociological inquiry over systems of their signification tends to erase economic considerations. While the postmodern disappearance of the Subject, in favour of the study of subjectivity, certainly does transcend tensions between Subject and object, the agency and structure of sociological analysis, it simply evades rather than resolves these analytical dilemmas. The conclusion explores the disappearance of the social in greater detail. The exploration of magazine reading discussed in the next five chapters benefits from post-structural theories of subjectivity but retains the ability to talk about the 'objectified' societal processes of subject formation which magazine texts represent. As Valverde (1991) notes, at the moment most post-structuralist critiques of the humanism upon which sociology is grounded take the form of negative rather than positive critique: they provide injunctions against established sociological formulations, telling us how *not* to think. In contrast, *Girl Talk* explores possible ways to think about the sociological study of texts like women's magazines within the context of both modernist and postmodernist critiques. This exploration emphasizes the agency of research subjects as meaning-makers. In order to do so it treats adolescent magazines as a text that mediates contemporary discourse on 'femininity.' This discourse is a process through which individual adolescent readers come to understand themselves as becoming 'women' and commercial institutions express their commitment to market relations. In the remainder of this chapter we explore how to study everyday meaning-making as an empirical rather than purely theoretical accomplishment.

Data Collection for *Girl Talk*

It seems to me that the sociological research which tells us the most about everyday social life takes the form of participant observation. As a consequence my initial proposal for the current study was framed along the lines of ethnographic research. However, as is true of most research agendas, in the long run the institutional context rather than intellectual requirements of the research determined not only how data would be collected, but what questions would be asked, by whom, and in what fashion. Given my day-to-day teaching, administrative, and other research commitments, ethnographic research would require release from teaching. Although the project was made possible through financial support by the Social Sciences and Humanities Research Council of Canada, release time from teaching was not funded, reflecting the expectation that data for academic research are collected through the waged labour of graduate students. Because the collection and analysis of ethnographic data cannot be separated, I was not comfortable with the prospect of appropriating the ethnographic fieldwork of a student. As a compromise, data collection was organized in a way which would allow graduate students to pursue independent work for theses by separating 'their' research from 'mine.'[4] Three students – Shelley, Nariko, and Kerri – were hired to conduct content and thematic analysis of magazines, and four students[5] – Alissa, Ann, Rebecca, and Jennifer – were hired to conduct tape-recorded interviews. Raewyn carried out archival and library research on the organization of the magazine-publishing industry. Both Shelley and Nariko subsequently completed a master's thesis in conjunction with the project; while the study was designed to allow one student to also conduct fieldwork suitable for her doctoral dissertation, maternity (regrettably) prevented the latter. All research assistants were female. Reflecting the demographics of the university population, the assistants ranged in age from early twenties to mid-thirties; five were Caucasian, and two 'minority' identities. Assistants were chosen on the basis of: their competence in social research; their interest in the project; and, for interviewers, my 'sense' that they were capable of developing rapport with young girls. The prior familiarity of assistants with adolescent magazines varied. My role in data collection consisted of designing coding procedures and interview schedules, supervising research assistants who coded texts and interviewed girls, and conducting group discussions with girls. I completed all data analysis, which occasionally overlapped with the type of work being completed by the assistants for their theses. In the final analysis, the project approximates what McRobbie (1991a: xi) calls 'social research': an 'investigative approach where the mode of research is more impersonal, where the subjects remain more or less anonymous respondents, where the procedure involves structured interviews supplemented with often short periods of observation [with] the whole process tak[ing] on a more documentary character.'

Given these considerations, the primary data for the current study were collected in two (overlapping) stages. The first stage entails content and thematic analysis of four adolescent magazines: *Seventeen*, *Young and Modern*, *Sassy*, and *Teen*. These titles were chosen because they are the most widely circulated commercial magazines for teenagers in North America; they are available at most of the everyday outlets where magazines are encountered and purchased – drug stores, grocery stores, and airports as well as magazine stands. *Seventeen* has been identified by commentators as the 'queen' of this genre, as a consequence of having the longest publishing history. In total, seventy-six issues of magazines were coded for different aspects of the study.[6] The second stage of data collection entails tape-recorded interviews and group discussions with teenage girls. Girls were chosen through referral on the basis of their willingness to participate in a study of 'teenage fashion culture,' subject to parental consent. In total, ninety-one girls participated in the study.[7] These two stages of data collection resulted in two sets of data: systematic summaries of the contents of magazines and transcripts of interviews with girls. The production of these data sets and their analysis are discussed below.

Meanings as Data: Analysing Magazines

The earliest reference to the value of content analysis in sociology appears in a work of Harriet Martineau's, written in 1834 (in Reinharz 1992; also see Lengermann and Neibrugge-Brantley 1998). Until recently, sociologists studied cultural documents through content analysis as a 'scientific' method that does not problematize meaning-making itself: the general assumption was that meanings are readily apparent and easily enumerated by trained researchers. McCormack (1982) argues that content analysis gained prominence in the 1920s, when the surveillance of mass media became politically important. Within this context, the goal of content analysis was to identify what kinds of appeals can change public opinion or attitudes. From its inception, therefore, content analysis assumed a relationship between symbolic systems and attitudes, opinions, and states of mind (McCormack 1982). It is not surprising, then, that feminists of the 1960s and 1970s adopted content analysis as a method that could support their claims that the public/mass media discriminates against women and perpetuates stereotypical attitudes towards women. We saw in chapter 1 the types of findings which are generated when content analysis is applied to women's magazines; here we consider its usefulness in light of its contemporary dismissal in cultural studies and discuss how it was employed in the current study.

According to Bernard Berelson (1952: 18), content analysis is a method which allows the 'objective, systematic and quantitative description of the manifest content of communication.' Berelson identifies four characteristics of content analysis which provide it with 'scientific' credentials and which have been seen to distinguish it from (mere) literary interpretation. First, the objective nature of content analysis through the application of 'codes' earns it the status of 'unobtrusive' measurement; here the claim is that, unlike in other research methods, the researcher does not have to contend with the possibility that she is influencing or changing research findings (Berger 1991). The absence of researcher effects means that interrater reliability will be high because different coders will produce the same results. Second, the systematic nature of data collection means that content analysis will provide comparative data; the same criteria can be applied to different texts, allowing the researcher to document historical trends or patterns of similarity or difference in comparable texts. Third, quantification implies both the standardization and the precision of measurement, which makes such a comparison both possible and valid. When samples are large and the data set complex, numerical summary assists evaluation, although I agree with Sumner (1979: 69) that repetition, in itself, is no guarantee of significance. Fourth, Berelson implies that content analysis is restricted to the measurement of manifest content, which does not require interpretation. Again, this has been seen to imply that reliability of measurement will be high.[8]

As a consequence of its scientific status, content analysis has been used extensively by researchers in sociology, as well as those in women's studies, media studies, psychology, and political science. In chapter 2 we saw that, since its introduction, content analysis has been extended to include the interpretive assessment of latent, or connotated, messages (see Kracauer 1952; Holsti 1969; Krippendorff 1980). This manner of working illustrates what has been called 'qualitative content analysis' (see Kracauer 1952). Qualitative analysis can pick up the nuances missed by a focus on manifest content, which can have significant meaning. The interpretive approaches of literary methods are being evoked; McCormack (1982: 151) maintains that what distinguishes humanists and social scientists is 'the disproportion between the data and the interpretation.'

This distinction aside, the most obvious difference between literary and sociological analysis of content is that the latter lacks a theory of signification. For literary critics meaning is a complex process not simply located in the text itself, but produced through interaction of reader and text. Once the text is viewed as part of an ongoing process that does not reflect but constitutes meaning, questions are raised which cannot be answered through analysis of categorical content alone. In the study of advertisements, for example, Gillian Dyer (1982: 114) argues that we require a methodology which can tell us not simply what is *in* the text, but what is *left out*: Why are certain images used rather than others, and how does their use help to construct a specific reality, as opposed to alternative constructions? These types of questions are better answered through semiotics, the study of signs and their role in the construction of meaning. Researchers favouring this interpretative approach[9] emphasize the limitations of quantitative content analysis as employed by social scientists.

Given the assumption that each category of analysis carries the same weight, Sumner (1979: 69) dismisses content analysis as 'repetition speculation' because 'its practitioners are merely speculating about the significance of repetition.' Also doubtful that quantitative analysis can adequately capture substantive meanings, Dyer (1982) points out that the separation of elements of communication for their enumeration removes them from the context which gives them meaning. In short, content analysis typically assumes that what exists at the denotative level is significant, and that significance is measurable as repetition (Budgeon 1993: 56). In contrast, semioticians point out that signs can vary in both nature and form. Depending on the relationship between their constitutive signifiers and signifieds, signs can stand for the actual referent which they resemble (acting as an icon);[10] they can point to further or additional meanings (acting as an index);[11] or they can be symbols with shared but arbitrary meaning.[12] This variation means that it is possible for the same sign to come to 'mean' different things: reports of high interrater reliability may simply signal that coders are trained to read signs in the same way. From this perspective, reliability is an artefact of research procedures and may not be meaningful when considering culturally different groups of readers (such as teenage girls rather than academic researchers).

The shortcomings of content analysis which treats meaning as transparent and texts as iconic 'reflections' of meaning clearly limit its usefulness when the goal is the discovery of meaning from the standpoint of the researched or the identification of processes that work to produce particular meanings. For this reason, although content analysis continues to be used by sociologists to detect cultural patterns, document historical trends, and compare cultural phenomena, it is not generally employed in cultural studies. In place of systematic content analysis, we are typically provided with either narrative descriptions of the general character of the text (such as a magazine) or, alternatively, the interpretive reading of a particular, selected text (such as an advertisement). Descriptive or interpretive or 'deconstructive' approaches provide much more compelling reading than quantified accounts. Moreover, these accounts can provide new insights and stimulate new questions. However, in the absence of an accounting of procedures through which descriptive codes and themes are identified, we cannot assess the extent to which claims are simply impressionistic or the possibility that additional meanings might become apparent through a more systematic approach. At the same time, the interpretive reading of select, isolated texts inheres the danger of treating the text as a 'specimen' rather than a process, primarily because interpretive readings seldom direct us to these texts as a *system*. By 'system,' I mean to the text as a form of social (rather than semiotic) power, produced within a particular institutional context. Along these lines, Sut Jhally

(1990) maintains that the analysis of single advertisements, for example, cannot reveal the role that advertising as an institutionally mediated discourse plays in our culture. This institutional form of communication can remain hidden because, in themselves, individual ads can be pleasurable. Furthermore, 'It is very difficult to criticise a single ad in isolation (even the ones that objectify women – we all objectify men and women in some way at some time ...). Parts of daily life have to do with sexuality and thus there is nothing wrong with individual messages that focus on sex and gender. (That is, unless one took a moralistic stance on advertising in which some messages are *inherently* unacceptable for public, or private, viewing ...)' (pp. 138–9; emphasis in original). I agree with Jhally's view that a critical analysis of advertising, as one example of an everyday social text, must direct attention to advertisements in their *totality,* as a system which results from a particular institutional context. As problematic as the enumeration of meaning may be, content analysis provides a systematic approach that allows us to identify meanings in a manner which provides a reasonably 'fair' re-presentation of cultural messages. It also allows us to compare similar texts and chart changes over time. Therefore, against cultural critics who draw attention to the open nature of these texts and the multiplicity of meanings, we note that magazines are constructed to capture a large readership among a specific audience. In practice, the construction of successful advertising 'campaigns' (to use advertising jargon) is facilitated by social research which helps to ensure that meanings provided by the texts will be received in specific ways by their intended audience. For example, *Mizz* carried out extensive market research before being launched and retains a group of 500 regular readers who test out and comment on magazine material every month (McRobbie 1991a: 136). This practice reminds us that shared meanings are necessary to sustain magazine circulation, and it is reasonable to assume that these meanings can be reliably identified by researchers who, coincidentally, are likely to share the age and class characteristics of magazine editors. Thus the coding of magazine texts assumes that researcher-readers can identify dominant meanings in these texts without inferring that these meanings are taken up as identified by actual readers.

In the final analysis, contemporary preoccupation with 'how' texts construct meaning, rather than 'what' texts say, contributes to the impasse in academic debates about the social significance of women's magazines. For us, this impasse arises, in part, from the kind of 'boundary marking' decried by McRobbie (1996: 30). While I do not want to oversimplify the matter, commentators drawing on post-structural theory have contributed to the view that content analysis, which assumes the existence of an 'extra-textual' social world and methods capable of its adequate representation, is an outdated mode of investigation. Against this view I maintain that, if it is correct to claim that texts construct (because symbolic systems constitute) the social, it seems even more imperative to discern exactly how that social is represented. This position is not to claim that meanings are subsequently taken up in the way that they appear to researchers; it may, however, help us trace how power is implicated in social texts as shared knowledge, a central task for the current project.

In summary, the usefulness of content analysis for the current study is threefold: historical trends inform us of the cultural constructedness of meanings, comparative data about competing titles help us explore reading preferences, and enumeration provides the researcher (and, one hopes, readers of *Girl Talk*) with a 'sense' of the nature of the magazines under investigation. The current study draws on content analysis to document the characteristics of femininity made available to readers and, subsequently, semiotic analysis to reveal how these texts are structured to engage readers in discourses of femininity. A detailed discussion of the (mundane) tasks of developing categories and classifying texts for enumeration appears in Appendix B. Although considerable energy was expended on these tasks, content analysis is only the beginning: whether or not (and how) texts actually engage readers can be answered only through interviews with girls. The following section discusses the collection and analysis of interview data. As we shall see, while the current study begins with researcher readings of the texts, these readings are not 'mis'taken as answers to questions about how texts are taken up in their everyday setting.

Interview Data: Talking with Girls

While the data from magazines tell us about the available messages of the text, the purpose of interviews with girls is to explore the relevance of magazines to their intended audience and the political significance of these contested texts by drawing on the practices of actual readers. Given the paucity of previous research, the study would necessarily have an exploratory character. Unlike in previous research, which was typically carried out on participants contacted through a local school or community centre, the ideal sample for an exploratory study would be heterogeneous, containing a cross-section of readers from differing socio-economic and ethnic backgrounds. A referral sample was developed, with initial participants recruited through advertisements distributed through my social network and those of research assistants. Participants were asked to suggest the names of two or three friends, but in order to avoid sampling a social network, no more than two 'generations' of referrals were used from each initial contact. Given that four interviewers were employed on the project, five different points for initial contact with girls were established. As a result, girls were recruited from Vancouver and the surrounding areas of Richmond, Delta, Surrey, White Rock, Abbotsford, and North Vancouver. In order to recruit both readers and non-readers, criteria for participation included simply an interest in talking with researchers about 'girls' fashion culture' and written consent from parents. Some girls were recruited into group discussions; others into follow-up interviews. In later stages, the sample of thirteen- to seventeen-year-olds was supplemented by a small number of interviews with pre-adolescent girls and eighteen-year olds. Since almost all of the thirteen-year-olds were familiar with fashion magazines, the pre-adolescent sample was included to explore the relevance of these texts to a younger audience. The eighteen-year-old sample allowed us to discuss more sensitive or complex issues and explore how most girls 'grow out of' once-favourite titles. Most of the girls seemed to enjoy the opportunity to talk about 'girl things' with an interested adult; this enjoyment may have been generated by the complementary movie passes which participants received in appreciation of the time which they spent in the study.

In total, ninety-one girls were recruited into the study (including pilot and supplementary interviews). The majority of data were collected through personal interviews rather than group discussion. While the latter practice is common in magazine research, a decision was made to collect all primary data for analysis through personal interviews and use group discussions to 'test' out various working hypotheses once data analysis was under way. I expected group discussions to be useful for primary data collection because much previous work on readers has been carried out through group discussion (Frazer 1987; Ballaster et al. 1991; Brown 1993). Furthermore, given the age of participants, I saw group discussion as potentially less intimidating than one-on-one discussion with an adult, and as more typical of the way in which magazines are shared and talked about in their everyday context. Against these expectations, however, follow-up discussion with one of the participants in the first group raised some interesting methodological issues. The session consisted of four girls who had not previously known on another, picked by Alissa because she felt they would form a comfortable group. Here is one participant's (unedited) recounting of the group dynamics:

The one thing that really, really, really hit me on the head and made me kind of shut up a little more than I think I – I think I stopped myself from saying certain criticisms because of the other two girls there. They, just because, it was so funny that – it really threw me that they said 'I'm anti-fashion' and 'I don't read magazines' but they knew the model's name, they knew every ad she was in. I swear to god I didn't know it was the same person [referring to a model who appeared in two different ads used in the discussion group]. I still can't see the resemblance! It killed me that they knew all the models' names but I didn't want to say anything – I didn't want to offend anyone.

I *liked* it [the session], but I'm kicking myself for not saying a little more. I probably should have but at the same time I'm going 'Wow – I wonder if I would have pissed people off.' I could feel myself sitting in the session during certain things they were saying that I just *didn't* agree with what they said and a lot of times I just shut up and I feel bad now that I did.

I just shut up. I admit it. I've just learned how to do that [laughs]. You just sit there and let the conversation take its path. And it's funny, 'cause leaving, well the other girl [fourth participant] and I we were just like – we just realized that if we said any more than that – the first thing I said is 'Did you shut up?' and she's like 'Yeah.' I'm like 'God, we shouldn't have.' And that's like the first thing. Why did we? And the first thing is if you disagreed you felt shut down – it's not just worth the fight and everything because what they said is so hypocritical but at the same time so *relevant*. The reason they are being hypocritical is because they don't want to be seen the way everyone thinks they're being seen. Does this make sense? And I'm not afraid to admit that I do read these things [fashion magazines]. But I mean, but at some level you sort of think 'Thank god none of my friends will be seeing this' because I don't want them to think that. They [two participants] are doing the same thing too. Why do we get sucked into this little cycle of worrying about how you should be? Reading magazines but not admitting it. Why?

Elizabeth Frazer (1987) interprets the kinds of responses given by adolescents in her group discussion of magazines as 'discourse registers': 'institutionalized, situationally specific, culturally familiar, public, way(s) of talking' (p. 420). A register both enables and constrains what is sayable in any context. From her analysis of interview transcripts, Frazer concluded that girls have a multiplicity of discourse registers available for use, with much of the differences in her group discussions explainable by the institutional context. For example, when Frazer initiated discussion the girls adopted a 'feminist' register; when the girls initiated discussion on their own, before the session proper started, the girls used the register, and values, of the tabloid press (p. 423). The transcript quoted above likewise shows that what any respondent may say to the researcher can be situationally specific, raising interesting challenges for researchers attempting to capture the 'meanings' of respondents.[13] However, for the current study the quoted transcript also seemed to suggest that personal interviews would be more likely to provide frank discussion.[14] Perhaps ironically, the difficulties of the group dynamics apparent in the quoted material above reappear in thematic analysis of interview transcripts: difficulties for the respondent are a result of both peer pressure and the tendency for girls to want to avoid conflict, issues that emerge in chapter 7.

In practice, interviewing young girls proved to be a much more challenging undertaking than I had anticipated and, as a result, the interviews varied in both length and quality. Consider, for example, these differing negative responses to the question 'Do you ever have fights with your parents about what you wear to school?':

No.

No 'cause I – I'm not really, I don't know. They seem to agree with what I wear – my mom always tries to pull up my pants though [laughs].

[pause] No, not really. I used to when I was younger, about certain tank tops and stuff. My mom would go like, you know, because they never wore stuff like that to school. You know, how, when it was jean shorts that people really cut up really *short* were in [laughs]. I used to wear *those*. And now I don't even like them, but I wore them at the time.
[Interviewer:] How old?
Fifteen, and my mom didn't really like those very much and I would kind of go like 'Okay, I'll wear longer shorts' but we never really *fought* about it, she just made little comments sometimes.

No. My mother has always approved of my clothes because I've always basically had a lot of the same taste that she has, and she has never really ever not liked the clothes I wear. Like she always – when we were young we went to Seattle and we'd go shopping together, so I always picked up her style more than anything else. And she always had – fashion is very important to my mother and she always had magazines lying around the house and I always look through them. And instead of dressing in kids' clothes when I was ten or thirteen, I'd be dressing more older. Like I never really got into 'teen fashion' as much as anyone else did. So in that sense I've never had a problem. If I'm going somewhere and – if I go to, say, a dance, or if I'm going clubbing or something like that, there'll be times when I wear a garter belt, or a skirt that's way too short, and they won't like it then. And my father would definitely comment on it. But they would never stop me from wearing anything, or have any restrictions. They'll just comment and say, you know, 'You look like a slut' and laugh, and that will be their comment, but they'll never stop me from wearing anything, or have any restrictions 'No, you can't buy that' or 'No, you can't wear that.' So I've never had any problems. I know it's working well if they comment on it.

While all except perhaps two respondents seemed enthusiastic about the interview, as seen from the responses above some girls were painfully shy in the research context. Moreover, these excerpts testify to differences in how adults and teenagers may interpret (or report on) the everyday encounters which interest researchers. One consequence is that not all completed interviews were suitable. I eliminated from the sample for analysis interviews in which the rapport seemed to be low, where too many questions were missed by the research assistant, where ambiguous responses were not clarified, where leading questions were used to elicit responses, or where I had the 'sense' that the respondent was trying to 'please' the researcher. While chatty respondents are a researcher's delight, I took care not to eliminate shy girls from the sample. While all interviews contributed in some way to a better understanding of the task at hand, the interpretive analysis presented in *Girl Talk* is based on a subsample of forty-eight (fairly) standardized interviews with girls between the ages of thirteen and seventeen. Two-thirds of this subsample are Caucasian; nine respondents are Asian Canadian, two African Canadian, and four from other ethnic-minority descent. In this group, twelve girls came from families with (at least) one professional parent with university education, ten from families with one parent in a skilled occupation requiring postsecondary education, ten from families with one parent working in trades, and one from a family with unemployed parents. In terms of family contexts, most of the girls came from two-parent families (often with parents in second marriages), although about one-quarter were in households with one parent at time of interview, and one respondent is a 'foster' child. Overall, these characteristics suggest that the sample is more or less 'typical' of the population from which it was drawn. A description of the girls is given in Appendix A. The girls in this study are not claimed to be 'representative' of teenage girls living in the Lower Mainland of British Columbia; at the same time we have no reason to believe that they are not 'ordinary' teenagers who can tell us something meaningful about their lives.

Data collection from interviews began when I hired Alissa, who planned to integrate aspects of her doctoral fieldwork into the opportunity provided by employment on the study. Alissa was chosen not only because of her research interests; she had extensive experience with young girls through previous work as a teacher and had produced a short documentary-style video with teenage girls as a project for another graduate class. Our plan was that research would be conducted in a style which would produce both ethnographic field notes for a doctoral dissertation and interview transcripts suitable for my project. A videotaped group discussion which I facilitated was held during the first few months of the research. Together Alissa and I developed a schedule of questions for interviews which would include both our research interests, based on a literature review of previous research,[15] the specific needs of the current project, and ideas from the group discussion. The provisional interview schedule was fairly

open-ended and was used for six preliminary interviews which helped to identify relevant questions; these interviews were useful in eliminating questions
and topics. Two early incidents alerted me to the 'dangers' of conducting
arm's-length research on non-adult populations. Questions which could be per-
ceived by 'interested non-participants' (such as parents and university offi-
cials)[16] as unsuitable (for example, those dealing with sexuality) would have to
be avoided in order to prevent adverse publicity for the research. Also, it
seemed to me that there was the potential for researchers to encounter interviews where girls might disclose situations requiring professional follow-up. In
the final run, this situation did not arise; however, the training of assistants
included discussion of how to deal with such situations in a way which would
protect the confidentiality of the respondent.

The initial stages of recruitment and piloting an interview schedule took about
five months, which was much longer than anticipated. In part, delays reflect the
structure of the research context, in that travel around the Lower Mainland for
appointments with girls was time-consuming (especially when girls cancelled
appointments without notice) and that student assistants are typically caught up
in other commitments, including course requirements, examinations, and so on.
At this point I became concerned about meeting the conditions of research funding and decided to hire additional assistants to conduct interviews following a
structured research schedule. Topics for these interviews centred around: getting
ready for school everyday; shopping for clothes and make-up; conflicts with
parents over dress or make-up; reading magazines; and relevant background
information, including questions to tap self-esteem. Most of the questions were
posed in terms of the respondent's *behaviours*, rather than her *beliefs,* a distinction which was not easy for all of the assistants to maintain. Questions about
magazines included: magazines (if any) usually read, reading habits, characteristics of favourite reading, favourite parts of magazines, sharing of magazines
with sisters and/or friends, and collecting images from magazines to decorate
bedroom walls or school agendas. A structured interview schedule was developed so that the same topics could be explored in each interview, with questions
asked in a similar manner. At the same time, most of the questions were suffi-
ciently open-ended to allow matters of meaning to emerge. Key elements of the
study topics were approached in more than one way. For example, the study
employed three different strategies to determine what parts of magazine texts are
read by respondents. The first approach was to simply ask girls 'what they
would turn to' when they first receive an issue of their favourite magazine.
Later, respondents were asked about specific parts of the magazine which they
might not have mentioned in an unprompted manner; for example, they would
be asked whether they 'ever read letters to the editor' if this text had not been

mentioned. Finally, in follow-up interviews the assistant showed the respondent a recent issue of her favourite magazine, asking her to point out what she had read in that particular issue. Reading was also explored through a series of twenty laminated magazine images taken from issues of *Seventeen*. Given the nature of magazine content, most of these images were advertisements. Respondents were asked to comment on these images; they were simply asked to 'say what they thought about the image' or 'what kinds of things come to mind when they see these types of images,' or 'whether they usually look at these when they read magazines, and why.' Because this aspect of the interview was conducted with as little prompting as possible, it proved to be the most difficult component of the interview. However, it was also one of the most fruitful aspects of the study (explored in chapter 4).[17]

During their interview, respondents were asked whether or not they would be willing to participate in follow-up interviews; only two respondents declined, one because she was moving away. I listened to all recordings shortly after interviews were completed, in order to brief assistants and prepare follow-up interview schedules. Follow-up interviews provided an opportunity to clarify ambiguous responses, probe interesting areas which emerged as unique to that respondent, and develop a second set of focused questions for all participants which explored the importance of dress and make-up at the respondent's particular school. They included the reading of images as well as general questions about school, leisure activities, and difficulties of being a teenager. Assistants carried recent issues of the respondent's favourite magazine to follow-up interviews; girls were asked to discuss what they had read in these issues, or to show the assistant texts which they would be likely to read if the respondent had not seen that particular issue.

Fifty follow-up interview schedules were prepared, with twenty-nine of these completed. Problems at this stage included the loss of research assistants as well as research participants.[18] Reluctantly I put closure on the collection of interview data, recognizing that I might never feel that I had answers to all the questions posed or that I had even come up with all the relevant questions.

Data as Text: Reading Readings

Although my initial intention was to transcribe interviews myself – to become 'immersed' in their content – after about fifteen transcriptions it became apparent that this was an unrealistic plan. The remainder of interviews were transcribed by Lisa, a paid assistant, so that I conducted analysis on transcriptions. The transcripts were organized in binders in order of chronological age. I resisted the initial temptation to compare readers according to variables which I expected to be important – age, social class, and race/ethnicity. Instead, I coded transcripts and completed thematic analysis in chronological sequence. During the first stage of thematic analysis, I identified common themes. For example, there was surprising similarity in terms of why girls read and what they enjoy about their magazines. I then questioned which types of comparisons would be important, based on what the data analysis had revealed. For example, I asked: Why do some girls read magazines while others do not? Do these two groups give different kinds of answers to the theoretically important questions? Which girls claim that they want to 'be like' an actress or a celebrity, and which girls want simply 'to be me' or refer to a role model such as their mother, an aunt, or a teacher? Which girls talk about magazines as 'realistic' and which girls begin from the self-conscious premise that magazines are 'constructions'? These groupings were then the basis for comparison on the key analytical issues: why and how girls read teenzines. The nature of the questions and data set meant that I made extensive notes and kept a reading diary during data analysis (a practice I began from the first moment of listening to the tapes).

Overall, the interviews provided answers to two types of questions: factual questions for which the respondent could give a conscious response (such as 'How old were you when you first started to read *Seventeen*?' or 'How often do you read *Seventeen*?') and theoretical questions which cannot be answered by the respondent, but must arise through analytic interpretation of data by the researcher (such as 'How do girls read?,' 'Why do these magazines appeal to these readers?,' and, ultimately, 'What is the effect of magazine reading?'). The answers to the former questions can be taken at face value[19] and also numerically tabulated; I coded all transcripts by hand and prepared summary sheets of the factual questions. The latter questions were answered through what I call 'symptomatic reading.' This interpretive method emerged during the *doing* of the project: in other words, it was not a methodological move adopted as a way to collect or organize the data. Symptomatic reading emerged from treating the data as 'texts': as texts the data are not seen to reflect a reality which the researcher re-presents, whether through qualitative or quantitative description. The data collected from the two stages of the project were seen as two 'stories' about what it means to be an adolescent woman; one story is found in the meanings identified in adolescent magazines, the other in the girls' talk about their lives. In the early stages of data analysis, these two stories were read against each other: one benefit of moving to suburbia was an 'extra' hour every day provided by commuting for uninterrupted listening to interview tapes, during the time that the coding of magazine content was undertaken. It struck me that at times the stories were harmonious, and that at other times disjunctures were apparent. A 'disjuncture' is a gap or inconsistency in the story of 'what it means to be a woman.' Disjunctures first became apparent as inconsistencies between magazine proscriptions and the experiences of readers. These types of disjunctures draw attention to distinctions between the cultural and the social worlds of adolescence. The analytical questions to be answered do not concern the ability of the text to adequately reflect the social (or vice versa), but rather what this disjuncture tells us about the constitution of the Subject through a discourse which draws heavily on commercial meanings. Thus the most interesting disjunctures appeared as gaps, inconsistencies, and uncertainties in narratives about 'Self' when girls talked about magazine reading or their everyday life in the context of interview discussions. I read these gaps and inconsistencies as 'symptoms' of an unstable Subject. In short, the symptoms for interpretive reading became evident after the completion of interviews, during their analysis, and were not 'items' on an interview schedule.

Symptomatic reading is not an empiricist approach which looks for a 'truth' which is reflected in the text: rather, symptomatic reading explores the 'faultlines' of the text in order to reveal its constructedness. Sigmund Freud developed this method of reading the Subject as a psychoanalytic technique. He identified symptoms in the ambiguities or lapses in self-expression which he read as arising from compromises which the Subject must perform to reconcile the conscious and unconscious. He thus read symptoms as effects of a struggle between the body, and the society upon which the body depends. These effects are manifest as jokes, Freudian slips, patterns of children's play, and, importantly, 'in the mutually affective relationship which human beings develop as a consequence of their past total helplessness and dependence on another person' (Wright 1984: 2). Symptoms are reminders that no experience of the body is ever erased from the human mind; each stage of becoming a Subject entails evasions which become relegated to the unconscious. The symptoms which bring human beings to the analyst's couch point to the mismatch between bodily desire and the cultural proscriptions of adult social roles. Thus symptoms point to processes which give the analyst access to the unconscious. This manner of symptomatic reading has been adopted by postmodern feminists, especially French feminist Luce Irigarary, who employs a symptomatic reading of Freud to identify the repressed problematics of patriarchal Western culture. However, as Hennessy (1993: 93) notes, postmodern symptomatic readings tend to remain within the ahistorical boundaries of the psychoanalytic problematic. She contrasts these readings to the more politicized potential of symptomatic reading as ideological critique: 'By opening the symptom and the text up to history and systematic analysis, the work developed out of a materialist appropriation of Freud's symptomatic reading offers a promising avenue for developing the political interestedness of the symptom and its implications for understanding the feminist standpoint as a critical practice. As a strategy of ideology critique, symptomatic reading draws out the unnaturalness of the text and makes visible another logic haunting its surface' (p. 93). For Hennessy, symptoms are silences which may be read as the irruption of counter-hegemonic discourses into an otherwise coherent story of patriarchal capitalism.

While Hennessy follows the Althusserian tradition of reading ideology, in the current study symptomatic reading is a useful way to identify the gaps and irruptions in the texts of girls' interviews that point to the struggle between the cultural realm of femininity and the social world of embodied practice. As we shall see, disjunctures point to the potential undoing of the speaking Subject, as an unstable subjectivity open to its own questioning. This questioning can be reformulated as a moment of 'crisis' for the Subject, in our case in 'becoming' a gendered Subject of the patriarchal order. Experienced as subjectivity and expressed as gendered identity, this moment of crisis is not read here as a psychoanalytic process, but as pointing to the problematic nature of a femininity constructed through the patriarchal culture of capitalism. It is also not to say that girls are in crisis; rather, symptoms express the 'everyday' experiences of becoming a woman in a culture which attempts to seal off meanings contrary to reconstitution of the dominant social and cultural order. This sealing-off occurs through discourses, such as those in teenzines, that have as their goal the restabilization of identity through reassurance that the everyday problems of teenage girls will be transcended as readers mature, biologically and psychologically, into adult women. This process of sealing-off is necessarily unstable because it is contradictory; the problems of being female do not 'go away' when girls become 'women.'

Chapter 4 begins to explore how symptomatic reading is employed in this study. As we shall see, the most readily apparent symptoms are gaps and inconsistencies in magazine texts themselves. These types of inconsistencies have been discussed by other researchers as contradictions in magazine discourse. In the current study, an example of contradictory messages within advice columns is messages which encourage readers 'to express themselves' and 'put their own needs ahead of those of problematic boys,' within the context of an overriding message about the importance of romantic heterosexuality and conformity to a womanhood which reconstitutes women's subordination. Postmodern writers like Fiske (1989a: 4) claim that contradiction is a key to reader agency because it provides a moment through which the reader draws upon her own 'resource bank of potential meaning.' Because he draws, as researcher-reader, on a counter-cultural resource bank, Fiske tends to emphasize the ways in which popular culture, as negotiated meaning, challenges hegemonic culture. Like many postmodern cultural critics, Fiske draws upon his own readings of social texts to illustrate how dominant meanings can be subverted. Likewise viewing the negotiation of contradiction as a point at which readers are agents of meaning, I was eager to assess how contradictions in teenzine texts offer moments for the reader to consider the constructedness of the Symbolic Order. In order to answer this type of question, however, I could not read magazine texts in isolation. Unlike writers like Fiske, I did not read the contradictions in magazine texts against a theoretical literature which would lead me to predict politicization of readers. Instead, I read the gaps and disjunctures in magazine discourse against interview transcripts. In this way, reading symptomatically entails a different kind of intertextuality than typically engaged by academic researchers. Specifically, the researcher does not 'read against the grain' in search of hidden, subversive meanings; rather, the researcher reads the texts in question against the meaning-making of everyday readers. Clearly, this manner of reading is difficult if the researcher expects, hence looks for, coherence and consistency on the part of research Subjects. In fact, I initially found the types of symptoms explored in *Girl Talk* as perplexing inconsistencies in interview transcripts. For example, the first symptom I encountered came as an observa-tion of the shift by girls from first person to third person when discussing their own behaviours and feelings about themselves 'as women.' Initially, I (uninten-tionally) read over these inconsistencies in an attempt to impose coherence upon girls' narratives of Self. However, by paying closer attention to the ways in which these shifts signalled changes in referent points[20] – from Self-construction to the construction of the Subject through the expectations of school or teenzine culture, for example – I came to understand them in terms of the 'doing' and 'undoing' of the Subject. 'Doing' refers to those moments when the interviewee spoke confidently from a coherent sense of Self; 'undoing' refers to those moments when self-doubt and incoherence 'leaked' unexpect-edly into interview narratives. Adolescent identity is thus treated as a practical accomplishment achieved through a contradictory discourse mediated by social texts that include commercial magazines. By 'identity,' I mean the ability of the Subject to sustain a narrative about Self and to answer critical questions about what to do, how to act, and who to be. As such, Self-construction is a reflexive project, requiring the subjective 'building up of a consistent feeling of bio-graphical continuity and ontological security' (Barker and Andre 1995). In this study, I employ the term 'Subject-ivity' to evoke an embodied rather than theo-retically constructed Self as a practical mode of consciousness. My task is to understand the doing and undoing of the Subject through the subjectivity sur-rounding teenzine reading and the everyday life of girls in this study. Symp-toms in both the discourse of femininity, and the social texts which mediate this discourse, led me to ask under what conditions do teenzines work to constitute the ideological Subject-ivity idealized by commercial texts? Under what conditions might contradictions and inconsistencies in the text encourage readers to challenge or resist the story of patriarchal capitalism? And finally, under what conditions can such inconsistencies and disjunctures constitute a problematic Subject-ivity, one in which contradictions play themselves out through the body as stories of compulsive disciplines of diet, exercise, and so on.

Drawing attention to these symptoms of the crisis of the Subject through a practice of reading is not to reduce these matters to simply a method of reading: the undoing of the Subject does not 'go away' by rewriting the symptoms or by reading them as 'resistance' or gender play. The symptoms have been well documented in an array of venues beyond cultural studies. The point here is to read these symptoms through a *critical* cultural studies. By using 'critical' we do not refer here to simply a 'negative' view of femininity, as postmodern celebrants of women's culture often claim that Marxists tend to do. Rather, this practice of reading provides a way of gaining access to the experiential world of female adolescence. In the final analysis this access provides a positive approach to feminist critique because it reveals the way in which lived experience can call ideology into question.[21] It therefore provides us with a way to think about resistance politically, as a social and not an individual process, to bring politics into feminist cultural critique.

The next five chapters explore the results of the fieldwork and this manner of working. As noted above, one of the most important requirements of reading data symptomatically is to (temporarily) displace researcher readings of texts in order to enter teenzine discourse from the standpoint of everyday teenage readers. This does not mean that as cultural critics and analysts we abandon the theoretical discourse which inspired our research in the first place; clearly, such a feat would be impossible. Rather, reading symptomatically means that we engage in a type of intertextuality which gives us access to meaning-making by our research participants. It is everyday meaning-making rather than academic meaning-making that becomes our analytical problematic. I do not reject the notion that the analytical techniques of the cultural critic can help us to understand social texts; I only argue that they are more fruitfully applied to the questions and problematics identified in adolescent rather than researcher readings of these texts. In order to explore what these different approaches each contribute to the study of social texts as process, chapter 4 employs techniques of textual analysis discussed in this and previous chapters. Through an exploration of advertising texts we identify the contributions, but also limitations, of both content analysis and literary methods of textual analysis as ways to access or to 'know' how texts work in the social world of adolescents. Drawing on Smith (1990b) here, we view limitations in current academic debate as ones of method, not theory; specifically of methods which treat the text as a 'specimen' for analysis. As we shall see, the type of text chosen for analysis in chapter 4 is not the favourite or preferred reading of the girls in this study. However, advertisements are a useful beginning point for *Girl Talk* because of their predominance in academic discourse on women's magazines and the (purported) effects of magazine reading. Given both the spatial and the visual prominence of advertising in women's magazines, cultural criticism has subjected these texts to extensive commentary. The purpose of chapter 4, therefore, is not only to explore the potential usefulness of different methods of textual analysis, but also to show the role of motivation in reading as the construction of knowledge. While this demonstration is not a claim that the current research is not motivated by the desires and interests of its author, it does highlight the importance of data as a means of discovery (of the world of adolescent femininity) rather than confirmation (of the theoretical world of the academic).

4

From Text as Specimen to Text as Process: Reading as Everyday Practice

Smith (1990b) warns against treating the text as a 'specimen' or 'sample,' a strategy common in cultural criticism. 'Specimen,' refers to 'working from within the textual, from this side, the reading and writing, seeing, hearing side of textual surfaces,' reading the actualities of people's lives off the text (p. 4). Clearly, this way of working reflects the legacy of cultural critique grounded in the analysis of texts as instances of literary 'works,' although, as we saw in chapter 2, it can also be found in 'scientific' analysis of texts. As McRobbie (1991b) notes, one of the problems which this way of working brings to cultural studies is that social texts are no longer recognized as material artefacts coming into existence through specific relations, under historical conditions of production which are also the context of their consumption. McRobbie, like Smith, advocates analysis which connects the text to both its making and its consumption through research which is structural, historical, and ethnographic.

Within film studies, Christine Gledhill (1988: 67) draws attention to the necessity to distinguish analytically between two elements commonly evoked in cultural studies: the 'feminine spectator,' constructed by the text, and the female audience, constructed by the sociohistorical categories of gender, class, race, and so on. For her, the question for feminist analysis is how to conceive their relationship. Along these lines, but going further, Mary Poovey (1988) argues that analysis must be extended to also include the texts produced by cultural critics themselves. She maintains that the inability of deconstruction – as a popular method of textual analysis within cultural studies – to account for its own existence places it outside politics or gives rise to conservative political expression. Against this trend, she maintains that deconstruction can be useful for materialist feminists if it pursues two projects simultaneously:

On the one hand, we need to recognize that 'woman' *is* currently ... a position within a dominant, binary symbolic order *and* that that position is arbitrarily (and falsely) unified. On the other hand, we need to remember that there *are* concrete historical women whose differences reveal the inadequacy of this unified category in the present and the past. The multiple positions real women occupy – the positions dictated by race, for example, or by class or sexual preference – should alert us to the inadequacy of binary logic and unitary selves without making us forget that this logic *has* dictated (and still does) some aspects of women's treatment. (p. 62; emphasis in original)

What Poovey alerts us to is the dialectical nature of textual analysis: the need to recognize texts as symbolic constructions which falsely unify women whose discursive positioning becomes the location from which embodied women, in all their lived diversity, must speak in protest of their positioning. Analysis by necessity must invoke the category 'woman,' but only in order to reveal the construction of its making and the interests which this discursive construction conceals. This means that deconstruction is an empirical as well as literary/discursive practice: after all, it is embodied women who have exploded the categorical 'woman' of white, Western feminist discourse.[1] We thus need social criticism which can bring to light the cultural construction of embodied as well as discursive, categorical women.

The purpose of *Girl Talk* is to develop such an analysis by employing a materialist analysis of social texts and the discourses which they mediate. As a dialectical method of analysis, this study views commercial texts such as women's magazines and their consumption as an opportunity to explore the imperatives concealed by the cultural construction of women as an interest group and the ways in which these imperatives play themselves out through readers' recognition of themselves as belonging (or not belonging) to this group. As we shall see, many of the worrisome effects of teenzine reading are linked to the importance for readers of 'belonging' to the constructed category 'teenage women.' *Girl Talk* thus provides an opportunity to observe the interface between the social and the cultural, between women as the objects and the subjects of cultural critique. At the same time, this study recognizes that both women's magazines and their analysis by academics are implicated in the practices through which the reality of 'women' and their interests are constituted. While previous chapters highlighted academic readings of social texts, the remainder of this chapter explores magazine reading as everyday practice and thus begins to connect the cultural world (of teenzines) to the social world (of embodied Subjects). It sheds light on the nature of Subject-ivity as the bringing-together of embodied women and cultural constructions of womanhood. It also demonstrates the necessity to differentiate between 'reading as research,' in which the text is a specimen for textual analysis and deconstruction by the academic, and 'reading as social practice,' in which the text mediates processes through which actual readers make sense of themselves and their world.

We have already seen that much of the academic debate surrounding cultural representation is inspired by the glossy advertising layouts of commercial magazines. While sociologists employ content analysis to chart messages and identify dominant values in advertisements, cultural critics draw upon literary methods in order to reveal hidden, connoted meaning which cannot be captured during quantification. In the main, researchers typically favour one approach as necessarily better. In this study, however, we reject the notion that *only* thematic analysis or *only* literary deconstruction can reveal the 'truth' of teenzine discourse. Instead, sociological and literary methods are taken as both complementary and necessary to an adequate understanding of social texts as systems (rather than instances) of signification. Systematic content analysis is necessary to tell us about the nature of teenzines as a cultural object that engages most of the girls in this study. Literary methods are necessary to help us connect this cultural object to its reading. Because readers encounter teenzines as instances (rather than as systems) of signification, we need to analyse discrete moments of the text. The problem remains, however, that even both methods used in conjunction cannot tell us how texts are taken up by intended audiences in their everyday setting. No matter how convinced we might be as cultural critics that teenzine messages play an important role in young readers' lives, we cannot simply read this role 'off the text.' In order to explore how social texts such as teenzines work as discourse rather than simply as cultural objects, we need to move beyond the text itself to its reading. Such an analytical move connects the cultural world of texts to the social world of embodied readers; it moves from the text as an object of analysis to the meaning-making that these texts mediate. Explicating the precise nature of this connection is the goal of *Girl Talk*. Given their predominance in both teenzines and academic debate, the focus for the exploration in this chapter is advertising texts; in subsequent chapters we analyse the texts favoured by readers rather than by cultural critics.

As noted in the introduction, this study began from interest in how women's magazines attempt to define women and assign them a place in the social order. Because the power of the text relates to its commercial nature, like previous analysts I gave advertising texts my full attention during the initial stages of research. Ads are an obvious beginning point for an analysis of fashion and beauty magazines: they comprise about half of magazine page space and are the major source of glossy imagery which makes these magazines such a visually pleasurable read. Dyer (1982: 86) maintains that imagery is so prominent in commercial media because pictures are easier for readers to understand and have more impact than words. The obviousness of advertising has led many cultural commentators to look for the effects of magazine reading in these glossy texts. We saw in chapter 1 that Winship and others link advertising layouts and pictorials to women's reading pleasures. At the same time, the purported negative effects of magazine reading have also been seen to lie in advertising. Smith (1988, 1990a) and others (Brownmiller 1984; Bordo 1993) argue that glossy advertorials for dress and make-up work to construct textually given forms of embodiment, all the while obscuring achieved femininity as skilled work. If for no other reason than the extent to which advertising generates scholarly debate, my analysis of teenzines began with advertisements in *Seventeen*.[2] What might young girls learn about 'being women' if the texts of teenzines work in the ways which previous commentators claim?

In the remainder of this chapter we answer this question by beginning from the obviousness of the text: we begin by identifying the manifest content of beauty advertisements in teenzines. Identification of content requires thematic analysis, conducted here on a systematic sample of ads published in *Seventeen* between 1951 and 1991. Despite changes in the appearance of advertising texts during the intervening forty years, advertising continues to signify femininity in surprisingly traditional ways. It thus becomes important to understand how contemporary readers, who have available to them the counter-hegemonic discourses of women's liberation, take meaning from these texts. We therefore move from researcher to everyday reading of advertising texts, in order to explore how ads work in the immediate context of their reading. While this move begins to ground our analysis of teenzines in the everyday discourse of femininity, our analysis does not end there. Everyday readings direct the analyst to problematics as yet undiscovered by researcher readings of the text. In *Girl Talk* these problematics are expressed through three analytical themes central to femininity as textually mediated discourse: *power* as the social effects of practices of signification, *agency* as the practices of embodied women that valorize shared meanings at the everyday local level, and the *cultural construction of the social* as the coordination of systems of meaning which act to reconstitute the conditions and relations which make particular significations possible. In order to understand how texts work in this way, rather than to understand simply their content, in this chapter we employ literary methods to answer sociological questions about social texts.

Femininity as Cultural Construction: Advertising Messages in *Seventeen*

Viewing femininity as textually mediated discourse directed me to question how feminine identity, as an individual practice of bodily signification, might be connected to magazine content. The curiosity expressed in the introduction

first led me to look for an answer through content analysis of beauty advertisements in a systematic sample of *Seventeen*. What are the categories and definitions offered by teenzine ads as the discursive 'truth' of being women? Because
I was interested in the ways in which these categories and definitions change
over time, advertisements were enumerated in four issues of *Seventeen* published during each of five years: 1951, 1961, 1971, 1981, and 1991. Together,
Shelley and I developed categories for coding and enumerating the glossy ads
which are such a prominent feature of teenzine texts. Between 1951 and 1991,
advertising accounted for anywhere from 49.1 per cent (for 1981) to 63.8 per
cent (for 1971) of the total page space of each issue of *Seventeen*. Regardless of
individual reading preferences (identified in chapter 6), advertising messages
are difficult to escape.[3] What do these texts have to say about femininity as the
culturally preferred way of 'being women'? Tables 4.1 and 4.2 answer this
question through a systematic enumeration of the subject matter and thematic
appeals of advertising copy.

   In table 4.1 we see that the vast majority of advertisements in any sampled
year concern clothing and beauty products, which together represent about two-
thirds of all advertised subjects in any year. While advertisements for domestic
products have never been a major category in *Seventeen*, they had virtually dis-
appeared by 1991. Of interest is the increased emphasis on beautification products: between 1951 and 1991, there was a twofold increase in advertisements
for make-up, and a threefold increase in those for hair products. During the
same time-frame, fashionable apparel decreased from 50.1 to 13.9 per cent of
advertising themes. In effect, femininity is increasingly presented through
advertising as a bodily characteristic. The primary message of ads is beautification of the female body, which is presented as an object of intervention and
improvement. This intervention requires the discursive and pictorial separation
of the female body into discrete, isolated parts. As Dyer (1982: 98) maintains,
representations of the male body are less often dismembered in this way. While
the female body is a subject of discussion across the various texts of *Seventeen*,
the dominant source of body themes is advertising: in any year, over 83 per cent
of all body themes were found in ads, with 93.6 per cent of body themes found
in advertisements during 1971. Overall, the female body has increasingly
become the dominant focus of ads: by 1991, 68.1 per cent of ads are for products associated with, or to be used on, the body for the primary purpose of aesthetic enhancement. Given the prominence of beautification, ads for beauty
products were thematically analysed as a separate genre. Clearly, beauty ads
play an important role in defining both what femininity is and how it is to be
achieved. Reflecting this role, it is common for them to accompany editorial
commentary on beautification; this textual strategy further links beauty and

Table 4.1: Subject Matter of Advertisements in *Seventeen*, 1951–1991

	% of total subjects enumerated				
	1951	1961	1971	1981	1991
Body topics					
Beauty products for skin, lips, eyes, nails, teeth	14.4	16.1	24.1	34.5	29.2
Hair products[1]	6.1	3.7	11.4	11.4	20.1
Perfumes and deodorants	3.5	8.0	8.1	5.7	8.3
Menstrual products and feminine hygiene	1.7	4.0	11.0	9.2	8.3
Slimming	–	–	0.5	0.4	1.4
% OF TOTAL	25.7	31.8	55.1	61.2	67.3
Non-body topics					
Fashion apparel	50.1	40.6	17.0	12.5	13.9
Entertainment[2]	3.2	4.8	5.1	6.8	6.3
Food	1.7	4.5	3.2	5.0	2.1
Engagement and wedding rings	2.3	1.9	3.0	2.1	0.0
Domestic[3]	8.6	6.7	4.1	1.8	0.7
Sewing, fabrics	3.5	1.9	1.6	0.0	0.0
Jewellery	0.9	1.1	2.7	1.4	0.7
Miscellaneous[4]	4.0	6.2	8.7	9.2	9.0
Total ads	343	370	366	280	143
Total subjects[5]	347	374	370	281	144

1 Includes products for the removal of unwanted hair
2 Includes music, films, videos, books, and magazines
3 Includes silverware, china, stemware, cooking equipment, and miscellaneous domestic products
4 Changes each year (includes luggage, careers, sports equipment, cars, telephones, photos, toys, stereo equipment)
5 Can be more than one subject per ad

commodity consumption. It also means that two types of messages can be found in beauty ads: messages which act to give meaning to the cultural construction 'woman,' and messages which give meaning to the bodily practices associated with the accomplishment of womanhood. Reflecting the nature of the influence I assumed these texts to have, I was particularly interested in the types of appeals that are made to readers who might (or might not) buy the advertised products. Table 4.2 summarizes these appeals under two headings: messages which give meaning to femininity and those which give meaning to the bodily practices of femininity. Coded messages thus concern qualities of

Table 4.2: Categories of Appeals in Beauty Advertisements in *Seventeen*, 1951–1991[1]

	% of all appeals				
	1951	1961	1971	1981	1991
To meaning of femininity					
Beauty, pretty	10.9	12.2	7.8	7.8	12.9
Soft, gentle, innocent	8.0	7.1	9.3	9.6	7.7
Natural, authentic	5.5	4.8	8.9	7.3	6.5
Sexually appealing, romantic	7.1	11.9	9.8	5.6	4.8
Exciting, dramatic outrageous	5.4	5.4	4.8	5.9	6.9
To meaning of bodily practices					
Solves a problem, fights, controls,					
provides security	12.1	10.9	17.0	17.9	15.7
Scientific, medical professional	9.6	7.1	4.6	7.8	9.3
Modern, new, advanced	9.2	9.2	7.6	6.4	6.9
Quick, easy, convenient	9.2	5.4	9.3	6.1	6.0
Improvement, change yourself	4.2	6.4	4.2	7.9	6.0
Unique, personal self-expression	2.5	5.4	3.5	6.4	6.0
Comfort, product is safe	7.1	3.7	6.7	6.6	5.7
Inexpensive	4.6	7.8	3.7	0.9	1.6
Perfection, excel over others,					
achieve ultimate	4.6	2.7	2.8	3.8	4.0
Total ads[2]	96	120	190	188	109

1 Four matched issues counted for 1961, 1971, 1981, and 1991; three matched issues
counted for 1951
2 Can be more than one theme per ad

advertised products as well as models because, as Williamson (1978) demonstrates, advertising implies that consumption will impart these qualities to the
reader.

Between 1951 and 1991, beauty advertising in *Seventeen* drew upon a narrow range of appeals to readers. About one-third of the messages enumerated
relate to the meaning of 'woman': among these messages, traditional descriptors dominate. Femininity as idealized womanhood is associated with beauty,
innocence, and softness. The majority of coded messages, about two-thirds,
concern the characteristics of the products. Beauty problems are consistently
presented as being solved by scientifically advanced, professionally endorsed
products which are inexpensive, convenient to use, and environmentally sound.
It is useful to note that, at the same time that advertising emphasizes the need

for intervention and remedies, ads claim to help the reader express her *authentic self*. This association between authenticity and achievement of the culturally prescribed norms of beauty implies that feminine beauty is an inherent quality of female being. Like the notion 'natural beauty,' one of the most enduring phrases in cosmetic advertising, appeals to authenticity obscure historical and political processes which underlie the text by inverting the relationship between the 'natural' and the 'cultural.' Natural beauty implies that femininity is something for the reader to 'discover' about herself; this discovery is aided rather than created through scientific and medical advances offered by the cosmetic industry. As we shall see in chapter 6, Self-discovery is an important source of reading pleasure; here we see that it extends to the practices of beautification.

In table 4.2, there is little change during the forty-year period in the way in which beauty ads idealize womanhood for their readers. Although developments in photographic technique and textual layout give the appearance that advertising has changed dramatically over time, written messages which accompany the pictorial treatment of femininity changed remarkably little. The explicit reference to beauty, softness, and innocence is consistent over time. This consistency is accounted for, in part, by continuity in advertisers. Cover Girl, for example, which draws on the traditional stereotype of natural beauty, reappears in issues across all years. What has changed is the frequency of messages over time: the increased proportion of cosmetic advertising means that the absolute number of beauty messages per issue was greater in 1991 than in the past. While letters to the editor during the 1970s often complained about *Seventeen*'s focus on beauty and fashion, cosmetic companies like Revlon, Maybelline, Breck, Noxema, and Ponds continued to endorse their products in similar ways throughout the forty years of the study, while advertising overall increasingly emphasized bodily improvement. In the most recent year of the sample, bodily beautification accounts for two-thirds of advertising messages in *Seventeen*. Significantly, the editors whom Peirce (1990) interviewed claim that *Seventeen* gives readers what they *need*; it is interesting to note that the girls themselves make a similar claim, discussed in upcoming chapters.

Chapter 6 explores in greater detail how beauty texts discursively position the reading Subject. Here we note that, however monolithic advertising texts may appear, the beauty mandate is a complex and contradictory process. Complexity arises from the way in which beauty messages, although emphasizing natural and authentic qualities of womanhood, must also exhort women to continually work over their natural bodily state. Advertisements thus mediate a contradictory discourse of femininity: femininity is natural but in constant need of improvement and intervention. Through advertising it amounts to 'prescribed authenticity.' The contradictory nature of the advertising texts which

Table 4.3: Texts and Subtexts of Beauty Advertisements in *Seventeen*

Dominant Theme	Subtext
OF BEAUTY STANDARD	
beautiful, pretty	*encourages objectification*
soft, gentle, innocent	*traditional femininity*
natural, authentic	*could subvert commodification*
sexually appealing, romantic	*endorses heterosexuality, male-centredness*
exciting, dramatic, outrageous	*could subvert traditional femininity*
OF BODILY PRACTICES	
solves a problem, fights, controls, provides security	*creates problems for proffered solutions*
scientific, medical, professionally endorsed	*promotes medicalization/naturalization of 'beauty'*
modern, new, advanced	*encourages need for change*
quick, easy, convenient	*induces sense of shortcoming for not practising*
unique, personal, self-expression	*endorses diversity – could subvert commodification*
comfort, product is safe	*induces sense of shortcoming for not practising*
inexpensive	*implies accessibility – could induce sense of shortcoming for not practising*
achieve perfection, excel over others, achieve ultimate	*promotes competitiveness*

mediate the cultural standards of femininity becomes apparent when we move from the level of pure denotation to an examination of the less visible subtexts of advertising discourse. The subtexts of advertising discourse are summarized in table 4.3.

As suggested by Smith and others, advertising contains latent messages which invite a sense of shortcoming in readers and encourage readers to identify with beauty problems. At the same time, signifying femininity in this way is a contradictory process. Perhaps ironically, the obviousness of beauty advertising which renders it a rather easy venue for individual enumeration also imparts a complexity when considering advertising texts as a genre. However monolithic these texts may appear to be as a consequence of their repetitive slogans and appeals, as a genre advertising texts have the potential to draw attention to their constructedness. As Gledhill (1988: 68) notes, this is the case because the use value of commercial texts, which lies in a complex of pleasures and meanings operating at different levels, is not easily predicted and controlled by their authors. The use value to a particular group of readers may be in contradiction with the ideologies that sustain the process of textual production in the long run.

In the current study an example of this contradictory process is found in 'alternative' themes of femininity in women's magazines which signify womanhood as 'exciting, dramatic, or outrageous,' for example. However, contradictions also arise from the fact that individual messages can become logically inconsistent when taken together as a system of meaning. For example, can ads successfully tell us to be ourselves and yet to still follow their cultural prescriptions? Clearly, answers to this type of question bring us to the limits of textual analysis. While thematic enumeration helps to characterize advertising as a distinctive system of signification, it cannot tell us how these texts work in the everyday context of their reading. It is necessary to now move from researcher readings of ads to their everyday reading.

From Researcher Readings to Everyday Practice

As we saw in chapter 1, the contradictory nature of magazine messages is the source of much academic debate over the everyday effects of magazine reading. Drawing on adolescent magazines, Helen Pleasance (1991) provides a succinct review of competing theoretical positions. On one side, commercial culture is theorized as the site where dominant power relations are successfully extended and reinforced; contradiction and readerly resistance are always recouped into dominant culture itself. On the other side, because culture is seen as a site of conflict and struggle, its power is never fully or permanently secured. Discursive contradictions are important as a site where dominant power relations can be pulled apart and challenged (p. 69). Within the first theoretical framework, ideology determines the meaning of cultural forms as narrative devices which make sense of, and tie us into, the 'real, material story' (p. 71). Pleasance cites the work of Judith Williamson as an example of this approach: within the narrative closure of her account the story is 'already told.' Drawing on magazines for adolescent girls, Pleasance illustrates that this approach necessarily leads the analyst to conclude that the unending logic of consumption secures tight ideological closure. She contrasts this pessimistic reading to that offered by postmodernist writers like E. Ann Kaplan and Angela McRobbie, who ask new questions about reading 'the cultural.' For example, Kaplan (1987: 5) suggests that youth culture, such as Music Television, which many feminists deplore for its apparent sexism, acts to fill an important cultural gap. It addresses 'the desires, fantasies and anxieties of young people growing up in a world in which all traditional categories are being blurred and all institutions questioned.' From this perspective, fantasy is given status in the everyday working of culture because fantasies about consumer lifestyles are as much an indictment of people's lack of real attainment of the benefits offered by the market as they are about incorporation into the market process (p. 81). On the basis of psycho-analysis rather than socialization theory, commercial texts are read as evidence of the constant undoing, rather than stability, of identity. The failure of identity is reflected in the continual searching for meaning through the pages of a magazine. Importantly, the gendering of identity is not read as a necessary *intent* of media like fashion and beauty magazines which create new dissatisfactions among readers. Furthermore, the unstable and contradictory nature of femininity offered by this venue can provide openings, rather than closure. Pleasance concludes that, 'in the narrative of openness, our relationships with pleasurable, dominant cultural forms does [*sic*] not sentence us to a social imprisonment, but can indicate our continuous refusals of, anxieties about and disassociations from those relations' (p. 83).

In the final analysis, Pleasance maintains that both versions of how social relations work through cultural consumption are valuable because each makes an important analytical contribution. While the first narrative gives a sense of the broad sweep of entrepreneurial capitalism and patriarchal relations, the second allows us to get beneath the monolithic dimension of power; it proposes a view of dominance as contingently constructed and suggests that culture is a site of struggle. Consumption, as a cultural activity, is seen to allow these openings (pp. 83, 84). Pleasance concludes that these two theoretical versions need not contradict each other, because at different times and for different reasons it would be important to argue for closure, at others for openness. Furthermore, she maintains that duality and contradiction resonate with the way dominance is experienced as lived relation.

While it may appear that Pleasance is able to 'retain the structuralist insight that subjects are not the authors of social meaning, but avoid the structuralist tendency to see subjectivity as singular and fully determined' (this volume: 92), in my view there are problems with the notion that we can sometimes advance modernist, structuralist views, and at other times a post-structuralist position. While the proposal to do so is attractive because it would provide closure on theoretical debate by allowing us to claim cultural consumption as both compliance and resistance, it does not provide solid ground for theorizing agency. In the final analysis this proposal merely repackages the problematic dualism characteristic of contemporary debate.[4]

It is significant that surprisingly few writers contributing to debates about the effects of magazine reading include actual readers in their study of women's magazines. One exception is the work of Ros Ballaster, Margaret Beetham, Elizabeth Frazer, and Sandra Hebron (1991), who challenge the tendency for commentators to conflate implied and actual readers. Like postmodern writers, Ballaster and colleagues take up the issue of pleasure in women's magazine reading; however, they move beyond the impasse that is constructed when debate is directed by the (overly simplistic) question of whether magazines are a source of women's oppression perpetuated by the capitalist market or a cultural expression of women-centred pleasure. Instead, Ballaster and colleagues explore how women's magazines, as commodities, orchestrate the relation between implied readers and actual reading audiences. Although their research emphasizes the historical construction of the femininity of magazine discourse, hence implied readers, they avoid a study of social identity that collapses into 'textual criticism' (p. 24). Their study includes tape-recorded group discussions with thirty-one women about magazine reading. The researchers asked readers what they like and dislike in magazines which they regularly read. In these discussions the researchers found that, at the same time that women enjoy magazine reading, they *are* conscious of the oppressive, ideological dimensions of their magazines and of the fact that these magazines address them through the commodity form. From discussions with readers, Ballaster and colleagues conclude that 'ease' and 'recognition' provide the major ideological pleasure of women's magazines (p. 168).

While their study of actual readers is a positive advance overall, the interviews by the Ballaster group supplement rather than challenge or displace their own researcher readings; the bulk of their research concerns the content and format of women's magazines from the eighteenth century onwards. In order to elaborate arguments which they develop from their reading of these texts, the authors present their interviews as 'suggestive' (p. 127). In contrast, the current study of everyday reading treats girls' recorded discussions as 'data' to be analysed for what they reveal about adolescent reading rather than whether (or how) they 'match' theoretical debates raised by researchers. In other words, my task is to problematize what is typically taken for granted: the act of reading. While a study of reading necessarily includes a study of the texts in question, it entails much more. It requires that we do not mistake the meaning-making of the researcher for the act of everyday reading. In the remainder of this chapter we begin to displace researcher readings by exploring the meaning-making revealed through girls' readings of teenzine texts. As outlined in chapter 3, this task requires that we take our analytical problematic from everyday rather than researcher readings. The problematic to be addressed in the remainder of this chapter is how embodied readers 'work over' the messages identified through researcher coding and enumeration. While their meaning-making includes semantic constructions which girls unselfconsciously deploy, here we look for the type of conscious negotiations which underlie decision making during reading. I take as my problematic the way in which girls themselves come to understand the texts which so interest researchers. As previous writers claim, the discursive negotiation of meaning becomes most evident when texts present readers with inconsistent or contradictory messages. However, as we shall see, while these openings in the text highlight reader agency in the construction of meaning, negotiation did not always occur in ways which I might have predicted from a standpoint grounded purely in theory.

'It Says What It Means': How Girls Read

A focal point of discussion that emerged during interviews with girls was whether or not particular ads represented a plausible reality, and it was on that basis that the reader typically enjoyed the ad – hence would spend time scrutinizing it in some detail as opposed to 'flipping' past it. In the following I draw on the readings of a series of twenty advertisements[5] for beauty products, fashion, and engagement rings (plus one car ad) taken from *Seventeen* (but which also appear in the other magazines). These images are listed and described in Appendix C. In order to explore how adolescent girls, rather than adult researchers, read the glossy images in fashion and beauty magazines, the analysis which follows makes transparent the rules and procedures through which girls come to claim that the images are realistic, hence pleasurable. Given the nature of the task, not all transcripts were suitable for analysis. Only those transcripts where discussion is relatively unprompted are used below; these transcripts include readings by girls who do not regularly read magazines.

Like researchers, adolescent readers did not passively accept the images presented; girls actively negotiated meaning as the basis for accepting – or rejecting – texts. As Gledhill (1988: 67) notes, by bridging the gap between textual and social subjects, the notion of 'negotiation' might take a central place in theorizing the relations among media products, ideologies, and audiences. The value of this concept is that it avoids an overly deterministic view of cultural production, whether economistic (the media reflects dominant economic interests outside the text) or psycholinguistic (the text constructs spectators through the psycholinguistic mechanisms of the Unconscious). It implies the holding together of opposite sides in an ongoing process of give and take. In the current study it allows us to think about the agency of readers. This agency is evident when girls reject ads outright, as many did, on the basis that elements of the message are not internally consistent. In part, this occurs because these readers employ logic in the creation of meaning:

I would think, 'Why is he painting her toenails? How would he know how to do it?' (Sixteen-year-old Alyssa reading ad for Liz Claiborne Fragrance)

I don't understand why she would be wearing something like that when it's all cloudy and stuff. And I wonder how they got the car in the middle of nowhere. (Sixteen-year-old Alicia reading ad for Saturn car)

As a consequence, girls rejected representations which do not make sense:

I don't get it, I don't get it. I mean I could read a whole lot into it – 'A Kiss is Not Just a Kiss' [reading slogan] ... I mean, I don't get this, I don't understand it. (Seventeen-year-old Jamie reading Bisou Bisou nouvelle couture ad)

This is strange, weird, like just a girl, a drink, and a car. If I looked at it, I wouldn't know what they're trying to do – it's confusing. (Fifteen-year-old Chelsea reading ad for Saturn car)

I don't think that makes any sense cause she's holding a jug of juice, and she's in the desert, and you see the back end of a car, and I see people playing music, but it doesn't mean anything. (Fifteen-year-old Heather reading ad for Saturn car)

[pause] I don't understand it. It says 'created for men' and then it has all these women-things, and then it says 'created for women' – never mind, I wouldn't read that part. (Fourteen-year-old Lauren reading ad for Lawman jeans)

However, as well as logic, lived experience was also a basis for making sense of representations, expressed by these girls looking at the same ad (in different interviews) which simulates a girls' pyjama party:

Oh this is neat! Like being with friends and having fun – a typical girls' night, this is a good one because I guess, like all girls have been there. (Fifteen-year-old Heather reading ad for Caboodles make-up kit ad)

This appeals to me because I can like relate to this, in the picture I can like relate to sitting around with your friends and everything and it looks sort of like an average – just getting ready to go out, and I'd probably read this and see more about what's on here [text] because I can relate to the picture. (Fifteen-year-old Kirsten reading same ad)

It kind of shows people doing real things. I would do that, sit at my friend's and have Sara pluck my eyebrows ... the models are on the realistic side – at least she's got curlers in her hair and they're not all perfect – they're in their underwear. (Thirteen-year-old Amanda reading same ad)

Conversely, readers could reject the same image because it does not reflect their experiences of being a teenage girl:

This one seems a bit *fake* to me. Like I'd read it over to see what it says, you know, but it's so like – [in a mocking tone] talking on the phone, curlers in your hair, like doing your make-up and laughing in your pyjamas, like it's so, like *TV* – that's what they do on TV. It's like a slumber party, it's a good one for a girls' magazine, but it's kind of fake to me. (Fifteen-year-old Elizabeth reading same ad)

These are commercials we laugh at! ... From a teenage point of view, from *my* teenage point of view, from where I am – this kind of thing doesn't happen in this kind of sense. We will do this, teenage girls will do this, but we don't all look like this. Like some of us would be shaving our legs, we wouldn't all be laughing, and we won't be this clean-cut, and looking this pretty – we'd be like no make-up, lying on the bed discussing things that we'd never discuss anywhere else. (Seventeen-year-old Jamie reading same ad)

While these readings suggest that girls do not uncritically accept discursive representations of their world, it is important to see what happens when young readers reach the limits of their lived experience. Ads were included which portray three signifiers of traditional adult femininity: a diamond engagement ring, a bride, and a woman with a child. While, across the group, responses to other ads were mixed, there was surprising uniformity among responses to these latter subjects. Responses were overwhelmingly positive:

I like this one ... It seems really, he seems really like he's *really* in love with her and it kind of shows, I guess, that guys care about girls and they're the ones that are kind of taking care of them and buying them stuff [laughs], which is *good* – plus it's also just kind of cute. (Seventeen-year-old Roshni reading ad for diamond engagement rings)

I like that – it says what it means. They're advertising for Beautiful [perfume] and she's in a wedding dress and you always think of a bride as beautiful and stuff ... It's nice. (Sixteen-year-old Lindsey reading ad for Beautiful perfume)

Yeah, like this is one of my favourites, too. 'Cause also it's Calvin Klein and that's my favourite perfume, 'Eternity,' yeah. And the picture's just – I don't know, I just think it's kind of cute and I think it really looks like a mom and daughter. Just two people really close. I don't know. It's kind of a loving picture. I like that one. (Fourteen-year-old Rachel reading ad for Eternity fragrance)

You know she's a model but she could be a mom still. And the little kid is really cute.

And that is how mommies and little kids interact – it's real. (Seventeen-year-old Jamie reading same Eternity ad)

I like this picture – it's in my locker [laughs].
[Interviewer:] Oh! Really?
I think it's really adorable and it shows – like because it's Eternity for Women and it has the two females in it, and it shows the sweet – like the sweetness like, the love – Like, you know, how Eternity has a sweet smell just like that [laughs].
[Interviewer:] And that's why you put it up in your locker?
Yeah. (Sixteen-year-old Alyssa)

While previous readings suggest that contradictory or overly ambiguous meanings may invite readers to reject messages that are subsequently deemed implausible, in these ads readers uncritically drew upon ideologies of romance and motherhood to arrive at unambiguous meanings. In many cases, readers did not feel it necessary to discuss the images at all, because they merely claimed that these texts 'say what they mean.' As Hall (1977: 325) notes, ideology as common sense does not require thought because it is spontaneously available, thoroughly recognizable, widely shared: it *feels* as if has always been there. Readers constructing unambiguous or 'absolute' meanings in this way typically found these ads pleasurable:

[Interviewer:] It looks good. Why?
Because 'two months' salary lasts forever' [reading slogan], like two months' salary maybe lasts, like, less than that, and a diamond 'lasts forever' so it's worth spending that money. I like that, the idea of that – showing how happy she is, you know. He gave her a ring and everything. (Seventeen-year-old Mary reading ad for diamond engagement rings; here it is important to note that the 'actors' in this ad are shadows on a wall)

I think it's appropriate to the title and everything. I like that one. 'Eternity' – life's like that: one generation goes on after another. (Sixteen-year-old Alyssa reading ad for Eternity perfume)

Okay, this is nice. It's peaceful. You can almost – I don't know. It's springy and it's nice. [pause] I like this one. It reminds me of – I don't know what [laughs]. You can almost smell the perfume. (Fourteen-year-old Kayla reading ad for Beautiful perfume)

Overall, the girls' descriptions of these three ads repeatedly employed words which connote traditional femininity: 'love' (for the image of the diamond engagement ring); 'innocent,' 'pure,' 'beautiful,' and 'happy' (for the bride);

and 'loving' and 'natural' (for motherhood). The excessiveness of reader descriptions is evidenced by sixteen-year-old Kelsey, who claimed that the bride in the Eternity ad is 'kind of sweet and serene and innocent and feminine.' Unlike the ad which portrays a pyjama party and thus provides an opportunity for readers to compare the representation to their own life, images that could be decoded as expressions of romantic heterosexuality were rejected by few girls.

The ideological appeals of romantic love and motherhood were so strong that they overrode the criterion of logic. As we see above, a woman playfully embracing a toddler in the Eternity ad was read as a 'loving mother' by the vast majority of girls. Clearly, the decision that she is the mother of the child is not made on the level of denotation, but rather through connotation, which draws on stereotypes of motherhood. Because stereotypes associate women with babies through the patriarchal institution of motherhood, readers drawing on this stereotype make that association in their reading. Central to this stereotype is an emotional bond between infant and mother, which the girls eagerly read into this image. For example, fourteen-year-old Kayla exclaimed:

This one is nice. I really like the Calvin Klein ads because they seem to have feeling in them, the Eternity one especially. This one – the mother is actually paying attention to the child, and the child seems to have some focus on the mother, saying that there must be some sort of attention there, or love, or whatever ...

It is interesting to consider the reactions of readers to an alternative, potentially liberating image of motherhood: a woman in a party dress dispassionately breastfeeding an unclothed baby. While readers were emphatic that the woman playing with a toddler is a mother, there was general scepticism that the woman breastfeeding depicted motherhood. For example, Kayla maintained that the woman did not represent a mother:

Hum [pause] well [pause], this one is kind of weird because it doesn't look like she's very loving, like the kind of person who'd, like, have a baby. First of all, because she's so skinny and, second of all, because you wouldn't be dressed like that, like in high heels and nylons [laughs]. The baby isn't even wearing any clothes [laughs]. She's barely touching it [the baby].

These sentiments were echoed by other girls:

It kind of bothers me that they put that there. I don't really think she looks like the motherly type, she's just kind of sitting there, kind of – I don't know, trying to make it look like something it's *not* ... I don't think that's the way most new mothers look. (Sixteen-year-old Lindsey)

It's totally unrealistic because, out of my experience with life, I've never seen a nursing mother dressed this way at all. I don't even know if I've seen a person that would wear nylons. (Sixteen-year-old Michelle)

She's wearing way too much make-up and she's too young to look like a mother. (Thirteen-year-old Stephanie)

In short, a woman breastfeeding is, logically, more certainly the mother of the infant than is a woman simply playing with a toddler. In fact, the latter image does not depict a relationship at all. Clearly, readers concluded that this woman is the mother by employing ideological associations for making sense. In contrast to their pleasurable construction of a 'loving' mother, the Bisou Bisou ad was not simply rejected as implausible by these young readers; it generated a fair amount of hostility:

I don't think they should have a picture like that in a magazine, I just don't think it's like, kind of appropriate – but her dress is really nice though. (Thirteen-year-old Ashley)

It's like really weird [laughs]. I don't like it too much. (Thirteen-year-old Brittany)

I don't like it [immediate response]. I don't think it suits, like a magazine, I think people might be offended by this. ... But you shouldn't be, but it's just – you don't want to see it in a magazine, like it's something which is 'reality,' not like something you want to see in a magazine. (Sixteen-year-old Alicia)

I don't know, it's weird, it's kind of fake. (Sixteen-year-old Alyssa)

I don't see the point, it's kind of stupid I think – like her breastfeeding a baby has anything to do with like – unless there's an article on it, or something but, maybe they're trying to show her family side, but I don't know. I just think it's kind of weird. I don't think there's a good point to it. (Seventeen-year-old Roshni)

The most common descriptors of the Bisou Bisou ad were 'weird,' 'inappropriate,' 'not loving,' and 'disgusting.' Suggested by these rejections is the possibility that the Bisou Bisou ad is 'too realistic,' in that it portrays the stark physicality of motherhood rather than its ideological emotionality. As a consequence, readers claimed that there was no reason to show the mother and infant in the Bisou ad, except as a 'ruse' to sell products. For example, sixteen-year-old Lindsey compares the two images:[6]

This ad [Eternity perfume] is really natural. It's just really natural-looking. It doesn't look as if she's gone and spent hours putting make-up on to go to a shoot. It looks like she's just gone and – just, you know, put a *little* bit of make-up on, not like tons of stuff. It doesn't really show anything having to do with the perfume, but, I don't know, it's a nice ad.
[Interviewer:] It's quite different from this other one. What do you think of that one? [Shows Bisou Bisou ad.]
Yeah, this one [Eternity] is sort of just being close, not being – I don't know – the other one is more shock value – you're attracted to the other one out of shock, but once you've looked at it you get turned off. This one [Eternity] you don't – you're not, it keeps you, like you can look at it and you can – it's very *real*. That's important, just to have that, to not feel that you're being tricked, or you're being conned into buying things.

Overall, readers could not see any reason to associate breastfeeding and a party dress:

I don't see the point for them putting that there at all. Women are the majority that read that magazine, so what would be the point. I don't really like it. It looks cheap. (Sixteen-year-old Melissa)

I'd probably look at this because I wear Bazoobazoo [Bisou Bisou], I wear that brand, but, uhm I don't really think the ad, really I don't like it – like what's the point of the baby, you know, it doesn't really seem like it's trying to say anything except a pretty girl with a baby [laughs]. (Seventeen-year-old Jamie)

This reasoning did not appear in the Eternity ad, however, where girls accept that the commodity and motherhood 'belong' together:

I like that [laughs] – it doesn't really have anything to do with perfume, either, but it looks neat.
[Interviewer:] Why?
I don't know, it's just neat. When I look at something like that, if there wasn't any name on it, I'd *know* it was 'Eternity.' (Sixteen-year-old Melissa)

I like Eternity, I like this one. Like, I have this one up in my bedroom.
[Interviewer:] This one's on your wall?

Yup. I like it because [pause] because it's a nice picture – it's like a mom, and a daughter, and 'eternity' says it all! [laughs]. (Fourteen-year-old Lauren)

In summary, the reality negotiated by these readers associates ideological femininity with the world of commodities in such a way that this association appears 'natural' or makes sense: this association does not hold if ambiguous or atypical imagery is used. The extent to which this association is naturalized is reflected in the tendency, mentioned by some of the girls above, to decorate bedroom walls, school lockers, or their daily appointment books with advertising images. In many cases, girls did not collect and display pictures from ads, simply brand logos: no matter how contradictory and unstable ideological appeals may be to cultural commentators, this study reveals a marked tendency for adolescent readers to assign ideology 'truth' status.

As a truth claim, the meanings available in commercial texts are no longer simply 'resources,' in the way many writers imply. Rather, many of the commercial meanings in this study have become incorporated into girls' 'knowledge' about the world of adult femininity. The notion of meaning as knowledge draws attention to the way in which the cultural constructs the social through incorporation of the cultural into readers' assumptions about the nature of social reality. Readers who reject teenzine texts may indeed be the discerning or playful consumers of meaning which postmodern cultural criticism often evokes; for the majority of readers in this study, however, teenzine reading is a much more complex process. As Pearce (1995: 89) notes: 'That I can, and indeed have, read them [texts] against the grain of their historical production does not alter the fact that they have *a preferred reader* who is not me.' Understanding this process is a primary objective of *Girl Talk*. Taking everyday reading as our problematic, we are led to ask, how do these texts, with so many obvious contradictions, come to be taken for 'the real'? In later chapters we look for answers in the everyday experiences of school culture. Here we identify how texts themselves encourage closure in specific ways. The final section of this chapter draws upon literary theory to help us understand how alternative, potentially subversive meanings (hence subjectivities) are reincorporated into dominant discourses in ways that encourage readings of traditional femininity. In this last section I analyse a specific beauty advertisement, following conventions of interpretative reading generally employed in literary rather than sociological study. Here I aim to identify procedures through which meaning is 'structured' into the text and its subsequent decoding. Contradictory elements are highlighted because they represent discursive disruptions in an otherwise seamless message. The reading presented below shows how a seemingly innocent text – an ad for underarm deodorant – constructs meaning which supports traditional femininity while actively discounting the feminist goal of women's liberation upon which it bases reader appeal. Recognition of this textual strategy draws attention to the shortcomings of content analysis as a method which treats individual parts of a message in isolation. For purposes of the current discussion, I ask whether the types of contradictions identified through the content analysis of ads invite readers to question, hence potentially reject, the contradictory discourse of 'post-feminism.' For this exercise I chose a rather ordinary advertisement from *Seventeen*: the product is an underarm deodorant and the accompanying illustration features a successful businesswoman. This ad is one of twenty discussed by girls during first-stage interviews. Significantly, it is the only ad which portrays a 'working woman.'

'The Modern Woman' of Soft & Dri

On the surface, the Soft & Dri ad (see facing page) concerns a conventional product associated with feminine hygiene: an underarm antiperspirant. Although this product is equated with 'success,' this message cannot be simply read off the printed text. This meaning is the result of a specific combination of visual images and printed text. Our purpose here is to understand how this connoted meaning emerges and to identify potential alternative meanings. This ad is interesting because it evokes a discourse of 'women's liberation.'

In decoding this text we begin by noting that the scene is intended to be a direct representation of reality, even though it of course has been contrived for this advertisement. At the denotative level this scene is meant to be understood as a woman having her shoes shined, sitting beside two men reading newspapers. To facilitate this meaning, a sign with the words 'Shoe Shine' appears in the photo. The image of the product is also iconic because it represents the actual product. Within this seemingly simple scene, however, there is a much more complex message. Contributing to the complexity is the indexical nature of the images: having one's shoes shined indicates status and success, and is traditionally associated with men. The newspapers further indicate that the people involved are 'active players' in the world, in that they have a need to be informed of the day's news. This does not apply to the man who kneels to shine the woman's shoes, however. Not only does he lack a newspaper, but both the job he performs and his positioning within the picture give him lower status. In this way, power relationships have been imputed among inhabitors of this scene. Those relations have been further gendered through symbolic signs. The colour of the woman's jacket is bright pink, symbolizing femininity; the pink flower on the product likewise serves as a symbol of femininity and identifies the product for exclusively female use. Because the shoe-shine stand, business

SHE'S NOBODY'S BABY.

SHE'S **NOBODY'S** FOOL.

SHE KNOWS WHAT SHE **WANTS.**

Your style is unmistakably confident with Soft & Dri Solid. With the hardest working odor and wetness fighters available. Also in Aerosol and Roll-on.

SHE JUST STAYS COOL. SOFT & DRI

suits, and newspapers symbolize traditionally male space, this scene can be read as standing in for other male-dominated domains.

As is true of the layouts in many advertisements, the coloured pictures in the Soft & Dri ad draw the reader's eye to the written copy. Fragmented into phrases which fit around the visual images are the words 'She's nobody's baby,' 'She's nobody's fool,' 'She knows what she wants,' and 'She just stays cool': most of the written text does not concern product information but rather communicates desired values such as self-assurance and success. For our purposes it is important that these values have been attributed to the lone female figure surrounded by men. This attribution occurs in part because of the way that the woman is associated with successful men. However, positive values also arise through oppositions which result from what does not appear in this scene. For example, business suits are among a broader range of identifiably male clothing which also includes jogging suits, jeans and T-shirts, and pyjamas. Clearly, the business suit carries higher, more positive values than these other ways of dressing. Likewise, the newspapers could be romance novels, textbooks, or women's magazines; the newspapers attain their significance because they are *not* romance novels, textbooks, or women's magazines. In a similar way the woman on the shoe-shine stand is defined in relation to what she is not: poorly groomed, fat, old, Black, and so on. Each of her physical characteristics gives her greater social value in a racist and patriarchal culture than would other possible characteristics.

Thus, given how the players in this ad have been given positive, valued associations, the primary exchange occurs between the product and the woman who has been linked to desired values. The product is hard-working, and so is the woman. She is successful. The product is soft, and so is the woman – that is, feminine, as indicated by the pink jacket. The woman is distinctly modern; she has successfully gained entry to a traditionally male domain. She uses the product, so it is distinctly modern. A secondary exchange elicited by the ad is between the reader and the woman who is the subject of the ad. The reader is addressed via the movement from the description of the woman pictured ('she') to a description of 'you' as this kind of woman, unmistakably confident in style. The appellation is assisted through the gaze of the model, which meets and connects with the gaze of the reader.

The viewer who positions herself within this symbolic system in a way to arrive at the dominant meaning is constructed as a 'modern' woman who might use the product, but also as a woman who endorses traditional feminine values. When we consider the depth of meaning constructed through this seemingly innocent scene, we find that, while the advertisement appears to advance the ideal of equality between men and women, it in fact perpetuates male and female difference and defines femininity in traditionally narrow terms. At first glance, the woman in the ad has been successful in gaining entry to the male domain of power and prestige. This meaning draws on the reader's desire for equality and incorporates values borrowed directly from the women's liberation movement. However, this advertisement is telling the reader that, since equality has been achieved, she can concentrate on the real work ahead – individual achievement, in this case linked to the use of Soft & Dri. Thus the confines of traditional femininity remain intact within a rhetoric of equality (see Budgeon and Currie 1995: 181, 182; Budgeon 1993). Finally, what does not appear in this scene but is necessary to preferred meaning is the successful woman who does not use feminine beauty products because she rejects the trappings of patriarchal femininity. This absent woman has the potential to bring dominant meanings into question by providing a feminist subtext which could position the reader as feminist rather than feminine. In the final analysis, this ad implies that the reader can enjoy what feminists want and have made possible without, in turn, the feminist rejection of patriarchal heterosexuality. This ad reveals how commercial media signify modern womanhood in a way which appeals to the utopian fantasy of gender equality while discursively discounting the struggle which will make this 'fantasy' happen. Semiotic decoding shows how the economic imperative of capitalism is linked to the construction of a specific meaning for 'woman': importantly this reading shows how discourses usually thought to be opposites (that is, those of feminism and femininity) have been broken down and rearticulated into a new discourse of 'post-feminism.' As illustrated in the cases of Kayla and Lindsey, such a discourse allows girls to read magazines within the everyday context of feminism without constructing the reader as 'feminist':

This is good 'cause she's like getting on in the business world and it's good for women to be in on that. But it has her alone, and I know that there's more than one woman in the business world. There's about 50 per cent now almost, well not 50 per cent but quite a few. So they've got her surrounded by men – there'd have to be more women [to make it realistic]. (Fourteen-year-old Kayla)

I don't understand why all the people she's around are men – it's not as if they are the only people that ever put pressure on women. Other women pressure other women too, so it doesn't make any sense. (Sixteen-year-old Lindsey)

We explore how teenzine texts work in this way in chapter 6.

Conclusion

The obviousness of advertising has made it a popular venue for cultural critique by academics. In part, the prominence of advertising in analyses of social texts reflects their importance within a tradition of media studies engaged in the scientific enhancement of marketing techniques. It also reflects the ubiquitous nature of advertising; teenzines devote about half of their page space to purchased advertising. In this chapter we have explored the seeming transparency of these texts. In order to do so, we entered their world phenomenologically, from the standpoint of adolescent readers. Approaching advertising in this way leads us to challenge the commonsense notion advanced by proponents of commercial media, that because readers recognize the constructed nature of these texts, they necessarily distinguish the cultural world of advertising from the social world of everyday life.

For sure, the young readers in this study distinguish between the cultural and the social, between fantasy and 'real' life. However, as we have seen in this chapter, there are important differences in how cultural critics and adolescent girls draw distinctions between 'real' and 'unreal' representations of femininity. Unlike adult readers, who are purported to separate fantasy from reality prior to reading, adolescent readers drew distinctions that are an effect of reading which blurs the boundaries between the cultural and the social dimensions of femininity. The most important finding of this chapter is a marked tendency for adolescent readers to assign ideology an ontological status. By 'ontological status' I mean the process whereby ideological associations are given the status of a truth claim: ideological representations are accepted as factual representations of 'the way things are.' As a truth claim, the meanings available for readers are no longer 'resources' but have been transformed into 'knowledge' about the everyday world. We pursue this theme further in chapter 7. Here we note that the notion of meanings as available resources implies that readers consciously choose among competing available meanings. In contrast, the notion of meaning as knowledge draws attention to the way in which meaning actively shapes the social as a result of its incorporation into the reader's assumptions about the nature of social reality. Writers who posit a social world which exists a priori to the text typically treat magazine discourse in terms of the former; embodied readers who reject ads which fail to deploy stereotypical associations are treating magazine discourse as knowledge.[7] This interpretation does not mean that readers are simply duped by texts; rather, it illustrates the importance of treating texts as process rather than as static objects of analysis. While our analysis begins from magazines as cultural objects which require textual decoding, as process we are directed to a chain of activities that transform meaning into material practices, a task begun here and taken further in subsequent chapters.

When we begin from the standpoint of adolescent girls, rather than of middle-aged feminists, we can see how teenzines offer not simply pleasure, but meaning about life and the social roles of women. We shall see in subsequent chapters how the knowledge provided by these magazines invites readers to understand themselves specifically as 'teenagers.' Here we have seen that readers do not passively accept all meanings, in the way in which sex-role research often assumes. As cultural critics have suggested, adolescent readers reject many of the messages and much of the imagery in their magazines. However, this rejection does not arise in the manner hypothesized by cultural critics. For example, Winship (1981: 55) claims that women's magazines 'are first and foremost fantasies for pleasure rather than practical action, and that they are recognized as such by the viewer.' She bases this claim on 'common sense' derived from her own reading experiences. While adolescent girls in the current study likewise maintain that they read magazines 'for fun' and readily acknowledge that not all images are 'realistic,' in contrast to Winship they do not distinguish reality from fantasy prior to reading: these readers drew distinctions as they read, *within* the text.

This difference between reading-as-research and everyday reading practice is important when we recognize that girls give the realities which they identify in texts ontological status: 'realistic' messages offered by the text are seen to convey truth about the social world. While this reality is scrutinized against experiential knowledge, we have seen that it also valorizes ideological definitions of adult femininity in ways that naturalize an affective association of femininity and commodities as sign values. This association made some ads 'feel' right, while images lacking affective associations were deemed unrealistic. While this association is not quite as seamless as argued here, it is the most striking feature of the data. This finding is significant in light of the fact that many girls treat these texts as a source of valid information about Self and interpersonal relationships (discussed in chapter 6).

In short, this incursion into the process of everyday reading illustrates how power works through venues of discursive 'knowledge.' In the following chapters we will explore how adolescence is signified in specific ways and how commercial magazines, as knowledge rather than simply pleasurable representations, engage readers in the construction of Self as becoming an adult woman. The view of magazines as 'knowledge' differs from the claim that they are vehicles for the pleasurable consumption of images, and from the notion that magazines are simply about behaviours such as consumption of advertised products. As objectified knowledge, adolescent magazines construct what

Smith (1980: 253) calls a 'mode of social consciousness': ways in which people think and talk with one another which originate outside actual relations of people going about their everyday business. She notes that, increasingly, modes of social consciousness are mediated by the social texts of commercial media, such as magazines, television, electronic knowledge – technological developments which can appear to be ideologically innocent because their photographic signifiers seem to exactly, and transparently, reproduce their signifieds. What remains hidden is the investment of signifiers with specific, ideological meanings through material processes and relations which produce the constructed text. As Hennessy (1993: 14) notes, meaning-making through commercial texts is an activity which embodies struggle over resources that are played out through the discourses of culture and the modes of reading they allow. While the discourses of commercial culture, and the modes of consciousness which they promote, work through the text, a critical inquiry must make visible the activities hidden by, but embodied in, everyday social texts. The challenge is to provide understanding which does not simply 'read' ideology off material processes and social relations, an approach which re-enacts Marxist base/superstructure formulations. Rather, for cultural studies to be truly critical, it must show how the ideology of commercial culture is constitutive of everyday relations, including gendered relations of domination and subordination.

In this study, ideology is constitutive of the everyday world of the reader when meanings in the text are assigned truth value. From this perspective, ideology is never just 'ideas' or 'beliefs': ideology is a way of knowing. As Smith (1990b: 34) notes, this understanding of ideology is 'radically different from that used and sometimes attributed to [Marx] by some sociologists and Marxists.' From the perspective of Marx's method, which insists on the discovery of relations and processes that arise (only) in the actual activities of people, ideology refers to 'procedures or methods of thinking and reasoning about social relations and processes. Ideology names a kind of practice in thinking about society' (p. 35). A material analysis of ideology, as methodological practice, is not about simply identifying mistaken beliefs and ideas in the cultural realm which are then analytically connected to the 'material' realm through theoretical relations, such as that expressed by the base/superstructure formulation. Rather, a materialist analysis discovers ideology and its working in the everyday activities of actual people. Within this context, systems of representation and processes of meaning-making are material expressions of ideology which make available as preferred meaning a 'frame of intelligibility,' or way of knowing. As Bill Nichols (1981) maintains, within discourse ideology is never just ideational: 'Ideology uses the fabrication of images and the processes of representation to persuade us that how things are is how they ought to be and that the place provided for us is the place we ought to have' (p. 1). As a cultural critic, Nichols argues that we need to theorize elements of representation, in order to understand the place set out for us in these processes. One crucial aspect of the discursive place provided through ideological representation is that it proposes a way of seeing invested with meanings that naturalize themselves as timeless, objective, and obvious (p. 2).

In summary, the social becomes fully meaningful only within a frame of intelligibility through which meaning is constructed. Social texts like commercial magazines provide such frames of intelligibility, and we are recruited by them into the social order through their discursive constructions. Thus ideology is not simply a mistaken or distorted representation of reality, but it becomes everyday practice because it is constitutive of reality. Semiotics and psychoanalysis can help us understand the discursive recruitment of readers to the Symbolic Order: these methods of analysis help us to see how magazine discourse addresses readers through their recognition of the social order. In subsequent chapters we see how the socially constructed notion of 'teenager' provides a frame of intelligibility through which young readers recognize their social world and their place within it.

One approach to the sociological study of texts which has had tremendous impact is Foucault's formulation of 'power/ knowledge.' Through the study of discourse, Foucault theorizes agency in a way which transcends established dualisms of object/ subject, structure/ agency, oppression/ resistance. One problem is that this manner of working often treats power as entirely textual. Against this legacy, the current study explores how social power works *through* *texts,* not *as text.* In chapter 5 we further explore how power works through textually mediated discourses to produce knowledgeable agents. Agency does not arise simply through the act of reading as engagement with the text, in the way which debates in cultural studies often imply. Rather, within the notion of discourse employed in this study, signification is integral to the social practices which make up the world of people and things. Because such practices draw on 'tacit knowledge,' knowledge cannot always be articulated as such (because it may simply 'feel' like the way people and things are or should be); however, it is not based (solely) on unconscious motives or drives accessible only through theoretical speculation or psychoanalysis. As Anthony Giddens, like Dorothy Smith, argues, 'the stocks of knowledge applied in the production and reproduction of social life as a skilled activity are largely "unconscious" in so far as social actors can normally only offer a fragmentary account of what they "know" if called upon to do so; but they are not unconscious in the sense given to that term by [structuralist] writers' (Giddens 1979: 40). When we implicate social texts, such as fashion and beauty magazines, in the construction of everyday knowledge through which readers make themselves and their everyday world intelligible, we will not look for the 'origin' of people's sense of Self or of people's actions in their conscious intentions, psychological configurations, or unconscious drives (even though these may tell us a lot about how social texts work). However difficult it may be difficult to trace the 'origin' of women's consciousness about their actions, [8] we can trace the material origin of social texts, such as women's magazines, which mediate women's self-understandings. In this study we trace lines of power which promote particular definitions of femininity and which are embodied in meanings which cultural institutions make available. In order to do so, we analytically move from magazine texts to their material origin in social institutions, from women's everyday experiences to the practices of multinational cultural production, from discursive to non-discursive sites of power. Magazine texts are thus a place to start, because they give us access to the constructed nature of social life, but they point us to the social organization of consciousness which links the individual and the social, the cultural and the economic.

While the ubiquitous nature of commercial texts renders them a universal feature of our everyday landscape which seems to 'come from nowhere while being everywhere,' Smith identifies these texts as 'objectified knowledge' which order, and are ordered by, activities of individuals whose relations and activities are mediated by these texts. A postmodern analysis which celebrates the 'death of the author' as an end of both 'intentionality' and the language of 'purpose' merely mystifies these actions and relations, ironically, by relegating the text to the status of a 'thing' to be analysed in and of itself. In contrast, the critical analysis presented in *Girl Talk* treats social texts as process, as constituent of the relations of ruling through which texts such as commercial magazines are produced. As we shall see, process allows us to think about the Subject in a state of flux rather than as occupying a fixed position. Although the representations in commercial texts may be experienced as realities without 'authorship,' we can trace their origins in institutional practices which organize society as textually mediated forms of social action (p. 122). Social texts with extensive readerships order social relationships because they have the potential to effect the coordination of individual activities with those of others. Smith claims that this form of textually mediated coordination represents a historically and culturally unique form of power. It is a distinctive form of communication in that it is a 'one-way movement of messages' which detaches the author from her particular location and appeals to an 'anonymous audience' dispersed over vast geographical locations. This form of communication, as knowledge, substitutes 'categorical forms for actual members' and 'accounts for actual events' (p. 123). The significance and the power of this particular cultural form therefore lie in its ability to structure social relationships through objectified knowledge of a social order which comes to be felt as an order which is 'as it is' or 'as it should be.' In this chapter we have begun to explore how textual power works in this way by treating the text as process rather than as a 'thing in itself or for itself.' The subsequent chapters continue this exploration.

5

Teenzine Reading: The Social Life of Texts

In chapter 4 we saw the importance of taking our analytical problematic from everyday rather than researcher readings of social texts, since everyday reading directs the cultural critic to processes and effects which remain repressed when theoreticians read Subjects and the social world 'off the text.' In the conclusion we confront the dilemma that all research, including that by social scientists, is a cultural practice that engages academics in the reading and rewriting of the social. In this chapter we enter the world of teenzine reading through analysis of girls' interviews. We do so in order to explore what adolescent girls rather than adult researchers identify as important about their magazines.

While people can seldom (if ever) tell sociologists why they engage in the behaviours which interest researchers, they can tell us about their activities, in our case, choosing magazines, sharing teenzine texts, going about the everyday business of being a girl at school. However, while girls' accounts testify to the agency of readers and map new terrain for sociological investigation, their accounts alone do not tell us how texts work. Rather, they redirect theoretical inquiry about teenzines and their reading, about the everyday operation of power and the connectedness of the cultural and the social. The purpose of this chapter is therefore to locate the problematics discussed in chapter 6 through further exploration of everyday teenzine reading. Despite the many theoretical advances which have been made in the field of cultural studies, fundamental questions about how texts work in everyday contexts remain unanswered. Specifically, why are commercial media so popular and (why) should they continue to be a concern for the feminist critic? In this and following chapters, we explore new ways of finding answers to these types of questions.

As we have already seen, commentators describe women's magazines as an easy, enjoyable read that invites fantasy: 'Bright colours, exciting headlines and layouts, elegant fashions and flawless faces draw the reader in as she turns the pages of a *Mademoiselle* or *Vogue*. Ideal images of the future self encountered on the front cover are multiplied and reinforced in feature after feature. Free to indulge in a narcissism based on fantasy, one can, for a moment, forget one's actual appearance in the mirror, replacing that memory with the magazine's concrete examples of ideal beauty' (McCracken 1993: 135–6). In the extreme, reading pleasure has been valorized as oppositional, and theoretically linked to qualities of a distinctly feminine cultural genre.[1] Specifically feminine texts have been identified as 'process-centred' and open, concerned with the interpersonal relations through which power works. This openness of feminine texts is seen to invite rewriting rather than the disciplined reading hypothesized by sex-role theorists. However, as Tasker (1991) notes, the problem with this approach is that every text is seen to contain the potential for subversive readings through a convergence of text, spectator, and setting: 'a certain group (women) reading certain texts within a specific setting (say, the domestic) can make manifest (draw up through the cracks and excesses of the surface) a subversive latent content, the meanings of which are essentially there' (p. 91). In other words, attempts to re-evaluate cultural forms which are the source of pleasure for so many women often conflate qualities of the text with qualities of reading. Without a study of everyday reading there is the danger that categories used by the critic to analyse texts are subsequently attributed to the audience, regardless of whether those categories are couched in terms of conformity/oppression or resistance/subversion. Along these lines, Tasker (1991: 85) complains that the language of resistance and crisis employed by the Gramscian legacy in cultural studies implicitly guarantees the political effectivity that is theoretically required by the analyst. For this reason, although the current trend to reclaim pleasures of the text may be a rhetorical advance, it is not an advance for the social-scientific understanding of these texts. While the language of the critic may have 'progressed' to include a more nuanced understanding of meaning-making and the constructedness of the social, without empirical study we cannot make similar claims about our understanding of embodied readers. We need a new beginning.

Getting Started: Girls' Choices of Magazines

Simply put, most of the respondents in this study claim to read magazines just because they are readily available. The ubiquity of women's magazines is reflected in how girls 'got started':

I first started noticing them [women's magazines] when I was in Grade 3 or 4, like really early. My mom and her friends used to always sit around and have those magazines. (Seventeen-year-old Alexandra)

I read [fashion magazines] when I go to the dentist's office [laughs]. When I'm sitting in the chair and they're putting fluoride in my mouth, they always give me *Vogue* [laughs], so I look through it. (Sixteen-year-old Alicia)

I was on a trip with my dad, visiting people in Calgary, and they had sixteen- and seventeen-year-old girls. I didn't have anything to do, so she gave me magazines and I started reading them. When I got home I got a subscription for *YM*. (Thirteen-year-old Stephanie)

In fact, sixteen-year-old Crystal claims that she does not need to buy magazines in order to read them:

My teenage friends seem to have a lot of magazines and then moms usually have them around the house and stuff, so I read them. I probably buy a magazine every month, maybe every two months, yeah, but I read a *lot* of them. A good friend of mine has a whole pile of all the women's magazines that you would ever read. So when I'm over there it's just like we sit there and talk and read magazines over and over again. So I don't really need to [buy them]. I've already read it [laughs] – why would I buy it?

Given the ubiquity of women's magazines, femininity and magazines seem to belong together as a matter of course. There is a widespread assumption that young girls enjoy teen magazines. As a consequence, many readers first received their now-favourite magazine as a gift subscription, typically from an older female relative. While readers could not always tell us 'why' they read magazines – indeed, they were not asked such a direct question – regular readers displayed strong preferences for favourite titles. The girls in this study were eager to discuss which magazines they like or dislike and, more specifically, what parts of their magazines they actively choose as the subject of their attention. We begin to explore *why* girls read teenzines, therefore, by looking at *what* they read.

Girls were not recruited into this study on the basis of their reading magazines: rather, potential participants were simply told that the research concerned girls' fashion culture and life at school. In fact, I expected that a comparison of readers and non-readers of magazines would be valuable if non-readers consciously reject fashion and beauty standards. First-stage interviews began with discussions of 'getting ready for school' and moved to magazine reading as, potentially, an extra-curricular activity for girls. I was initially surprised that only two of the thirteen- to seventeen-year-olds in this study have never seen, or do not read, adolescent magazines. However, while virtually all the girls were familiar with teen titles, the extent of magazine reading varies among girls in the study sample.

In this sample, 70 per cent of the girls are avid or regular readers of magazines. Regular readers read at least one title every month and typically read magazines every week:

[I read] *Seventeen, Allure, Mademoiselle* – religiously, every month. I *should* have a subscription, but I don't bother. I should, like I know I should. (Seventeen-year-old Mary)

In contrast, avid readers usually identified models by name when browsing through magazines and exhibited familiarity with the careers of models as well as the histories of their magazines:

I read a lot of magazines ...
[Interviewer:] Do you read *Seventeen?*
... *Seventeen*, it's not a very good magazine at all because when this new magazine *Sassy* came out, they totally gave them a big scare, and so *Seventeen* was forced to really change their format and everything. They still, it still is the bigger one I think ... [flipping through]. The art direction isn't very sophisticated, I don't think. The pictures are good and stuff, but when you read it, it's always, it's just that, for example, these two models, Niki and Chrissie Taylor, they've done five articles on them in the last year or two – it's true! (Seventeen-year-old Laura)

Avid and regular readers are the most important sources of information about magazine reading in the analysis for *Girl Talk*. However, as noted already, this does not mean that they can articulate *why* they read teenzines. From this perspective, why girls consciously choose to not read is a significant question. In contrast to regular and avid readers, a number of girls in this sample are occasional readers or non-readers. In this sample, 19 per cent of the girls read magazines only 'once in a while.' An occasional reader makes no attempt to ensure that she reads any title every month. Her reading is erratic, because she simply reads magazines when they happen to be available, such as when she visits a friend. Occasional readers are interesting because they are often (but not necessarily) critical of teenzines; like readers who quit, they can articulate reasons why they do *not* read teenzines more frequently. The sample for this study also contains a number of girls who are currently non-readers but who were readers in the past. This type of non-reader, comprising 7 per cent of the sample, is typically an older girl. These non-readers are interesting because reflection on their reading history helps us to connect teenzine reading to age-specific issues surrounding identity formation:

[Interviewer:] What made you stop?

Table 5.1: Magazine Reading of Participants, by Age Group

	% of entire group		
	13–14 yrs	15–16 yrs	17 yrs
Young & Modern	73	95	58
Seventeen	53	95	58
Teen	33	20	0
Sassy	13	10	33
Vogue	20	40	50
Mademoiselle	0	20	33
Elle	0	15	33
Allure	7	10	25
Cosmo	13	10	17
Chatelaine	0	10	17
Rolling Stone	7	5	17
Interview	0	5	8
Shape	0	5	8

Base *N*: 48 girls aged 13 to 17 years

Well, they're all the same [laughs]. All just clothes and make-up, and once you've learned how to do your make-up I don't know why you have to read it anymore. (Fifteen-year-old Hannah)

Only two girls never participate in girls' magazine culture. Given the ubiquity of teen magazines, like readers who quit, these non-participants help us explore why some girls refuse the text. As we shall see, however, non-reading is not necessarily associated with a rejection of fashion and beauty culture in the way I had initially imagined, nor is it an indicator of critical awareness of the arbitrariness of the text. As in the case of Laura, avid readers are likely to express the most pleasure from magazine reading, but to also be teenzines' greatest critics. In the chapters which follow, we draw on these types of differences among readers to explore why teenzine texts successfully address some girls, but not others. In order to do so, we begin by identifying reading preferences. Table 5.1 summarizes the titles given by respondents when asked 'what magazines' (if any) they usually read.

As noted above, the girls in this study are not homogeneous in their reading habits. As well as differing in their frequency of reading, the girls vary in their reading repertoires, as shown in table 5.1. Overall, the number of magazines mentioned in unprompted identification of reading ranges from none to ten titles. For example, while thirteen-year-old Brittany reads *Teen* and *YM*, sixteen-year-old Erica ended her list of nine titles with the comment 'all the fashion magazines.'[2] However, despite differences in the extent of magazine reading, an age-related pattern emerges when we look at the titles preferred by different age groups and the reading histories of individual girls. As we see in table 5.1, *Seventeen* and *YM* are the most popular magazines overall, especially among fifteen- and sixteen-year-olds. Reflecting its editorial appeal to younger readers, *Teen* is read by about one-third of girls aged thirteen to fourteen. Although many of the seventeen-year-olds often indicated that they read *Teen* in the past, none is a current reader of *Teen*, and older girls often listed adult titles in their current reading. While *Sassy* is read by a minority of girls, its popularity is greatest among older girls, who are drawn to its 'alternative' approach. Given that *Sassy* contains the most discussion of social issues and the least text on beautification of the four teenzines in this study, *Sassy*'s lack of reader appeal is a problematic taken up in chapter 7. Here we note that many more girls reject *Sassy*. According to fifteen-year-old Elizabeth, this is because *Sassy*, unlike *Seventeen* and *YM*, is not 'useful':

I don't know. It's [*Sassy*] just like really boring. Everyone says 'Don't get it' because it's a rip-off. Like there's nothing you can benefit from – like tips on make-up and fashion, and stuff like that. *Sassy* doesn't have any of that.

The notion of an age-gradient in reading preferences is also reflected in older girls' recounting of their reading histories. Although seventeen- and eighteen-year-old readers were typically familiar with all the titles in the study, many of them reported that they had 'outgrown' specific titles by the time of the interview:

I read that one in the past when I was younger. I think that one's more a younger teens' kind of thing.
[Interviewer:] Why?
It was the rage, kind of. It's like this boy star said 'this' and 'How do you kiss?' or 'How do you like it?' – it was dumb but you liked it when you were younger, kind of thing. I don't know – that's what I thought *then*. (Seventeen-year-old Mary)

While the age at which readers felt that they had grown out of earlier favourites was variable, the sequence of titles remained fairly constant:

[Interviewer:] Do you remember when you first started reading magazines like *YM*?
[Pause] It would have had to have been in, like – oh, okay, it would have been when I was in love with the 'New Kids' [laughs – New Kids on the Block]. It would have been

like in Grade 5, when I started reading like *Tiger Beat*, then *Teen* and *Seventeen*, and like all those ones. Then after a while I graduated from those little 'teeny bopper' ones and into, like BIG teeny bopper ones [both laugh] – into older ones like *YM*. (Fourteen-year-old Kayla)

Eventually, you get into Grade 6 and you start reading *Teeny Bopper*, like *Tiger Beat* or whatever – those like Bop magazines with all the sitcom guys, stars, and stuff like that [laughs]. And then from there you work your way up, I guess to *Seventeen*. It's actually a kind of chain – it's like they're building a staircase. You start at like *Teeny Bopper* and you work your way up to *Teen, Seventeen*, you go to *YM*, then you go to those magazines like *Glamour, Mademoiselle* and, you know – if I look around someone's house – my friends' mom's houses, in their bedrooms they have *Vogue* – they wouldn't have *Teeny Bopper*! [laughs]. I think it's definitely like climbing through an age thing, or whatever – maturity, I'm not sure. (Sixteen-year-old Crystal)

In the main, this age-gradient was explained by girls as reflecting content they can relate to:

I usually read *YM*s and *Teen* and *Seventeen*, and that's about it ... They talk to kids that are my age about things that I'd be interested in. Whereas, opposed to *Vogue* [laughs] – they talk about things for older people. I like *YM* the best.
[Interviewer:] Why is that?
Because they're really focused on, like the fourteen and fifteen [year-olds] like, right in my area ... It appeals to my age group and it's got interesting things. (Thirteen-year-old Brittany)

I used to be into like *Teen* – that's when I was in Grade 7, 8. And then *YM* just seemed kind of like older and more my style – like it has stuff more like, *useful* stuff that I'd read. All the questions – they aren't too young, and they aren't too old or anything. They are kind of right for me, so I've had a subscription for that for a while. *Seventeen* is just – it seems basically pretty much the same to me as *YM* but maybe *YM* is one step up, age-wise ... I read *Vogue*, but it's not really interesting to me cause it has nothing to do with someone *my* age, like someone I relate to – it's kind of older. (Fifteen-year-old Kirsten)

As evidenced here, girls are not attracted to magazines by glossy, pictorial texts; these readers want 'people's life stories,' answers to everyday problems, and 'useful stuff' to read. We explore these types of texts in detail below. For the moment it is important to note that the girls often reject the glossy elements of women's magazines which have been the subject of extensive feminist analysis in favour of texts that they claim address girls their age:

Yeah, I think *Seventeen* is better. It has more stuff in it. There's a lot of articles and stuff in this one [points to magazine]. This one has articles and stuff about the readers' poll and everything and I thought that was interesting ... Usually if it's in these magazines it has something to do with teenagers or whatever, so I just like to read them [articles]. (Fifteen-year-old Tiffany)

[Interviewer:] Why is *YM* better than the other ones you mentioned?
It's more – like *Allure* is more of a fashion magazine and that's all. I like the stories [in *YM*]. It describes people's life stories, what they've gone through. Like, if you have a problem usually it mentions something that you need to know. (Fifteen-year-old Rebecca)

Importantly, the relevance of age cuts across racial lines. In part, this finding may reflect the fact that the sample is self-recruited: girls who do not relate to dominant notions of a 'girls' fashion culture' would be unlikely to volunteer for the study. However, among this volunteer sample, rejection of adolescent magazines was not based upon perceptions that these magazines perpetuate Caucasian standards, even though some regular readers commented on the racist characteristics of magazine content. For example, thirteen-year-old Stephanie identified *Essence* as her favourite magazine:

Because it's a Black magazine – you don't find a lot of those here in Canada – and it deals with people in their communities who are doing something, even though it is an American magazine. Uhm, it kind of gives me an overview of what people are doing out there – it picks up your spirit to know that there are people out there – it has junior achievers that are Black. And I can also relate to the hair products and stuff – they have models, too, really gorgeous models [laughs] and all the hair-care stuff that is 'made for you,' and of course you can't forget the fashion section!

Stephanie is an avid reader of women's magazines, starting with *Glamour* when she was eleven years old. As well as *Essence*, her current reading includes *Seventeen, YM, Mademoiselle, Shape, Glamour, Sassy, Allure, Cosmo, Tell*, and *Ad Busters*. As evidenced here, she enjoys *Seventeen*, a magazine which has historically perpetuated Caucasian beauty standards:

I look at the horoscope first, then check out whose wearing what, where, uhm, in the ads – but I don't really read a lot in the ads, like the make-up ads. And then I go through the ones that they have in every issue, like the 'Ask Jane,' or the 'Beauty Tips' section – that kind of thing [laughs]. *Then* I go to the '[Table of] Contents' and see what the theme article is and see if it interests me.

This enthusiasm was expressed by other minority readers:

I read *YM*, *Sassy* – I like those magazines, and like the music magazines with the posters, I like reading about famous people and what they're *really* like and [pause] I like it in *YM* and *Seventeen* magazines how they have like your horoscope and what you're like – your colour and if you're an 'earth person,' or something like that. I like reading, they have like all these things about if you're an earth person, a water person. I like reading that. They tell you what you are. (Fourteen-year-old Lauren)

YM is more of a reading magazine and it's got more information. *Bopper* and *Teen* don't have anything on how to improve yourself, but *YM* has, like what fashion is going to be in soon. (Thirteen-year-old Jessica)

I like to see how they put on make-up and stuff. When they talk about that or some experience – something that happened to you and you feel that you need advice or something, then I read that ... I want to look at how to do make-up, I just want to see how the make-over is different.
[Interviewer:] The before-and-after shots?
Yes, I like looking at that. (Fifteen-year-old Nicole)

As suggested by these readers, the 'adolescent' referred to by magazine texts can be experienced as a universal category based on chronological age rather than cultural identity. This appeal is explored in the remainder of *Girl Talk*; for the moment, the transcripts quoted from above show that, in contrast to researchers who read magazines in order to understand how texts work, girls are motivated to read, at least in part, by the desire to know about themselves as 'teenagers' and to solve everyday problems. As a consequence, reading choices are determined by a search for texts which provide 'something more' than entertainment.

Beyond the Pleasure Principle

If asked directly, the girls in this study claim, as feminist researchers do, that they read magazines 'for fun.' At first glance, this response may appear to support the characterization of magazine reading as a search for pleasure. The problem is that this interpretation places reading pleasure outside the realm of the social. However appealing, pleasure as an effect of reading is never 'innocent' or separate from its societal role. In this and following chapters we explore the pleasures of teenzine reading. In order to do so we must identify which texts the girls in our study enjoy, why these texts sustain reader interest, and how these texts bring together the cultural and social realms of adolescence. As a number of writers note,[3] the construction and maintenance of any social order entails the construction of pleasures that secure participation in that order. In contrast to the notion gaining currency in cultural studies that pleasure can escape ideological manipulation and act as a form of disruption and resistance, Ballaster and colleagues (1991) point out that many commercial venues in a consumer culture will be both pleasurable and ideological – they ask, 'What else could pleasure be and how else could ideology work?' (p. 162).

Pursuing the types of questions which also motivate our study through discussions with readers, Ballaster and colleagues find that the pleasures of women's magazines derive from the magazines' ability to act both as a 'time-keeper' in women's lives and as fantasy. They link time-keeping to the way in which magazines address the particular circumstances of women's experiences at different points in their lives. They link fantasy to the opportunity provided readers to gain a sense of participation and belonging to an imagined community of women. Assigning fantasy status to this community does not mean that Ballaster and colleagues view the constructions of femininity in magazines as innocent pleasure, however. While readers are free to pick and choose the texts they read, the magazine text determines the range of possible meanings because it contains implicit assumptions about womanhood and therefore defines what kind of life can be taken for granted and what is open for struggle and renegotiation. Ballaster and colleagues advance the interesting suggestion that the fantasy element of magazines works by providing readers a fleeting sense of safety through the absolute dominion of women's domestic world:[4] 'The pleasure in safety is to be had from many elements of magazines, not least in forging of a homogeneous domestic community in contrast with the threats and confusions of the world outside it. That world is constantly on the margins of the magazine's field of vision, understood both as threat and [as] *unreality*' (p. 165; emphasis in original). In short, although Ballaster and colleagues support the notion advanced by postmodern writers that women's magazines occupy fantasy status in readers' lives, they do not celebrate this status as evidence that women's magazines are an innocuous source of pleasure for women.

Similar to the (imputed) adult readers who dominate academic debate, girls in the current study found magazine reading a readily available pleasure. Some girls *did* refer directly to the 'fantasy' element when describing the pleasures of magazine reading. This fantasy typically arises from the visual pleasures provided by glossy beauty and fashion layouts:

Actually, I kind of like the pictures; they're sort of interesting, exotic, but, uhm, most of the stuff I wouldn't wear. I don't know. I guess it's like a mental fantasy of what it would look like. [Later, looking at *Elle* with interviewer] I don't know. I guess it's like fantasy land for me [laughs]. Like I don't really have any clothes like this, so it's the only thing I can do! [laughs]. (Seventeen-year-old Amy)

Usually after school I have friends coming over and we sit there and we fantasize and read all these magazines articles and 'Oh, I wish that was me,' and stuff like that [laughs]. (Fourteen-year-old Lauren)

Fantasy themes also surrounded depictions of romantic relationships or future roles as adult women:

Uhm, I really like this one just because it's kind of different for a guy to be actually kissing the girl's – or look like he's *about* to kiss the girl's foot. Most of the time maybe the guy would be saying that to the girl 'Kiss my feet,' or something ... I've actually heard guys say that [laughs]. I've never [laughs] heard a girl say that to a guy, so it's almost like a reversal. (Sixteen-year-old Melissa, looking at ad for Converse shoes)

I like this ad. It's really natural and it's sort of like the future. You look at this and you think about what your future is going to be like, and stuff. It sort of makes you think about that. (Sixteen-year-old Erica looking at the bride in the ad for Beautiful perfume)

Despite the appeal of these utopian themes, however, the comments quoted above exhaust the references to fantasy themes in interview transcripts. Readers referred more frequently to favourite magazines in terms of their realistic qualities. Overall, 'realism' rather than fantasy emerged as the most important characteristic in descriptions of favoured reading. This means that, while girls cited different magazines as preferred reading, a favourite magazine was chosen from the available competing titles because it was deemed to refer to 'real' people or to address 'real' problems which readers face:

Teen, I don't know, it's just more to my liking. It just seems more *realistic*. I think it deals more with the problems that people *actually* have. (Sixteen-year-old Crystal)

And in *Seventeen*, the articles are better than *YM* ... The ones in *Seventeen* are about like real life, or sometimes they're stories that people have wrote, and I like reading that. [Showing an example to interviewer] Well, we have had a family friend that had breast cancer, and sometimes I like things like this – that have say happened to my friends or something. (Fifteen-year-old Christina)

Sassy is a little better than *YM*. I mean it's in the same category but it's a little better because they put real people on the cover and real people inside the magazine ... *Sassy* seems to pride itself on being more realistic than the other magazines. (Thirteen-year-old Stephanie)

In contrast to the adult readers who are purported by researchers to enjoy the fantasy status of pictures and ads, the emphasis on reality by girls in this study underlies their rejection of both fashion and (other) advertising:

I never look at the fashion stuff. 'Cause it's stuff that's almost like too weird to wear for me. I don't know, I would never think of dressing like they've dressed [pointing out fashion pages in *YM*, her favourite]. It's all – it's not real.
[Interviewer:] It's not?
No. A lot of it isn't real because like they all have these 'drop dead' bodies and they're not going – you know, not everyone's going to wear clothes that way. So I just, I don't know, I never look at the fashion. They're too weird. (Sixteen-year-old Melissa)

We shall see later that this rejection of magazine fashion is not an indication that dress is unimportant to these readers; on the contrary, this rejection is based on the grounds that magazine fashion is, simply, not real enough. When the girls were asked what might make their favourite magazine more enjoyable, a dominant theme which emerged[5] concerns the prominence of fashion models who are 'too perfect' or who are seen to perpetuate unrealistic body standards. This dissatisfaction does not lead girls to reject the beauty mandate itself; it does lead them to reject individual titles which emphasize fashion or contain too many ads:

I've read that [*Sassy*] a couple of times, and, ah I don't like it.
[Interviewer:] Why?
There's no articles, every page is ads.
[Interviewer:] Really?
Yup, the whole thing. (Fourteen-year-old Rachel)

I just found that I like *YM* better.
[Interviewer:] Is there anything in particular that is better about it?
Seventeen has columns in it too, like *good* ones, but I found that I like *YM* because it's got more – it doesn't have as much advertisement; it – it's got more writing in it. (Thirteen-year-old Ashley)

Seventeen [is here favourite] 'cause I find I can relate to like the articles, and what they're saying in the stories, and this and that. I like the pictures – like they're kind of just fun, but the other ones, I just end up flipping through them and it's just ads and stuff – I'd rather go for a little bit more. (Seventeen-year-old Mary)

Most of the time *Seventeen* is boring because it doesn't have as much stuff as the other two have [*Teen* and *YM*]. It's just got mostly pictures, like it's not interesting articles – it's got, like, no writing, it's just pictures and credits.
[Interviewer:] What things make *YM* better than *Seventeen*?
I don't know, it's got like interesting stories and people writing in to tell their problems and just stuff, like it's more interesting. It has lots of pictures, but it has writing too, whereas *Seventeen* just has pictures, just ads for stuff. (Fifteen-year-old Elizabeth)

What these comments tell us is that, in contrast to the emphasis which postmodern critics give to the pleasures of reading as escape from reality, girls in this study want magazines that address the reality of teenage life:

I like reading other people's things and seeing what happens with their lives and then I'll try and make sure it doesn't happen with mine [laughs] ... I like that [shows interviewer] – 'Problems at Home, How to Cope.' Like, if you're having family problems you could probably find out what the problems were and see how they solved their problems. (Thirteen-year-old Brittany)

They [magazines] teach you a lot of things, like what you should do, what you should think. Sometimes they're really helpful – like your Mom dies, right? They might have advice on how to struggle through this. Like problems and things like that. And maybe make-over. Like you know, 'how to *do* a make-over.' I mean you can just look at those for suggestions. (Fifteen-year-old Nicole)

Soap operas [another of her favourite pastimes] are sometimes a bit unrealistic – you can't really follow them to make decisions. But in magazines, they give you advice, realistic advice that you can follow. (Sixteen-year-old Lindsey)

Because of this emphasis on what readers can learn from magazines, the girls indicated the following:

I mean, a magazine is fine to look through, but you don't really want to pay for something that you're not going to sit down and actually *use*, you know what I mean? Like *Sassy*, there'd actually be stuff I want to read, stuff I want to know about inside of it. I mean, I like looking through the fashion and stuff as well, but if I'm going to buy a magazine I want to have something that's going to *do* something [laughs] for me, you know what I mean? (Seventeen-year-old Jamie)

I used to be into like *Teen*, that's when I was in Grade 7, 8. And then *YM* just seemed kind of older and more like my *style*, like it had more, like useful stuff that I'd *read* – like all the questions ... they were kind of right for me so I've had a subscription for that for a while. It's not like a *Vogue* or anything, you know – *Vogue*, like I read it but it's not really interesting to me 'cause it has nothing to do with someone my age, or like someone I can relate to. (Fifteen-year-old Kirsten)

Vogue, it's kind of a waste because what's the point if all you're going to do is flip, like for five seconds to look at a magazine [laughs]. If I see it on the stand it's fun to look at, but I wouldn't buy it because it's a waste of like four dollars, right? (Sixteen-year-old Erica)

In summary, while the girls in this study, similar to adult readers, claim to read 'for fun,' most reject the glossy ads and photo-spreads of magazines in favour of written texts. As a consequence, their reading does not include very many of the magazines or specific texts studied by academic critics. While we saw in chapter 1 that the content of teenzines is very similar to that in adult magazines, we still know very little about girls' reading pleasures. In order to understand why girls enjoy teenzines, therefore, we need to pay attention to what girls rather than researchers find important. In the next section, we explore the specific parts of teenzines that the readers in this study enjoy. In chapter 6 we explore the nature of girls' favourite texts.

From Pictures to Written Texts: Girls' Choice of Texts

When examined only for content, the written texts of teenzines appear monolithic. Repetition could, in fact, be one of the reasons why some girls do not read very many teenzines. Sixteen-year-old Crystal quit teenzine reading because she found them boring:

It doesn't really do much. It's like the same magazine over and over again. Like a *different* way to put on every shadow, and a *different* hairdo [laughs]. You know. So that gets boring, I guess, so I don't usually buy it [*Seventeen*] unless, like I'm going somewhere on a long trip.

Magazines are not experienced this way by those who choose to read them, however. Despite the kinds of similarities noted in chapter 1, teenzines are described by enthusiastic readers as offering a diversity choice of reading:

The first thing I read is the beginning where it tells all about what is in the whole magazine – the Table of Contents. Probably the first thing I read, *YM* has their article – 'disasters of the month' or 'nightmare of the month.' It's an article about a whole bunch of bad things that have happened to people and stuff. Just like embarrassing situations that have happened to people. Like you see a guy and you trip and fall, and make a fool of yourself. Things like that. And, I don't know, mainly the stories about relationships and stuff like that. Then the quizzes, I usually do those. They're about like relationships and matchmaking and things like boyfriends. I read them. (Sixteen-year-old Lindsey)

I go for *YM* because they have romantic stories, they have like funny stories – embarrassing moments, it's just like a fun thing to read ... As soon as I buy a magazine I have to read *every* part. I see what's on the cover, like the real headlines, and see what one interests me more, and then I'd read *that*. And then after I read whatever, I just go from beginning to end, I go through the whole thing. I read *everything*. (Fourteen-year-old Lauren)

YM has like interesting stories, and people writing in to tell their problems and stuff. Like it's more interesting. They have advice columns and they have the 'Say Anythings,' which is like embarrassing moments and stuff. And horoscopes. And people writing to 'Dear Jill' or 'Dear Jack,' or whatever. I kind of just read through the whole magazine. (Fifteen-year-old Elizabeth)

For the large part this sense of diversity, hence choice, in reading is a result of textual format rather than textual content. For this reason, when asked about their 'favourite' parts, the girls were more likely to mention the type of text rather than specific topics.

Although thematic analysis requires that researchers give each unit of text equal emphasis during enumeration, adolescent readers freely 'pick and choose' their way through their magazines:

When I read, like I usually don't just look through the magazine. I kind of go to wherever it is – the stuff – and just look through it ... I see what interests me and then I might flip through it – like just flip through the articles and then the ads and stuff. (Sixteen-year-old Melissa)

If I'm reading I kind of, what I'll do is like skip through all the little letters and see if there's anything that kind of relates to me, and then if it's interesting, or if I want to know what the answer is, I'll read that, or whatever. (Seventeen-year-old Jamie)

This manner of reading is made possible by the format of teenzine texts. Much of the written material in adolescent magazines appears as small, self-contained blocks of text; very few articles are longer than the equivalent of two full pages. This format means that magazines are seldom read from 'front to back':

I usually do the tests, and then if there's certain articles or stories, I want to read them first. And then I go back and read the whole thing over again, but first I go to the parts I want to read first. Mostly the stories interest me – the stuff on the cover that they say is inside. (Fifteen-year-old Tiffany)

It also allows magazine reading to fit into fragmented bits of available time:

Usually once you've flipped through the magazine [and] you've looked at every page, then you go back and look for articles you wanted to read. I usually put the magazine down and a couple of days later, when I've done my homework and no one's calling me, I'll pick up the magazine and read [them]. (Sixteen-year-old Crystal)

During lunch break I had nothing else to do so I went to the library and the only books that were short enough to read during lunch were magazines. So I got magazines. (Fifteen-year-old Christina)

The discontinuous nature of magazine reading thus means that some parts of magazines are read more widely than others. The types of texts which girls like to read are shown in table 5.2.

As seen in table 5.2 and already discussed above, the glossy texts of teenzines are not the most frequently read part of adolescent magazines. About half of the girls claim that they look at the fashion sections of magazines when they read, while less than one third of these readers claim that they (consciously) look at ads. Fashion spreads captured interest near graduation, when girls scoured magazines for styles of dresses and new hair fashions. During the rest of the year, however, most girls indicated that they would never wear the stuff in magazines, in part because 'you wouldn't be able to get the advertised clothes even if you wanted them':[6]

I would never wear those clothes, just because I don't dress up. It's more like dressy clothes, like things you would wear to expensive dinner parties ... I can't imagine myself in any of those things. I don't know, it's all boring. It's just like 'Ehk,' whatever – 'Nothing special.' (Seventeen-year-old Brianna)

I'll look at a magazine and say, and just kind of think to myself 'Oh, I would really like to have *this*,' you know. 'It would be really cool to have that kind of image.' But when it comes to shopping, I can't usually look for anything because the magazines we get are

Table 5.2: Parts of Adolescent Magazines Read by Participants, by Age Group

	% of entire group		
	13–14 yrs	15–16 yrs	17 yrs
Advice (includes relationships, beauty, and health)	73	89	36
Quizzes	60	56	36
'Say Anything' (or funny stories such as 'It Happened to Me!')	53	61	27
Fashion	47	56	45
Stuff about guys (or about romance)	47	11	27
Real-life stories/tragedies	33	67	27
Horoscopes	27	56	36
Feature article (only if 'interesting')	33	22	36
Stories/interviews with celebrities	20	17	9
Advertisements (usually only if 'catches my eye')	27	28	27
Letters from readers	27	11	9

Base *N*: 44 girls who currently read adolescent magazines or 'used to' read adolescent
  magazines regularly

usually – like, the stores we have don't actually carry the stuff shown in magazines.
(Seventeen-year-old Amy)

Maybe like once or twice I'd seen something, like sometimes they have, like you know,
a really nice shirt. I wouldn't go out and look for *that* shirt, but something like it. You
know what I mean, 'cause usually all the fashions from magazines are from New York
or whatever. I can never find it. Like I've seen stuff that I really want, and if it was
around I'd go out and get it, but it's usually in New York or Seattle or whatever, so I
never end up getting it [laughs]. (Seventeen-year-old Laura)

Very few girls indicated that they always read ads. More typically, girls claim
that they look at ads 'if they catch their eye.' This finding is significant, given
that the academic study of women's magazines (whether in criticism or support) has given disproportionate emphasis to the analysis of advertisements.
While adult women may be attracted to the spectacle of consumption as 'wish-
fulfilment' in the ways which Winship and others suggest, the girls in this study
prefer texts that they claim resonate with their everyday lives. While fashion is
widely read by the seventeen-year-olds in this study, readers between the ages

of thirteen and sixteen prefer advice, quizzes, and real-life stories. As seen in table 5.2, almost three quarters of thirteen- and fourteen-year-olds, and 90 per cent of fifteen- and sixteen-year-olds, mention advice pages as regular reading. McRobbie (1991a: 165) also draws attention to the importance of this reading preference among young girls. It is in the problem page that she finds the strongest definitions of teenage femininity. What gives these pages such readerly appeal?

Despite their dismissal by the world of 'serious' journalism, McRobbie points out that the advice column provides an open forum for an audience with little or no access to conventional therapeutic venues. She thus claims that the question-and-answer pages of teenzines play an important social role; 'it is listening and responding to, a discourse which so far has found no other space' (p. 156). This listening and responding valorizes sexual knowledge, which is uneasily avoided in our culture, despite its cultural coding in the normative language of romance, love, and marriage. Moreover, advice columns are a distinctly feminine form because it is not only women's lot to suffer personal unhappiness in a particularly acute form, but also their duty to try to alleviate the unhappiness of other people (p. 158). Within this framework, the power of adolescent magazines can be linked to their role as a regulative, controlling mechanism which operates along the terrain of the provision of knowledge in a culturally specific way which addresses women:[7]

From this viewpoint the problem page would represent a privileged site in the creation of a number of discourses designed so that they may be used by teenage girls to make sense of their complex and frequently contradictory feelings in relation to their own sexuality. It might even be described as a focal point for the construction of female sexuality which exists alongside other discourses, sometimes in harmony with them and on other occasions and in other contexts at odds with them. The problem pages, therefore, add to the clamour of already-existing organizing discourses, such as those found in the school, the home and elsewhere in the mass media. (p. 165)

Commentary by the girls in this study supports McRobbie's claim that advice columns appeal to readers as a source of knowledge about otherwise culturally repressed or devalued topics. The readers in this study continually refer to the usefulness of advice columns, a claim which links magazine reading to the everyday experiences of teenage girls. And yet I have also argued that it is not content alone which gives these texts appeal. As we saw in chapter 1, regular columns and feature articles similarly provide information about beauty, romance, and sex. What gives these topics more appeal when information is framed as 'problems' rather than as 'information'?

Winship (1987) maintains that 'agony' columns can actually be a source of reading pleasure. For her, the peculiar pleasure of advice lies in the relief provided by confirmation that other people's problems are worse than the reader's own. From this perspective, Winship claims that, however appealing, problem pages are not in women's interests because they reinforce both the privatized nature of magazine reading and notions that women's experiences of oppression are 'personal' rather than social problems. Like McRobbie, Winship argues that advice columns are anti-feminist because they demarcate boundaries between the private and the public: both McRobbie and Winship suggest that problem pages individualize and personalize women's experiences of oppression.

In contrast to both McRobbie's and Winship's claim that advice columns offer reading pleasure, however, McCracken suggests a somewhat opposite effect: 'The technique of question and answer encourages readers to think that their peers have written to the magazine with such problems. If a reader hasn't yet thought about herself in these fragmented terms, she should begin to do so if she wishes to be beautiful and share the concerns of her peers' (1993: 138). From this kind of reading McCracken characterizes advice columns as a potential source of anxiety and self-doubt. She claims that the authoritative tone which underlies answers to problems induces guilt and thus acts as a corrective to the otherwise pleasurable transgressions offered by fantasy elements in the text. In this way, McCracken maintains that although fantasy elements of women's magazines offer temporary release from the normative mechanisms of social control, advice columns guarantee ideological closure: while pleasurable inducements to consumption challenge or disrupt the boundaries of everyday life, advice to readers about their practical problems corrects any potential transgression of prescriptive femininity by encouraging readers to conform to established behavioural codes and standards.

Along with Winship and McRobbie, McCracken argues that, although appearing to address women's interests, women's magazines operate to reconstitute their oppression. What their analyses above have in common is reliance upon researcher rather than everyday readings.[8] In this chapter we begin instead with girls' readings. By starting our analysis from girls' accounts we have already begun to question many claims being advanced about the effect of teenzine reading. For example, we have seen that the community of teenage reading is real as well as discursive. Sharing favourite tidbits from magazines was a frequent pastime among readers:

My friend *loves* doing the little surveys, like the 'Friends' survey and stuff. She always gets me to fill them out with her, or she'll ask me questions and we go through – actually, lately we've been going through them like crazy because it's grad. So we've been all going through those magazines you've listed, basically just for styles of grad dresses, and stuff like that. We've been going through them together a lot lately. (Seventeen-year-old Alexandra)

If we're reading the magazine we'll talk about stuff in it. Like quizzes and – I don't know, if there is a question-and-an-answer like 'Dear Jill' and 'Dear Jack' – which is younger people's questions – we kind of read them and discuss them. Like if your boyfriend didn't talk to you or something and you don't know what to do and they [reader] asked what to do, then we'll start a conversation like 'What would you do?' and 'What would *you* do?' and everything. It gets into a conversation like that. (Fifteen-year-old Chelsea)

This sharing goes against the notion, described above, that advice columns individualize readers' experiences and difficulties of 'being women.' As we shall see, in this study advice columns are implicated in girls' construction of their social, as well as personal, world. We explore this process within the context of school culture in later chapters. Here table 5.2 directs our attention to the advice columns, quizzes, and 'embarrassing moments' in teenzines:

I read them with my friends and we might do the quizzes, or read through the questions. We have talked about the 'Say Anything' with my friends at basketball. It'd be like, 'Oh, you read *that* – eh?' and we'd laugh about it ... If I find the 'Say Anything' hilarious, I'll phone up a friend and be like 'Oh my God, listen to this!' Or I'll tell my mom because she thinks they're funny. (Fifteen-year-old Kirsten)

I do those little quizzes and tests with my friends. Usually after school I have friends coming over and we sit there and we fantasize and read all these magazine articles, and 'Oh, I wish that was me' and stuff like that [laughs]. We go, 'Oh, you should really like this article' or something like that – I'd go to school and say that to my friends. (Fourteen-year-old Lauren)

We have already seen from girls' accounts that their reading preferences are shaped by texts which the girls deem to be 'realistic.' This notion of realism is important because it is the basis for girls' claims that their magazines give them 'something useful' that they can 'relate to.' In subsequent chapters we take this finding as our problematic.

Pleasure Revisited

In chapter 4 we compared how researchers and adolescent girls read the glossy advertising images of women's magazines. We saw major differences between researcher and adolescent reading, primarily in terms of the status which these images have for readers. Importantly, we saw that, unlike cultural critics, girls tend to assign ontological status to stereotypical representations of femininity. This means that while girls draw distinctions between real life and the discursive fantasy of magazines, they make these distinctions much less critically than adult commentators often claim. In this chapter we have seen that, however visually appealing, the glossy images of commercial magazines do not sustain the reading interest of these girls. In contrast to researchers, adolescent readers want 'something more' than pictures. Most girls in this study prefer written over pictorial text. We thus began to explore how adolescent girls read the written texts of teenzines by identifying favoured texts. However, unlike previous researchers, we do not conflate qualities of these text with qualities of their reading. Very often, when writers describe texts as demeaning to women, reading has been assumed to be oppressive; when texts are described as pleasurable fantasy, reading has been taken as resistance to patriarchy. In the chapters that follow we move beyond this type of reductionism which conflates the text as cultural artefact and the social effects of its consumption. In order to do so, we have begun to problematize not only the text, but also its reading. While a study of the text helps us to understand the social world as cultural construction, it cannot tell us how this world is experienced by embodied rather than hypothetical readers.

As cultural critics point out, the regular reading of magazines signals the immense pleasure which these texts can offer women. If asked directly, girls maintain, as do many adult critics, that they read their magazines 'for fun.' To claim from such a response that teenzines are an innocuous source of pleasure would be to seriously misinterpret girls' reading however. A critical analysis must go deeper. It must locate pleasure itself within the cultural and social realms of adolescence. Pleasure is clearly an effect of teenzine reading; to imply that it somehow resists or escapes its cultural and social construction is to reduce it to an essence. At the same time, treating pleasure as an effect of the text does not mean that girls are simply 'duped' by their texts, or act as discursively disciplined readers. Instead, it renders pleasure part of our analytical problematic, something in need of explanation. Included in our explanation is girls' search for 'something more.' Girls in this study are drawn to the text in search of 'useful' information about themselves, their relationships with boys, and the day-to-day problems of being a teenager. The two most important qualities of favoured texts are that they address the reader as a teenage girl, and that they deal with 'real life' situations and relations. These qualities give rise to an age gradient in reading habits, expressed both in terms of what girls like to read and what they dismiss as not relevant. During interviews, assistants asked the respondent whether or not she 'had ever read or seen' specific magazines

(*Mademoiselle*, *Glamour*, *Allure*, *Harpers*, *Vogue*, *Cosmopolitan*) if she had not mentioned them in unprompted responses. While many of the girls had not seen some of these titles, as seen in table 5.1 most girls were not regular readers of these magazines. Typically, respondents dismissed these titles as 'adult' magazines, suitable for 'older' women:

I don't really like that one [laughs]. It's [pause], for like older girls, I think like twenty-year-olds or something.
[Interviewer:] What makes it for older girls?
It talks alot about sex and stuff, and nothing's wrong with that. It's just, like, I'm still a virgin and stuff like that, so it doesn't make any sense to me. (Thirteen-year-old Amanda, reader of *Teen* and *YM*, discussing *Sassy*)

I don't really read it [*Mademoiselle*]. I've looked through it, but I've never read any of it – I just don't know, they're adult magazines, I just don't find it interesting. *Teen* and *YM* have more stuff to do with my age of people, but *Mademoiselle* is just like – I don't know. (Fifteen-year-old Elizabeth)

I think it's [*Mademoiselle*], it's not for younger people, so it's not too interesting.
[Interviewer:] How can you tell it's not for younger people?
Uhm, I don't know. It's just like the articles are more for older people like, 'how to cook' and stuff [laughs]. They have like recipes and all the fashion is like more [pause] – they're nice suits, but they're for *women* and they have like the dress skirts and stuff – and I don't wear that [laughs] (Fourteen-year-old Lauren)

Given the popularity of *YM* and *Seventeen* among the fifteen- and sixteen-year-olds in this study, it is important to note that the content of these titles emphasizes three themes: physical attractiveness, heterosexual romance, and stardom.

We will see in chapter 6 that these topics resonate with readers' everyday preoccupations. While adult women may gain pleasure from romance reading, for example, as an escape from the domesticity of their everyday life, many girls in this study treat texts about romance as a source of practical information:

I'd probably read that too [pointing out 'The Five Weird Ways Guys Show You that They Like You'] and then try to compare – see if any of that's happened [laughs]. I usually will call up – like one of my best friends is a guy. I'll call him up and read them to him and ask if it's true. And we'll usually laugh about it! He'll laugh and he'll go 'Yeah,' and then a couple of times he'll go '*What* are they talking about?' I don't know – it's kind of funny just listening. I'll call different guys and get all their opinions on it. (Fourteen-year-old Rachel)

It just interests me, what guys say about things to do with girls. Just like I'd like to know. Wishing my boyfriend would do something like that [laughs]. Uhm, all this stuff. Like, 'How to make the first move' – I'm not saying I'd *actually* go out and do what they say ... (Fifteen-year-old Kirsten)

Given that this information can be found in other teenzine texts, we are directed to the importance of the question-and-answer format employed by advice columns and quizzes, the two types of texts girls 'liked most' or 'turned to first' in their favourite magazines. The question-and-answer format, rather than the content alone, contributes to the reader's sense that their magazines offer 'something useful':

I like to read, like these questions, 'cause lots of them is true and it might be happening to you too, so –
[Interviewer:] Can you give me an example?
Like what should I do and stuff, like if I broke up with my boyfriend and like that, you know. (Fifteen-year old Nicole)

In conclusion, while the manifest messages of adolescent magazines may not be dramatically different from those identified in women's magazines, girls' reading differs from that hypothesized by many writers. Specifically, girls are attracted to teenzines because they are seen as a source of 'something useful,' something 'you can benefit from.' Drawing on thematic and literary analysis, chapter 6 explores why advice texts, in particular, are the source of adolescent reading pleasure, and how they invite the construction of feminine Subjectivity. In chapter 7 we link the discursive attraction of teenzines, and the effect of their reading, to the social world of adolescence at school.

6

From Pleasure to Knowledge:
The Power of the Text

In chapter 5, the study of everyday reading helped us to identify the question-and-answer format, prominent in advice columns, as a teenzine text with reader appeal. The purpose of this chapter is to further explore advice columns by taking as our problematic the claim by girls that these columns address real-life problems and situations. In taking teenzine constructions as 'real,' however, we are not mistaking the cultural world of adolescence for the social world of our readers. Instead, we question the ways in which teenzine reading brings together the discursive and everyday worlds of being a teenage woman. As we have already seen, teenzine readers differentiate between the cultural and the social, although not in ways implied by cultural critics. In this chapter the pleasure afforded advice columns, and the boundary-making which these columns provoke, are linked to the two-part format of question and answer. Ostensibly, questions are framed in terms of a 'typical' teenage girl, someone who the reader may relate to. The question re-presents the everyday preoccupations of this hypothetical Subject. In contrast to questions, answers are constructed as an empathetic but knowledgeable response to typical teenage experiences and concerns. We will see that answers, often characterized as a 'parental' response, in effect construct a societal response that conveys approval (or disapproval) of the hypothetical 'reader with a problem.' In this chapter we explore how this two-part format of question and answer positions the reader in ways which frame messages as self-discovery and connect the reader to a constructed community of 'typical' adolescents. This self-discovery and connection account for much of the pleasure afforded by advice columns; they also challenge the notion that teenzine reading isolates individual readers from the social world of women.

Advice columns invite discursive analysis because their dialogical nature evokes an 'other.'[1] Understanding this dialogical character is important because, as I have already argued, women are encouraged to judge themselves from the position of an absent 'other' which, historically, has embodied patriarchal definitions of what is normal and desirable in women's behaviour and attitudes. Moreover, because this 'other' evokes a universe of female readers, advice pages can act to construct an imaginary 'community of women' united by their commitment to feminine pursuits. In this way, teenzines construct not simply a reading Subject, but a social world of female adolescence. While it may be true that advice columns encourage readers to personalize their everyday problems of 'becoming women,' in this study 'personal problems' signal membership in the world of teenage women. In chapter 7 we explore why this may be so by looking at girls' experiences of school culture. In this chapter we look for answers to this apparent paradox within the text itself.

Many critics of teenzines imply that readers actively follow advice provided by their magazines. From this perspective, commercial texts are seen to adversely affect readers by shaping their behaviours. This assumption underlies much 'commonsense' criticism of mass media. For example, *People* (3 June 1996) explores 'how media images of celebrities teach kids to hate their bodies.' This assertion is based (in part) on the finding that 15 per cent of girls diet or exercise in order to 'look like one of the many images they soak up on TV' (p. 67). It is interesting that conventional social scientists do not share such strong convictions about the influence of commercial media. In fact, because viewers have very poor recall of advertisements, for example, many researchers in the field of communications and mass media claim that popular worry about media effects is grossly exaggerated. In the chapters which follow, we may begin to suspect that these researchers have been asking the wrong question. Instead of asking whether readers can recall or recognize texts – such as specific advertisements – here we look at the ways in which the reader comes to recognize herself as a teenage woman through the commercial media of teenzines. Taking the position that the Subject is an effect of teenzine reading, we begin this chapter by identifying the behaviours encoded in teenzine texts that may, or may not, be adopted by readers. However, we also note that question-and-answer texts provide more than a behavioural message. The choice of question which frames responses, together with messages encoded in the corresponding answer, convey a normative framework of what is both 'usual' and desirable for adolescents.

Advice pages construct the Subject-ivity of the reader by offering goals and values which orient the reader towards traditional pursuits of beauty and heterosexual romance. This chapter systematically maps these goals and values in the four magazines in this study. We shall see that this map of adolescence is not as straightforward as simple content analysis might lead us to believe. We have already seen that, in the case of beauty advertisements, magazine texts embody contradictory messages; advice columns are no different. While I do not disagree that these contradictions may lead some readers to question or outright reject the proscriptions of teenzine discourse, in this study young readers often question themselves rather than textual constructions. In chapter 7 this questioning becomes significant if the contradictions identified in teenzine texts reappear in readers' everyday lives. Our task as cultural critics, therefore, is to examine question-and-answer texts in order to explore where, and how, the experiences of the embodied Subject and magazine discourse coincide. In the remainder of this chapter we identify the behavioural goals and attitudinal values through which teenzine readers are addressed. We then explore how the discursive presentation of these messages encourages closure in ways which support dominant meanings of adolescent femininity. Ultimately, the solutions to personal problems appearing in teenzine texts act to reinforce the very forces which give rise to readers' problems in the first place. Through a close reading of three typical question-and-answer pairs, we identify how these texts address young readers in ways which promote heterosexual romance and preoccupation with physical beauty, despite the presence of other messages which admonish readers to 'accept themselves' and to put their own needs and desires ahead of those of men. In doing so we necessarily emphasize a coherent Subject and the stability of meaning; in chapter 7 we call this treatment into question. While the power of the text is demonstrated through the actions of readers who behave in ways prescribed by magazine writers, we will also see less obvious ways in which teenzines impact upon the lives of teenagers.

Beauty, Boys, and the Body: Exploring the Goals and Values of Teenzine Advice

We have already seen that, during interviews, girls pointed out articles and stories which they believed would be helpful to readers, and some identified 'useful things' that they themselves have taken from their magazine reading. These 'tips' are most obvious in advice about beauty and health:

You can get some tips out of that [pointing to text in *YM*], like what you can do with split ends, and that kind of thing. It sounds kind of superficial [laughs] but you can get information out of them. (Sixteen-year-old Chelsea)

I love the colour of her hair [pointing to model in her favourite magazine].
[Interviewer:] Really?
Yeah, I love it. I just cut my hair a few months ago, but I wanted to dye my hair that

colour. But then I wanted it to be really curly and that's too much, so I just cut it. I could always dye it still, though. (Sixteen-year-old Crystal)

Every little bit helps [laughs]. Little tips, from like you know, you can do this with your hair. Sometimes they do people up. Like they add highlights to their hair and they change their make-up and everything. It kind of makes you think 'Gosh! I wouldn't have invented that.' Like, I mean I would like to see what I would look like after that. Some people actually do look like that person and so it gives them tips, like if your hair is this colour you could do your lipstick a shade darker, or something. (Fourteen-year-old Kayla)

It just gives me ideas about what I can do with my hair, face, how far I can go with what I wear, which is really interesting.
[Interviewer:] How far you can go?
Yeah, it gives me ideas, like some of the stuff is *really* pretty strange, and I'm not planning on wearing it to school, but sometimes I think 'Oh, that's a pretty good combination. I could do that.' (Thirteen-year-old Stephanie)

This kind of advice reading was typically associated with 'fun':

I read them sometimes for make-up tips, and fun things like that. Like things you can do – how to really apply fake eyelashes, and stuff like that, just like little weird things like that ... Oh, the tips in *Cosmo* are also good. Like they have little fun things. They have 'How to create cleavage' and stuff like that, which another magazine [like *Seventeen* or *YM*] would not have. (Seventeen-year-old Allison)

In many ways, Allison's account resembles the reading hypothesized by postmodern writers who celebrate the pleasures of magazine culture. For example, she went on to say:

I never read anything seriously ... Never as – well, like if 'this' is what the magazine says is 'fashion,' then I believe 'that's fashion.' Like I'll just take what I like out of each month's issue and that's what I like. I'll never go for something I don't like. I don't know, there are people who I know who subscribe and love them and live by them. If they [magazines] say 'something is good,' then that something is good. And they say 'this is fashion' and 'this' is what to wear that month, so they will wear that, even if they don't look good in it and they don't like it. *I* don't do that at all.

In this reading, Allison remains very much 'in control' of the text, picking and choosing which messages to accept or reject. Her reading is not typical of those by other girls in this study, however.[2] As we have seen, many girls were likely to say that, while magazine reading is fun, they also learn something from their magazines. How girls learn from teenzines is less obvious than why these magazines are fun to read. In order to explore magazines as an avenue of learning, we turn to readers who argue that their magazines provide them with 'something you need to know.' While this type of 'serious' reading does not mean that girls slavishly imitate magazine fashion in the way Allison suggests, it directs us to the stories of readers who describe teenzine advice as 'useful':

I read this one [pointing out an article in *YM*, 'How to make the first move and make it work.'] How to make the first move – I never make the first move. It's always this 'does she like him,' 'does she like me' kind of thing. That's what I don't like – the game.
[Interviewer:] The game?
That you play, before you actually get together.

[Interviewer:] Did you get anything out of that article, after reading it?
Yeah, 'cause sometimes some of my friends, my *guy* friends – it says something about the guy friends when he's your pal, and you like him, but you don't know if he likes you, when he does things, like to show you that he likes you – you don't know, you're not sure. Because you don't know if he's paling around, or joking around, or what. I think it was interesting to read, and a bit helpful. (Seventeen-year-old Erin)

'What guys love to hate' [pointing to an article she read in *YM*], just their opinions on things, what they like about girls or they didn't like. I was talking about that one with my friends. Some of them [answers], you've – *I've* never thought 'Oh, they actually think this way,' but some of the things are actually true, in the ways that guys react. You would be able to tell if they liked you, or if they didn't like what you were doing, or something like that ... [We] just thought it was helpful, kind of helpful. Just to know what we should do, or shouldn't do. I don't know. It's kind of bad to follow a magazine article, but it gives some [good] advice. [Points to] 'What guys love and hate on the first date.' Tips on what to wear, what to do, what to talk about, and how to act. (Sixteen-year-old Erica)

Usefulness can only be established by comparing advice columns to everyday life:

I'll read, I don't know if I always read the advice that the people actually give back to people who send the letters, but I'll read the letters just to see if I've ever heard of anyone say the exact same thing, or something. (Sixteen-year-old Jasmine)

Later we discuss the significance of reading only the questions appearing on problem pages. Most readers give attention to the answers as well as questions. In fact, many readers gave examples of how they have applied magazine advice to actual situations:

It's funny because, uhm, I broke up with my boyfriend a while ago and I was just really like, uhm, upset or whatever and, I just wanted to get a magazine – like just to kind of *do* something, to read through. And they had an article about it! Like how to get over it [breaking up]. And I ended up getting it [the magazine] because of that and it was really good. Like it had 'Ten steps' and things you had to do and things you had to think – like 'always blame him' and then they went on about that. Always 'think about his bad qualities' and stuff like that. It did help. I noticed by the end of the time I read it, it was kind of like 'Yeah, that's right!' (Seventeen-year-old Roshni)

These readers fail to critically distance themselves from the text in the manner expressed by Allison (or at least failed to do so during interview dialogue). In exploring their accounts we replace the notion of texts as a source of information with a treatment of the text as knowledge. While information implies that readers consciously choose from among available messages according to their needs and interests, knowledge draws attention to the way in which the needs and interests of readers are actively shaped by the text, as an effect of reading. The notion of knowledge thus draws attention to Subject-ivity as process, and allows us to explore the way in which the cultural helps to construct the social. However, by locating reading within the everyday context of school culture, we will not simply read the social world off the cultural. Thus distinctions between information and knowledge, the cultural and the social, are important analytically because they help us understand how power works through the text.

The interconnectedness of the cultural and the social is evident in the claim by readers that teenzines offer them 'something you need to know.' These readers typically attribute realism to the text:

I usually read all that kind of stuff [pointing out things in *Sassy*]. I just read it, just 'cause, uhm – all these little short stories, like all the letters that they write in and that kind of stuff, it's people writing in, it's not just a bunch of fiction. (Sixteen-year-old Lindsey)

Usually they get picked to write it, so it's not as if someone has interpreted someone else's feelings. And also they usually have, when they're writing an article about – like this one here [pointing to text in *YM*] – 'My boyfriend wants me to have sex with other guys' – it would have like the *facts* or whatever and then it has the person's story. Like someone's *experience*. So it's not as if you're reading it and thinking 'This never happened' 'cause it's got someone's experience right there. (Sixteen-year-old Michelle)

This realism is often credited to advice columns which are argued to be especially relevant to everyday life because they help readers solve actual problems:

It [*YM*] describes people's life stories, what they've gone through. Like if you have a problem, usually it mentions something that you need to know, like teen things. (Fifteen-year-old Rebecca)

When people write letters, with their problems, they give you good advice to follow and it's fairly easy to, it's not like something that will be really difficult for the person to do. [Interviewer:] Do you have any examples?
Maybe like if you were being picked on, being a bit of a social outcast, or maybe – I don't know, if you were a bit shy [it might tell you] to become a bit more outgoing, like to 'try a bit harder.' Things like that. (Sixteen-year-old Jasmine)

[I read advice columns] when they might apply to you, or you'd think this is so similar to your friends – you just want to know what they might say about it. Because if it is *happening*, you just want to know what you could do, or one of the suggestions that you can follow. (Fifteen-year-old Nicole)

Given that many readers claim to follow teenzine advice or describe it as a source of useful knowledge, it is important to look at the kinds of behaviours these texts prescribe. In order to systematically map behavioural messages, content analysis was undertaken on all issues of *Teen, YM, Seventeen,* and *Sassy* published between June 1993 and May 1994.

Teenzine Behaviours

In this study, the behavioural messages of advice pages are coded and enumerated as goals. A 'goal' refers to an actionable component of editorial advice. In total, more than forty goals were initially identified during coding, as shown in Appendix B, table 2; in order to summarize findings here, categories which did not reoccur in more than one title are omitted from tables. Table 6.1 summarizes goals identified in the advice columns of the four teenzines in this study. In table 6.1, a 'dominant theme' refers to a category which occurs in at least (about) one in five questions of a respective text; 'minor themes' are relatively infrequent, found in (about) less than one answer out of ten. Despite their relative infrequency, minor themes are important; while a dominant theme allows us to characterize the general nature of magazine text, as Sumner (1979) notes, readers do not relate to messages simply on the basis of their frequency. For our purposes minor themes are important because they are often the source of dis-

Table 6.1: Goals Given in Advice Pages in Four Adolescent Magazines

Category	% of answers in a typical issue with themes[1]			
	Teen	YM	Seventeen	Sassy
Dominant Themes				
1 Do what's right for you	5.5	6.5	15.9	88.3
2 Accept yourself	5.5	13.1	37.8	18.6
3 Take care of your body	21.6	15.9	13.4	13.8
4 Make the best of the situation	23.5	11.2	2.4	14.5
5 Be patient, wait	4.1	11.2	7.3	19.3
6 Get professional help	8.0	21.5	18.2	16.6
7 Look better	36.6	16.8	4.9	15.9
8 Develop a new, practical skill	23.5	11.2	2.4	14.5
9 Understand guys better	16.6	21.5	11.0	43.4
10 Improve communication in relationships	11.1	15.9	24.4	7.6
Minor Themes				
11 Assert your own needs, desires	5.0	4.7	12.2	2.1
12 Get a boy, have a romance	2.5	9.3	2.5	6.2
13 Tolerate boys' undesirable behaviours	0.3	1.9	4.9	0.0
14 It's not your fault that something happened	0.3	4.7	6.1	2.8
15 Fight an injustice	5.5	4.7	11.0	2.8
16 Help others in trouble	1.1	2.8	2.4	0.7
17 Know about the world and your place in it	0.3	1.9	2.4	0.7
18 Resist pressure to conform	0.0	0.0	6.2	4.8
19 Be open, truthful in relationships	2.5	3.7	8.5	1.4
20 Change the behaviour of others	0.8	6.5	4.9	0.7
21 Question your own behaviour, motives	3.6	5.6	7.3	4.1
22 Make new friends	0.8	1.9	3.7	1.4
23 Improve relationships with family members	5.5	4.7	11.0	2.8
24 Obey parents	0.3	1.9	4.9	2.1
Base N^2	361	107	82	159
No. of question/answer pairs per issue	32.8	10.7	6.8	14.5

1 Each question/answer pair can have more than one theme.
2 Taken from all issues published between June 1993 and May 1994

cursive contradictions or sometimes contain 'alternative,' potentially politicizing messages, such as 'fight an injustice.' The importance of these types of messages is dealt with in more detail later. For the moment, systematic enumeration is used to characterize and compare teenzines in order to better understand girls' reading preferences.

As table 6.1 shows, a cluster of three behavioural themes dominates the advice pages of the teenzines in this study. This cluster, which allows us to characterize teenzines as a genre, emphasizes: being attractive, being knowledgeable about boys' culture, and doing 'what's right for you.' Beautification is such a ubiquitous goal of adolescent magazines that its prevalence in advice columns hardly comes as a surprise. What is more interesting, perhaps, is the lesser emphasis given to beauty problems in magazines read by older girls. For example, while over one-third of the questions in *Teen* concern beautification, less than 20 per cent of questions in *YM* and *Sassy*, and only 5 per cent of questions in *Seventeen*, deal with this thematic topic. This pattern does not mean that beauty themes are any less important in *Seventeen* than in *Teen*, however. In large part, it reflects differences in textual format. As shown in table 6.1, the frequency of question-and-answer text is the highest in *Teen*. *Seventeen* has the least number of questions per issue, about one-fifth of the number in *Teen*. An assessment of overall magazine content shows that beauty and fashion are dominant themes across all titles. We saw in chapter 1 that fashion and beauty topics account for almost two thirds of the topics discussed in the feature articles of *Seventeen*. Added to these editorial features is the impact of advertising, which accounts for almost half of the page space in all teenzine titles and concerns primarily the use of cosmetics, perfumes, hair products, and fashion accessories. The lesser emphasis given to beauty in question-and-answer format, therefore, directs us to the importance of textual form as well as content. Specifically, differences in format may reflect assumptions on the part of editors that older readers are already knowledgeable about beauty techniques. As a consequence, beauty tips for older girls are found less frequently in advice columns, where they are framed as direct appeals for 'help' from inexperienced readers, and more frequently in feature articles, where they are framed as a specialized discourse for women well versed in the basics of make-up use. This difference in framing is apparent in the following two excerpts, one from *Teen* and the other from *Seventeen*. While the excerpts are similar because both deal with 'problems' associated with mascara use, their authorial tone belies different assumptions on the part of editors about the competence of their reading audience:

I'm Asian. My eyelashes are really straight. I use mascara to make them look longer and thicker, but they still need help. What can I do?

Before applying your mascara, use an eyelash curler. Don't press down too hard. Squeeze quickly and gently three or four times. Apply a coat of mascara, and wait a few minutes to let it dry. Then apply a second coat. (*Teen*, July 1994)

Whenever I use mascara, my eyelashes stick together and look spiky. How can I prevent my lashes from clumping?

Your mascara is probably too thick. If you choose the right formula, you should never have to use a lash comb or remove excess. Try a thinner mascara (avoid thickening formulas) and layer on two or three light coats. (*Seventeen*, August 1994)

The difference in these two texts is not simply that they address different concerns. In the first example, the reader needs help in making her eyelashes look 'longer' and 'thicker.' In responding to her plea for 'help,' the editor introduces the use of an eyelash curler, as a supplement to mascara use alone. Because the editor assumes that the reader has not used such an instrument, the answer contains instructions on its use. The reader is told to use the curler 'gently,' squeezing 'quickly' three or four times. She is also instructed how to apply several coats of mascara. While the second text contains a similar, if not identical, message for the reader – that lashes should appear 'longer' and 'thicker' – here the reader's problem is not explicitly stated as lashes that are 'straight,' or not 'longer' and 'thicker.' Rather, the reader's problem is lumpy mascara: she does not need advice about how to make her lashes appear 'longer and thicker,' or how to apply mascara, only about the correct formula. Thus the editor refers to a lash comb as something which the reader might have already tried. For our purposes the main difference between these two texts, therefore, is not found in their messages, but rather in underlying assumptions about the nature of information required by the reader.

Comments from girls in this study support this interpretation. The reading of fashion and beauty magazines typically began at that point when girls were initiated into make-up use, about the age of twelve. Many readers learned how to 'do' their make-up from magazines like *Teen*:

I started to wear make-up in Grade 7 – but I didn't tell my mom [laughs] ... Like my mom would let me wear eyeliner, right, but I know *now* I would overdo it ... Like we always went to everyone's houses [on the way to school] because we lived in a small town, and her parents would be at work so they weren't home when she left. So there would be like five of us girls and we would all, you know, 'fix our make-up' at her house. And I guess 'cause we were so excited about being able to wear it that we used to kind of want to show that we're wearing it. So we would put a *lot* of make-up on. Like really *tacky* colours and stuff [laughs]. (Seventeen-year-old Roshni)

Like other girls in this study, Roshni had to learn to wear make-up 'properly':

Actually, I learned a lot of how to wear make-up from magazines because you know, they always used to have these techniques like about how to wear eyeshadow, eyeliner right. Because I used to wear it all wrong, I guess, because I used to put the liner on the inside of my eyes and stuff, just little things like that.

Ironically, however, an emphasis on beauty and instructional tone are also stated reasons why older girls 'grew out' of *Teen*. Once knowledgeable, readers like sixteen-year-old Crystal found these characteristics tedious:

The stuff they focus on is kind of fun, but it's just like hairdos, how to put on make-up, like what's the newest rage, and it gets boring after a while. It doesn't really do that much. It's like the same magazine over and over again. Like a *different* way to put on eyeshadow, and a *different* hairdo [laughs]. So that gets boring. So I don't buy it any more usually unless I'm like going somewhere on a long trip and I need lots of magazines to read.

However, even girls who might mock these columns during interviews claimed at the same time that they could find them useful:

Yeah, these beauty question-and-answer things [showing interviewer what she reads in *YM*]. They have them in just about every magazine. Usually it's like thirteen-year-old girls asking for advice on like how to put on lipstick and stuff! [mocking tone] I think it's really funny when they do that [laughs]. It just kind of makes me think 'What the hell!' [laughs].
[Interviewer:] Do you ever get anything from them?
Sometimes, like when they have things that say like 'Tips on how to do your make-up a little faster.' I always look at those because it takes me like sometimes half an hour, so I want to be absolutely accurate and not screw up because if you screw up you have to start again! [laughs]. (Fourteen-year-old Kayla)

As seen in these examples, the ubiquity of the beauty mandate means that the desire to 'look good' can be taken for granted by magazine writers; the editors can assume that readers 'naturally' want to look their best. This naturalness means that teenzines will appeal to minority readers, despite the fact that they embody a Caucasian beauty standard. For example, here an African-American reader who wants 'natural skin make-up colours' is advised to avoid emphasizing her Blackness:

Makeup girl Christine Hoffman says you should find a lippie that's as dark or even darker than your skin. Stick with brown shades and never go the burgundy route! She says too many people make that mistake, and it won't give you the look you're after. (*Sassy*, June 1994)

We have already seen that these types of contradictions do not necessarily call the constructedness of the dominant beauty standard into question for minority readers. In chapter 7 we will see that the mandate to 'look good' plays an important role in school culture; it is therefore one point of convergence between the discursive and experiential world of female adolescence.

The second dominant goal in teenzines as a genre is to 'know guys better,' expressed in terms of learning more about what boys think, how they behave, and what they prefer in female partners. As we might anticipate, this goal is typically linked to the importance of 'having a romance':

... First, just because a guy doesn't utter those three magic words, doesn't mean that he doesn't care for you. Some people find it difficult to express their emotions ... It's possible he has been busy and hasn't had time to talk on the phone. Give him a chance to explain his side of the situation. Also, keep in mind that some people just aren't as comfortable talking on the phone. So be sure to talk to him in person. (*Teen*, July 1994, answered by 'Jack')

As in the case of beautification, editors can assume that romance is a shared goal of readers. As a consequence, the goal of having a romantic attachment is not stipulated as frequently as we might expect. For example, it was coded for less than 10 per cent of advice texts in all four titles. However, as we shall see below, because this goal takes the form of an assumption rather than assertion of the text, romantic attachment is a dominant message of teenzine advice.

Given that the heterosexual orientation of women's magazines is a well-documented finding of previous research, the prominence of this theme in teenzine advice is not surprising. What is more important here is the way in which learning about guys, their likes and dislikes, is one of the attractions of teenzines for some readers:

[flipping through *YM*, showing interviewer what she likes] That's one I would want to read — 'What guys love to hate.'
[Interviewer:] Why do you find it interesting?
Well to see what kind – like what guys are into now. Like what kind of girl they like and, uhm, what they hate about girls. All that. (Thirteen-year-old Caitlin)

With *YM* they seem to have more selection and stuff and not only do they have, like they have more stuff on guys. Like not what *we* think of guys, but what guys think of guys. You know, it has more guys' opinions and stuff in it. (Fourteen-year-old Kayla)

I have that one [points to July 1994 issue *YM*].
[Interviewer:] What were the things that you read?
Uhm, I guess I always tend to go, like they always have something about guys, what guys think. And I always find that kind of interesting, so I usually end up going to that first [laughs].
[Interviewer:] Any reason why?
Just 'cause I find it interesting because they have like little sections on a guy's point of view. Like they ask a guy a question and see what he says, and stuff. It's just kind of interesting to know, like what they say about things. (Seventeen-year-old Roshni)

As in the case of make-up, learning to identify the right guy interests many readers:

See, they [*YM*] also have, uhm little things like [pointing out to interviewer] 'Guy Quest.' – 'What makes you dive into a relationship?' [reading from text]. Just 'cause all the guys there – I don't know, you can just tell that they're going to have all their opinions and stuff [laughs]. And it helps that they give pictures of them so you can see what they look like. And it doesn't necessarily say, like 'that guy's good looking, so I'd want to go out with him.' After you listen to what he has to say about things you totally change your mind and stuff. (Sixteen-year-old Melissa)

In chapter 7 we will see that boys' opinions and preferences are a powerful influence in school culture. Because boys have the ability to determine a girl's reputation, learning about guys' culture is a second point of convergence between the discursive and the experiential world of female adolescence.

The third dominant behavioural goal in teenzines is 'doing what's right for you.' This is an interesting goal because it is associated with messages that the reader is a unique person who is valuable and should be cared for:

Is it worth putting up with a friend who cares more about attention from boys than your feelings? (*Seventeen*, July 1994)

There's no need to conform to the preconceptions of your parents ... as you achieve stuff on your own terms, your parents might come around to respect you. (*Sassy*, June 1994)

That doesn't mean that you can't try to emulate models; it simply means that you shouldn't go to extreme measures to do so. Try out their hair or clothes styles, if you like, but don't constantly compare your look with theirs. You'll drive yourself nuts, and you won't be able to appreciate all the things that are special about you. (*YM*, August 1994)

We will see below that the goal of 'doing what's right for *you*' is frequently associated with the value of self-esteem, coded in almost one-quarter of all advice in *YM*, *Seventeen*, and *Sassy*. It is further reinforced by the less frequent message to readers that they should 'assert their own needs or desires.' Framing advice in this way could enhance the appeal of teenzine advice, as is the case for seventeen-year-old Roshni:

Like they have [social] issues in *YM*, but they have two sides to things sometimes. Like when they have controversial stuff, I found it tells you to do what *you* feel rather than [telling you] 'don't do it.'

The goal of 'doing what's right for *you*' may strike feminist critics as a vindication of adolescent magazines. McRobbie (1991a) draws attention to the feminism-from-within adolescent magazines that reflects the way in which many editors of women's magazines have been influenced by feminism. As we saw, in chapter 4, however, the discursive incorporation of feminist messages and slogans does not result in 'alternative' meanings about 'being a woman.' In chapter 7 we see that the ensuing contradictions can present dilemmas for young readers. Messages which encourage the reader to 'accept herself' for what she is, while giving overall emphasis to 'getting a boyfriend,' can construct a reading context that makes it difficult for readers to accept themselves if they, in fact, do not have a boyfriend. Below, we see how the message to 'accept oneself' not only places the reader in opposition to competing messages found elsewhere in the magazine, but appeals to a 'Self' that evokes a secure and stable Subject. In chapter 7 we will see that girls' experienced Self may not be so coherent and well-defined.

Three dominant themes in table 6.1 point to differences as well as commonalties among the behavioural orientations of the teenzines in this study. Advice to 'make the best out of the situation' or 'be patient, wait' was typically given to suggest that teens may 'grow out of' current problems:

You may not be ready for sex ... waiting until you're older – and when you're more comfortable with physical intimacy – might be a better idea. (*YM*, February 1994)

This theme of 'waiting' and suggestion that problems will 'go away' with maturity is found in about one-quarter of the answers to questions in *Teen*; it also appears in about one-fifth of the answers in *Sassy*. This theme was the least likely to appear in *Seventeen*, where readers were more frequently told that better communication in interpersonal relationships is important in solving problems:

As you realize, telling them [parents] you think they should get a divorce wouldn't be very helpful, but I do recommend saying something. At a time when things are relatively calm, try letting your parents know how much their fighting freaks you out. (*Seventeen*, September 1993)

This theme of better communication is found in about one-quarter of answers to questions in *Seventeen*, reflecting its greater emphasis on getting along with family members. Significantly, readers of *Seventeen* were also told more frequently than other readers to 'be open or truthful' in their relationships.

A large part of the advice in teenzines is framed as 'self-help,' suggesting to readers that solutions to problems lie within their reach, hence their control. However, occasionally readers are advised to 'get professional help':

By recognizing your mother's alcoholism, you have already taken an important step in addressing alcoholism in your family. There are a number of groups that can provide support to the family members of alcoholics. Ask a school counselor, or check your telephone book for more information about such groups. (*Teen*, August 1993)

It sounds to me as if you are seriously underweight. You should see a doctor to find out how you can put on some pounds. (*YM*, August 1994)

As we shall see below, reference to 'professional' help is important because it often directs the reader to male professionals employing patriarchal definitions of womanhood.

Advice pages are not simply a source of practical information for readers. Whether or not readers actively subscribe to the goals identified above, we have already seen that they may turn to advice pages to 'check out' other people's problems:

[Showing interviewer what she reads in *Teen*] I like that – 'Problems at home, how to cope.' Like if you're having family problems you could probably find out what the problems were and see how they solved their problems.
[Interviewer:] You mean you could get some advice?
Yeah ...
[Interviewer:] Do you ever take advice from them?

No.

[Interviewer:] No? So why do you read them?

It's just to see how – what other people's problems are. (Thirteen-year-old Caitlen)

For some readers, this checking includes a comparison to their own experiences:

I can relate some of the stuff with my life. Like, just things that have happened and things that they talk about – like things that guys do or something I can relate to ... It interests me to see what happens to other people, [what they] think and say, and [to see] if it actually happens to other people, what happens to me [laughs]. Just things like that. It interests me. (Fifteen-year-old Kirsten)

I guess it's kind of corny but sometimes I'll read a letter and like, I thought it was a good idea – you know, that they wrote. And I read those [answers]. Some of the questions just really surprise me in some of the magazines. Usually what the – whoever is answering the letter, says what *I* kind of tend to think at the same time, so that's kind of nice. (Sixteen-year-old Kelsey)

I read the question or what they ask and then I see if it has anything to do with me. And if even sometimes if they say [reader's question], 'Oh, this mascara doesn't look good on me. What should I do? Oh, I'm like distraught,' then I read what they say. Sometimes I feel like it's a really poor answer, and other times I'm like 'Well if that is all you have to worry about, you're laughing,' but sometimes – yeah, I usually see what the question is and I skip through [the rest]. (Seventeen-year-old Victoria)

Like Victoria, some girls read only the questions on advice pages:

Whenever I read the advice columns I'll read the problem not, like *not* the resolution, it's just sort of – I want to get to the next. (Sixteen-year-old Michelle)

I like reading those question-and-answer things [flipping through a magazine]. Where people send in like their problems and stuff, and then this person answers them ... I like reading the questions better than the answers, though. The questions, I just find them interesting, but the answers, I don't even care to hear. I just like to hear what people are sending in. (Sixteen-year-old Jasmine)

When read in this way, teenzines do not simply prescribe actions which readers may or may not follow; they provide an opportunity for readers to learn about the social world through other people's problems as a reference point for the reader to assess the normalcy of her own experiences. As a point of reference, advice pages define behaviour that is both normal and socially acceptable. This normalization occurs in the way that behaviours are also linked to attitudinal messages. As well as behavioural goals, attitudinal values were enumerated in all issues of *Teen*, *YM*, *Seventeen*, and *YM* published between June 1993 and May 1994.

Teenzine Values

In this study attitudinal messages are coded as values. In the main, values follow logically from stipulated goals. For example, when readers are instructed to 'accept yourself,' the value of 'self-esteem' is promoted. Similarly, 'do what's right for *you*' corresponds with 'independence,' 'get a boy' with 'heterosexual romance,' 'look better' with 'physical attractiveness,' and so on. Regardless of whether readers actively follow the behaviours prescribed, the advice pages construct a normative adolescent femininity by outlining both what is taken for granted as normal and what is desirable. This type of information is important to readers, whether they use magazines to 'check out' their own experiences or to assess the behaviours and attitudes of others. Table 6.2 summarizes the values coded on the advice pages of our four teenzines. As in the case of goals, a cluster of four values characterizes teenzines as a genre. Overall, teenzines promote as desirable: scientific information, physical attractiveness, physical health, and guys' culture and point of view.

As shown in table 6.2, the most frequent value for the sample as a whole is the promotion of 'faith in science.' This value is dominant in all titles, found in over half of *Teen* question-and-answer pairs, and about one-third of those in *YM* and *Sassy*. This value is typically found in topics concerning beauty or the body:

That would be a little cyst, also known as a sty or chalazion. It's common around the eyelid where there are many glands which can get blocked up. The Man of Skin, Dr. Peter Wisch, suggests that ... (*Sassy*, May 1994)

Even the non-acne-prone can suffer from *acne mechanica* ('athlete's acne') ... Shower as soon as possible with an antibacterial cleanser (like Hibiclens, available in drugstores), and exfoliate gently with a Buf-Puf or loofah to open clogged pores. After toweling off, treat the area with an astringent or medical acne pads ... Source: Rodney S. W. Basler, MD, dermatologist and chair of the Task Force of Sports Medicine, American Academy of Dermatology. (*Seventeen*, May 1994)

As seen here, scientific or medical knowledge gives these texts an appearance

Table 6.2: Values Promoted by the Answers of Advice Pages in Four Adolescent Magazines

Category	% of answers in a typical issue with themes[1]			
	Teen	YM	Seventeen	Sassy
Dominant Themes:				
1 Promotes faith in science	54.6	37.4	22.0	33.7
2 Promotes men's values, points of view	16.9	22.4	12.2	6.1
3 Physical health	12.7	15.9	18.3	33.7
4 Heterosexual romance, intimacy	1.7	17.8	43.9	13.8
5 Physical attractiveness	30.5	25.2	7.3	14.9
6 Self-esteem	5.3	16.8	18.3	13.2
7 Assertiveness	7.2	17.8	22.0	6.2
8 Independence	0.5	3.7	22.0	3.9
9 Friendships with same sex	8.3	7.5	12.2	5.5
10 Introspection	4.1	5.6	11.0	5.7
11 Consumption	31.0	8.0	2.0	12.6
Minor Themes:				
12 Good relationships with parents	5.5	6.5	20.7	4.4
13 Self-control, patience, determination	3.0	13.1	11.0	0.0
14 Honesty	2.2	5.6	7.3	1.2
15 Initiative	2.5	9.3	3.7	6.2
16 Suspicion of boys, men	3.6	3.7	9.8	2.5
17 Tolerance for difference	0.3	0.9	4.9	0.6
18 Courage	0.0	0.5	3.7	0.6
19 Altruism	0.8	2.8	2.5	0.6
20 Anti-racism	0.0	0.0	2.4	1.2
21 Sexual equality	0.0	0.9	0.0	2.5
22 Good relationships with siblings	1.1	0.0	4.9	0.6
23 Education	0.0	6.5	0.0	1.2
24 Empathy	0.0	4.7	3.7	0.0
Base N[2]	361	107	82	159
No. of question/answer pairs per issue	32.8	10.7	6.8	14.5

1 Each question/answer pair can have more than one theme.
2 Taken from all issues published between June 1993 and May 1994

that the information presented is 'value-free,' an appearance assisted by the professional credentials of the 'experts' referred to by editors. It is not coincidental that the experts referred to in both of these examples are male. While questions about the female body or beautification typically appear in columns written by female editors, scientific and/or medical knowledge is the domain of men. Despite their value-free appearance, these texts legitimize patriarchal standards because men are advanced as authorities on what it means to be a woman. Furthermore, appeals to science also impart a sense that the problems encountered in teenzines are not simply normal, but also 'natural' because the biological rather than the socially constructed nature of 'problems' confronting teen readers is emphasized. Thus, appeals to medical or other 'scientific' discourses imply that technical solutions are at hand.

The naturalization of cultural standards of feminine beauty also occurs when scientific knowledge is also advanced for beauty problems. In these cases 'beauty' becomes a health problem:

What to do: Coat your lips with a rehydrating treatment (Blistext Lip Ointment contains an aspirin-like ingredient to soothe sore lips). Once a week *gently* brush lips with a moistened soft-bristled toothbrush to remove dead skin or use a lipstick with built-in exfoliating grains (Coty Lip Doctor). (*Seventeen*, November 1995)

As seen in this example, appeals to the medicinal qualities of the solution not only conceal the constructed nature of the beauty standard being advanced, but also disguise the promotion of commodities. The above answer is an example of what Earnshaw (1984) calls an 'advertising editorial,' or McCracken (1993) an 'advertorial.' Advertorials blur the boundaries between commercial messages by advertisers and the concerned, empathetic messages from editors. This blurring is important because, as we saw in chapter 5, most readers reject overt advertising: 'too much' advertising was often a stated reason for the rejection of specific teenzine titles, and less than one-third of the readers in this study consciously looked at ads, doing so only when the text 'caught their eye.' In short, advice columns in teenzines, similar to advertising pages, solve readers' problems through consumption, although consumption was coded as a dominant theme only in the case of *Teen:* this finding reflects the emphasis which *Teen* gives to beauty rather than relationship questions. While most (if not all) beauty problems are solved through the use of commodities, here the value of consumption was coded only when explicit reference was given to brand-name products. As we shall see in the conclusion, the promotion of consumption in teenzines reflects the relationship between the economic interests of cosmetic and fashion industries and those of publishers. Because this relationship affects both what editors can say and how they frame their messages, it acts as an invisible censor of adolescent magazines.

Given the prevalence of 'looking good' as a stipulated goal, it is not surprising that physical attractiveness reappears as a dominant value. However, its prominence in *Teen* and *YM* is an interesting contrast to *Sassy*, which gives more emphasis to physical health. This difference is apparent in the following comparison taken from the beauty columns of *Teen* and *Sassy*. Here both the question chosen for discussion and the answer reflect quite different editorial value-orientations:

I have almond-shaped eyes with very narrow lids. Can you suggest some makeup tips to make my lids look bigger? K.M., Eugene, Ore.

To make lids appear more prominent, use eyeshadow and an eye pencil to create a crease between the upper and lower sections of your eyelids. Begin with a light, brown-toned pencil, and draw a new crease line from the top of the lid across the eye down to the corner of the lashes. Smudge with a cotton swab. Go over this line with a shadow that's in the same color family, and blend. Using a slightly darker pencil, draw a line along the base of the lashes. Bring this line up and out at the corners to the new crease line. Once again, smudge with a cotton swab. The sweep shadow across the lid, and apply mascara to your lashes. (*Teen*, February 1994)

I was thinking of getting an eyeliner tattoo. Is it harmful? Amy

Hello? Is anybody home? Why on earth would you want to have permanent makeup on your face? First of all, styles change, and one year down the road you will surely regret that you have an indelible line on your eye. Not to mention the dangers involved. Using a needle in such a delicate area can't be safe. Who knows if you'd have a weird reaction to the ink, or get an eye infection or something? Need I go on? If you want to look like you have eyeliner on, why not use a little? Apply an eye pencil close to the bottom, then add a coat of mascara. Won't it be nice to be able to take it off when you want to? (*Sassy*, July 1994)

As in its editorial advice about boys, *Sassy* presents readers with a much more critical stance towards the traditional pursuits of femininity than the other titles. It is significant, therefore, to learn that *Sassy* is not only the least popular teenzine among girls in this study, but that it received the greatest proportion of negative assessments by our readers. We consider this finding at greater length in chapter 8.

Because an important goal of teenzines is to 'know guys better,' it is not surprising that men's point of view is promoted as a value. However, it may be surprising to learn that not all information about guys' culture and preferences is associated with the immediate goal of 'getting a boyfriend' or 'having a romance,' in the way we might expect. For example, messages about boys' behaviours are also framed as criticism about boys or about patriarchal standards:

Oh, anyone with a hefty bra size is automatically a floozy now, Right? God, I'm so tired of these restrictive stereotypes – especially when it's girls doing it to each other. Yeah, maybe some guys get turned on by big breasts ... How sadly misguided. (*Sassy*, June 1994; answered by 'Kate')

The above example from *Sassy* is interesting because it espouses feminist values and shows how discussion of guys does not necessarily present boys as the object of romantic interest. However, the blatant feminism of this example is also an exception. While the teenzine titles in this study contain (limited) discussion of women's issues, such as gender discrimination, violence against women, or abortion, the use of male editors on advice pages allows teenzines to be critical of boy's behaviours without giving the appearance of 'male bashing':

A closer look, however, should clue you in. This guy is enjoying the fact that you're interested in him. He's not considering your feelings when he's flirting with you. He's enjoying an ego boost at your expense. Hard as it may be, you're going to have to see this guy for who he really is. It won't be easy, but set your sights on someone else. (*Teen*, August 1993; answered by 'Jack')

Even when teenzine discourse contains elements of feminism, as shown here a feminist Subject position is not necessarily constructed for female readers.[3] In part, this is because a female reader will be less likely to assume the position of the speaking Subject of male-authored discourse; in part, it is because feminism is overshadowed by male approval and the value given to having a boyfriend. Here, as elsewhere, readers are advised to 'get rid of problem boys' as a strategy that enables them to look for 'someone else.' Although male points of view and patriarchal values might be questioned by readers, they are seldom given critical treatment in teenzine discourse. Similarly, although *Seventeen* and *YM* encourage readers to 'do what's right for *you*' and 'assert your own needs and desires,' the socially approved femininity of teenzines is linked to non-feminist values: the importance of physical beauty and male authority or approval. While editors may explicitly encourage girls to accept their feelings as valid and to feel good about themselves, *feeling* good is implicitly linked to *looking* good and to having a boyfriend. This connection reappears in girls' accounts of their everyday life at school in chapter 7.

In summary, this section highlights how teenzine advice constructs a reading Subject by addressing readers as unique and valued individuals. However, we have also seen that this process is fraught with difficulties. Readers are told to 'accept yourself,' yet beautification is a primary goal, setting standards that are not achievable by all readers; they are told to put their own needs first, yet they are also told that a girl needs a boyfriend. In short, while readers are addressed as unique and valuable individuals, approval comes through the pursuit of goals and values which conform to traditional norms of femininity. As we shall see in chapter 7, the need for approval is an overriding concern in girls' accounts of everyday life at school. For most girls in this study, it places sharp restrictions on their search for individuality as a dominant theme in teenzine discourse.

As shown through the content analysis here and by others, the messages in women's magazines are neither coherent nor unambiguous; in fact, individual messages often contradict each other. Given that readers pick and choose their way through these texts, is it possible that they merely choose 'good' messages – such as 'assert your own needs' and 'do what's right for *you*' – and reject the 'bad' ones – such as the importance of 'looking good' and 'having a boyfriend'? More centrally, do these types of contradictions encourage readers to question the constructedness of teenzine discourse? These questions are important in considering the impact of teenzine reading and the potential effectiveness of programs of media literacy. What I suggest here is that, while these types of reading are certainly *possible*, they are not likely to be the dominant effect of teenzine reading, for two reasons. One reason will be found when we examine girls' accounts of everyday life at school in chapter 7. The other reason comes from closer inspection of the readings which advice texts invite. In the remainder of this chapter we explore how advice columns invite a taken-for-granted story of adolescence that promotes traditional femininity and all the contradictions which this femininity embodies.

Beauty, Boys, and the Body: What's a Girl to Do?

In this chapter we have seen that teenzine advice concerns three topics: beauty, boys, and the body. While these topics also dominate other editorial texts, in advice format these topics appear to be raised by a reader. This discursive framing is important because it evokes the sense of intimacy and of adolescent community that encourages girls to claim that these texts are 'realistic.' In this section we explore in detail how this framing occurs and how it encourages the disciplined reading that constructs dominant definitions of femininity. As before, here we emphasize the text as constructing a unified message and posit a coherent reading Subject; later, we explore lived Subject-ivity as a much less stable process.

While attributes of authorship to 'a reader' evokes the sense of community, this feeling is also facilitated by the question-and-answer format of advice texts. Typically, the question is placed in a social location which could be 'anywhere.' No matter how specific an individual reader's question may be, it will not be presented in terms of the peculiarity of her individual existence, but rather her gendered membership in the social world of adolescence. This membership is not constructed through use of the third person 'we,' however. In fact, the use of the empty signifier 'we' – which would provide entrée to the collective world of women – is conspicuously absent in teenzine texts. Rather, the discursive opening which is created for the reader occurs through the use of the first-person singular, 'I.' As an 'eye' created for the reader to view the social world of adolescence, this positioning has the paradoxical effect of transforming questions about membership in 'the social' into questions about 'personal relations.' Consider, for example, these two seemingly different problems:

I'm fifteen and I've been going out with a twenty-two-year-old guy for three weeks. My friends say there is only one reason someone his age would be interested in a fifteen-year-old: sex. Do you think they're right? (*YM*, July 1994)

I have a lot of male friends, so when I meet guys it's natural for me to be friendly and treat them just like anyone else. Unfortunately, a lot of them have been confusing this with a sexual advance. How can I make it clear that I'm only interested in them as human beings? K.C. (*Sassy*, July 1994)

These two examples are interesting because although they at first appear to raise two different types of problems, both problems arise because of a (heterosexist) culture that sexualizes gender relations. In both cases, the reader has a problem because her behaviour and expectations do not follow cultural norms. In the first case a fifteen-year-old reader interprets her relationship with a twenty-two-year-old as 'romantic,' about love rather than sex; in the second, a reader interprets her interaction with boys as appropriate for 'friendship' rather than sexual encounters. Two specific scenarios have been constructed where the (hypothetical) reader is uncertain about her situation; while *she* does not define her current situation or expectations as based on sexual relations, *others* do. Her uncertainty thus arises because she has violated the expectations of others: that 'love' should be based on emotional, psychological compatibility, here reduced to age; and that an active expression of interest in boys amounts to a sexual invitation. Thus both questions are actually about problems which many girls can encounter because of cultural norms which sexualize relationships between girls and boys. Presented here through first-person narrative, they have become 'personal' problems.

It is not simply the question, however, that gives this social problem its personalized form. Reflecting the manner in which these questions are framed, answers are also presented as personal solutions:

He might be just after sex but there are other possibilities ... But even if his motives are pure, you might think twice about a relationship that's bound to have problems – seven years is a big age difference at this point in your life. Going out with a much older guy may force you to grow up too fast. And you probably won't hang out with your friends as much or do the things other people your age do ... Go out with other guys your own age too. Answered by Catherine Clifford

There is nothing wrong with the fact that you choose to ignore old myths that boys and girls can't just be friends ... If, in the future, you meet a boy you think is boss, but you just want to be friends, tell him. Answered by Jeff McDonald

These two answers are interesting because in one case (taken from *Sassy*) the reader is advised to go against 'old myths' which dictate that 'boys and girls can't just be friends.' However, like the advice to 'go out with guys your own age too,' it is the reader's behaviour that remains the focus of attention. Both readers are similarly advised to put their own needs ahead of those of men, but neither answer encourages readers to think critically about the gender dynamics which lie at the root of their problems with boys. As we shall see in chapter 7, this omission is important. While many girls told interviewers that dealing with boys was 'one of the hardest things about being a girl,' their concerns were framed within a school culture that valorizes the sexual double standard, racism, and violence. We will see that experiences at school can discourage readers from calling the constructedness of teenzine discourse into question; here we explore how advice columns frame topics of interest to girls in ways which close off the cultural, hence political, dimensions of girls' problems. In order to better understand how teenzine texts work in this way, we look in detail at the treatment of the three topics which dominate advice pages: beauty, boys, and the body. In the following we explore the discursive form of advice rather than simply its content in order to understand how the absence of the social, hence political, dimensions of adolescent problems is not simply a case of 'missing' information.

I'm too embarrassed to go barefoot!

We saw above that the pursuit of beauty is a mandate of adolescent magazines, appearing as both a desirable goal and a positive value. As in the case of the photographic cropping used in advertising (see Millum 1975), the female body is fragmented into discrete, isolated parts, each requiring specialized attention. Here attention is directed to readers' feet.

> Dear Beauty Editor,
>
> The soles of my feet are hard and callused, and I'm embarrassed to wear sandals or go barefoot. Any suggestions? M.R., Pensacola, Fla.
>
> To get your feet in shape for spring, follow these simple steps: 1) Soak feet in warm water for 10 minutes; 2) Pat dry feet with a towel; 3) To smooth calluses away, gently rub rough areas with a pumice stone. Another option? Try a pumice scrub, such as Naturistics Mandarin Pumice Scrub. With fingertips, massage the scrub into rough skin using circular motions. Rinse off thoroughly. (*Teen*, May 1994)

At first glance, this question may not appear to address a matter which deserves extended commentary. However, this straightforward and innocuous appearance is what makes this text worthy of our attention. While the bottom of one's foot may hardly seem to qualify as a serious problem, this reader is too embarrassed for her feet to be seen in public. Because feet represent our means of locomotion, figuratively speaking this question can be decoded in terms of women's autonomy. Readers are not likely to decode this text so figuratively, however. Here we read the literal message of this text to be that no feminine body part escapes public assessment. As a specific case in point, the reader is identified as 'M.R.' who lives in Pensacola, Florida. No further details about the reader's identity are provided. We do not know her age, weight, hair colour, ethnicity, skin type, or other characteristics which are usually the focus of attention in beauty columns. One possible reason for this lack of detail is that this type of problem – embarrassment because of hard, callused feet – is a problem for all women, not just specific types of women, or even just women in Pensacola, Florida. Identification with the reader who needs a remedy for 'embarrassing feet' is facilitated by use of the first-person singular '*I'm* too embarrassed.' Given the obvious urgency of the situation, the reader is given immediate, practical advice.

As for the reader with embarrassing feet, the identity of the editor remains anonymous; in fact, we have no hint of first-person dialogue in her reply. Further, advice is given in an imperative form 'To get your feet in shape, ... follow these simple steps.' The reader is not reassured that her feet are normal or advised that she should do something other than worry about the condition of her feet. Instead, three 'simple' actions are provided. Included in these actions is the use of a commercial product, Naturistics Mandarin Pumice Scrub. While the absence of pronouns gives this message a terse and seemingly value-free message, presented by an expert as three easy steps, we recognize it as an advertorial, a hidden form of advertisement. While the actual product is not pictured, the words 'naturistics' and 'mandarin' conjure up a fragrant product which is environmentally friendly.[4] The quest for beauty mandated here appears natural. The problem has been framed in terms of body parts, and the solution in terms of a natural-sounding product. What is hidden is the nature of social embarrassment for women to reveal feet which have calluses – a physical condition historically associated with the hard work of manual labour.

This advertorial is interesting in that younger readers of *Teen* may not be familiar with the use of 'pumice stones' or a 'pumice scrub.' However, the reader need not be embarrassed by her ignorance of such womanly knowledge; this text instructs young readers about the use of these beauty products. The directions are clear and specific. Readers are told to massage 'with fingertips' using 'circular motions' and reminded to 'rinse thoroughly.' The ease of such instructions implies that anyone *can* (hence everyone *should*) have feet which are 'in shape for spring.'

Overall, the types of beauty questions are remarkably similar from magazine to magazine. More than other questions, beauty problems are given urgency through the word 'help!':

I'm African-American and have long hair. I use a curling iron almost every day. Lately, I've been noticing that my hair isn't as shiny as it used to be. Help! (*Teen*, July 1994)

Help! When I use a conditioner my locks go totally limp. But if I don't use it, I can't get a comb through my hair. Any tips? (*Seventeen*, November 1995)

Dear Elaine,
I have an interview with a modeling agency soon, and I don't know what to wear. Help!
Lorena, Rochester Hills, MI (*YM*, August 1994)

These examples are interesting because they raise 'problems' which again reinforce a cultural norm, in this case that of feminine beautification. While the problems raised stem from the universality of this norm, here it is taken for granted; the need for beautification does not require explanation because readers already understand it. Unlike the relationship question discussed below, there is no uncertainty about societal expectations. In fact, its currency is witnessed by the African-American girl who wants long, smooth hair; for her, a specific standard of beautification – a Caucasian standard – is the cause of her problem. However, this standard is not the 'cause' of her questioning. As in the other questions, her appeal for 'help' is not an appeal for escape from restrictive cultural norms, but it gives discursive urgency to her pursuit of feminine beauty. This urgency closes off discursive space for beauty norms themselves to be a topic of discussion.

Will I ever get a boyfriend?

In table 1.3 we saw that, with the exception of *Teen*, topics concerning boys were the most frequently coded theme of advice pages. Despite some variation in emphasis among titles, advice about boys is framed in terms of three general topics: *heterosexual pairing*, discussed as how to get a guy to notice or like you (dominant in *Teen* and *YM*); *(hetero)sexual relations*, discussed as advice about sexual activities with boys (dominant in *Seventeen*);[5] and *boys' culture*, discussed in terms of boys' interests and experiences, what boys like or dislike about girls' appearance or behaviour (dominant in *Sassy*). These values are tabulated in Appendix B. Here we analyse advice to readers about 'getting guys to notice or like you.'

Dear Cathi,

Will I ever get a boyfriend?
I'm sixteen and I've never had a boyfriend or even kissed anyone. I'm not really ugly or anything, and I have an okay personality – I'm outgoing, funny (I try to be, anyway), and not stuck up.

My best friend and I catch guys looking at us like they want to talk, but they never do ... All I know is, if I don't kiss someone this year I'll kill myself! Why don't I have a boyfriend? And how can I get one?

Well, I can tell you that killing yourself is definitely not the way to solve this problem, or any other one. (You were kidding when you said that, right? If not, talk to an adult you trust or a counselor *right away*.) I can also tell you that your question – how can I get a boyfriend? – is the most common one I receive for this column.

There's no magic formula for falling in love or getting a boyfriend, but here are a few thoughts that might help. 1) It's not something you can control ... 2) Sometimes the more you look for love the more it eludes you ... 3) Things are just as rough for the guys ... 4) Changing yourself to get a boyfriend is bad news, especially if it involves the three D's: drinking, drugs, dressing sleazily ... 5) Just because you don't have a boyfriend doesn't mean you can't have boy *friends* ...
(*Seventeen*, September 1993)

Many commentators have already pointed out that 'getting a man' is a dominant theme in women's commercial culture. Reading the text quoted above, we are likely to arrive at this dominant theme of heterosexual romance as the path to a (normal) girl's success and happiness. Through close reading, we can see that the normative prescription of heterosexuality arises through three messages which act as assumptions rather than assertions of magazine discourse.

Similar to the message about beautification, the first assumption encoded in this text is the universality of heterosexual desire. Universality is already suggested by the reader, who refers to 'my best friend and I.' This reference to a friend makes it clear that the reader is not the only sixteen-year-old without a boyfriend. This question reassures other readers finding themselves in a similar situation that they are not alone. More importantly, however, the state of being without a boyfriend is identified here as a 'problem,' such an urgent problem, in fact, that this reader claims 'I'll kill myself.' Stated as a problem, it becomes self-evident that the reader *wants* a boyfriend. The idea of wanting a boyfriend becomes excluded from the framework of dealing with this reader's 'problem.' Again, she is not the only sixteen-year-old who wants a boyfriend. Her best friend also wants a boyfriend as well, and Cathi claims that 'your question – how can I get a boyfriend? – is the most common one I receive for this column.' The second assumption gives us the reason why all normal teenage girls would want a boyfriend.

Having established the universal nature of heterosexual desire, the reader can already anticipate the second message, articulated by Cathi, that this desire is natural. In fact, she claims that 'it's not something that you can control' because 'for the most part, love's about chemistry, timing and luck'; 'if the chemistry's there, it's there; if it's not, you can't force it.' The dialogue has already shifted from the first person, 'I' who has 'the problem' to second person, 'you.' While Cathi begins her reply in the first person, 'I can tell you' – which she repeats twice in the opening paragraph – the discourse shifts to 'you.' The discursive Subject offered by this text is the 'reader with a problem.' Despite use of the name 'Cathi' to give the answer a 'personal touch,' advice is provided in a neutral, authoritative tone which cannot be linked to identifiable characteristics of its author. We know that the reader is sixteen years old, 'outgoing, funny and not stuck-up.' In contrast, we are given no clues about Cathi's identity: the shift is from the personal and specific problem to its social and universal re-solution.

At a superficial level, it appears that Cathi provides information to reassure readers. For example, she points out that 'it happens for some people at fourteen and some at forty. So if you're blaming yourself for being alone or setting deadlines for having a boyfriend, you're being unfair to yourself and adding unnecessary pressure to your situation.' Here we note that Cathi equates the state of being without a boyfriend with 'being alone,' despite the statement by the reader that she has 'a best friend.' Because heterosexual love is natural, being without a man is being with no one; further, being alone is unnatural. In order for nature to play its role, the reader should 'relax. Be patient. And give yourself a break, okay?'

Further reassurance appears to be extended through Cathi's admonition for the reader to 'be herself.' This third message is important, because it appears to counteract the notion, suggested by the reader, that she must be doing something wrong. This reader begins by pointing to her 'normalcy': she is 'not really ugly or anything' and has an 'okay personality.' Again, love must be natural because the reader assumes that she is acting in a way which prevents her, an 'ordinary' girl, from having a boyfriend. In fact, the reader has already tried to actively change her behaviour; she has tried 'wearing sluttier clothes and even going for younger guys.' Given the failure of these efforts, she now asks Cathi whether she is doing 'something wrong.' It is interesting, then, that Cathi does not take this view. In fact, she suggests that 'sometimes the more you look for love, the more it eludes you. I suggest putting the energy you've thrown into boy-hunting into other, more productive things, stuff that will make you feel better about yourself rather than feeling like you "failed." For me, this means reading, working, seeing movies, renting blades and flying all over town, or just spending more time with friends.' It may appear, therefore, that Cathi is suggesting that it may indeed be okay to forget about boyfriends, pursue other interests, and even consider that 'because you don't have a boyfriend doesn't mean you can't have boy *friends*.' Along these lines Cathi suggests that the only thing which the reader is doing wrong is *not* being herself: 'Changing yourself to get a boyfriend is bad news, especially if it involves the three D's: drinking, drugs, and dressing sleazily ... don't risk your body, mind and self-respect.' However, lest this message appear to contradict previous assumptions that romance is the universal and natural desire of women, Cathi points out that, 'whatever *you* choose to do, remember that what's really important is feeling good about yourself, and once you do, guys are more likely to be attracted to you ... One last thought: Love can come when you least expect it, and it usually shows up just about when you stop looking.' This shift away from an emphasis on getting boys to 'being yourself' is an important one. At first glance, it may appear to make the advice in this answer qualitatively different than the imperative tone of 'beauty tips.' However, on closer inspection we can see that this is not the case. While the first two assumptions are framed as general, social principles, the third message moves the discourse back from the general, natural world of heterosexual attachment to the reader without a boyfriend: from the world out there to *you*, the reader. Personal 'genuineness,' rather than acting as reassurance, now becomes an issue when any anxiety is raised by the situation of being without a boyfriend. A genuine person would do stuff to feel good about herself and be more relaxed around boys. Because boys are more likely to be attracted to this kind of person, a genuine person would not have the problem of no boyfriend. This theme of being your *genuine* self is reinforced by the message that the reader should not do things like drink or dress in a sleazy way to attract boys: 'Even if this stuff does get you a guy for a while, it won't be the guy you have in mind.' Thus genuine people are the people most likely to find 'true love,' the importance of which is the dominant theme of the entire text.

In conclusion, textual analysis helps us to understand how a dominant reading of the text works to reinforce traditional femininity even while appearing, on the surface, to encourage young readers to 'do more productive things than boy-hunting,' to 'feel good about themselves' and to avoid the unnecessary pressure of self-blame. Here self-esteem is tied to successful heterosexual relationships: while readers may be attracted to individual messages about feeling good and being themselves, the dominant message is that heterosexual love is the true path to women's happiness; that being without a man is being alone. While content analysis also reveals messages to the reader to 'accept herself,' 'assert her own needs and desires' and 'do what's right for *you*,' here we see how the same text emphasizes that a genuine woman always has a man. The disciplined reader of this text accepts the heterosexism of dominant femininity as an avenue for both self-expression and self-esteem.

What is the morning-after pill?

While preoccupation with make-up, hair, and other beauty practices dominates the advice pages of *Teen*, questions about the body – more specifically, the female body – were the second most frequent category of questions in *YM*, *Seventeen*, and *Sassy*. In these three titles, about one-quarter of questions concerned body topics, which included questions about healthy skin and hair, as well as questions about general health. Surprisingly few questions about contraception and the prevention of sexually transmitted diseases appear in advice pages. While these topics are often covered in informative feature articles, we shall see below that the format of the text may be of more consequence than the provision of information itself. In order to see how the framing of advice about contraception works, here we explore a typical question about birth control, taken from *YM*.

> **What is the morning-after pill?**
>
> I've heard about a pill you take the day after you've had sex so that you don't get pregnant. What is it? Where can I get it?
>
> 'The "morning after" pill is an emergency backup to prevent pregnancy in case you "forgot" to use birth control, or a condom slips or breaks, or your diaphragm is dislodged, or in cases of rape or incest,' says Hakim Elahi, M.D., medical director of Planned Parenthood of New York City. The method is about 98 to 100 percent effective if used correctly, under a health-care provider's supervision. The 'morning after' pill is actually a series of high-dosage, specially prescribed birth-control pills. Two pills must be taken no later than 72 hours after unprotected intercourse (within 12 to 24 hours is better). The pills work by changing the lining of the uterus, so a fertilized egg can't attach to it, says Dr. Elahi. Side effects, which are usually minimal and short-term, include nausea, breast tenderness and a delayed period. These pills are available through a doctor at many college health services and at Planned Parenthood clinics. Cost: $50 for an exam plus up to $25 for the pills. (*YM*, July 1993)

This question is a good contrast to the problem of not having a boyfriend. While the discussion about boyfriends suggested that falling in love is a result of body 'chemistry' and that heterosexual romance is a universal desire of readers, the missing context of this discussion is the problem of teenage pregnancy. By now researchers have shown that most unwanted pregnancies among teenagers are a consequence of failing to use contraception, not lack of information about pregnancy and contraception. The above example is particularly relevant, therefore, for the discussion in the concluding section of this chapter. This text is also interesting because it appears to be value-free. This appearance arises because of the clinical nature of the information provided and also because personal pronouns are absent from the answer; in fact, the discussion shifts from the reader, indicated by the use of the first person, 'I,' to a discussion of 'it,' 'the pill,' which is a 'thing.'

To begin, this discussion opens with a rather straightforward question. The reader has 'heard' about the morning-after pill and wants to know 'What is it?' and 'Where can I get it?' No other information is given about this specific reader: we are given no identifying initials or suggestions about where she lives. Ostensibly, she is interested in something she 'heard' about. However, the nature of her questions might lead us to suspect that she is sexually active; otherwise, why would she ask 'Where can I get it?' From this question we might further assume that the hypothetical reader is engaged in unprotected sexual intercourse, on a regular basis. Knowing where to get the pill, which needs to be taken 'no later than 72 hours after unprotected intercourse' will help her only in the future. Research on teenage pregnancy suggests that a number of readers may relate to the problem addressed here.

In contrast to the anonymity of the reader, the editor is a specific and identifiable person. Her photo is provided and her name, 'Kathryn Keller,' appears on the top of the column: she is white and appears to be in her thirties. However, the voice of Kathryn Keller does not dominate the text, which begins with factual information: the ways in which unprotected sex occurs are given, the effectiveness of the morning-after pill is described, as well as side effects and instructions on how to get it. Here the authority of information comes from a health-care professional, Dr Hakim Elahi, the medical director of Planned Parenthood in New York.

Like the questions discussed above, this problem is given urgency. Dr Elahi refers to the pill as an 'emergency' back-up; however, anxiety raised by the urgency of the problem is eased by learning that the pill is 'about 98 to 100 percent effective.' Importantly, these results are guaranteed only if the pill is used 'under a health-care provider's supervision': unlike the two problems above, the solution to 'unprotected intercourse' does not lie directly within reach of the typical teenage girl. Here the solution lies in the hands of 'health-care providers,' in this case the male director of Planned Parenthood: he is an authority on women's sexuality and the female body, he can provide a solution to unwanted pregnancy that is more effective than the reader's 'failed' efforts. Furthermore, most of the information which Kathryn Keller, an adult woman, provides also seems to come from him. In this way, although men are included in this discourse about unwanted pregnancy they are associated with the solution rather than the problem.

In this case the solution to the problem of unprotected intercourse is a technical one: the 'morning-after pill.' The cost of obtaining the pill is included, so that the reader is constructed as a potential consumer of Planned Parenthood's services. No advice is given for readers who may not be able to afford $75 for these services. This answer is not unlike the advertorial above: it provides information about a product as well as how to use it. This effect is assisted, in part, by a shift from the second-person pronoun, 'you' used in the introductory sentence but not repeated elsewhere. The text shifts from addressing 'you' to a discussion of the pill and how the pill works. The answer tells us more about the morning-after pill than it does about adolescent sexual life.

As in the other problems discussed above, the social context of unwanted pregnancy is lost, although here it is alluded to. The reader may be someone who has forgotten to use contraception, or she may be someone who was raped or whose contraception failed. Significantly, the word 'forgot' is placed in quotation marks by editors, suggesting that it is a euphemism. The researcher familiar with the social context of teenage pregnancy might suspect that the hypothetical reader did not simply forget her contraception, but that she does not use contraception. Intercourse may not have been 'planned' because you cannot plan to 'fall in love' – above we can see that the reader might have already been told elsewhere in her magazines that love is 'not something you can control' and that it 'can come when you least expect it.' Furthermore, true love only comes when a girl is 'genuine' and acts herself; unless a reader defines herself as sexually active – an identity which many girls discuss as problematic in chapter 7 – planning to have intercourse does not allow her to 'be herself.' However, the problem is not simply that the reader receives contradictory messages about heterosexual romance, but that this text on unprotected intercourse does not invite construction of a Subject in control of her situation.

In summary, this reading suggests that magazine discourse surrounding contraception which is framed in 'value-neutral,' clinical terms does not construct the reader as a knower. In the previous example we saw that 'having no boy friend,' for example, discursively addresses readers in ways which invite personal identification with the hypothetical girl with this problem. This identification is not encouraged by the frank and impersonal discussion of dealing with the emergency situation of unprotected intercourse. Absent here is editorial attention to self-doubt, as was given to the reader who worries about not having a boyfriend, even though we may expect that the topic of unwanted pregnancy is anxiety-provoking for readers. Also conspicuously absent is reassurance that the problem of unwanted pregnancy is shared by others, and that questions about birth control and contraception are 'common.' In fact, girls who might have the problem of unprotected intercourse have been constructed as 'victims' of rape or incest. The reader who simply did not use contraception for other reasons thus falls outside the bounds of normalcy established here: she is a deviant case. What this researcher reading suggests is that, despite the frankness with which contraception is discussed in contemporary teenzines, the contradictory nature of the Subject constructed actually contributes to the problem of adolescent pregnancy.[6] As tempting as it may be to connect these contradictions to the social problem of unwanted pregnancy, however, we cannot read this effect off the text alone. Regrettably, while questions on the body were important motivations for magazine reading among the girls in this study, very little discussion about sexual activities appears in interview transcripts on this aspect of adolescent magazines. This absence reflects the research context, discussed in chapter 3: interviewers were instructed to avoid sensitive topics such as sexual activity. While the girls were obviously comfortable talking about 'getting ready for school' and the nature of interpersonal relationships, the opportunity to discuss sexual practices was not structured into the interview. A further possibility, however, which requires further research is that the absence of discussion on contraception use reflects the fact that teenzine discourse places the reader who actively uses contraception outside the bounds of 'normal' feminine behaviour (see Holland et al. 1996). Future research which explores what adolescent girls actually 'learn' from teenzine texts providing 'sex education' is required.

Question-and-Answer as Self-Discovery

In chapter 4 we saw that, unlike adult cultural critics, teenage readers often assign truth status to the text. It is important for us to understand how social texts constitute 'reality' for their readers because this understanding will tell us how social texts work as power. To begin, therefore, we need to ask *which* texts girls view as addressing the reality of their everyday lives, and how texts, through their reading, construct the reality of adolescence in ways which resonate with traditional patriarchal definitions. In chapter 5 girls identified the question-and-answer texts typically found on problem pages as a favourite source of reading pleasure; they directly link this pleasure to the realism attributed these texts. In this chapter we explored how texts work in this way, limiting analysis to the immediate context of their reading. Here two types of researcher readings were employed. In order to map the discursive context of reading, content analysis was employed to identify topics, behavioural goals, and attitudinal values. This mapping was not meant to imply that all parts of magazines are given equal attention. As interview transcripts illustrate, teenzines are typically encountered as discrete 'moments' of text. Not all readers scan their magazines from cover to cover, although most of the thirteen- to sixteen-year-olds give extended attention to advice pages. Because readers thus encounter teenzine messages as discrete 'bytes' of texts, it is necessary to begin our study of texts as isolated 'moments' of meaning-making. The moments examined here correspond to those favoured by adolescent readers.

While ostensibly about 'objects' of consumption, teenzine messages concern social activities, personal practices, individual attitudes and values. If we look at the overall content of advice pages, we can identify messages which direct girls to look attractive, value their relationships with boys, and take care of themselves. Directing girls to these goals means that traditional femininity is promoted, despite messages which also tell girls to do what's right for them as unique individuals. However, in identifying these types of messages we have not argued here that teenzines simply prescribe behaviours for readers to follow. Rather, the effects of teenzine messages follow from their engagement of readers in the construction of a reality which resonates with the dominant social order. It is the reality of adolescence evoked by teenzine discourse which encourages readers to think and behave in specific ways. This reality is a consequence of both the manner of reading employed by girls and a textual format which invites closure in specific ways. The specific textual format studied in this chapter is the question-and-answer format of the problem pages. Here we have seen how this format invites readers to identify with textual messages through membership in the world of teenage girls. We have also seen that this invitation depoliticizes teenaged readers' everyday problems.

Depoliticization occurs through forms of address which reassure the reader that her question is natural because it is asked by other girls. It also occurs through solutions framed as medical or scientific advice. In this way, the distinction between problems associated with puberty – as a process of physical and psychological maturity – and adolescence – as the social and personal experience of that process – is blurred. The social aspects of adolescence are thus mystified through a disappearance of the socially constructed nature of readers' everyday problems of being a girl. Because these problems stem from the patriarchal nature of our culture, promoting a male point of view on adolescent problems reassures readers that editorial solutions will secure male approval, further obscuring the nature of girls' 'personal' problems. We will see in chapter 7 that becoming a woman in a patriarchal culture is fraught with contradictions and anxieties. We will also see that girls can be well aware that their anxieties are related to the patriarchal context of 'being a girl.' It is interesting, therefore, that the pursuit of traditional femininity is so pleasurable when connected to magazine reading, an activity girls eagerly pursue in their 'leisure' hours. In this chapter we have identified textual factors which make Subject-ivity as an effect of reading a pleasurable experience for many girls. In chapter 7 we explore sociocultural factors which enhance the attraction of teenzine texts.

In this study girls identify 'questions and answers' as their favourite reading. While this format is most obvious on problem pages, it is important to note how extensively questions and answers are employed in teenzine texts in total. Perhaps acknowledging its popularity among readers, advertisers frequently employ question-and-answer format, in the case of sixteen-year-old Kelsey successfully:

I like these ads actually. They are kind of appealing in some ways. I don't know what it is about them, but they're either – I guess it's the questions on top of her. 'Are there limits?' Not for some women.' That kind of question. And sometimes they have 'Is it natural?' You know, I guess.

[Interviewer:] Why do you like that?
I don't know. It's just something about it that kind of zones me into it. I guess it's quite a big advertising campaign or whatever you want to call it. But it works. I have a few things that are Maybelline thanks to these ads. (Sixteen-year-old Kelsea reading Maybelline mascara ad)

A question-and-answer format is more commonly employed by editors, however. For example, the titles of feature articles are typically posed as a 'question' which the editor answers at length. These topics follow much of what we have already studied in advice columns. The covers of *Teen*, for example, lure readers with bold titles – 'Want him to notice you?' or 'No guy? Find out why,' – while *Seventeen* invites readers to find out about themselves by asking 'Do you have a big mouth?' or 'Are you in love?' The appeal of this discursive format accounts for the popularity of quizzes, ranked as the second most favourite reading in this study: about 60 per cent of readers between thirteen and sixteen years of age read quizzes while, as is the case for advice columns, only about one-third of seventeen-year-olds read these texts.

Quizzes are interesting in that they share the discursive form of advice columns. However, while topics are posed as questions, in quizzes the answer is open for negotiation. In *YM*, for example, this negotiation takes place in a regular column entitled 'The Inner You.' As a form of self-discovery, quizzes allow the reader to assess herself:

Are you an emotional mess? (*YM*, November 1993)
Are you a drag? (*YM*, August 1993)
Could you be a star? (*YM*, May 1994)
Are you a drama queen? (*YM*, July 1994)
Are you a great date? (*YM*, July 1993)
What kind of girlfriend are you? (*Seventeen*, November 1995)

They also help the reader assess her knowledge of the skills required for successful femininity, such as:

Beauty questions – Do you know the answers? (*Teen*, June 1993)
Is your hair-style right for you? (*Teen*, October 1993)
Which cleanser is right for you? (*YM*, September 1993)

The self-assessment implied by these types of open-ended questions carries over into other magazine text. For example, a fashion feature for swimwear in *YM*, May 1994, is titled 'Can you bare it?' In answer to this question, the reader's eye is drawn to attractive, slim models in skimpy beachwear. Notable in these types of texts is the repetitive appeal to the individualized reader. Readers are seldom, if ever, asked 'What do women want?' – a form of address that would give voice to women as a political collective. The construction of an individualized reader in this way is important because it directly invites the reader to compare herself to the norms of femininity constructed by the text. In chapter 7 we will see that, while such a comparison, in theory, can invite rejection of textual constructions, for many girls it calls extradiscursive constructions of Self into question.

In the same way that advice columns often give voice to a male point of view, articles framed as questions extend the assessments of girls to guys:

Would you date a girl your friends can't stand? (*YM*, July 1993)
What makes a girl irresistible? (*YM*, May 1994)
What makes you ask a girl to the prom? (*YM*, March 1994)

In these cases, not only are readers invited to compare themselves to discursive constructions, but this comparison is based on male standards of feminine behaviour. The open-endedness of this format not only obscures the coding of patriarchal values, but also acts to actively engage the reader:

I'd take a quiz like this – 'Is he serious about you?' [pointing out text in *YM*]. I always take the quizzes. I'll always do a quiz if it's like about boyfriends and love, and all that kind of thing. I'd take a quiz about it – just for the fun of it. That's why I like this magazines so much, because it always has quizzes in it [laughs]. (Sixteen-year-old Melissa)

This open-ended format invites engagement because the reader inserts herself into the text through self-assessment:

[Interviewer:] Why is *YM* better than the other ones?
There's more writing in it, I guess. It's got a lot of pop quizzes, like 'Are you too sensitive?' and then they'll have ten questions and then your results under 'a,' 'b' and 'c' – I think those are neat! (Fifteen-year-old Amber)

In these cases, the pleasure of teenzine reading takes the form of self-discovery:

Like I don't think if I wrote one of, like actually wrote out one of the quizzes my personality would change, but I would think inside of me how different I was, and stuff. I think it just helps [readers] think better about themselves, sometimes. (Sixteen-year-old Alyssa)

I love quizzes. They're something to do. Like even though you know, you could just read the three [items] and know what you are, but like you have to take the whole quiz. I'd like do the whole thing and then add it up down here [shows interviewer in *YM*] 'cause I always want to find one that says 'Are you a spazz?' 'Cause I just want to know if I'm a spazz. Like I've done every other quiz, but they don't have one that says 'Are you a spazz?' (Fourteen-year-old Kayla)

Unlike the problem pages, where answers are clearly stipulated, quizzes leave the Subject open to negotiation. The Subject constructed by the text emerges as the reader herself fills in the discursive space provided for her answers. However, the open nature of such text does not mean that discursive closure is not exercised by editors. For most quizzes, scores are rated and evaluated according to where they fall on a range of desirable outcomes. For example, in the quiz 'Are you a great date?' scores classify the reader according to whether she is a 'date disaster,' a 'first-rate date,' or a 'first-date failure.' The disaster date is chastised by the editor, Eileen Livers: 'Do you have to give your date such a hard time? Being overly demanding of the guy you're with can be a way of hiding your own insecurity. (You'll point out his flaws before he notices yours!) This is not healthy, says Kate M. Wachs, Ph.D., a psychologist ...' (*YM*, June/ July 1993). In contrast, the first-rate date is praised: 'You're warm, friendly and positive, three important qualities for a good date, according to Dr Wachs. And you don't analyse every move your date makes. Plus, you're into meeting lots of guys, so when Mr. Right comes along, you'll know enough about guys to recognize him.' The first-date failure is given instructions to improve her date-ability by 'being herself': 'Guys will ask you out once, but then they usually lose interest. Maybe that's because when you go on a date, you get so nervous. Relax, and remember that dating is supposed to be fun. Open up and let him know what you'd like to do ...'

In the final analysis, this quiz contains many of the elements which we saw in advice columns about 'getting guys to like you.' As in the advice texts examined in this chapter, here the reader's ability to be asked out by boys is linked to 'being yourself' for the purpose of finding 'Mr Right.' Omitted from this text is any questioning of dating itself or the fact that some boys date only girls who engage in sex, an issue discussed in chapter 7. Instead, readers are advised that girls with successful dates have 'important qualities,' while those who fail to be asked out for subsequent dates probably have psychological problems. As in advice columns, the reader's self-esteem is measured by her ability to please others, in this case boys. While the text offers the seeming pleasure of 'writing' Self, if the reader is to be rated as a 'successful' – hence 'normal' – person, this writing must fall within the narrow confines of the values promoted elsewhere in the magazine.

Self-discovery as an effect of teenzine reading differs from the notion that readers 'imitate' behaviours in the way implied by many critics of popular media. While imitation implies that the reader attempts to mould herself to an external other, self-discovery implies a genuineness because the Subject-ivity which is constructed is to be accepted by the reader as an expression of her 'true' Self. From this perspective, the self-discovery promoted by question-and-answer texts reveals the power of teenzine texts. It corresponds to Foucault's identification of the importance of self-scrutiny and the incessant production of self-knowledge about our thoughts, feelings, and fantasies in the operation of modern bio-power. As MacDonald notes, according to Foucault, 'the subject produces herself as a normalized subject whose actions and desires are increasingly knowable and predictable. This subject then becomes ever more available to be used and controlled, thus facilitating the connection between knowledge and power' (1991: 59). Thus Foucault's major contribution to theorizing the Subject is the identification of discourses which enjoin the Subject to participate in her own subjection.[7] *Girl Talk* extends his observation to those discourses promoting 'femininity' through the commercial texts of women's magazines. While the normative femininity discursively constructed in teenzine texts offers a reader pleasurable identification as 'a woman,' it incites a reader to 'know the truth of oneself,' producing a Subject-ivity constantly engaged in self-regulation and normalization.

7

Doing and Undoing: The Everyday
Experience of Subject-ivity

Although a time of drastic physiological change, the primary tasks of adolescence are psychosocial: to integrate the components of identity into a coherent whole as the basis for adult sense of Self. John Mitchell (1986: 15) lists these components of identity as including a sense of personal importance; continuity of experience; and solidarity with family, community, and society. He notes that the integration of these diverse elements into a coherent unity presents an enormous challenge to today's youth. Because teenagers are not valued as important by society and because they do not do much of importance in their everyday life, a sense of personal importance can be elusive. Further, everyday life for most teenagers is not characterized by continuity of experience, but rather by unexpected failures and disappointments. Finally, many adolescents do not have a sense of solidarity with their families or their community; Mitchell claims that, if anything, adolescents may harbour hostility towards these institutions (p. 15).

Mitchell's claims are supported by research which shows that Canadian teenagers experience significant strain in their relationships with their parents, and even with each other. This strain is especially pronounced with girls, who have lower self-esteem than boys. King and Coles (1992: 96) relate strain for girls to adjustment problems they experience in career aspirations, body image, and dealing with the traditional values associated with marriage and family (see also Holmes and Silverman 1992).[1] In her study of the experiences of being young and female, Mary Pipher (1994) links women's mental health to the ability for women to 'own' their experiences. She points out that, because our culture has been written from the standpoint of men, girls have no language or discourse through which to do this owning. As a consequence, the significance of teenzine discourse is not so much that it prescribes behaviours, which readers may or may not follow, but that it gives meaning to the experience of being adolescent. As we saw in chapters 5 and 6, teenzines discursively construct a speaking Subject who then can 'name' adolescent experiences and problems, employing definitions offered by commercialized culture. Importantly, Pipher (1994: 43) maintains that in real life girls can respond to the cultural mandate of traditional femininity in one of four ways: they can conform, withdraw, be depressed, or get angry. Whether girls feel depression or anger is a matter of attribution – those who blame themselves for failure feel depressed, while those who blame others feel angry. Generally, outward blame is directed towards parents. As a clinician Pipher is interested in the everyday dangers which accompany the transformation from a girl to a woman. Her study draws on the stories of girls she encounters in a clinical setting. In this chapter we examine the stories of the 'ordinary' girls recruited into this study, interviewed in a research setting. The purpose of this chapter is to read the everyday lives of the girls in our study against teenzine texts. Our task is to explore whether, and how, the everyday life of readers enhances the appeal of teenzines, thus encouraging young girls to 'name' their experiences and problems through the categories offered by these texts.

In the previous chapter we studied the construction of reading Subject-ivity through the transformation of textual information about femininity into practical knowledge about womanhood. We saw that the teenzine world of adolescence is narrowly defined in terms of looking good, having boyfriends, and being accepted by peers. We noted in chapter 6 that these personal pursuits are re-presented as universal interests, lifted out of their social and political context. In this chapter we identify everyday processes which encourage girls to take up these pursuits as the normal and desirable expression of a gendered Self. However, we will also see that girls' sense of Self is often in a state of flux. One of the striking themes which emerges from transcripts of girls' interviews is uncertainty, expressed during discussion of what it means to be a girl and to fit into school culture. In this chapter I read girls' stories of everyday life at school symptomatically, exploring the fault lines in these stories in order to reveal the constructedness of adolescent Subject-ivity as the search for a social Self. Here symptoms of adolescent femininity take the form of self-doubt, which can lead to anxiety – anxiety about looks, about being accepted by peers, and about societal expectations. This uncertainty renders adolescent Subject-ivity unstable, captured here in terms of the 'doing' and 'undoing' of the Subject. 'Doing' refers to those processes, such as getting ready for school and reading magazines, which facilitate girls' sense of individuality and of being a Subject in control. 'Undoing' refers to processes, such as worrying about looks and being labelled by others, which unsettle girls' emerging sense of Self and worth as social beings. While we can read this undoing politically as researchers, for many of the girls it is experienced as a loss of control. We will see that, while teenzines address this loss of control by offering to help girls feel secure about their feminine identity, everyday experience can call the constructedness of this femininity into question. Within this context, magazine reading is a contradictory process of Subject formation.

In this chapter contradictions do not arise from the teenzine messages discussed in chapter 5; rather, contradictions arise from the processes identified in chapter 6 which work to construct the boundaries of 'normal' teenage life. In this chapter we will see that the problem to be considered is not whether the teenage world constructed in magazines reflects the actual experiences and problems of actual readers. Rather, we will see that, while experience can encourage readers to call the constructed world of adolescence into question, reading teenzines 'against the grain' requires readers to place themselves outside cultural prescriptions at a time when they are searching for social acceptance. The question that is raised, therefore, concerns the ways in which the everyday, socially structured experiences of teenage life encourage girls to accept (or reject) the teenzine mandate to look good and win approval from boys. In this study, school culture reinforces the definitions of femininity and ways of being female offered by teenzine discourse. As we shall see, the importance of dress as a signal of belonging is a recurring theme in girls' interviews which suggests that, although school culture is a potential source of alternative definitions and knowledge of teenagerhood, it actively reinforces the patriarchal messages of commercial culture.

Because chapter 6 emphasized the formation of the Subject through reading, it analytically bracketed off other avenues through which girls gain a sense of Self. Sociologically, these avenues include the influence of significant others (such as family members, teachers, and friends) as well as other leisure pursuits (such as television, music, movies, and hobbies). In this chapter we explore the importance of peers, experienced through school culture. In the first section we examine how school culture bases acceptance, hence social membership, on particular forms of dress and self-presentation. The discussion presented here is (briefly) read against a tradition within sociology to romanticize the teenage emphasis on dress as resistance. In the second section we explore how school culture, as well as being a venue where social Self is formulated and consolidated, is also a source of 'undoing' of the social Self. This undoing occurs when girls 'get a reputation' through labels which gain currency from patriarchal standards of femininity. As in chapter 6, here we emphasize dominant readings of girls' conformity to school culture and acceptance of teenzine definitions. In chapter 8 we will explore stories of resistance for what they tell us about a feminist politics of culture. While the findings in this chapter are necessarily exploratory and require follow-up,[2] they help us locate commercial media such as teenzines in the everyday life of adolescent girls in order to better understand their impact. This exploration informs subsequent discussion in the conclusion.

The Same but Different: Getting Ready for School

Given the limited avenues of self-expression for adolescents in our culture, it is not surprising that clothes play an important role in school culture. This role is much more complex than I initially expected. Because interview schedules opened with discussion of getting ready for school and the daily practices which identify readers as women, as a researcher (but not as a feminist) I was somewhat disappointed that the girls, on the surface, appeared to be somewhat ambivalent about their everyday appearance. Over half of girls were wearing blue jeans, often with sweatshirts or loose-fitting tops, at the time of interview.[3] Among the girls who were not required to wear a school uniform, the vast majority mentioned 'jeans' as what they 'usually' wear to school (94 per cent) or as their 'favourite' thing to wear to school (76 per cent):

I love jeans. I *love* jeans. They are the most comfy things in the whole wide world ... I've got a close friend who got me into wearing men's jeans. I'm glad she did. [Interviewer:] Why?
Well, because the legs aren't as tapered as women's jeans, and I'm not crazy about tapered legs. And the pockets in the back are bigger, and – at least in Levi's. And the distance between the crotch and the waist is shorter, so I don't feel as though my waist is way up in the middle of my chest. That's why I like to wear men's jeans. (Sixteen-year-old Kelsey)

Moreover, many girls specified that their favourite clothes are baggy:

I like either straightlegged or pretty baggy jeans – not *too* baggy, but I like those. And maybe a blouse and a vest – I have this baggy kind of jogging vest from Club Monaco. [It's] sleeveless, [so] I like that under a blouse. I like vests. (Fifteen-year-old Kirsten)

The really big and baggy ones – I've got a couple of pairs of those, but my parents don't understand that most people – the reason lots of people wear them is because they're really comfortable. That's why I wear them. My mom goes 'Well, at least they're not skin tight' [laughs]. (Thirteen-year-old Brittany)

Does this mean that these girls have rejected the mandate of traditional femininity? Unfortunately, no. The ability to appear as if dress does not matter can actually signal that kids have dressed with a lot of care:

Some of my friends say they don't care what other people think, and this is what I find confusing because, uhm, they're basically grunge. They have pink, yellow, purple, neon hair and it's all in dreads and they have rings everywhere and none of their clothes match, but that in itself is a fashion statement. I mean, to some people that is looking good. So they might say 'Oh I don't care,' but when you dress yourself [like that] in the morning, the act of dressing yourself actually shows that you care what other people think. (Thirteen-year-old Stephanie)

As already suggested by Kelsey above, despite the *apparently* casual nature of girls' dress, the 'right' jeans for school require attention to detail. Danesi (1994: 80, 81) points out that, while blue jeans historically may not have been a 'fashion' item because of their origin as work clothes for blue-collar men, the meaning of jeans has changed dramatically during recent decades. Jeans represent the way in which the transgression of established fashion norms itself has become a 'fashion statement.' Moreover, they symbolize the diffusion of fashion across all socio-economic classes while now maintaining new social gradations through details such as brand of jeans, quality of fabric, cut of leg, and so on. In short, while jeans may not be a traditional fashion item for women, their contemporary importance means that they are central to a carefully planned school wardrobe. For example, both fifteen-year-old Nicole and seventeen-year-old Mary usually just wear 'jeans and a top, probably five or six days a week I wear jeans.' However, like many other girls they also indicated:

I have this thing where I don't like wearing two things in the same week. So I think about [clothes for school] at the beginning of the week. Like 'This day I'll wear *this*' – unless I don't feel like it that day. (Mary)

I prepare clothes the night before already or I'm thinking while I'm sleeping because I usually don't have time in the morning because I can't try things on first to see if they look good. So I always prepare the night before. (Nicole)

In order to not wear the same thing too often, Mary coordinates her entire wardrobe according to things that 'mix and match':

I always go for basic things. Almost everything I have is totally plain or can go with everything else, 'cause that makes it easy. I guess I have my general style of what I like, so I get all my clothes kind of really basic to *that* [style] and then I'll pick like a few things that are totally different, so that I've got some fun stuff.

Like many other girls, Mary's coordination extends to her make-up:

I match my lipstick usually to what I'm wearing [laughs]. Like I know that I have a green outfit [so] I'll wear this lipstick, and like that one goes with my plums, and kind of like that.

As in the case of many other girls, achieving the 'right' look for school can be a lot of 'work.' This work includes earning money which enables girls to buy things that they 'want.' In this study, most of the girls earned money through baby-sitting, tutoring, office work, or waitressing. Having their own money is important because, while parents usually pay for clothes that the girls *need*, most of the girls have to pay for things which they do not need, but which they *want*:

My mom buys like dress shoes – like my Doc Marten boots, she would never have bought me them. I had to buy them on my own. I don't know, she buys me clothes that she thinks I *need*, where I buy clothes I just want. (Sixteen-year-old Alyssa)

My mom buys me like the *necessities*. Like if I have enough jeans, enough sweaters, shirts and nice things or whatever and then I want something extra, I have to pay for it, but if I don't have enough jeans or something we'll go together and buy another pair. (Fifteen-year-old Tiffany)

It depends if I need it or not. Like, if they [parents] think I need a pair of jeans they'll buy me a pair of jeans. But if *I* think I need a pair of jeans and they don't, then I'll have to pay for it. Or they might throw in *some* money – depending. Especially if it's expensive I'll have to throw in some money. (Fifteen-year-old Kirsten)

The work of planning a wardrobe also includes shopping:

Actually, yesterday was the last day of school, so we dressed up and I wore a dress to school – it was from Le Chateau. It was like a summer dress, and I wore a nice T-shirt underneath it, like not a T-shirt, but [a top]. It came down to my knees, and it had buttons down the front. It's just green with little flowers on it. I wore sandals and I wore my hair straight down, it was flowing, just natural. Like I went shopping and just bought something for the occasion. I had it all ready that day and I knew how I was going to do my make-up and my hair. (Fourteen-year-old Jennifer)

Whereas Fiske portrays shopping as guerrilla warfare, most of the girls shopped for things which conform to school norms. For example, Jennifer bought the dress she described (see above) while shopping with three of her friends who agreed to dress more-or-less the same. Against the view of shopping as resistance to the mass market, seventeen-year-old Allison prepares for a shopping spree through magazine 'research':

Usually if I'm going to Seattle or on a [shopping] trip I will usually, or my mother will, buy like piles [of] every single fashion magazine possible from stores and bring them home. She'll go through them and I'll go through them after her. I'll tick pages of outfits that I like and usually I'll try to find – I mean I've never actually, except for once – once I actually went and found something in a magazine because I liked it so much. It was a pair of velvet pants and I got them exactly, I copied the *exact* outfit out of the magazine, but I've only ever done that once. Usually it's the *idea* that matters. Because I have that idea in my mind, I'll be looking for that idea in the store and I'll usually find it. Yeah, it's almost subconscious that I don't really realize that I'm doing that.

We saw in chapter 5, however, that Allison is not typical of the girls in this study. Most of the girls do not use magazines as the basis for choosing their clothes. In part this is because they claim that 'you could never find the stuff anyways,' which implies, of course, that they *have* looked for styles from magazines:

I'll look at a magazine and say, just kind of think to myself 'Oh, I'd really like to have *this*,' you know – 'It would be really cool to have that kind of image.' But when it comes around to shopping I can't usually look for anything because the magazines we get are usually – like the stores don't actually carry the stuff shown in magazines, so it's kind of hard. (Seventeen-year-old Amy)

More typically, girls looked to their classmates rather than magazines for ideas what to wear:

Usually they're [magazine fashion] kind of things that nobody wears. Like I would wear them if everyone else did, but I'd feel kind of dumb wearing them when no one else does, 'cause they're usually kind of far-out things. (Fourteen-year-old Rachel)

Like, if I know what my friend's going to wear tomorrow and it's sexy – if she's wearing like a nice top that she looks really good in, then I don't want to come to school in like, sweat pants. Say Sara and I are together and she goes 'Yeah, I just bought this new top and I'm going to wear it tomorrow,' you can assume it's nice. (Fourteen-year-old Jennifer)

In Kelsey's case, copying friends meant that she might buy, but not necessarily wear, the same things:

Generally, I go along with what's in. I guess my friends help to influence me too, if they've got something that I like a lot, I'll get something similar to it, not exactly the same, but sometimes I'll just see something that I really like and I probably won't wear very often but I get it anyways. Well, a lot of people have been wearing clogs lately, so I went and bought myself a pair of clogs this summer. I've only worn them twice and I haven't worn them to school at all, so it's kind of pointless why I got them. And then a lot of people have been wearing those cameo chokers, and so I got one of those too, and I haven't worn it to school at all.

What these stories tell us is that the rejection of magazine fashion, described in chapter 6, is not a sign that these girls subsequently reject the mandate of fashion magazines to 'look good,' as we might suspect if we were to look at teenzine reading alone. Rather, girls reject magazine fashion because it does not match the 'reality' of everyday life at school:

Like all the clothes they wear [in teenzines] are just so, 'typical' almost. Like no one would wear most of the clothes that you see in magazines. They're so conservative and fancy, and like something that you could see people on television shows wearing, but no one really wears them in real life. (Fourteen-year-old Kayla)

I'm just looking at these things [showing interviewer a fashion page] and I'm like 'You're not going to catch me dead in one of these things!' It's for pale-skinned, blue-eyed, long wavy – it's for Niki Taylor [name of the model]. There's no way you're going to any high school in this country – unless she's a freak or likes surprising people, you're not going to find a pink mohair A-line dress on anybody! (Thirteen-year-old Stephanie)

Like other minority readers in this study, thirteen-year-old Stephanie rejects teenzine fashion, but not the teenzine mandate to 'look good':

There is a dance in December, it's pretty formal [I thought] this might help me, so I bought the magazine. And there were ruffled taffeta sequin dresses that cost thousands of dollars that were way beyond my range. It was nothing of how you could use your own wardrobe, how simple things could get you there. Nothing to do with my hair [laughs]. There was just long, shiny blonde hair.

As the transcripts quoted above show, magazine fashion has no practical value for most girls when it comes to their everyday dress. For school, girls want something that makes them feel 'the same as but different from' their friends.[4] The notion of dressing 'the same but different' was the most important theme of interview transcripts in total:

[I dress] similar but with my own style. Like I have cords and everything that no one else has. And, uhm, I don't know I just try not to look like everyone else [laughs]. But a lot of the same stuff too! Like everything I like's in style, or whatever [laughs]. (Fifteen-year-old Kirsten)

The friends that I hang around with wear just jeans, and you know, T-shirts and jeans the way they *should* be worn – you know, on your waist ... We all just basically have our own personal style, but it's kind of around the same style, you know. (Sixteen-year-old Erica)

In effect, most girls claim that they got ideas about being 'me' from others:

The way you get a new idea is you just look at something and go, 'Ooh, that looks cool!' And you find your own version of it that you like, or whatever. I just make it more *me*. (Seventeen-year-old Mary)

This ability to be able to dress the same as but different from other girls requires careful attention to small details which might be missed by a casual observer:

Like I don't want to look the same as I think everyone else does. Like I want to look so that people go 'Wow, look what she's wearing!' or 'I like that. I want to wear that too.' I want to create my own style.
[Interviewer:] What do you do to be different than other kids?
I don't know, just something *different*. Like maybe some weird ribbon in your hair or just something different that starts a trend with you, and the next thing you know, everyone's doing it. I don't know, all different things, like make one jean leg roll bigger than the other. (Fifteen-year-old Heather)

I usually have a different style from everyone else, I like to be *different*. Like, I'll wear pigtails one day, just to be different. I'll wear my socks up high with shorts, you know [laughs] so I'm different. I don't know. I like to be the same sometimes, but I just want to be different sometimes. (Fourteen-year-old Lauren)

Despite the emphasis Heather gives to being different, in the final analysis her style is like that of all the other girls: 'My style is just casual. Just like jeans and a T-shirt.' While the emphasis on being 'yourself' by dressing different may appear to offer an opening for the expression of individuality, in fact kids who fall out of what is expected by their classmates are quickly labelled. In large part, these labels are derogatory, evidenced by this explanation of 'geek':

I feel really bad saying this, but it's a lot to do with the 'geek' complex kind of thing, you know, so I feel bad saying that, but –
[Interviewer:] What's a geek?
Well, there's this girl at school who has worn the same thing every day – [same] kind of style since Grade 8 and she's going into Grade 12 now. It's just been a navy blue skirt with a little ruffle just below the knee, white tights, little dress shoes, a turtleneck or a T-shirt and a sweater, like a cardigan sweater. She wears the *same* thing *every* day. (Sixteen-year-old Kelsey)

It is not surprising that most girls wanted to avoid being classified in this way. Moreover, labels are difficult to get rid of:

And if you get a reputation it usually can follow you. If you change schools it'll follow you.
[Interviewer:] Really?
Yup. Like someone will know someone from the other school and then they'll tell them about it and then everyone knows ...
[Interviewer:] Can you give me an example?
Like people would say like 'the nerds' or 'the dreebs' [laughs] or whatever. If you hang around with them, it's like people are all like, 'Oh, you have no life. You don't do any-thing. Like, get away from me.' (Thirteen-year-old Caitlin)

We discuss the importance of labels in the next section. Here we note that, although girls lauded the virtues of dressing to 'suit themselves' or to express their 'creativity,' most were careful to remain within the bounds of what has been defined as acceptable by peers. Being careful in this way requires working knowledge of group norms:

God, I feel rotten saying this [laughs] but you want to avoid the label, you just want to go with the flow. Unless you want to do something really rebellious, you know, be seen as totally *different*, you mainly go along with it, clump together with everyone, so you fit in. In mean, there are certain things that you can wear that stand out, it just depends on what's acceptable and what's not.
[Interviewer:] What's something that stands out but that's acceptable?
Dying your hair black, wearing a bunch of earrings and nose rings, just that kind of thing, you know. Dark, dark, dark, dark, dark eyeliner or dark lipstick – like black we're talking here [laughs]. (Kelsey)

Danesi (1994: 81) observes that teen codes of dress are highly unstable, ductile, and short-lived: wearing these codes is thus a demonstration of social skill on the part of their bearers. This means that the failure to exhibit knowledge of acceptable dress can be read as a personal shortcoming, a reading which encourages girls to be intolerant of femininity which falls outside that established by their particular school culture. For example, although Kelsey does not agree that people should be labelled by their clothes, she feels that the girl described above could easily avoid being labelled as 'geek' by paying better attention to cultural cues and by improving herself:

I don't think it's fair that people should be labelled like that, but, then again, I think she could kind of think that a couple of people have noticed this kind of thing and have, you know, have mentioned it to her. I don't like the idea of labelling people by their clothes, if you feel comfy in that, I guess you should stick with it. I still think – I don't know, you *should* kind of make yourself feel better, if you just dress up a little bit sometimes.

In the final analysis, while 'getting ready for school' may strike adults as an activity too 'trite' for scholarly attention, dress is a complex phenomenon in the life of adolescent girls. In our study, for example, we have seen that, in teenzines, dress is presented as an avenue of self-expression, while at school it is experienced a signal of belonging to a social group. Given these contradictory demands, it is not surprising that girls' discussions often sounded illogical or difficult to follow:

At school there's different *types* [of people], so – Like, some people dress like, you know, like people dress *differently* at school, but I guess how I dress can be *similar* to people. Like I don't dress the *same* as my friends, but people at school dress – like we wear the same clothes too and we dress the same. Like, if I were walking in the hallway and I saw someone, you know, like someone I don't know, you can see that there're dressed sort of like me. Or I dress sort of like them. (Sixteen-year-old Alyssa)

Like Alyssa, many girls had a difficult time articulating to researchers exactly what is expected in terms of dress for school. As in Crystal's case, girls often strive to reconcile otherwise opposing goals: sixteen-year-old Crystal, for example, explains her dress as 'stunning' and yet 'natural,' as manipulation yet as expressing authenticity:

You should look stunning, [but] you shouldn't like – you want to hit people but you don't want to put them on the ground, you know what I mean? ... When I get up in the morning and I dress, I think of making a subtle impression but I want to stand out. Really, I want to look nice but not to the point that people are [saying] '*Look* at her!' Just subtle.

In the final analysis, the social significance of teenzines is not necessarily found in girls' attempts to directly follow magazine fashion; of more importance is their mandate for girls to be knowledgeable about 'proper' dress through the contradictory message that clothes are an avenue of both self-expression and social acceptance. According to this magazine mandate, we can 'read' clothes for what they tell us about their wearer, but we can also read them for what they tell us about social relations. In the next section we explore how this contradiction plays itself out in the everyday setting of girls in our study.

Doing and Undoing: Subject-ivity as Process

Interpretations of teenage fashion first appeared as a topic of serious academic interest in the 1970s. At that time the outrageous apparel of British youth – Teddy Boys wearing Savile Row Edwardian jackets, Mods wearing Italian suits, Punks in bin-liners – shocked the general public and captured the imagination of the academic Left. In an attempt to counter the moral panic which surrounded the styles of unemployed working-class youth in postwar Britain, writers such as Stuart Hall, Tony Jefferson, and Dick Hebidge theorized their outlandish appearances and rituals as a form of resistance. Following their work, sociological inquiry into fashion moved away from dress as conspicuous consumption to dress as 'production': subculture theorists interested in youth theorized dress as an activity through which adolescents 'write' themselves as texts to be read by others. Researchers then read youth styles as an existential solution to age and class domination,[5] as illustrations of how popular culture is created through the active appropriation of the texts and practices of culture industries. Drawing on Lévi-Strauss's notion of bricolage, sociologists like Hebdige (1979) and Willis (1990) emphasize how youth combine or transform cultural products in ways not intended by their producers. Within this work the sign values of commodities are rearticulated to produce alternative, subversive meanings. Attention was shifted away from the claim that capitalist consumption degrades social life and stifles individual creativity through the 'mass' market, towards the notion that consumers actively and creatively participate in the production of popular, 'common' culture. While less emphasis has been historically given to gender, this theme reappears in the postmodern position, discussed in the introduction, that women's fashion is a venue of personal experimentation and social change.

However appealing this approach, one problem with it is that these types of accounts conflate agency with resistance. While writers acknowledge that the outlandish styles which originally signalled rejection of dominant culture have been taken up in mainstream fashion and worn because of a commitment to, rather than rejection of, a consumer lifestyle, they nevertheless emphasize dress as an avenue of social change. An example is Paul Willis's study of the symbolic work at play in the everyday cultures of the young. In an attempt to challenge the hegemony of institutions which 'keep alive the myth of the special, creative individual artist holding out against mass consumerism' (1990: 1), Willis finds vibrant symbolic creativity in everyday activity and expression. He describes this activity as necessary, because it 'ensures the daily production and reproduction of human existence' (p. 9). Importantly, the necessary work of symbolic creativity produces and reproduces individual identities – who and what 'I am' and could become. From this perspective, the symbolic creativity of youth through language, music, haircuts, clothes, and so on is a rich venue for academic decoding and analysis. Like subculture theorists before him, Willis begins from the premise that 'young people seem to turn deliberately to the informal and to resist administered symbols' (p. 15). As a consequence, he describes teenage dress in terms of the symbolic work of appearing different in order to express and explore specific individual identities. He defines clothes specifically as resources used 'not only to attract the opposite sex, but also to gain friends, win peer-group acceptance, and to appear different or interesting' (p. 89). He further notes that, because more is at stake for young women than for young men in the realm of fashion, it is not surprising that they embellish it with rich significance (p. 91). Even while he admits that fashion texts like teenzines are a product of women's powerlessness in patriarchal culture, Willis nevertheless treats them as cultural resources which young readers 'work' on: while he (at least) pays lip-service to the fact that dominant images and definitions constrain young women's participation in the social world of adolescence, his readers remain very much 'in control' of social texts.

For the most part, research on teenage culture ignores the gendered nature of fashion as a social phenomenon or, as in the case of Willis, gives it superficial treatment. As Roman and Christian-Smith (1988) point out, much subcultural work on adolescence is outright sexist. They link this sexism to three masculinist tendencies of cultural studies: the use of male samples and practices as the norm; the celebration of spectacular aspects of male subcultures as evidence of 'opposition' and 'resistance'; and the focus on masculine public discourse which obscures both feminine themes and the significance of women's consumption and use of various media (p. 15). However, the tendency to conflate agency and resistance is so pervasive that it often reappears in the work of researchers who self-consciously advance a feminist interpretation of girls' dress. For example, McRobbie (1991a) notes that, despite their conformity and the conventionality in their dress, girls in her study invested their appearance with added cultural meanings. She interprets these meanings as resistance to the official ideology of the school: 'In conclusion, the Mill Lane girls certainly did not conform to the rules and regulations set out by the school. Without resorting to violence in the classroom, or continual truancy, they undermined its authority. But they did this by elevating and living out their definition of "femininity." They replaced the official ideology of the school with their informal feminine culture, one which was organized round romance, pop, fashion, beauty and boys' (p. 51). In the final analysis, McRobbie draws attention to the way in which girls' resistance to official school policy – that the girls wear school uniforms – acts to propel them along the path of traditional femininity. While I think this interpretation is an advance over ones which celebrate teenage struggle against the dominant order, McRobbie, as do her male colleagues, reads the meaning of dress off girls' clothing; we are given little sense about the meaning of dress to the wearers. In order to interpret the importance of dress to teenage girls in the current study, below we explore how girls, not sociologists, read clothing. Here we find little evidence that girls (consciously) employ dress as resistance to authority. One result is that very few girls claim that they ever have fights with their parents about what they wear to school. Overall, three themes emerge from girls' discussions about what dress means within school culture: clothes are a vehicle for creativity and self-expression, clothes are an indication of group membership, and clothes are a sign of social status. In the next section we explore these themes through symptomatic reading of girls' accounts of dressing for school. Here we see how dress is experienced as an expression of social rather than individual identity, revealing the importance of teenage conformity rather than resistance.

Doing Self: Getting Ready for School

With very few exceptions, girls in this study did not exhibit the outlandish and provocative styles of dress which have been the focus of so much sociological commentary. We have already seen that the vast majority of girls usually wear jeans to school, and many emphasized a preference for baggy, comfortable clothing. When discussing how they decide what to wear to school, girls who referred to a 'personal' style of clothing typically exhibited a well-formulated sense of Self, reflected here in fifteen-year-old Christina's discussion of how she decides what to wear:

For me, it's whatever feels comfortable and I feel like I look good.
[Interviewer:] How do you decide that you look good in something?
It just feels right [laughs]
[Interviewer:] Feels right?

Yeah. If I just put it on and then stand in front of the mirror and it looks the way it was *supposed* to look, then it's okay.
[Interviewer:] What's the way it's supposed to look?
The way I pictured it would look before I put it on [laughs].

Given the importance which academic writers give to clothing as the production of Self, there are surprisingly few descriptions by the girls themselves of dress as an expression of individuality. As we might expect from previous research, these discussions are framed in terms of the 'creativity' of clothing:

It's kind of like my own creative expression is how I portray myself [pause]. Not getting extravagant, though. Like I would love to wear really weird clothes, but I don't have the funding for it, so I just kind of wear what I've got now ... I like clothing. It's kind of fun. Making new outfits and stuff and trying to match colours and patterns and – it's creative expression, really. (Seventeen-year-old Amy, who attends an alternative school)

I felt like doing something a little more creative today, so I just looked at what I had, and the colours seemed to go well so I chose it because I was feeling in a good mood – I felt like being different than I had been the other days. (Fifteen-year-old Christina)

This view of clothing led Christina to claim that dress can express the 'real' person:

I think that make-up is a lot of fun and clothes are a lot of fun ... I see clothes as a way of expressing yourself and showing people *more* of yourself and helping them to understand what you're really like and what you feel like.

When viewed in isolation Christina's comments seem to support the view, advanced by writers about subculture, of dress as a semiotic resource through which the wearer creates herself as Subject. Her case, which is exceptional, is discussed at greater length in chapter 8. In this study girls were much more likely to emphasize the importance of looking like others. The most significant others, of course, are classmates. We saw above that many girls consciously copied what they saw on other girls at school. Thus many girls shopped with friends in order to have the security of a 'second' opinion:

I usually go [shopping] with my friends. I usually go by what they think looks good on me, what feels good on. And the price has a lot to do with it ... Well, if my friends like it then they can tell me whether it looks good. If they think 'Oh, that looks good,' then I get it. (Fourteen-year-old Jennifer)

Importantly, girls are not always as aware as Jennifer that clothing is about peer approval. Typically, girls mentioned that their 'mood' has a lot to do with what they chose for school. Even girls who like to be creative in their clothes are not always 'in the mood' to be expressive:

[Yesterday I wore] black boots, baggy pants, and a big wool green, red, and black Silo shirt that I had bought the day before. I really didn't feel like getting dressed up that day, but, actually, when I wear baggy jeans and stuff, I just feel like blending in, because everybody else in school wears baggy jeans – it's kind of my 'blend-in' mode – I don't feel like drawing too much attention, but generally I don't exactly want to look like a slob, so – if I feel like drawing attention to myself, I break out my big orange skirt or, if I feel like getting dressed up a bit, my black skirt, if I feel like mopping around school, my jogging pants or something. (Thirteen-year-old Stephanie)

Despite Christina's claim that dressing up can be a way of 'expressing yourself,' she also told Rebecca that

I tend to dress is more normal clothing, I guess – jeans and T-shirts and stuff – when I feel lousy.
[Interviewer:] Why do you think that is?
To be less noticeable.

As suggested here, wearing creative clothing 'draws attention' to oneself. For this reason, although girls typically discuss wearing what 'is comfortable,' they are often alluding to the psychological comfort of 'fitting in,' of not being self-conscious:

I just like to be comfortable. It's like I don't really care if I look nice or not, just as long as I'm comfortable [laughs].
[Interviewer:] Could you give me some examples of things that make you feel uncomfortable?
Well, uhm, shorts that I think are too short, or like pants I think are too tight, or skirts that I think are too tight – they really make me feel self-conscious. (Fourteen-year-old Kayla)

I just wear what's comfortable, 'cause it's what I like better [laughs] ... I usually buy the colours that I like and if it seems like it'll fit, 'cause I don't like clothes that are tight-fitting. I just feel super self-conscious, so just basically if I like the colour and the material and how it looks, you know, the fit. (Seventeen-year-old Cassandra)

While dress can be an expression of individuality, the creative self-expression of most girls in this study was moderated by their desire to be 'socially comfort-able.' As seventeen-year-old Amy notes, being comfortable is about 'belonging':

[You] always have to find somewhere that you'll find comfortable.
[Interviewer:] And you find that hard?
Sometimes. I'll kind of see people and you kind of say – Oh, someone you'll think would be interesting to hang around with or something. And it doesn't really – I don't know, you kind of sometimes make yourself be almost like them. To try to find similar-ity for whatever reason.

A key theme which emerges in this study is the importance of being 'similar to friends,' read within school culture as a sign of social membership. When describing different groups at school, most of the girls referred to social groups in terms of dress more than other characteristics, such as gender, age, or race:[6]

I find it [school culture] tends to categorize people and put them into a little box and that ends up creating a kind of competition that comes out in clothes and stuff. It decreases your individuality and won't let you be yourself and it won't let you do what you want to do in any way, shape, or form, generally. (Sixteen-year-old Kelly, now attending an alternative school, explaining what she didn't like about public school)

It's more bopper.
[Interviewer:] What's bopper?
Well, I guess you don't find too many of them any more, but a bopper would be hair high up in a ponytail, lots of make-up, giggle, giggle, giggle. Uhm, I guess that would be it. The clothes would be a little fancier [than grunge], just that kind of thing. (Sixteen-year-old Kelsey)

I think within certain groups people feel like they should act the same way as other peo-ple, and dress the same way. But if you hang around different groups which are more kind of like [into] you wear what you want, then there's not pressure there. (Sixteen-year-old Erica)

As a case in point, even though Erica describes her group as into 'you wear what you want,' members of this group dress the same:

We all just basically have our own personal style, but it's kind of around the same style, you know.

Because dress signals group membership, girls are well aware of the way in which fashion maintains group boundaries:

It's not so much sticking with a fashion, it's just not going over your boundaries kind of. There's like different sets of cliques at school. If you started dressing like another group, you're kind of – you've overstepped your boundary and you're just expected now you have to be part of their group. (Sixteen-year-old Michelle)

Boundary maintenance through dress means that very small clothing details are highly significant:

It might seem all the same to adults, but to kids it's all different. Like you can tell the difference between a homey and a skater by: a skateboarder cuts their jeans, right? And a homey like pins them, right? So it's like weird differences. (Thirteen-year-old Samantha)

As a consequence, the expression of social rather than individual identity introduces pressure to dress a certain way. This pressure could take the form of disapproval of styles which are visibly outlandish according to the established school code. For example, fifteen-year-old Hannah, a foster child, moved from an inner-city school to a Christian school in the Lower Mainland. While her grunge wardrobe had served her well at her previous school, it was rejected by her new classmates:

I get a lot of, uhm, criticism at school, for my clothes and stuff like that ...
[Interviewer:] What do people comment on?
Really weird. Just, 'That really looks bad' and stuff, but it's just kind of the grunge look isn't in our school, so I guess people think things. I guess I have my own style in a lot of my clothes and people don't appreciate it, so that's fine. I don't care what other people think [laughs].

It is also significant that Samantha claims that 'she doesn't care.' As suggested by this offhand comment, because clothing styles are used to assess the desirability of their wearer it is very likely that some respondents would be reluctant to admit to interviewers that they wear clothing not approved by peers.[7] As we see repeatedly in this chapter, girls are more likely than Samantha to discuss the nature of peer pressure through examples of 'other kids" experiences. Few respondents claimed that there was pressure in *their* group to dress according to a specified code. Discussions of conformity to group standards were usually couched in terms of groups which are visibly different from that of the respondent, while girls discussed their own dress in terms of conscious choice. This choice extends to respondents' preferences for brand-name clothing. As observed by fifteen-year-old Nicole, peer pressure could include wearing brand-name clothes:

People would like, yeah, look down on you and they wouldn't accept you as their friend, and stuff like that ... Brand names *shouldn't* be such a major factor for having friends, like I mean you should accept the way they are, right? But really, it's really hard to do that because some people can't take the embarrassment, you know; they can't face it. It's sad that people get accepted or don't according to what they have for clothes.

Because of the cost, not all kids can afford 'big name' brands. As a consequence, wearing brand names can be a sign of status:

You get a lot of 'Oh, that must have cost a lot if you got it from the Gap.' That kind of thing, and that's kind of – I don't understand why, but if it cost a lot, 'Hey, that's good!' you know, it's not *really* [laughs]. It's kind of pointless. (Sixteen-year-old Kelsey)

They're recently wearing a lot of brand-name clothes. I've seen one girl, her hair in a pony tail right up here [shows interviewer]. And that's the only time she put her hair up in a pony tail – like it's a plain white T-shirt – it looks really plain but only in the back, it says 'Calvin Klein' right up here. So she did that, and I've seen a guy at our school wearing his jeans really low but his underwear said 'Calvin Klein' on it and, basically, that's what people like, they love showing it off. (Fifteen-year-old Heather)

Conversely, fourteen-year-old Rachel recalls how her inability to wear brand names was a source of peer rejection in earlier grades at her school:

I was like embarrassed, 'cause I didn't [wear brand names]. 'Cause they're like expensive and if you didn't have the money to buy it, then you would have to wear other things. People would laugh and it's kind of embarrassing, so [laughs] ...

Unlike these girls who are consciously aware of the nature of peer pressure, most other girls did not read the popularity of brand-name clothing in terms of boundary maintenance or group membership. For example, when asked what they wore to school, it was common for girls to matter-of-factly identify their clothing by brands:

[Interviewer:] Can you remember what you wore to school yesterday?
Yup. I wore Ikeda lock-up jeans and a green Club Monaco T-shirt. (Fourteen-year-old Rachel)

[Interviewer:] What's your favourite thing to wear to school?
My favourite kind of outfit to wear would be like a pair of loose-fitting 501s and then Docs. (Sixteen-year-old Crystal)

[Interviewer:] Can you describe what you're wearing today?
Yeah. I have on some jean shorts that are cut off at the bottom so they're kind of frayed, and a Gap striped T-shirt, and a jean jacket and Doc Martens. They're purple. Like those are called 'monk sandals.' (Seventeen-year-old Cassandra)

Rather than explain their dress in terms of peer pressure, respondents were more likely to claim that they 'just happen' to like brand names as a matter of 'coincidence':

I don't know if it's coincidence that I like the big names or if it's some subliminal thing [laughs]. But I like the brand names. Some of the stuff I can't afford, so I go with stuff that I can that I like and the brand name I like. Like I like Big Star jeans but can't afford them, so I buy Club Monaco, because I like them too and they're cheaper. (Fifteen-year-old Kirsten)

It doesn't really affect me that much 'cause I guess you get into a habit of always buying it. Like when I was younger my mom always dressed me in like clothes from Woolco [laughs] and stuff. Once you start buying your own clothes, you kinda go out shopping with your friends and stuff and end up buying like, I guess the kind of clothes everyone else wears. So it doesn't really affect me much because I'm used to buying them [brands]. (Seventeen-year-old Roshni)

The brand name is still – it's sort of like, I mean you can wear tight-fitting jeans, or baggy jeans, but they have to be 'cool' – you know, they have to have the cool name, they can't be, oh, I don't know –
[Interviewer:] How do you feel about that?
I don't mind. I usually find that most of the clothes that I like are in there, in the area, anyways. So it doesn't really affect me. I buy my own clothes, so I have to save up my own money, but it doesn't matter. I mean, I like 'quality' clothes. (Sixteen-year-old Crystal)

That's a big thing now [brand names].
[Interviewer:] How do you feel about that?
I think it's stupid, but you have to feel that way [accept it] because of the people at school. But, usually the brand names are good, otherwise people wouldn't like them so. So they're usually comfortable and nice-looking or something. It doesn't bother me that much any more. I just buy them, I don't really think about it any more. (Fourteen-year-old Rachel)

In summary, despite the fact that most girls comply to the dress code of their school culture, very few complained about pressure to conform. Instead, girls emphasized that they like to wear what is socially comfortable. For the large part, 'comfortable' clothing is similar to that of friends, even though girls often went to great lengths to explain how their wardrobe is 'different.' Difference is signalled by specific details in the cut of their jeans or fit of T-shirts. What their stories tell us is the significance of school culture as the context within which girls develop a sense of social Self. This culture is all the more important if school is the only avenue for girls to meet potential friends. Fitting into school culture means adopting not only the activities and behaviours of peers, but their distinctive modes of dress. Group membership is signalled through clothing, and boundaries between groups are maintained through very subtle distinctions. Thus attention to clothing detail is important not only because it signals group membership, but also because it is a sign of cultural competence. If girls want to be a recognizable member of a social group they are required to dress in ways which make them recognizably similar to their friends. For girls, friendship entails shopping for clothes, doing make-up together, or swapping clothes. This does not mean that girls do not value experimentation or do not attempt to 'be different'; rather, it means that individual creativity must fall within limits set by the group. Falling outside the boundaries of one's group or failing to con-form to the general principles of dress established by school culture carries the risk of being labelled, for example, as a 'geek.' Given the negative associations accompanying these types of labels, it is not surprising that most of the girls place great importance on the opinions of their peers. Thus, compliments on their dress boost girls' self-confidence and contribute to their experience of 'having a good day':

If someone compliments me when I look good, like if I get dressed up and someone says 'Oh, you look really good today. Your hair looks really nice,' it totally boosts my confi-dence ... I feel the worst when I don't *feel* that I look *good*, because people kind of look at you and think 'Oh, what are you doing?' because you don't look good. That's proba-bly the worst I feel, when I don't feel like I look good. (Fifteen-year-old Kirsten)

I guess you have that feeling if you look good, if you know other people look at you, and then you get that – like 'fixed up' image: 'Oh, I look good today.'
[Interviewer:] That makes you feel good?
Yeah. (Fifteen-year-old Heather)

If I looked good for school, and if you were complimenting me on what I was wearing, then I'd feel pretty good. (Thirteen-year-old Amanda)

Significantly, when asked about the kinds of things which make the respondent 'feel good' about herself, girls were much more likely to mention how they look than what they accomplish through other activities.[8]

Given the significance of peer assessment, definitions of Self are not always controlled by the individual Subject. As we see below, the ability of peers to label others becomes a source of 'undoing' as well as 'doing' of the Subject. For girls in this study, two processes contribute to undoing experienced as self-doubt and anxiety about social Self. The first process, apparent above, arises from the emphasis that school culture places on appearance, which can result in worry about how one 'looks.' The second process arises from the ability of others, especially boys, to affix socially undesirable labels to girls. Both of these themes emerged in discussions which moved away from descriptions of how girls 'do' a social Self for school, to how girls feel about themselves as women. Girls do not have control over the definitions which contribute to their sense of social Self; as a consequence, identity can be experienced as unstable, in constant threat of 'undoing.' As we discuss later, undoing reflects the transformation of the gendered Subject into an 'object' of assessment – by boys, by other girls, and by Self. We examine the undoing of social Self in the next section in order to subsequently explore the doing and undoing of the Subject as both the context and the effect of teenzine reading.

Undoing the Subject: The Power of Naming

Because the interview schedule intentionally focused on 'doing' the gendered Self, I was initially surprised at the way in which self-doubt often 'leaked' into these discussions. In some cases, self-doubt emerged as a spontaneous 'confession' to the interviewer:

I didn't used to be like this, but I'm really quite shy. I'm very shy around people that I don't know very well. This has only happened in the last few years. It's really weird. I don't know why, but I'm like almost a lot of times, like *scared*. I don't know. I'm really scared of people when I go to parties and stuff. (Seventeen-year-old Laura)

I think I spend too much time thinking about what other people think, even though I don't always fit in with what they want. I still seem to do a lot of that and I spend too much time thinking about how it look and all of that. (Sixteen-year-old Kelly)

In other cases, self-doubt emerged in responses to questions about who the respondent admires or 'would like to be like.' In these cases, girls express a longing for qualities which they feel they currently lack:

[I would like to be] like a fashion model – one of those people 'cuz they seem like they have everything. Like they seem so happy and everything all the time 'cuz they're pretty and they don't ever feel bad about themselves. If they're not looking very good that day – it always seems they always are, but I don't know – everyone really likes them and everyone notices them and they're in pictures and stuff. (Fourteen-year-old Katherine)

I'd like to be someone [pause] like that had *confidence*, more confidence, that would be *sure* of themselves, but not too sure of themselves, and that sometimes didn't care what they said, like they didn't think back afterwards and go 'Oh, maybe I shouldn't have said that, I feel kind of dumb now.' (Sixteen-year-old Jasmine)

I don't know if this sounds stupid, but I'd kind of like to be like Madonna [laughs]. Just – *not* because of the way she looks, but attitude-wise. I like her attitude because she seems really kind of daring and like, some of the things she does are really wacko, like they're really stupid – like not stupid but, you know, they're like 'Oh my god, I can't believe she did that!' She seems really *gutsy*, and she seems sure of herself and, she doesn't seem like she cares about what anyone else thinks as long as – she likes to kind of surprise people and do things that, you know, are 'socially incorrect' [laughs]. (Seventeen-year-old Roshni)

It is significant that the girls link feelings of social inadequacy to worries about looks. In this study, most of the girls expressed concern about their appearance at some point in their interview:

I *should* be feeling good about myself all the time, but that's when I feel the best about myself – just if I think other people think that I look good, that's usually – I mean, I kind of thrive on what other people's, like on what other people think, you know. (Seventeen-year-old Jamie)

When I've eaten a lot and I'm not active and I just think 'Oh god, I'm so fat!' You know, just those days when you're just like – like everything in your closet is so ugly and you're like 'I look fat in everything and everybody else is so thin.' Just when I'm like, so fat. I just don't want to eat ever again. (Seventeen-year-old Victoria)

In the final analysis, most of the girls in this study discussed personal worry about their looks because they consciously acknowledged that there is a cultural mandate for women to look good. It is not surprising, therefore, that many girls directly link feeling good about themselves to looking good:

[How I feel] It's judged by hair, face and body, and also clothes. If like the clothes are right – but clothes go into the body category and it's more of a self-conscious kind of thing – but I realize I do it when I'm getting into the car. If my hair is working, and my make-up is working, and there's not too many blemishes on my face and I don't feel fat, and I don't think I look fat in what I'm wearing, and everything is – not necessarily comfortable – comfortable isn't even an option, really – and I like what I'm wearing and everything is not binding, or I don't feel like I can't do anything in it, like if everything is okay, I will feel great, yup, definitely [great]. I won't go somewhere if I don't feel good about what I'm wearing. Like I have to have not necessarily the 'right' outfit, but I have to feel good in my clothes before I go somewhere, and if I don't feel good in my clothes, I usually will not have a good time at all. Like I will be really uncomfortable the whole night. And I'll go 'I wish I was wearing something else' and I will be obsessive, almost. (Seventeen-year-old Allison)

I got my hair done a while ago for my grad pictures and I really liked it, and it looked good and it made me feel better about myself. I was kind of glowing – I guess I was more confident walking around because I knew I looked all dressed up and good. I'm not trying to brag, but you know it's underneath that – you look at yourself in the mirror and you kind of think 'Oh, my hair turned out nice today' or your make-up turned out good. (Seventeen-year-old Roshni)

[I feel bad] when I've tried everything that I have in my closet and nothing feels right, it doesn't feel too good [laughs]. I guess when I feel the worst is when I feel like [I'm] being put down about something and I can't get comfortable and I can't feel right and I don't look right, and things just aren't coming together. (Sixteen-year-old Kelly)

It also means that girls can feel perpetually on display:

The toughest thing about being a girl is that you always have to be concerned about what you look like. That's another thing, you get into the frame of mind that – [laughs] well most of my friends get into a frame of mind that somebody's always watching. You always have to look good for that person. He's coming to school today, or she's coming to school today, so I gotta look good. I gotta look good. (Sixteen-year-old Stephanie)

In fact, most of the girls claimed that the hardest thing about being a girl has to do with looks:

Ninety per cent of what we care about – and it's the same with me – is how we *look*. I don't know if this is true of all people our age or just us ... that's what I care about mainly. I still do care about my schoolwork and everything, but I don't – I don't go out of the house if like, I don't get my hair cut every two months, I won't go out of the house like a day after the two months. (Seventeen-year-old Laura)

Living up to the standards of like the 'girl thing.' You know, like being all feminine and stuff like that, because I'm just like a sporty type of person who – like I don't get all dressed up and all made up to go to school and stuff, and a lot of people do. The stress is on looking excellent and beautiful and whatever, and I just don't, that doesn't interest me. (Sixteen-year-old Melissa)

I think there's a lot of pressure as far as having a boyfriend and looking good. It's really like, just as a girl, you're supposed to look good and, you know. It's also, there's lots of pressure that not so much, well sometimes, you find that if you do sports, it's sort of well 'You're a girl. Why do you want to be serious in sports?' (Sixteen-year-old Lindsey)

As reflected in the cultural 'truth' that beauty is 'in the eye of the beholder,' physical appearance can be assessed only through the reactions of others. Given the importance of a girl's looks, negative comments about appearance can be devastating in their effect:

And if someone even as a joke would say 'Oh, you cow' or something, it really made me upset and that would make me go a week without eating a thing. (Fourteen-year-old Rachel)

They can also contribute to the worry, expressed above, about getting 'fat':

[It's hard] trying to keep that perfect figure. Like you don't want to bloat out and like be huge 'cause then you know you're not going to – like people are going to treat you differently. You don't want to be treated differently, you want to be treated the same. (Fifteen-year-old Heather)

While sexist comments by others are a worrisome finding, a discouraging number of girls expressed dissatisfaction with their looks. Because self-disparaging comments were fairly common in first-stage interviews, during follow-up interviews research assistants asked whether there was anything the respondent would change about herself if she could. Very few girls responded that there was nothing that they would change about their physical appearance:

I'm not the kind of person who feels really bad about myself. (Fifteen-year-old Rebecca)

I'm quite independent, so I don't really feel that I want to be someone else. (Sixteen-year-old Alicia)

We explore these types of positive assessments in greater detail in chapter 8.

Here we listen to those girls who provided a detailed inventory of physical flaws which they are either working to improve or would like to change:

I look exactly like my dad. My mom has really nice – yeah, my cheekbones, I don't really have any, but I look exactly like my dad, and my mom is really pretty and I don't have any of her features. Like she has like nice cheekbones and the kind of lips that, you know – I think that I have a really ugly mouth, it kind of goes up here and it's like, kind of *puffy*. (Seventeen-year-old Laura)

I'd like to have lighter eyes – I have green contacts.
[Interviewer:] Why?
It actually attracts more people, I've noticed.
[Interviewer:] Does it?
Yeah, 'cause it's not very common for an East Indian or a brown person to have light-coloured eyes. (Seventeen-year-old Erin)

I would lose a bit of weight. Yeah, I'd probably lose a bit of weight and I want longer eyelashes, and less zits, and straight teeth. (Fifteen-year-old Danielle)

[I'd like to] get like skinny, for one thing [laughs]. That's number one. And my nose – it's big [laughs], and then I'd get a – I don't know, it sounds really dumb but my lips are too thin [laughs]. And I hate freckles! (Fourteen-year-old Rachel)

[I'd like to] change my face, how it like [laughs], like get rid of all the pimples I have, uhm, get my teeth straightened, like make them go more inwards and nice like models' [teeth] because I want to be a model. Sometimes they have auditions for being a model in there, and I want to be a model, so I – *Teen* magazine for the last year has a model thing in it, so I'm going to send away for it. (Thirteen-year-old Caitlin)

These types of negative self assessments could invalidate positive feedback from others. Rachel, for example, does not believe her boyfriend's attempts to reassure her:

He says I'm being stupid. He thinks, he goes like 'You're *beautiful*' [laughs] and all this and then it's like –
[Interviewer:] You don't believe him?
No, I don't. I just think he's saying that to be nice and I tell him that and he gets really annoyed. He's like 'Oh, Rachel, you're skinny' and everything [laughs], and I'm like 'No.'

Similarly, fourteen-year-old Lauren does not trust compliments from friends:

I don't really believe people when they tell me that I look good though.
[Interviewer:] Why not?
Not *people*, just my friends 'cause most of my friends are false.
[Interviewer:] Really?
Yeah, they're false. They're not really – like they'll say one thing and mean another ...
They say 'Oh, you look good' and then to the next person say 'Oh my gosh. Did you see
what she's wearing?' So how do you know when I – when someone's telling me that I
look good, I just want the truth.

In many ways, Rachel's case is unusual, because other girls were more likely to
discuss the negative labels that boys, in particular, affix to girls at school:

They're always like, if you don't have big breasts they like make comments, like 'Oh,
you're flat-chested,' and it's like they don't like you. You can't really say anything back
to them. You just kind of have to take it 'cause you can't – like you couldn't say 'Oh,
your face is ugly,' you know. You just have to take it. Like it's hard to say something
back because there's nothing that they have that you can comment about ... Like I really
couldn't say something back. It would have to be like about their face or like, I *couldn't*,
like I couldn't really say anything really bad that would actually hurt them. (Thirteen-
year-old Ashley)

You can get a lot of abuse from guys. Like they say, they can make fun of your – comment on your chest size or whatever, right, and they'll mean it as a joke, but it hurts. Like
it can hurt, you know. A lot of things that are tough about being a girl are about looks.
(Sixteen-year-old Kelsey)

As well as getting sexist comments about their looks, girls also worried about
getting 'reputations.' The most serious reputation concerns a girl's sexual
behaviour. This type of labeling (which was often applied by girls as well as
boys) was the second most frequently mentioned source of anxiety for girls at
school:[9]

[I feel bad] when people give bad comments about me, like call me a 'slut' – I had a few
like that. They [other girls] just didn't really like me so they started spreading rumours
around school last summer. (Thirteen-year-old Caitlin)

It's not really right, but girls can get – like a girl can do one thing wrong and she can be
labelled, that type of thing. Like girls can get labelled easier like for being a bitch or a
slut, you know, stuff like that. If a guy did something, someone might say he did something, but they won't label him, like say anything about it. And if it's a girl, then you

hear, you know, 'She slept with someone.' It's like, 'Yeah, she's a little slut.' It's just right away. (Seventeen-year-old Roshni)

A lot of that happens. If you do [have sex] they'll go telling all their friends, if you don't they'll tell all your friends that you're a freeze, 'Don't go out with her. She won't do anything. It was a whole two weeks that she wouldn't have sex.' That type of thing ... When I talk to my guy friends, they all tell me that, like they're saying 'Oh, get *her*. She's a slut.' (Fourteen-year-old Rachel)

This power for boys to label girls led many girls to recognize the 'double standard' used to assess the behaviours of their peers. Thus Rachel went on to say:

It's the thing where girls are considered sluts but guys are studs, type of thing. That type of thing, and it's not just having sex. It's anything. A guy will break up with a girl and an hour later be going out with a different girl and he's just considered a stud and the girl's like 'Oh my god. What a slut.' And all that type of thing. I just don't think it's really fair [laughs]. It really bugs me.

However, the power of labels can also discourage girls from speaking out against this practice. Although Rachel claims that she does not like the way in which her school culture labels girls, worry about being labelled herself keeps her silent:

They'll talk to me. They'll [say that] and I'll just like 'Uhum' like and nod and [laughs]. Like I don't really say anything because I don't really want them giving a bad opinion of me or thinking I'm a geek or something, so I just don't say anything. But I just don't go along with it, yeah, whatever.

The (apparent) freedom of boys from censure led some girls to claim that it is harder to be a girl than a boy:

The guys that I know, uhm, you know, they come to school in green jeans and purple shirts and they probably haven't washed their hair in the past two months, but nobody cares. Okay, so what if a girl – But if a girl did that, now oh gosh [laughs]. It would be 'Have a shower,' 'Nice colour co-ordination!' 'Where'd you buy that!' (Thirteen-year-old Stephanie)

I don't think you have as much freedom as guys. Just from noticing my friends and stuff. Parents tend to let guys go out and party and drink and that kind of stuff and girls are like 'No, you have to stay home.' You know, 'Bring your friends over here' [pause]. Also, I don't know, being a girl also you have to [pause] not necessarily work harder but you work the same to get not as much recognition. It's kind of hard. (Seventeen-year-old Mary)

Like if a guy did a certain thing it would be different than for a girl, the punishment. Like a guy could pass it off, but a girl couldn't. It wouldn't be – a girl would have to live with that for the rest of her life, kind of thing. (Seventeen-year-old Erin)

And guys, they just don't have much problem. And girls get so much pressure about their looks, their figure, everything, right? If guys, if they're overweight, it wouldn't be such a big problem, not that much. But most guys, they would prefer skinny, really skinny girls, you know [laughs]. And girls, they don't really look at their [guys'] looks. Most girls look in their inner, you know, inner personalities. (Fifteen-year-old Nicole)

The process of labelling could be so pervasive that even girls who consciously maintain that it is wrong got caught up themselves in categorizing other girls according to patriarchal standards:

Like I'm guilty myself for doing it [laughs] and I wish I didn't. I kind of feel like almost everybody does it. And I just don't like when I do it. I feel so guilty I just feel like I wish I wouldn't do that and I wish other people wouldn't do it too.
[Interviewer:] Can you give me an example?
Like if I was walking in the mall or something like that and I saw this girl that had like blonde hair and she's wearing a skin-tight little tiny top and all this stuff, I'd automatically say 'slut' in my head. Like I know that's mean, but I'd say something like that. But you don't know because she could be a completely nice and intelligent person and not sleeping around or anything and then she's not a slut. It might just be the way she chooses to dress. (Sixteen-year-old Melissa)

We have already seen above that Rachel disapproves of the way in which boys label girls' behaviours according to the sexual double standard. It is interesting, therefore, to take note of how she describes one of her female classmates:

I guess there's people like that, but she just doesn't care. Either she's with a different guy every night, and I'm kind of like, well, if she gets – I'm not going to feel sorry for her if she gets a disease or something because it's her own fault. She knows everything, all the facts, but she doesn't care.

In summary, these types of stories help us to identify two processes which can erode girls' self-confidence: the cultural emphasis on girls' looks and the power of labels applied by others to determine social Self. Both of these processes undermine girls' emerging sense of an autonomous Self. Importantly, both processes embody patriarchal definitions of what it means to be a woman. The ability of these definitions to call Subject-ivity into question reflects the way in which becoming a woman in a patriarchal culture transforms girls into objects of cultural censure. While teenage boys are also subjected to classification and the application of gendered labels, traditionally this process is based on what boys 'do' and less on how they look. It is not coincidental that patriarchal definitions of femininity can conflict with definitions which girls might otherwise apply to themselves. For example, we have seen above that Melissa describes herself as the 'sporty' type: significantly, this Self definition brings her into conflict with definitions of femininity based on 'looking beautiful' which are dominant in her school culture. For the most part, however, these types of conflicts are not always identified by girls for what they are – a double standard for adolescent behaviour. In fact, we have seen that girls often adopt – sometimes consciously – dominant definitions for desirable behaviour on the part of other girls. As we have seen in the previous chapter, these definitions dominate teenzine discourse. Moreover, we also saw that, while advice on girls' problems in fitting into school culture addresses readers as gendered Subjects, it typically does so from the standpoint of dominant, patriarchal definitions of feminine behaviour. Below we discuss how girls' experiences of patriarchal culture can contribute to the appeal of teenzine discourse, which, in turn, normalizes the problems of being a woman. This discussion highlights the power of social texts, but also raises questions about the way in which experience can, potentially, challenge the social construction of the feminine Subject and the patriarchal social order. We explore these questions in chapter 8.

Teenagerhood as the Search for Social Self

As noted by psychologists, the task of adolescence is the consolidation of identity as an autonomous Self required for a healthy, socially functioning adult. While this task is required by every culture, it does not mean that the nature of this process is either universal or natural. The types of developmental crises which adolescence entails are very much social products. They are shaped by social roles – what adolescents 'do' – and cultural definitions which enable participants to attribute meaning to what they do. In our society, the primary activity that adolescents 'do' is attend school. The purpose of this chapter is to explore school culture as the everyday context of teenzine reading.

In listening to girls' stories it is tempting to suggest that, outside school, nothing much happens for many of these girls. While this temptation merely reflects the nature of the research, boredom is a recurring theme in girls' accounts of what they do. Although they also engage in casual forms of paid work or sometimes participate in athletics, the typical response to queries about their favourite activities outside school is to 'hang out' or just be with friends:

[I do] Nothing, Absolutely nothing. Just sit around with my friends and listen to music. That's it. (Fourteen-year-old Kayla)

Just stuff with friends. Anything – rent movies, go to the movies, shopping, beaches. Anything, as long as it's with friends. (Fourteen-year-old Rachel)

[I like to] to hang out with my friends.
[Interviewer:] Why?
'Cause they're fun people to hang out with. We listen to music or we go and hang at the mall. (Thirteen-year-old Ashley)

I can't wait for school to start.
[Interviewer:] Why?
Well, school's interesting. During the summer it's kind of boring. Like all day you and your friends get to together and you figure out what you want to do [laughs]. There's not much to do in Richmond, right? So you don't know what to do, and we hate going to the mall because we always get into trouble at the mall. (Thirteen-year-old Samantha)

As noted by Samantha, hanging out with friends requires doing something, explained here by sixteen-year-old Michelle:

When we're bored we'll go to McDonald's or the Seven–11 and just kind of hang around ... [But] You get classified as having no life if you hang out at McDonald's too much, so we just kind of go through, the drive-through. We'll go to McDonald's, quickly through the drive-through, and come home and eat it.

What this (perhaps) amusing anecdote reflects is the ability for teenagers to 'make something' out of the lack of structure which characterizes their daily lives outside of school. Structurally, a boredom that accompanies 'hanging out' finds relief through attending school. Like Samantha, virtually all the girls in this study emphasized that they liked school, although typically for its social rather than academic aspects:

[School] it makes me feel like there is a schedule in my life because I don't like being totally carefree and doing nothing 'cause it feels like I'm wasting my time, and then also because my friends are at school ... When I'm not in school, [laughs] my favourite thing to do is sleep. Either sleep or hang around. (Sixteen-year-old Alicia)

Yeah, I like school.

[Interviewer:] Why?

Well, because if you didn't go to school you wouldn't know any people, and you'd be very bored. Like I don't mind it. I don't like the working part of it, but just being there, the social part of it I like. (Fourteen-year-old Rachel)

Well it's fun to go and see your friends and everything at school, but sometimes the work is kind of hard. It's like kind of stressful, but it relieves your stress seeing all your friends and stuff like that. (Thirteen-year-old Ashley)

I do like school because I like being around my friends and that's the only time we get to see each other a lot, like on weekends. Like right now [summertime] I can't even see my friends. Like you know, it's just really hard to see them. But – I guess learning's good for you [laughs]. (Sixteen-year-old Alyssa)

For the large part, girls find the academic side of school 'boring':

If I'm sitting in science class and the teacher's saying something that's relevant to me, I'll sit up and listen. If, uhm, I think to myself 'Is this going to help me?' I'll listen. But if he's just prattling on about the bubonic plague in some unknown godforsaken country, like I guess I'm concerned, you know, but then he goes onto the next subject and he just starts going on, I'll just fall asleep. And I'll *pray* for lunch time to come so I can go outside and talk to my friends. (Thirteen-year-old Stephanie)

The boredom of schoolwork can make teenzine reading a welcome distraction:

If you've got like a boring class, and somebody brings it to class and, you know, people read horoscopes, or right now with prom dresses everyone's bringing in magazines to class 'Oh, look at this dress – it's exactly what I want' and that kind of thing. (Sixteen-year-old Crystal)

Usually I won't read any of the fiction stuff until like, maybe two days later [after purchase] when I have a lot of homework to do ... I buy them when I have a lot of homework and I don't want to do it, so I'll just comb through them and spend hours looking at them. Just cutting out things and fun things like that. (Seventeen-year-old Allison)

Given the apparent freedom which this boredom reflects, it might surprise adults to learn that kids nevertheless find it difficult to be a teenager. Difficulties stem from what Alyssa describes as 'learning to be yourself' and 'to stand on your own.' For the girls in this study, the process of figuring out 'who you are' is not always easy:

Like just I think finding out who you are is the most hardest thing to do. I mean like most of the time – well, for me, like I've no idea really what kind of person I am, you know – what I want, finding out what you want and who you are. I think that's hard [laughs]. (Sixteen-year-old Erica)

I'm just finding out this year, is like you have to decide so much. Like, what am I going to do? You're going to somehow decide on some career and know who you should be and what you should be doing and everything. I think when you're my age, it's too much to know. There's too much pressure put on you. (Seventeen-year-old Mary)

Some girls suggest that dominant stereotypes of teenagers make the search for a positive identity difficult:

[It's difficult] dealing with some people's views about teenagers. Views that generally homogenize teenagers, homogenize them into an unpleasant group, as opposed to a pleasant one.
[Interviewer:] Unpleasant as like?
Smoke, take drugs, be really really rude to anyone who's older, and don't like authority etc. etc. etc. [laughs]. (Fifteen-year-old Christina)

I think there's two things.[10] One is a stereotype that everybody's given us. The stereotype that all teenagers steal. It's a bad stereotype where, you know, you're shoplifters and hooligans! It's really tough to get past that sometimes when you're not. It's hard to get over that and show everyone, I'm not who you think I am. (Seventeen-year-old Alexandra)

Predictably, girls experience being a teenager as being 'in between' identifiable social roles:

I guess one of the hardest things is just the fact that you're kind of 'in between' so you're a child when it's convenient and you're an adult when it's convenient. You never get to really be in one place that's convenient for *you*. Well, not never, but it seems that a lot ... If they [adults] don't want us doing something they'll say 'Oh you're too young, you're too irresponsible.' And then if they need something done, they say 'Oh, you can do it, you're a big girl now.' It gets kind of annoying sometimes [laughs]. (Sixteen-year-old Kelly)

You're 'in between.' Like you're for sure not a kid and the kids realize that, but you can't do everything that adults do. You can't even do anything like people two years older than you can do, you know. So, you're kind of stuck. (Seventeen-year-old Brianna)

One result of being neither a child nor a adult is the lack of clear guidelines:

It's probably just an oxymoron, but you get too much freedom and you don't get enough freedom. Some areas I think we are given a lot, way too much freedom, and other areas I think we're not given nearly enough. It's hard. There's no real boundaries set for teenagers, so they have to screw up to figure out where they are [laughs]. At least that's what I've found. (Sixteen-year-old Crystal)

The hardest thing is dealing with the people around me, like dealing with your friends, and your parents, and your boyfriend, and just kind of, you know ... like everyone goes through a different stage, so it's kind of hard, like to know what's right from wrong. (Seventeen-year-old Roshni)

I wanted to go on the merry-go-round, but they wouldn't let me because I was too old. Right? But you're too young to do the things that you're sort of expected to do. Like the obvious, uhm, parent–child situations. They always tell you to 'act mature,' but they always want you to be their little baby. It's a bit confusing after a while [laughs]. You don't really know what to do. (Thirteen-year-old Stephanie)

For girls, trial and error can be costly, however. We saw above that, while it is easy for girls to earn 'reputations,' it is much more difficult to loose negative labels affixed by peers. Thus girls encounter special difficulties in achieving the autonomy required for experimentation. For girls in this study, barriers to autonomy sometimes come from concerned parents:

I think even parents don't know where they want to put the line, because they're not really sure. Well, 'They're [teenagers] a kid, but they're not an adult.' I think that's the hardest part. The stress, 'cause you're figuring out a lot of stuff. I mean the first twenty years of your life you're probably learning the most about yourself that you ever will. And it's hard. It's emotionally really hard on people. (Sixteen-year-old Crystal)

You can't go out because blah, blah, blah, blah – 'cause you're a girl, because you don't walk by yourself to wherever, like even a short distance because you're a girl, somebody's going to get you or something. That's what my parents say. And if I hang around with all my guy friends, they say 'Oh, you're the only girl there, don't go, something's going to happen to you,' even though they're like my Church friends. And they think because we also go out with other people not in Church, uhm, my parents, sometimes they're worried [laughs]. It's annoying. (Sixteen-year-old Alicia)

Parents think that you shouldn't be allowed to do that much and, you think 'I can do that' and your dad's like 'No, you're not old enough.' That type of thing.

[Interviewer:] Can you give me an example?
Well, being out after dark alone, like walking home kind of thing. We got into a lot of fights about that kind of thing. And Lollapalooza [concert] type of thing. I'm going to that now but my dad was a little bit 'iffy' about that because of everything that happens, and Tammy's mom won't let her go. (Fourteen-year-old Rachel)

Other times the nature of school culture makes it difficult to just 'be yourself.' Peer pressure is the most frequently mentioned restriction on girls' budding autonomy. As we saw above, social acceptance, which is required for the development of a healthy sense of Self, requires conformity to seemingly arbitrary codes of behaviour:

You've got to develop yourself completely without offending anybody. Again, school comes into play because you have to be psychic to be in high school, I swear. You constantly have to look at people, constantly watch what you're doing, see what they're saying 'cause if you do one thing wrong, friends tell friends and you get the whole school after you, which is not a good thing. And so again, you have to prove yourself to people, especially being a girl. (Thirteen-year-old Stephanie)

[At school] you're around teenagers every day and if you're not up to top notch amongst the people you hang out with, it's just, you don't feel comfortable. I mean you *could* hang out with other people – right, there you go – but that's not always the case.
[Interviewer:] What kind of pressure are we talking about?
Act a certain way, dress a certain way, laugh at certain jokes, you name it. The stupidest things can bother somebody. And it's just, if you're too much into computers you're just not worth the bother. It's just, I don't know. (Sixteen-year-old Kelsey)

I don't know how to say this, but there's really like [the notion of] cool people, *better* people, and some of the things – 'Oh yeah. I'm not cool' and all that [so] I have to go and do something. Some people go ahead and try smoking. They start smoking and you don't want to be around smokers, and they go off with others and they all smoke and stuff like that. (Fourteen-year-old Emily)

This requirement for conformity can introduce self-doubt:

I don't know, when you go to school and see all these people all pretty and stuff and you just feel kind of plain and normal. Well, it just kind of feels like 'Oh, maybe I should do that too' ... And then I just, you know, sometimes I feel like 'Oh, maybe I should start wearing something like that.' (Sixteen-year-old Melissa)

As argued by Melissa, the discovery of Self occurs in the face of peer pressure to conform to group behaviours. Among peers, boys were identified as a special source of pressure, particularly to engage in sexual activities:

I guess guys are kind of tough because they can have ideas about you before you even know them. I mean, just like what they think of you. You know, you can hear things and you get a story, like 'Oh she said no and she really means yes,' and like *no way* – if you said 'no' you mean 'no,' right? (Sixteen-year-old Kelsey)

Yeah, guys are a stress. They've always been a stress. Always will be.
[Interviewer:] What kind of stress?
You, like you know, 'We have to be together forever' and they always lead you on and they just mess with your mind.
[Interviewer:] Do they?
Yeah. I just find that guys do that. Like it works both ways, but girls aren't like that though. Like I found a lot of girls don't do that 'cause they don't find the point. It always hurts them in the end. But guys don't think like that, so I just find guys a stress. (Fifteen-year-old Heather)

Pressure from guys about sex – it's really hard. They're really pushy. Like you're like 'No, leave me alone' and they just don't listen. They're just relentless, they just don't listen. Like, 'What part of *no* don't you understand?' Leave me alone. (Sixteen-year-old Michelle)

Fourteen-year-old Kayla claims that friendships with girls are not necessarily easier:

All the girls are such spazzes and you're always in fights with each other. We're just so uncas [not 'cas'ual] compared to guys ... Like, we just have to be like 'I'm not talking to you,' 'You're not my friend anymore,' and, you know [laughs] like it's so dumb! It's annoying when it happens 'cause then the girls are like 'Oh my god, she's just a bitch.' You know, like 'I hate her' [laughs] and we all say like 'Yeah, we do [too].' And then it all comes out and then people find out later you're talking about them and everybody's in trouble [laughs].

In this brief discussion,[11] school culture is a complex venue within which to develop a sense of Self. Acquiring a sense of Self requires carefully negotiated trade-offs between asserting individuality as an expression of Self and being like others in order to gain approval from frequently unsupportive peers. In this chapter we have seen how this negotiation takes place through dress and gendered identity as the route to social acceptance. Although purportedly about academic achievement, school has a hidden curriculum – learning to 'fit in.' Given the lack of social space or positive identity for adolescents generally, fitting into school culture is important because it offers one of the few venues through which teenagers can develop a sense of 'belonging.' Unlike academic performance, fitting in is not always under the control of individual participants. Acceptance by peers is based on conformity to social codes which for the large part remain unspoken: in many cases, the girls themselves had difficulty articulating the precise nature of group expectations. However, from their stories we have seen that these expectations are based very much on gendered norms which accompany being female. Despite the outwardly unisex style of school fashions, girls are directed towards patriarchal definitions of femininity rooted in very traditional notions of what it means 'to be a woman.' This can make it difficult for girls whose sense of Self draws on definitions which place them outside the bounds of traditional femininity. For example, as a skateboarder thirteen-year-old Samantha considers herself to be very different from other girls at school. The price which she pays for this identity is dealing with peer rejection. Samantha thus maintains that the hardest thing about being a girl is 'being herself':

I'm being made fun of at school for being a female skateboarder. Some guys think that girls can't skate, but they're wrong ... Since I'm a girl skateboarder most people like reject me 'cause, you know, there's not too many of us. But I don't listen to it because I know the truth myself.

As we have seen here and as mentioned by a number of other girls, because sports are a venue for boys but not girls to gain sense of Self, girls often (but not always) find that their interest in athletics places them in opposition to definitions held by their peers of feminine dress and behaviour. We explore this process in chapter 8.

The power of peers to affix the labels that determine social acceptability means that girls (as well as boys) are subject to continual assessment by peers. Within school culture, these labels are based on girls' looks and their acceptance by boys. We saw above that the emphasis on looks can make girls feel continually 'on display' or become hyper-critical of their physical appearance. At the same time that definitions of femininity revolve around girls' emerging sexual identities, sexual activity is risky and, like assessments of physical appearance, not subject to girls' control. While girls can become 'popular' with boys through sexual activities, overt displays of sexual autonomy are labelled negatively by peers. In the final analysis, fitting into school culture is a complex and risky task. As a consequence, it can throw girls' Subject-ivity into a state of flux, which some girls labelled through a discourse of the 'excessive emotionality' which accompanies the biological fact of 'being a girl':

> We seem to have a lot more emotional fluctuations than males do. And that's sometimes hard to deal with. Things come up, and you don't know why ... Maybe it has to do with PMS, or whatever. (Seventeen-year-old Amy)

While Amy understands her experience in terms of the physiological transition to womanhood, the purpose of the current study is to explore the social construction of adolescent femininity. In *Girl Talk* the social construction of teenagerhood includes social texts, such as teenzines, which we can now read against school culture.

In chapter 4, we questioned whether contradictions and inconsistencies in teenzines lead readers to question adolescent femininity as a social construction, in ways suggested by some cultural critics. These critics suggest that gaps and contradictions in social texts are a point of instability in dominant systems of meaning which invite rewriting and the construction of alternative, subversive meanings. Against this claim, I have located these contradictions within the everyday experiences of adolescent girls. In conclusion, the lived experience of adolescence does not invite critical decoding of teenzine texts for most of the girls in this study. The first reason is found in the experiential reality of school culture. While girls recognize that magazine standards of feminine beauty are unrealistic, experience tells them that the cultural mandate to be beautiful conveyed by these texts is real. Criticizing magazine images is thus an indictment of the reality which requires girls to look good; the reality of this requirement means that the teenzine emphasis on dress and physical beauty accurately reflects aspects of their experiences of being a girl. Placing oneself outside, or against, the experienced reality of dressing to fit into school culture requires a secure sense of Self, at a time when girls actively seek peer approval. While the majority of girls in this study were more likely to question themselves than they were the cultural proscription of adolescent femininity, in chapter 8 we explore cases of girls who question – hence reject – this mandate.

The second reason that school culture reinforces teenzine messages is found in the discursive naturalization of patriarchal definitions of 'being a woman.' In chapter 6 we explored how the everyday problems of being a woman are lifted from their social (hence political) context in order to be re-presented as personal problems. In this chapter we have seen that many of the experienced problems of readers stem from the patriarchal nature of dominant definitions of femininity, and the power of boys in particular to label girls according to these definitions. While this power of boys makes it understandable that girls will want to learn more about guys and their opinions, the way in which male attitudes and world views are presented in teenzine texts acts to mystify the nature of the social forces which shape readers' lives and which give meaning to dominant definitions of the femininity which readers are encouraged to adopt. For example, while readers are often advised to get rid of problem boys, and issues such as date rape and sexual harassment are discussed in feature articles, in the main this discussion is devoid of critical analysis. As we saw in chapter 6, themes of 'doing what's right for you' and 'get rid of problem boys,' common in advice and feature stories, are typically used to reinforce the importance of finding the 'right' guy. In conclusion, therefore, the power of the text lies in its demonstrated ability not only to construct a reading Subject who accepts dominant definitions of being a woman, but also to normalize the dominant order as it is experienced through school culture. In the final analysis, regardless of how innocuous or entertaining middle-aged researchers find women's magazines, teenzines provide stark illustration of social texts as power.

8

Calling Cultural Constructions into Question

As noted by the girls in chapter 7, society does not offer adolescent girls a sense of belonging through provision of a specific social 'place.' In the absence of positive definitions of adolescence, many girls feel that they exist in a state of limbo, 'between' childhood and adulthood, with few guidelines or clear boundaries. The absence of positive definitions and sense of social place can make it difficult for girls to find a voice to name their experiences of adolescence. From this perspective teenzines are significant to the process of becoming a woman because they offer a discourse which speaks specifically to young girls about their adolescent experiences. In doing so, they construct 'teenagerhood.' However, it is not simply that teenzines fill a discursive void or that readers are 'seduced' by the social texts of commercial media. Girls are discriminating readers with distinct reading preferences. In this study we have seen that, although teenzine preferences vary, most girls favour titles which address 'the reality' of their teenage life. As a consequence, popular titles are those which are deemed to address readers' everyday experiences. The purpose of chapter 7 was to identify ways in which experiences of school culture in particular enhance the appeal of commercial texts.[1] In chapter 7 we saw similarity in the dominant messages of school culture and teenzine texts: that a girl should always look good and that guys' opinions and preferences are important. Teenzine texts associate these goals with girls' self-interest by constructing a social Self and, subsequently, evoking this Self when encouraging readers to 'do what's right for *you*.' Girls' accounts of their everyday life at school suggest that teenzine messages resonate with teenage experiences of school culture and, as a consequence, reassure readers that their experiences fall within the boundaries of 'normal' teenage life.

Despite this reassurance, however, many girls mention that it is difficult to 'be a girl,' especially to pursue the cultural mandate to 'look good.' Because physical attractiveness is based on the assessments of others, comments from peers can be both reassuring and devastating when self-esteem is linked to physical appearance. As a consequence, learning how to look good is important for girls growing up in a patriarchal culture. From this perspective, teenzines simultaneously address the experienced need of girls to acquire the skills of feminine appearance and reinforce the message – identified in both teenzines and in girls' stories – that feeling good is the result of looking good. This message means that teenzines contribute to both the doing and the undoing of the reading Subject.[2] In terms of 'doing' Self, magazines are a source of practical knowledge about gendering the female body, and many girls claim to make use of these practical tips in their magazines. It is interesting that while respondents typically have difficulty identifying the precise nature of what they must do to fit into their school culture, they can be surprisingly articulate about how to 'do' their gendered bodies. Fourteen-year-old Kayla explains to Rebecca (who does not wear make-up) how she gets ready for school:

I just try to make my face look more even [laughs].
[Interviewer:] More even?
Well, just, you know, even out the skin tones and bring out the eyes ... I put concealer to cover the eye bags I have [laughs] under my eyes, and then I put on my first coat of eye shadow, which is like the same colour as my skin, actually – but it sort of takes away any little veins or something that might be on the top of my eyes that I can't see. And then I put on a sort of pinkish colour around the creases of my eyes, and then I follow that with a dark brown – just around the creases. And then I 'define' my eyebrows, and put on lipstick and mascara.

As shown here and argued by Smith (1988), although taken for granted, the everyday act of 'being a girl' is an accomplishment; it entails gendering the female body. For girls who are at a crucial stage in learning to be a woman, gendering requires acquisition of technical knowledge about make-up, dress, diet, and self-presentation. In chapter 7 we saw that school culture provides a context which supports the pursuit of these practices. More importantly, school culture is often the source of many of the 'personal' problems which dominate teenzine discourse. As a result, many girls claim that their magazines have the potential to be 'helpful.' For example, fifteen-year-old Heather explains that, because her school culture does not accept fat kids, a lot of girls want to lose weight:

I just think, like guys – 'cause a girl might think 'Oh yeah, if I'm big and ugly and hefty-looking no one will look at me and no one's going to want me.' That's how most girls have that stress. Everybody, in general. 'Cause like they might think 'Yeah, I'm hefty and big and have no friends and no one's going to want to be with me. No one's going to hang out with me.' So maybe that's a problem [for them].

She then claims that teenzines might be useful for this reader:

They [teenzines] have things like 'Ten ways that you can become thinner' that might help them. Maybe the magazines will help them change and maybe push them a little more, 'cause maybe they'll read it and go like 'Yeah, maybe this'll work.' I think it might help them.

Heather's comments are important because they show how teenzines work in the context of everyday reading: readers do not simply imitate magazine images, but rather see in their magazines practical information on 'fitting in' and thereby 'belonging,' a process which I argued underlies teenzine reading.

As noted in chapter 7, an emphasis on 'fitting in' does not encourage girls to question the source of personal difficulties in being accepted, in 'belonging' to the patriarchal order. On the contrary, to remain outside the dominant discourse of femininity, or to be critical of accepted behavioural standards, requires a sense of Self and of belonging that places individual girls outside the bounds of 'normal' feminine behaviour. While a coherent sense of Self and belonging may accompany the adult reading of women's magazines, it was an infrequent occurrence among teenage readers in this study. The purpose of this chapter is to further explore instances of refusing the Subject-ivity offered by the text. Unlike commentators who explore resistance as a quality of the text, however, here we link resistant reading to the everyday context of reading. Chapter 8 explores how, and why, experience can call cultural constructions into question.

In this study, constructing a social Self that fits into school culture is described as the 'doing' of the Subject. At school, it is based on the display of an appropriately gendered identity. Teenzines contribute to the doing of the Subject in two important ways. First, teenzines help readers 'fit in' through the provision of solutions to the dilemmas which school culture presents to girls: dilemmas about how to attract boys, make friends, improve self-presentation, and so on. We have seen in this study that girls claim to actively follow many of the 'tips' and suggestions found on problem pages. When this occurs teenzines are implicated in the construction of a social Self. In order to explore the Subject constructed through teenzine advice, we identified the behavioural goals and attitudinal values which give meaning to adolescence. Overall, this Subject is constructed around the pursuit of beauty and heterosexual romance, through patriarchal values that are an important source of self-esteem.

However, in this study we have seen that the effect of teenzines is not found only, or even primarily, in their prescriptive messages. The second, potentially more common, way teenzines affect readers' lives is through the construction of the social world of adolescence. Through a format which invites comparison reading, this construction offers a venue for reassurance that readers' experiences fall within the bounds of normal teenage life. When the reader identifies with the problems and stories submitted by others, this recognition reassures her that her situation is comparable to the 'typical' teenaged Subject of teenzine discourse. We have already seen, for example, that the girls in this study often compare the texts of advice columns to their everyday life. Some girls read problem pages for the questions and not the answers; in effect, they 'check out' the problems of other readers in order to compare these problems with their own experiences. This comparison helps establish the boundaries of 'typical' teenage experience; its analytical significance includes the ways in which comparison brings together experiential and discursive knowledge. Importantly, comparison is not limited to question-and-answer texts:

[Showing interviewer what she reads in *YM*] And that type of thing – 'What's Hot, What's Not.' I don't usually go based on that, I just like to see what they think and how much of it is actually true. Like if they say a belly ring – in my last one I read that the belly ring was the top thing of 1994 and I'm just like trying to think how many people have that and everything.
[Interviewer:] Do you know a lot of people with them?
I've got one [laughs]. Actually I only know two [other] people. I don't know them, I've just seen them at school. I just wanted something different [laughs] so I went downtown and got it pierced. (Fourteen-year-old Rachel)

Clearly, Rachel's reading reveals a desire to gauge her own practices of self-expression against teenzines accounts of 'what's hot.' She gains reading pleasure from the recognition of her gender practices in a discourse that affirms the social desirability of her attempts to 'be different.' As in the case of getting ready for school, here pleasure arises from comparison reading which affirms the 'sameness' of the reading Subject to the Subject constructed by the text; it helps to impart a sense of 'belonging.'

Affirmation of social Self is not linked only to reassurance of being the same as the discursively constructed Subject. In this study, comparison also can account for the enjoyment of 'Say Anything' and other 'embarrassing' but humorous moments in other readers' lives. We saw in table 5.2 that over half of thirteen- and fourteen-year-olds and almost two-thirds of fifteen- and sixteen-year-olds like to read embarrassing anecdotes of other readers' lives. In these cases, pleasure arises from difference between the reader's everyday experiences and those constructed through stories of embarrassing moments:

'Say Anythings' [showing interviewer in copy of *YM*], I read this whole thing. I just took this out and read them all. They're so funny. They're really funny. They're just like the funniest stories and it makes me laugh. I don't know, it's just like they're *so* embarrassing and it just makes you so glad it never happened to you! (Fourteen-year-old Kayla)

Some of them ['Say Anythings'] are like realistic, but some of them you just – they're still really funny. So I guess it just makes you think 'Oh, if that ever happened to *me* I'd die!' (Sixteen-year-old Michelle)

As suggested here, the embarrassing experiences of others can offer reassurance because no matter how awkward her own social situation may feel, the reader's experiences pale in comparison to those provided by others. These texts thus reinforce a sense of normalcy about the reader's life. Like the problem pages, these stories facilitate the doing of the Subject. This doing also appears in comments about true-life tragedies which are frequently the topic of feature articles. About one-third of thirteen- and fourteen-year-olds and two-thirds of fifteen- and sixteen-year-old girls in this study identify 'real life' stories as regular reading:

See, this is the kind of stories I like to read [shows interviewer in *YM*]. 'My best friend was kidnapped and killed' [reading title].
[Interviewer:] Why do you like those?
I don't know. I think I've read about this girl before, seen her on some kind of thing [laughs]. The whole town like put a thing across saying 'Bring Polly Home' or something to the person who kidnapped her. 'Cause my friend who I was with last night, she got lost, and we spent like an hour and a half walking all around looking for her. She just came back. So, when I looked at it [article] I just like, because those were all the things that were going through our heads last night 'Oh my God. What if this happened?' (Fourteen-year-old Kayla)

I saw an article one time about a prostitute in *Seventeen* or something and I guess I could – it explained how horrible her life was. [It made me think] It's not worth it to run away, and stuff like that. (Fifteen-year-old Tiffany)

There's a true story on this girl whose ex-boyfriend attacked her when they weren't going out anymore. I read this one because it's kind of scary that, uhm someone could actually do that to a person ... After reading it, it kind of scared me. I was kind of shaken up a bit because you could almost picture it happening to you. (Sixteen-year-old Jasmine)

Like embarrassing (but humorous) stories, tales of personal tragedy put the reader's own worries or dilemmas into perspective: however difficult her current situation, for most readers it is likely to lack the tragedy of the types of stories typically featured in teenzines. The tragedies in teenzines thus impart a sense of security to readers 'belonging' to the dominant categories and definitions appearing elsewhere in the text.

In summary, while comparison reading draws on experiential knowledge, it also blurs the boundaries between the discursive and experiential aspects of teenage life. Through comparison, teenzines reassure readers about the normalcy of their own situations; in doing so they actively construct the social world for teenage readers. While the effect of commercial media is readily apparent when readers directly adopt the styles or attitudes of these texts, the power of teenzines is much more subtle when they act to define the reality of adolescence. Definitions arise through discursive processes that categorize experiences, prioritize issues, and repackage dominant values in forms relevant to readers. We have seen that specific formats, such as quizzes, encourage reading as 'self-discovery,' repackaging dominant goals and values as self-knowledge.[3] In chapter 6 the self-knowledge promoted by teenzines invites comparison reading. Comparison reading is most obvious in quizzes, where readers are invited to score themselves according to dominant behaviours and attitudinal values. Girls' accounts of reading reveal, however, that comparison reading, as a process through which readers assess the normalcy of their experiences or sense of Self, is characteristic of teenzine reading generally. Comparison, which is central to the doing of both the reading Subject and the social, testifies to the agency of readers. For our purposes, however, comparison reading signals the power of the text, because, in this study, comparisons testify to the truth status which readers assign to commercial media. However important personal experiences and systems of understanding may be to individual readers, as social texts teenzines work to support the dominant order by addressing the existential dilemmas facing young girls in ways which perpetuate the problems of being female in a patriarchal culture. In doing so, teenzines naturalize the world of constructed femininity which supports patriarchal definitions and the power of boys to label girls according to these definitions. As others have noted, magazine texts seldom, if ever, critically question the social origin of problems which require solutions: how to look good, how to be popular, and how to attract boys. Rather than question the goals implicit in advice columns, teenzines construct a Self in ways which normalize traditionally feminine behaviour and attendant values. Readers who resist the text by questioning teenzine messages are thus required to question the normalcy of their Self-constructions: as a consequence, the power of the text rests not simply in the doing of the Self and the social, but also in the undoing of the Subject.

As in the case of doing, undoing occurs when readers compare themselves to constructed texts, an unanticipated theme that first emerged when girls read the advertisements discussed in chapter 4:

I've seen this [ad] a few times. It's kind of intimidating to me 'cause there's like five models right across there, and it's making it look like if you wear this, then it'll look as good as it looks on these people, and so I don't like it too much. (Sixteen-year-old Erica reading ad for Revlon make-up)

This is one of the ones that you just kind of flip past because you know you're not like her. [Interviewer:] When you say 'like her,' what do you mean?
Well, she's really pretty and everything, and I guess it intimidates the person who reads it. Like myself. It would intimidate me because she's more pretty than me. (Fifteen year-old Rebecca reading an ad for Conair Wavemaker)

As noted here, comparison reading draws attention to the way in which the boundaries between the discursive and material world are not as distinct as supporters of commercial femininity often claim. Given the age of readers, it is not surprising that comparisons of Self to textual constructions focus on standards of physical appearance. While readers may not yet have developed a secure sense of Self with which to gauge teenzine constructions, the physical Self provides a concrete point of comparison. The power of comparison is not only enhanced, but mystified, within discourses which present beauty as a physical rather than cultural standard, as a natural rather than accomplished aspect of womanhood.

In the final analysis comparison reading blurs the relationship between the discursive and everyday worlds of adolescence. However, as we have seen, this process is fraught with difficulties and contradictions. Can the contradictory nature of comparison reading encourage readers to call cultural constructions into question, in ways suggested by postmodern critics? The remainder of this chapter explores this potential. Here we look at those moments during which girls discuss the constructedness, rather than reality, of teenzine texts. So far, I have emphasized the disciplined nature of girls' readings. While disciplined readings dominate the current study, I am not claiming them as a universal manner of reading: in this chapter we explore readings which resist closure in ways which support the dominant order.

Negotiating Contradiction

Like Heather, seventeen-year-old Mary begins by claiming that magazines can help girls master the femininity required to fit in at school:

> If you're into all the stuff that they talk about and they focus on, I guess for you it's 'I've learned how to put on my lipstick properly' and you've learned what everyone else will be wearing next week, so you can keep up. I think it makes you feel really secure.

However, she went on to point out that not all readers would find these texts reassuring:

> But, if you're not that kind of person, it doesn't help you because you look at it and think 'What am I supposed to be?' 'Cause, like anyone who doesn't fit into that exact stereo-type isn't really going to get anything from it. That almost could be negative, too. Like, 'Should I be like this?'

As Mary notes here, at the same time as they provide readers with reassur-ance, magazines can contribute to anxiety through the undoing of the Subject. Sixteen-year-old Kelsey is likewise aware of the contradictory nature of teen-zine messages which she feels might confuse readers:

> They [*Seventeen*] say, you know, like you should think for yourself and you should respect people for who they are, and then they have all these – you know, it's kind of contradictory. I mean, they have ads of how you should dress and what you should look like and this and that, and then they say 'but respect people for what they choose to be like' Okay, so which do we do first?

Thirteen-year-old Stephanie extends this process of undoing to quizzes:

> Some of the magazines really make you feel bad about yourself. Like some of the quiz-zes that they give. 'Are you a back stabber?,' 'Are you a drama queen?,' you know 'Do you deserve to be with your friends?' – 'Are you a good friend?' Things like that. You come to doubt yourself.

Stephanie went on to say:

> It's a whole cycle. I mean you read the thing and you may brush it off, but it's always there. And you do something that the magazine said and all of a sudden it's a big deal.

You *really* start to feel insecure about yourself. And all that's going to do is put you in the same position because you're going to go back to the magazine for an answer, right? But it's not going to give you one. It's just going to give you another problem.

Unlike Stephanie, most girls do not recognize how their magazines contribute to the construction of 'another problem.' Most of the girls, like sixteen-year-old Michelle, resolve the contradictory nature of teenzine discourse in a much more 'matter-of-fact' way:

Sometimes you look at the models and you feel worse. But I guess sometimes when they have like different – like what you can do to detract from something that you don't like [about yourself]. Like ways to cover it up, I guess that kind of makes you feel better 'cause you think that – say if you really think you have big hips, sometimes they'll give you kinds of clothes that you can wear that will make them look, like make you look slimmer.

As postmodern writers emphasize, contradictions are discursive 'leaks' in the hegemonic discourse of femininity. They are analytically important because they are a point at which the reader can be alerted to the constructed nature of social texts. In chapter 6 we ignored these leaks by emphasizing coherent readings and stable reading Subjects; in chapter 7 we saw that coherence and stability are not characteristic of many girls' accounts. Instability is most apparent when girls come to doubt themselves; importantly, self-doubt can be triggered by teenzine reading. However, in this chapter we look at cases where discursive ambiguities and contradictions lead readers to question the dominant meanings of the text rather than self-constructions. We do so in order to explore readers' reflexivity and the notion advanced by postmodernists of reading as resistance. As pointed out in chapter 7, the exploratory nature of this research means that findings are suggestive and further research is required. Nonetheless, findings in this chapter challenge us to reassess many of the assumptions which currently shape theoretical debates in cultural studies, a task taken up in the remainder of *Girl Talk*.

'Too bad it doesn't work': From Disciplined to Sceptical Reading

Previous chapters emphasized the disciplined readings of texts, interpreting these readings within their everyday context in order to treat the text as process. In this and the following section, we explore instances of critical reading which resist or challenge dominant meanings. By 'critical' I refer to readings in which girls draw attention to the constructedness rather than [purported] 'reality' of texts. Critical reading is important for both theoretical and political consider-ations. Theoretically, it corresponds to the postmodern characterization of reader resistance. Politically, instances of critical reading can help us identify processes which encourage readers to reject unachievable goals or attitudes that are not in their best interests. As for the analysis of disciplined reading, it is not simply a case of identifying examples of reading resistance. While we begin by taking note of instances of critical reading, these readings are assessed within the context of the entire interview transcript. In other words, examples of readings which do not lead to dominant meanings are interpreted within their everyday context in order to assess whether critical reading can be meaningfully inter-preted as 'resistance' to patriarchal proscriptions for women. This assessment results in the identification of two types of critical reading, one which supports and one which does not support the material expression of dominant definitions constructed by commercial texts. In this study, no evidence was found for gen-der insubordination through semiotic subversion of the text; alternative identi-ties are associated with methods of reading which resemble those discussed in previous chapters. Like the girls who subscribe to the dominant messages of teenzines, girls who reject the traditional femininity constructed by these texts negotiate meaning through comparison reading. In these comparisons resistant meaning comes from the experiential knowledge which girls bring to their read-ing of the text. Understanding why these experiences are found in only a minor-ity of cases among the girls in this study helps us to identify social forces which act to enhance the appeal of commercial media to our young readers.

The first type of critical reading exhibits scepticism towards the text. As Barker and Andre (1995) found, young readers often recognize the constructed nature of social texts. However, this recognition is not the end of the story, as many commentators imply. For many readers in this study, recognition of the constructed nature of social texts became part of their negotiation with the text. It required these readers to reconcile beliefs that their favourite magazines, unlike rejected texts, are 'real.' Although previous chapters emphasized disci-plined reading and the construction of dominant meaning, most readers actually expressed cynicism towards magazines at some point in their interviews. For the most part, cynicism was directed towards advertising texts:

Oh no! [laughs] 'Giving you the guts to go out and get what you, or who you want, in this big wide world' [reading caption]. Just because your hair is curled doesn't mean that you're going to conquer the world – sorry, lady! Not this one.
[Interviewer:] So you don't like it?
It's kind of unrealistic. I mean, they're telling you that if you curl your hair with Conair

Curling Rods that you're going to conquer the Japanese stock market. I highly doubt it [laughs]. (Thirteen-year-old Stephanie reading ad for Conair Hair Curlers)

Just kind of 'Maybe she's born with it, Maybe it's Maybelline' [reads slogan in mocking tone]. Like [they're] really using the idea that their make-up's going to make you look beautiful. I think this is a major misconception [laughs] because I don't think mascara's going to make you look beautiful. And like, '*unlawfully* long' [reading slogan] – I don't know. It's a good commercial, but usually when I see stuff like this in a magazine I just flip the page. (Sixteen-year-old Crystal reading ad for Maybelline Mascara)

Overall, this cynicism contributes to the finding that fewer than one-third of readers indicate that they (consciously) read ads in their magazines. In short, it leads to the rejection of specific teenzine texts.

Cynicism can also be directed towards advice columns and personal stories, although this occurs less frequently. However, unlike the case of advertising, scepticism towards advice pages does not necessarily lead readers to challenge their ontological validity.

The thing that always strikes me is okay, they write in, it takes a while for the magazine to be printed, then you have to buy the magazine, see if your answer is in the magazine, and so it's like a month later, two months later that you're going to see even if they choose that question. You know, you don't even know if it's going to be answered or not, so really, by the time it's answered the problem may be over ... [Less than one minute later] I think you can learn stuff. You can learn stuff from other people's experiences that they've written in to figure out. (Sixteen-year-old Kelsey)

I feel sorry for anybody who actually puts into action advice that they hear here. I think you have to be really in serious need of help.
[Interviewer:] Why?
If your best friend is a magazine! This I recall reading on Friday [shows interviewer]. It's about this girl whose boyfriend wants her to have sex with his best friend while he watches. Who writes into a national magazine and says these things [laughing]. And for one, two, three, four [counting] columns, all she's telling her is 'drop him.' I'm sure somebody else could have told her that. My friends and I just laughed. We laughed – I mean we felt [sorry] for her, but gosh, she must be feeling really stupid right now. (Thirteen-year-old Stephanie)

Despite cynicism, in both of these cases respondents are referring to embodied rather than constructed readers with problems. While they may be cynical about the nature of problems discussed or the situation of readers who would actually use magazine advice, they nevertheless invoke a reality consistent with these readers and their situations. As a result, Stephanie went on to say:

Every girl is not the same in the world, and that's what these magazines are trying to portray. They're trying to give the image, you know, that they're [girls] all the same. You all have the same problems, everything happens the same to all of us. And it's not. And that would be a very hard thing to do, to give specific scenarios, but there are levels that at least they could try.

As suggested by Kelsey and Stephanie, these types of critical readings express disappointment with representational failures of the text. Because they do not question the texts themselves as constructions, sceptical readings do not necessarily lead to a rejection of teenzine discourse. For example, sceptical readers often criticized specific advertisements, but not the desirability of the advertised product:

It's really unrealistic.
[Interviewer:] Is it?
When's the last time you had a guy kiss your feet? It's never really happened to me, so it's kind of being staged for the camera. You can tell 'cause it looks like there's other people in the room. I don't think a guy would kiss your feet with other people in the room! [laughs] I like the shoes, though. (Sixteen-year-old Michelle reading ad for Converse shoes)

I don't think they should have a picture like that in a magazine. I just don't think it's like, kind of appropriate – but her dress is really nice, though. (Thirteen-year-old Ashley reading ad for Bisou Bisou dress)

Not this one [showing interviewer an issue of *Seventeen* she did not read last month].
[Interviewer:] Why not?
Just because it has Niki Taylor, but –
[Interviewer:] What's wrong with Niki Taylor?
[Laughs] I just think she's *too* beautiful. I can't look at her. I have the other ones [issues] where it's just like runway models on the cover and they've just got these fashions in them and I think that's much better. (Fourteen-year-old Kayla)

However sceptical readers are in these particular instances, they do not question the commodification of femininity or the role of their magazines in the construction of undesirable images of femininity. Like Stephanie, sceptical readers wish that magazine editors would 'try a little harder.'

For our purposes, a more interesting disjuncture occurs when readers criticize the magazine's use of beautiful models with 'perfect' bodies, but not the cultural mandate for women to look good. Because these readers do not question what Wolf (1990) calls 'the beauty myth,' the contradictions which result can lead to an undoing of the Subject:

I hate how they always have pretty girls in advertisements [laughs]. [I would] just like to see, like just more average girls, like more not so skinny and perfect, type of thing. It makes you feel really ugly reading it [laughs]. (Fourteen-year-old Rachel)

The one thing that's actually always bothered me about all magazines is that they always have these perfect models, and that's something that I would say is really annoying sometimes because every page you open to there's like a girl who's absolutely perfect. You know, she's got gorgeous hair, gorgeous features, she's thin and tall, and everything. I think that that's one thing that affects all girls, you know, because the average girl that's looking or buying this magazine is not going to look like that. I think even for myself sometimes, sometimes you tend to compare yourself to it without even noticing it. Like you'll see these girls and like the way they look so good and everything and you try to look really good, and you want to be really thin and stuff. I just wish for any magazine that would have girls that are, like average. (Seventeen-year-old Roshni)

It is interesting that a significant number of both regular and avid readers admittedly dislike the fashion models used by teenzines or wish that their magazines would portray 'ordinary women' (and men):

I don't understand why they can't put in people who aren't – and plus, some of these models aren't even like really beautiful, you know [laughs]. I mean I guess they have good bodies and stuff, but why can't they just put in ordinary people, like everyday people, so that people might be able to connect better. And they have gorgeous-looking guys throughout all the pages, which kind of makes people think – I'm not sure what it makes people think, but I think it's just fine to go out with someone whose not totally gorgeous, or even like good-looking – someone who's just kind of average. (Sixteen-year-old Erica)

I don't like the way that they have like these girls here with, you know. Everything has to be these girls that look absolutely gorgeous and it's like they're trying to say that if you do this [points to article on exercises] then you'll get looking like *that*. It's fine for girls to be like that, because people are like that, but every single thing that you look at has girls like that and it could just be like normal people [instead]. (Sixteen-year-old Melissa)

If readers do not connect these images to the imperative for their magazines to market femininity, confusion could emerge in their reasoning about the realism which they impute to their favoured text:

I'd want them [*YM*] to make their magazine more realistic, more like – I don't know, it *is* realistic, but the models are wearing clothes that people aren't going to buy. Like maybe having models that aren't really that pretty. Like I mean, I know girls who go nuts because they think they should have this skinny body because that's what they show in the magazines. Maybe they should show a beautiful fat – *fat*'s mean: like a *large* girl – like maybe they should show someone who doesn't have a perfect body. (Fifteen-year-old Kirsten)

Given readers' criticisms of teenzine representations of feminine beauty, it is interesting that *Sassy* is the least popular of teenzine titles. As noted in chapter 5, the majority of girls in this study express general indifference or dislike for *Sassy*, the teenzine with the least amount of discussion on make-up and the most likely to criticize cultural standards of beauty for women. This finding raises doubts about the potential viability of an alternative, feminist text for teenage women. While further research is required, here I suggest that *Sassy* is not accepted by these young girls because it places them, as the reading Subject, in opposition to cultural standards of acceptability during a period when girls most need reassurance that they are 'normal.' Magazines promoting oppositional readings require audiences with a firmer sense of Self than do teenzines which promote dominant attitudes and values. While this suggestion requires further investigation, here we note that sceptical readers are often aware of the tension which exists between their criticism of teenzine femininity and their experienced necessity for girls to look good:

She looks really, really skinny, and pretty.
[Interviewer:] You like that?
No. It makes me feel fat.
[Interviewer:] Do you mean that they should have women that are less skinny?
Yeah. I don't know. That depends. Like sometimes I think when girls see pictures like that – lots of my friends I know are anorexic and stuff, they'll say 'I'm not going to stop until I look like that girl.' But then if you had bigger girls modelling the clothes, that looks bad. And you might think 'If I look like that, I don't want to buy it' [laughs]. I don't know. In between. It depends, I guess. (Fourteen-year-old Rachel)

The problem is that they'd probably lose readers [if they discussed social issues] because the people who do care about these issues wouldn't think of looking in *YM* unless they started to advertise until there was no end and completely changed their image. And then the people who do read these magazines would just find it a complete downer [laughs]. 'What happened to the pimple fixes, man? What are they doing?' (Thirteen-year-old Stephanie)

If girls did not identify the source of the contradiction between their criticisms of teenzine models and their reading preferences, they had a difficult time explaining their rejection of *Sassy*, the teenzine which articulates criticisms which readers themselves expressed during interviews:

[Listing what she would like to change about *YM*] Put in more [social] issues about what I just talked about, and uhm, maybe put some not bigger people, but maybe some not-so-pretty ones, you know what I mean?
[Interviewer:] But you just said you wouldn't pick *Sassy* because the girl on the cover wasn't pretty enough.
Oh, yeah, well like, I guess I did, but you know what I mean. (Fifteen-year-old Danielle)

I don't know, it's just [pause] it seems like, in a way they're [*Sassy*] trying to be *too* different and it just is *weird*. They're not realistic in a way with some things – I don't know what it is, I guess *Seventeen* isn't realistic either, but there's something about it [*Sassy*], something about it isn't right [laughs]. I can't really place it. (Sixteen-year-old Crystal)

YM I think caters more, its more fashionable to read and its just more like, it's more fashion-conscious in that way. It has a lot more, uhm, like current styles that everyone wears, but *Sassy* is sort of, it's weird [laughs]. It's like a little bit more offbeat and uhm, sort of ... I don't know. It's hard to explain. (Sixteen-year-old Lindsey)

While these types of contradictions and leaks in meaning making are read by researchers as invitations to challenge or outright reject the mandated femininity of magazine discourse, rejection of teenzines is not characteristic of the majority of readings in this study. In fact, when asked 'who they would like to be like,' even critical readers evoke magazine imagery:

In all honesty I'd like to be what the magazines advertise, not necessarily just in body and looks, but the confidence they advertise. Someone who can wake up in the morning and not care what she looks like and still look good when she goes out somewhere. That's the kind of person I want to be like. There's a part of me that wants to be absolutely beautiful in the fact that I don't have to care, and there's another part of me that want's not to care whether I am or not. These two things are constantly fighting, and constantly doing it, and just, I'd like to be happy and secure, and above all, I don't want *that* to depend on my looks or on what I'm wearing, or anything like that, most of all. (Seventeen-year-old Allison)

Several girls mentioned celebrities, three of whom were (coincidentally) featured in *Seventeen*'s 'Who's Hot, Who's Not' during the period when interviews were conducted:

I'd like to be like probably Kate Moss. She's skinny. She's really pretty, but she doesn't care what people think, like she just goes *natural*. Like she doesn't wear lots of make-up like the other models, and she wears jeans and stuff all the time. In interviews and stuff she sounds pretty friendly. (Fourteen-year-old Courtney)

So like attitude-wise I really like her [Madonna] and look-wise I would say that I kind of would like to be like Janet Jackson, because I think she's kind of got a really – you know, like innocent look, kind of sexy look to her. (Seventeen-year-old Roshni)

Cher, Madonna, and Tina Turner all rolled together because they're all – they *all* have attitude and they know what they want. Well, Cher's kind of plastic, but she does what she wants and she doesn't really care what other people think. Madonna's really made something out of herself and even though it's kind of strange and I don't really listen – watch any of her movies, or particularly like any of her videos, she's got that 'get out of my way' personality. (Thirteen-year-old Stephanie)

Halle Berry. Like she's completely natural and she doesn't have a weave or anything like that, and she's just really pretty and I guess a lot of guys like her. She has a good body and stuff, and she's also really, really smart. (Thirteen-year-old Amanda)

 If girls chose everyday role models, their choices were often women who embody magazine values:

Looks-wise probably someone like Niki Taylor or someone at school. Just one of the really popular girls that have all the friends and the nice clothes. Yeah. (Fourteen-year-old Rachel)

My aunt. She's really into fashion and, she's a legal secretary and she's really into fashion stuff. Like, she helped me pick out my grad dress and she's – like she's in her late thirties but she's really into it, like with styles and stuff like that ... Like most of her clothes are working type clothes, but she's got really good taste and I admire her. I'd like to be able to wear nice clothes and stuff like that when I'm her age. (Seventeen-year-old Victoria)

While a few girls did cite their mothers as role models, choices of women whose public recognition does not emphasize the femininity espoused by teenzine discourse do not appear very often. Female athletes or politicians, for example, are not mentioned, although seventeen-year-old Cassandra admires Dian Fossey 'for what she has done.'[4]

In summary, I characterize the critical readers cited above as 'sceptical' readers: although critical of the text, a sceptical reader has not rejected its promotion of the cultural mandate for women for women to look good or questioned the role which commercial venues, like fashion magazines, play in perpetuating this mandate. A sceptical reader is therefore not a politicized reader; her reading cannot be claimed as expressing a critical awareness of herself, or her social role, as a woman. While sceptical reading escapes discursive closure in ways which result in dominant meanings, it is not likely to challenge patriarchal proscriptions for women. In the final analysis, the reader remains within the dominant discourse of femininity: in fact, sceptical readers typically express disappointment with a text which fails to live up to patriarchal standards. Thirteen-year-old Stephanie is a good example of a sceptical reader. We saw above that she expressed criticisms of teenzines at a number of points throughout her interview. However, we also saw that she is a faithful reader of teenzines who wishes that the creators of these texts would 'try a little harder.' Sceptical readers typically base their criticisms on representational failures rather than the fact that teenzines offer readers constructions which, by their very nature, can never present the reality which respondents long for: that is, their wish that teenzines could promote make-up use, for example, without overemphasizing the message that beauty is important or in ways that in fact encourage readers to 'accept themselves' as they are. Although sceptical readers may be critical of particular individual messages, they otherwise accept the overall goals and values espoused by teenzines. Again, Stephanie is a good example:

Oh, 'Cover Girl' ads [looking at an ad with interviewer]. I have a grievance with Cover Girl [laughs]. I'm pretty negative about these things.
[Interviewer:] That's okay. We want to hear what you have to say.
'The Cover Girl look is yours, in 147 shades' [reading caption]. No! If they're going to advertise these things in this country, please supply it. I've gone to every London Drugs store, the closest they come to my colour is like honey beige, which is like streaking white on my face. They really don't live up to what the ads portray them to be ... Like I used their clarifying makeup. It didn't match my skin tone, firstly, and for some inane reason they put silicic acid in the thing. What it does is just peels your face and turns you white.

Stephanie (African Canadian) continues to criticize the racism of make-up advertising, reading the ad, which features five models from differing racial groups:

I guess the one thing I do like about the ad is that they give Asian and darker-coloured-skin girls in the ad. But there's only two of them. And three of them are green-eyed, blue-eyed, mousy brown and blonde, right? Even in TV commercials, all of them are blonde. All of them are white.
[Interviewer:] Um. I've noticed that.
And then all of a sudden they hit you with 147 shades, 'We've got it all for you' [reading slogan].

However, like other non-Caucasian readers who are consciously aware of the racism of the current beauty standard, Stephanie does not reject the beauty mandate or the industry which benefits from its promotion:

And you go out there and you're expecting this and you look for it and you're like – Cover Girl is one of the cheapest make-ups, that's what attracts people to it. You can get a bottle of make-up for about 5, 5 or 6 dollars. It's too bad it doesn't work! [laughs] Okay. So basically you end up going back to Revlon and paying $12 or $13 for a bottle of Colourstone make-up, which is the only make-up that really suits people of colour. Revlon, they have done a very good job of doing that.

The purpose of this citation is not to suggest that gender is a more important factor in teenzine reading than is race; further research is required to explore the way in which racialized identity is related to the reading of texts, such as teenzines, which are based on Caucasian representations. Rather, the above citation illustrates the power of the text voiced by sceptical readers, in this case to naturalize the commodification of femininity and women's pursuit of beauty in ways which obscure racist dimensions of patriarchal domination. In the final analysis, Stephanie's reading does not place her in opposition with the dominant meanings promoted by teenzine discourse. Sceptical reading does not mean that readers simply pick acceptable meanings and discard others, however. Despite the criticisms of the text voiced by sceptical readers, many examples of undoing come from the transcripts of their interviews. Seventeen-year-old Laura is presented as illustration.

Laura: 'It's just for your own self'

Laura's transcripts contain the most articulate criticisms of magazines expressed by girls in this study, evidenced by her commentary on the Eternity ad, cited at length below. As noted in chapter 4, the vast majority of readers uncritically accepted this representation as a pleasurable image of a loving mother. In contrast, Laura decodes this ad as a representation constructed to appeal to potential consumers of Calvin Klein perfume. As a consequence, she does not incorporate stereotypical associations into her meaning-making:[5]

Uhm, this is a more high-fashion ad for Eternity – Calvin Klein. It has a super model in it. [pause] It's very 'WASPy' [White Anglo-Saxon Protestant]. Even though all you can see is the woman and the girl, they're both white, they're both wearing white. It's kind of like they're in the 'great outdoors' – they're in the country. Uhm, it's appealing I think to people that can't afford the Calvin Klein clothes but can afford the perfume. It's just selling a really nice yuppie image I think – but this would appeal to *all* people, but they sell the perfume to people who can't afford the clothes. And it does say 'Calvin Klein' in big letters at the bottom, so – It's a nice picture and everything. It's not – they're not using sex or anything, they're just using like – it's *affluence*. It looks affluent and, I don't know, I like it. I think that she's pretty and stuff. She's obviously not the kid's mother though. I don't know if they're trying to make it look like that but it's *never* in these ads, it's never struck me – maybe it's because you see her all the time, she's such a big model, but it's never struck me that it's supposed to be a parent-and-child kind of thing.

In many ways, Laura's reading resembles those by cultural critics. As we might suspect from her familiarity with the model, Laura is an avid reader of women's magazines, including *Allure*, *Mademoiselle*, *YM*, (sometimes) *Seventeen*, *Shape*, *Sassy*, *People*, and her mom's 'house and home' magazines. Her familiarity extends to the publishing histories of many of the magazines discussed in the study, including teenzines. Consider this response to Alissa's request to 'tell me what you think of *Seventeen*':

Seventeen? I thought it would have been *Sassy* that they have chosen [looks for a copy of *Seventeen*, which she leafs through during the interview]. *Seventeen*, it's not a very good magazine at all because, when this new magazine *Sassy* came out, they totally gave them a big scare and so *Seventeen* was forced to change their format and everything. They still, it still is the bigger one I think, but it's just – it's almost patronizing, I think, or however you'd describe it. *YM* magazine is not. It's very, it's very – Mary [friend] says it's anti-woman. She called my attention to that. It's kind of true. Uhm, *Seventeen*, it has good fashion, but not as good as *YM* and it's – there's not much in it. You can read it in about five minutes ... *Seventeen* is really, uhm, it's very, like it appeals to Middle America more, I think. The fashion is a bit more – it's not as, it's a bit more interesting I guess. It's not really more fashionable or less fashionable, it's just that I like – these girls in *Seventeen* all look like they're from some, you know, some small town in wherever. They're really like clean-cut and in *Sassy* they're more urban, the fashions and stuff.

Laura also connected magazine culture to economic imperatives:

Shape is a good example of a magazine we really didn't talk about. It's owned by the Weiders, who own everything in fitness you can imagine. They are like I guess the expert family of fitness. He owns, you know, the companies that make the machines and the food and the clothes and the videos and *everything*, and he also owns the magazine and all the ads are for – not all of them, but a lot of the ads, the vast majority are from *his* company, but it's a good magazine. It's not a *scam*, I wouldn't say, it's just a good example of how people use their magazines as, like for a consumer kind of cause.

We might expect from these kind of comments that Laura would have been classified with the readers in the following section who reject the dominant definitions of commercial magazines. In fact, when asked if there was 'anything she might like to add' after commenting on specific ads, Laura reminded Alissa, 'you can't expect too much, you can't say "Oh that's ugly" or "It's tacky" because normally it's tacky on purpose. It's more business than art.' Despite her critical readings of these texts, Laura's everyday acceptance of the dominant messages of femininity is signalled elsewhere in interviews, when the discussion turns to Self. We have already seen, in chapter 7, that Laura expresses doubts about herself and also claims that 'looking good' is the hardest thing about being a girl. Despite her awareness that the beauty mandate serves economic interests, Laura never goes out of the house without make-up:

It started out like when I was younger, that I wouldn't go out without powder, and then powder and concealer, and then foundation [laughs]. But, uhm, I did once, when I was in Mexico at spring break with friends – I went for breakfast without make-up on ... If you – if someone saw me on the street they'd probably think that I wasn't wearing make-up because it's just like 'skin make-up' – it's not like loud colour. And I mean, I *could* [go out without make-up] if I really want to, like I don't have really bad skin or anything.

It is interesting to note that, like most of the girls in this study who wear make-up, Laura went on to claim that she does so 'for fun':

[Interviewer:] Why wear make-up then?
I wear make-up because it's fun. And like I think it's just, I feel better, like just – I don't know. I guess [that's] why everyone wears make-up [laughs].

Clearly, this claim by Laura that she wears make-up 'for fun' cannot be interpreted as 'gender play.' Her commentary clearly testifies to the extent to which the practices of looking good have been incorporated into Laura's self-esteem and sense of Self. We saw earlier that Laura maintains that '90 per cent of what we [adolescent girls] care about, and that's the same with me, is how we *look*':

If I put on my make-up and everything, I probably don't look that much different, so I feel better if you've done that. But it's just for your own self, but I think that it's all connected at my age to how you look, when you feel good about yourself, or like when people – yeah, that's *mainly* the most – you also feel good about yourself like if your friends say something nice to you, or you do well on something or whatever, but it's not, it's not as big a thing, you know what I mean?

As a consequence of worrying about their physical appearance, Laura and her friends started wearing anti-ageing creams when in Grade 7. As signalled by the shift in her discussion from first person – '*I* feel better' – to second person – 'if *you*'ve done that' – Laura's reflexive assessment of her own practices of beautification are a source of undoing. Because she is aware that linking self-esteem to beautification is not in women's interests, Laura believes that she and her friends[6] 'aren't very well adjusted':

Like my friends aren't very well adjusted [laughs].
[Interviewer:] What do you mean?
Well, I think it's just because we, most of us went to like the girls' school for a long time and we're not just really, like we don't, we're not really like well adjusted. Like a lot of my friends care a lot about how they look. But, like we could all go out and put on a kind of show and get all dressed up, but we can't, it's really hard for us to make friends with people and be like normal.

Laura elaborates why she feels that she and her friends are not 'normal':

Just like the total, like the obsession – maybe our parents put it on us, about how you look and what you're wearing. We're always like way more dressed up than other people wherever we go ... They say this happens at all-girls schools and stuff, like being a lot more concerned about weight and how you look and like, being more catty.

The purpose of discussing Laura's story is not to claim that her low self-esteem is a consequence of her avid reading of women's magazines: rather, her story reveals the power of cultural over individual choices and reminds us that isolated readings of specific texts cannot be taken out of their everyday context if they are to be 'reread' by researchers for what they tell us about embodied Subjects and everyday Subject-ivity. There is an obvious disjuncture between Laura's 'intellectual analysis' of magazines as serving economic interests through 'anti-woman' messages and her everyday practices which resonate with these very messages and which she acknowledges to be a source of anxiety. This disjuncture is not (simply) a shift between discourse registers, in the way which Frazer (1987) suggests.[7] Rather, it points to what Smith (1987) calls 'fault lines' in women's consciousness. Smith attributes these types of disjunctures to contradictions between official discourses about what it means to be a woman (such as those which are replete in women's magazines) and the reader's experiential knowledge of living as a gendered Subject. In this study, fault lines are leaks in the process through which teenage readers are discursively positioned as women in a patriarchal culture. Through symptomatic reading by the analyst, fault lines direct us to research problematics surrounding the ways in which women's experiences and their understandings of 'Self' and 'the social' are constructed by patriarchal culture. This manner of working is further elaborated in the conclusion. For the moment we note that the disjunctures identified above draw attention to what is bracketed by much academic criticism of women's magazines and their reading: everyday life 'outside' its textual re-presentation. Interpretations of reading which do not consider this context can misrepresent the process through which readers are constructed as Subjects. The importance of this point becomes apparent when we examine the transcripts of girls who are not simply sceptical towards the text, but who actively reject teenzine discourse as a venue for the construction of Self and their understanding of the social. Unlike sceptical readers, these critical readers challenge dominant constructions of femininity in politically meaningful ways because their everyday practices embody resistance to patriarchal prescriptions for women.

From Scepticism to Rejection

In the accounts noted above, instances of critical reading do not signal an alternative expression of gendered Self or the reader's recognition of traditional femininity as a patriarchal construction. In this section we explore cases where critical reading is associated with alternative definitions of 'being a woman' which lead to a rejection of the social constructions of teenzine discourse. Three criteria are used to classify critical readings in this way: an awareness by respondents that adolescent magazines do not unequivocally serve women's interests, aside from whether or not they enjoy reading women's magazines; refusal by the respondent to judge her acceptability according to teenzine standards of femininity; and the choice of role models which is not based on the values promoted by teenzine discourse – good looks and acceptance by men. Only this type of reader can enjoy the text in the ways described by Winship and others because they do not 'confuse' the discursive and material worlds of being female. These criteria resulted in six cases[8] of critical reading which refuse the discursive positioning offered by the text. The stories of these respondents offer cases where teenzine discourse does not construct reality for the reader and, hence, does not hold the power to undo the reading Subject. Three examples are described in detail below; as in the case of disciplined reading, the rejection of teenzine massages is examined within the context of everyday reading. The purpose of this section is to answer the difficult but important question of why self-doubt and anxiety do not necessarily accompany magazine reading. Rather than theorize Subject-ivity from transcripts of critical commentary, we read these transcripts symptomatically to ask why most, but not all, girls in this study adopt the dominant meanings constructed by commercial texts. However difficult this question may be, it is clearly of more practical value to a feminist politics of culture than the unexamined claim that reading embodies resistance: as we shall see, refusing the text is accompanied by the adoption of alternative paths to adult womanhood.

Samantha: 'They should call the magazine "Cover Girl"'

And here again [showing ad to interviewer]. If you look on every page, if there's like not a story or whatever, there's a Cover Girl ad on every single page mostly. They should call the magazine 'Cover Girl' instead of *YM*, because it's all Cover Girl. They're everywhere [laughs] ... I know only one girl out of all my friends that looks like one of these people and I know a lot of people, so it's really weird.

Thirteen-year-old Samantha quit reading magazines only about two months before her interview with Ann. She laughs at magazines like *YM*, calling them 'nothing but dumb ads.' Like other girls who reject teenzines, she quit when she 'found out that they are not at all like real life.' Since then she reads old copies of *YM* only when she's 'really bored.' For the most part, Samantha has replaced *YM* with new favourites – *Thrasher* and *Trans-World Skateboarding* – which reflect her interest in skateboarding, a predominantly male sport. Samantha's involvement in skateboarding places her self-definition in opposition to the femininity of both teenzine discourse and her school culture. Samantha deals with conflict which arises by dismissing teenzine discourse and the way in which it represents the teenage world. In doing so, she draws on specialized knowledge:

Well, I used to read *YM* when I was like eleven and twelve. But then I became a skateboarder I realized how dumb they are too. Like how they're non-realistic, right, and like this [Pointing to text] this issue makes fun of models everywhere ... [Pointing to fashion pages in *YM*] Okay, there's a picture of some bopper with Roller Blades in it, skateboards which obviously don't mix ... Skateboarders would usually hate jocks. And here you see in these magazines they have like pictures of girls with skateboards that probably don't even know what they are. And sometimes they have like really old kinds of skateboards that aren't even around any more and they think they're cool with them! [laughs]

Like other girls in this study, Samantha wears comfortable clothes to school which at first seem similar to those described by other girls. For example, on the day of her follow-up interview, Samantha was wearing baggy jeans and a long, baggy shirt. However, Samantha claims that there are only about three other girls at her school that dress like her, and a few more guys. She then emphasizes that because her group are 'skateboarders and not homeys' they dress differently from other kids at school. As she told us in chapter 7, the biggest difference between her group and other kids is that skaters cut their jeans, while homeys pin theirs. Although she wears cover-up make-up occasionally, Samantha does not wear make-up to school. What sets Samantha apart from other girls at school, however, is her interest in skateboarding. As we saw in chapter 7, kids at school reject Samantha because she is a 'girl skateboarder.' Samantha notes that it is usually the boys at school who reject her, 'but sometimes there's the off females too.' However, Samantha claims that she 'knows the truth' herself, and dismisses their opinions because 'probably they're not used to seeing a girl skateboarding, they probably think it's a men's sport, but it's not. It's just a board with wheels on it.' Overall, Samantha feels the best when she is with her skateboarding friends because 'they're fun to be around.' They make her laugh. Despite the fact that Samantha is rejected by classmates because she is different, when asked who she would like to be like, Samantha responds confidently, 'Myself.'

Kelly: 'It ... seems a bit superficial to me'

It also seems a bit superficial to me [looking at the Caboodles ad].
[Interviewer:] Why?
I guess because they're so engrossed in the details that are only on the surface.
[Interviewer:] The make-up and stuff?
Yeah. I think that make-up is a lot of fun, and clothes are a lot of fun. They can be a great expression of character, but when you spend your whole day on, like when you spend day after day on these things, uhm, it gets to be a way of covering up your natural stuff. I see clothes I guess as a way of expressing yourself and showing people *more* of yourself,

and helping them understand what you're really like and what you feel like. What they seem to portray in advertisements is that it's more covering up and showing what somebody else wants to see, instead of what *you* are.

As indicated above, sixteen-year-old Kelly enjoys dressing up. She claims that 'it can really encourage certain moods and can really get you into the spirit for something.' However, her everyday dress is casual. Like most of the other girls, at time of interview Kelly was wearing jeans, in this case with black socks, a grey wool jacket, with a black tank top and a short, button-up shirt. She claims that she wears 'what's clean in my closet and whether I feel like something colourful, or what activities I'm going to be doing, what would be appropriate, what's comfortable.' She wears make-up once in a while: 'occasionally, just a little bit of eyeliner, a little bit of mascara or something. Very rarely very much.' Kelly enjoys dressing up for what she considers to be special occasions, such as dances, meetings with her meditation group, or dinner with her father. For these occasions she would probably wear 'nylons and a dark brown dress, basically down to my calf and either flat shoes, or not too high.' Despite her enjoyment of dressing up on these occasions, Kelly does not read fashions magazines very often. 'I'll pick up one here and there and look at it, just look at the faces and read little bits,' but 'I don't go through each one specifically.' In the main, her magazine reading is limited to times when she and her sisters are 'just doing something that's not terribly active and [we] pick up a magazine and make comments.' About teenzines, Kelly maintains:

I guess I'd say the majority of them seem to portray quite a superficial image, but I also – like I don't condemn fashion or make-up or anything because it doesn't have to be that way. It can be played out differently.

When asked in her follow-up interview to show Rebecca something that she considers to be 'superficial,' Kelly commented aloud as she browsed through a recent issue of *YM*:

Oh yeah. I was looking at a friend's the other day, with another friend who doesn't generally read them. And we were laughing away and having a good time [laughs]. [Shows Rebecca examples in *YM*] I tend to be Canadian, so 'Stars and Stripes' kind of outfit doesn't really do it for me [laughs]. Uhm, I don't know, 'Babe Alert – Hollywood's Hunkiest' [reading title]. For me those kinds of guys are a little bit too much. Too much on the body and not enough in the mind. You know, it tends to be off-balanced and you tend to get sick of it pretty soon. That's just kind of pushing that and getting guys to be more and more like that, and that's not really what I want in my life. That seems kind of silly. It all seems kind of just a little bit silly because none of these pictures are something that I would be doing in my life. Uhm, I don't know. What else can I say?

Kelly also describes the fashion and beauty industry as 'a bit annoying':

Well, for example, I picked up one magazine cover – it's some catalogue or something, that had, you know, four or five pictures on the front and I was looking at one the other day and the majority were women with like jewellery or babies or with technology or something. And like, their main customers seem to be women here, or – I don't know, sometimes I guess they could be aimed at men too, having women in the picture. But it just seems that when I go out shopping or if I'm walking through a mall, it seems a lot of the people there are women.

In the final analysis, Kelly would rather read *Nature*. Perhaps reflecting the fact that she lives with her father in a single-parent household, for Kelly, unlike many of the other girls, fashion magazines are not part of the home environment. Instead, her household has a lot of 'alternative newspapers and environmental publishing or something. I might be looking at some *National Geographic* or something,' otherwise 'I don't get into a whole bunch of media in that sense.' Also unlike other girls, Kelly attends an 'alternate school.' Kelly describes public school as 'just like a day-care.' Unlike the case in the public school which Kelly attended previously, most of her classmates 'stay away from stuff like Guess.' In fact, she maintains that 'with the people I hang out with it's more likely to be pressure *not* to wear certain names': kids would be likely to ask 'Why are you supporting them?' Kelly feels the best about herself when she's 'having a good time with friends' or taking part in an activity that she really enjoys. While Kelly closes her first interview with the reflection that although 'I'm sure I can think of things I'd change in myself, I would always want to be myself.'

Mary: 'The stupidest things in the world'

I think Benetton ads are the stupidest things in the world. They're trying to sell clothes and yet they use like all these political controversies to get attention, to get talked about. I think it's really dumb. I don't see what it has to do with a store that sells clothes that are just way overpriced. I don't know. I think they're dumb [reading Benetton ad].

Although seventeen-year-old Mary usually wears jeans to school, on the day of her first interview she was wearing 'black fitted ski lodge pants, I guess you'd call them, a hunter green ribbed turtleneck sweater, and a plaid vest.' Because

Mary does not like wearing the same clothes twice in one week, she plans her school wardrobe a week ahead. She wears lipstick and mascara to school, and 'a bit more' when she goes out for special occasions. Like the readers quoted above, Mary is critical of the advertising in teenzines. Overall, she claims that advertising is insulting to readers:

I guess they want to relate to women, they want them to be able to go 'Oh yeah. That's exactly how I feel sometimes. Here's something just to pamper me.' Or whatever. But to me it's just the stupidest thing 'cause it just totally makes you out as stupid. Like you can't make a decision. You have no feelings. I don't know. I don't read those [reading ad for New Freedom sanitary pads].

Furthermore, Mary does not compare herself to magazine representations:

I don't look at it and go 'Gosh, I'm not that skinny' or 'I'm not that pretty' or nothing like that. I'm just kind of, like for me they're not that serious. It's just I want to flip through. I want to have a look. Like you're kind of bored. I'll just look through, find something a bit different, or I'll just read some little article or something.

While Mary does not name a specific person as a role model, she describes the type of women she admires:

I like people who are totally into whatever it may be, kind of like, say, a woman who's totally, like she knows what she wants, whose independent, whose like well put together and like well respected, confident, and like has a fun side as well. I can't name a specific person, though.[9]

As indicated above, unlike Samantha and Kelly, Mary still reads some women's magazines. She relates this to the fact that 'they're just so easy, you just sit there and kind of glance.' What makes her story different is the fact that Mary was once an avid reader of teenzines. She claims that she simply 'grew out of' *YM*:

Yeah, I read that one [*YM*]. I read that one in the past when I was younger. I think that's a younger teens thing.
[Interviewer:] Why?
The rage of it. It's like, like this boy star said this and 'How do you kiss?' and 'How do you like it?' It was dumb, but you liked it when you were younger kind of thing. That's what I thought [then].

She connects these personal changes to changes in school culture, comparing her experiences of Grade 11 with those of earlier grades:

I think more things are acceptable now. You know, no one cares as much, like [about] what everyone else is wearing. It starts to really not matter any more. It's just whatever you're comfortable in, or whatever. I think before your personality had to conform a little more. Like now you probably have your friends and they're probably not going to care what you wear.

Mary's case was chosen because it captures the nature of personal changes discussed by some of the older girls. In fact, Mary's reading preferences were changing so rapidly that they differed in her two interviews.[10] At the time of her first interview, Mary read *Seventeen*, *Allure*, and *Mademoiselle* 'religiously, every month' and told Rebecca that *Seventeen* was her favourite. By the time of her follow-up interview about eight months later, however, Mary no longer read *Seventeen*, which she then described as hilarious:

Seventeen just seems like, it's for like thirteen-year-olds. I don't know even how I liked it before.
[Interviewer:] So you've outgrown it?
Oh, I read it and laugh, it's so funny. It's honestly funny to read. It's all little problems and stuff. It's hilarious. Like things are so stupid in it. Like you know, I'll still flip through them or whatever, but I just think they're dumb. Like little stories, little problems. Those are just frightening.
[Interviewer:] Can you give me an example?
Yeah. Like they're so stupid. 'I want to get my ears pierced and my friend says she can do it. Should I let her?' [showing Rebecca text in *Seventeen*]. Like just the stupidest things. I just, like it's amusing to me more than anything else.

Despite these derisive comments, Mary candidly suggested that in her younger years she must have been like the typical reader addressed by these texts:

They should make it fit more people. Like to me that fits the total stereotype. A little twelve-year-old who's infatuated with make-up and clothes and little trends. Like even now they seem trivial [but back] *then* they didn't. Like I'm sure I was exactly like that.

She claims to have once been the stereotypical Subject of teenzines:[11]

I think that everything they do in that magazine, in a lot of magazines for that matter, kind of gives you one impression and that leaves you with one impression the entire time. They're kind of really constant about that. Like to me it just seems like to like that you'd have to be a certain kind of person and you'd have to fit that stereotype and I'm sure I did. That's probably why I liked it and stuff.

Mary attributes current reading preferences to her development of a broader perspective on life: 'When you get older I think you can kind of look at things from other perspectives and appreciate other points of view and other reasonings, other logics, other ideas, and stuff.' Because Mary attributes her rejection of teenzines to her own 'maturation,' unlike Samantha and Kelly she continues to read fashion and beauty magazines: her new favourites are *Allure* and *Glamour*. In the final analysis, therefore, although Mary rejects teenzines, she has not rejected commercial magazines; rather, Mary has simply grown out of teenzines and into women's magazines.

Discussion: Rejecting Teenzine Texts

The above three stories presented above are sketchy; further research is required which would provide in-depth reading histories. Although the emphasis has been on the critical rejection of teenzine messages, it is important to remember that such rejection does not characterize the readings in this study. For the moment, resistance to the text reminds us that acceptance of patriarchal femininity is not an 'inevitable' effect of teenzine reading. Further, the stories noted above challenge the temptation to theorize the embodied Subject off magazine reading alone. If the critical reading comments of Samantha, Kelly, and Mary were assessed in isolation from their everyday lives, on the surface we might not find that they differ from those of sceptical readers. What qualifies these three cases as resistance to patriarchy cannot be not found in readings of the text alone. In this study, resistance to the patriarchal proscriptions of commercial culture is claimed only for those cases where resistant readings are incorporated into definitions of Self. Because this study takes the view that the primary effect of teenzine discourse is the construction of the gendered Subject, resistance can be meaningfully claimed only when the reader's definition of Self does not arise through comparison to the text. This is not to say that these readers do not compare cultural constructions to their everyday lives. Here comparison leads these readers to reject cultural constructions rather than to question Self. What the six cases of reading resistance in this study have in common is the refusal to assume the discursive positioning of teenzine texts as a point from which to establish what is 'normal' or 'desirable' for themselves as adolescent women. Why do these readers, who represent a minority of our sample, maintain the reading distance needed for a critical assessment of the text? Why do they, unlike the other girls, distinguish between the discursive and the experiential world? As an empirical rather than entirely theoretical question, we are led from text to context; from analysis of reading 'as a woman' to analysis of the everyday life of 'becoming a woman.'

In the final analysis, this chapter is about the way in which everyday experience – itself mediated by the meanings available through dominant culture – is a source of alternative understandings of the social world, including that of 'the adolescent.' In chapter 7 we identified public-school culture as an experience which disciplines reading by directing girls towards dominant definitions of femininity. When school culture emphasizes the need for girls to 'look good' and to understand the patriarchal norms that determine social acceptance, experiences at school can give resonance to teenzine messages. What the three readers above have in common is marginality to this culture. In Samantha's case, her interest in non-traditional sports is an alternative avenue for the formulation of a sense of Self; this interest also sets her apart from the dominant culture at her school. In the case of Kelly, as well as two other resistant readers in this study, reading occurs in an 'alternative' school context which does not support the goals and values of traditional femininity through consumption. Three of the six girls who reject the dominant messages of teenzines are not located in the everyday culture of public school. Finally, Mary no longer operates within a school culture which supports teenzine world views, not because she has relocated to an alternative school, but because the nature of school culture itself changes as girls advance from public to high school. Growing out of teenzines is important because it signals the way in which teenzine reading is transitory. It also suggests that what Mary in fact rejects is not so much the patriarchal proscriptions of teenzine discourse as her own previous immaturity about 'doing' gender. As we saw in chapter 5, the most frequently cited reason for reading teenzines is their age-relevance: it is also the most frequently cited reason for quitting teenzine reading. However, the transitory nature of teenzine reading does not mean that we should dismiss or downplay their social significance. Rather, as feminists we should ask what role teenzines play in making the transition from girlhood to womanhood so difficult for many women. As sociologists we further ask why this current study finds so few cases of resistant as opposed to disciplined reading. Clearly, our answers to this latter question directs attention to the way in which society, generally, is complicit in the difficulties expressed by the adolescent women in this study.

Comparison Reading and the Power of Naming

Ang (1988: 188) argues that as feminists we must understand reading pleasure because it can empower women. In chapter 6 we explored the pleasure of teenzines as recognition: many readers in this study expressed pleasure when they recognized themselves and their teenage experiences in the text. This recognition does not mean that girls are simply 'duped' by the text: recognition is the result of negotiation, described here as 'comparison reading.' Comparison reading draws attention to the intersection of experiential and discursive knowledge. In this study, readers draw on their understanding of social reality in order to assess the truth status of the text. In Chapters 4 and 7 we saw how this understanding is rooted in both 'conventional wisdom' of traditional stereotypes and experiences of school culture. Specifically, chapter 7 suggests that the culture of public school is likely to reinforce traditional definitions of gender. In the final analysis, correspondence between teenzine messages and school culture supports comparison reading which empowers women by reaffirming the normalcy of their experiences and by giving girls, as reading Subjects, a voice to claim an authenticity for these experiences. In *Girl Talk* this pleasurable aspect of teenzine reading is equated with the 'doing' of the Subject in ways which allow her to 'fit in' to school culture and gain a sense of 'belonging' to the social. The problem is that this doing is framed within the goals and values identified in chapter 5 that emphasize self-interest in terms of looking good and knowing men's attitudes and opinions. Teenzine reading is thus a contradictory experience. One consequence is that it is not always, or necessarily, a pleasurable experience. The pleasure of recognition arises precisely because the reader assigns truth status to the text; ironically, this means that the potential of the text to do the Subject brings with it the potential to also contribute to the 'undoing' of the reading Subject. In *Girl Talk* undoing is expressed as self-doubt and anxiety about oneself or one's place in the social order; this self-doubt and anxiety was an unanticipated finding of the current study that was subsequently taken up as the research problematic. Specifically, we explored why teenzine reading, as a common and pleasurable pastime for many young girls, is also a source of marked displeasure.

As in the case of 'doing' the Subject, teenzine reading contributes to undoing when readers compare their embodied Self to magazine representations. Given the unachievable standards set by beauty magazines, it is not surprising that comparisons result in an unfavourable assessments of physical Self. While adult women may, indeed, fail to compare themselves in this way or successfully dismiss unrealistic standards, in this study comparison reading can lead to a questioning of Self-worth. Even readers who criticized the beauty standard perpetuated by commercial representations of women provided an extensive inventory of physical characteristics that are a source of personal dissatisfaction. In some cases (but certainly not all) this dissatisfaction gave rise to conflictual Self-definitions. In this study, conflict often surrounded a conscious acknowledgment that, while cultural representations are a source of anxiety for many girls, readers themselves accept these images as valid messages about femininity. While these types of conflicts are often characterized (and treated) by concerned adults as evidence of psychological pathology, here we have seen how the mandate of school culture to 'look good' contributes to a lived experience that reinforces the everyday importance of cultural standards of feminine beauty. When we take the standpoint of our young readers, questioning the dominant meanings of the text amounts to a questioning of the reader's own meanings of herself as becoming a woman. While it may be the case that individuals have the power to reject social messages which they consciously recognize to be against their best interests, in this study the reading context of school enhances the social over personal relevance of patriarchal definitions of being a woman. In short, the everyday experiences made available to girls through institutionalized modes of social organization reinforce commercial meanings of the social world.

In *Girl Talk*, the power of the teenzine text lies in this ability to both do and undo the reading Subject and readers' understandings of the social. However, we have seen that the text does not operate in this way for each and every reader. The purpose of this chapter is to question why some girls, but not others, read in ways which resist this power of the text, however pleasurable its reading. In order to answer this question we looked at instances where reading escapes the discursive disciplining of the text. This type of reading is important because it can be a practice through which readers control their reading pleasures by actively rejecting discursive messages which they deem 'unrealistic,' irrelevant, or against their best interests. Importantly, critical reading engages readers in what Frazer (1987) calls a discourse register which distances them from the text. This distancing prevents the reader from assigning ontological status to the text and can provide a position from which the reader can reject the text, however pleasurable its reading. Because most readers articulated criticisms of their magazines at some point during interviews, our goal is to understand why the distancing which occurs through critical reading allows some readers, but not others, to reject messages which contribute to the undoing of the Subject. Our investigation identified two types of critical reading practice, one which supports and one which does not support the patriarchal meaning of commercial texts.

The first type of critical reading is described in this chapter as sceptical reading. Sceptical reading expresses disappointment with the representational failures of the text, rather than with its actual message. Because sceptical reading does not question the ontological validity of messages such as the importance of looking good and gaining male approval, as in the case of disciplined reading teenzines remain relevant to sceptical readers. In the final analysis, sceptical readers do not reject teenzines as social texts. In chapter 7, we have seen that the relevance of teenzines is encouraged by their everyday reading context, in particular the context of school culture. While I agree with Frazer (1987) that readers' reflexivity can bring into question the nature of constructed messages of womanhood, when reflexivity is grounded in the experiences of school culture, dominant messages of femininity may not be challenged. In fact, when teenzines are read within the context of school culture, teenzine messages appeal to girls because they address the experiential dilemmas of 'being a girl.' The problem is that teenzines provide personalized solutions for readers which, in the long run, act to reinforce the dilemma of being female in a patriarchal culture. Regardless of the criticisms which many girls expressed, sceptical reading cannot be interpreted as politicized reading in any meaningful sense. Instead, what interests us is the disjuncture between readers' intellectual analysis and their everyday practices which embody the goals and values of teenzines. As a symptom this disjuncture appears through the questioning of Self rather than the text. It suggests that *as a process* the text is much more complex than many commentators suspect: as researchers we cannot read the effect of teenzines off the text alone.

A second type of critical reading has been identified which is associated with refusal of the text. Like sceptical readers, these readers may criticize the text for its representational failures. The difference is that their refusal of disciplined reading is grounded in the questioning of teenzine discourse itself. In this study questioning is facilitated by a reading context which does not support the dominant definitions and majority experiences of being female in a patriarchal culture. In our case, readers who rejected teenzine discourse are marginal to, or located outside of, public-school culture. In this exploratory study we saw three ways in which this marginalization might occur: through participation in nontraditional sports, through attendance at an alternative school,[12] and through the progression from junior high to high school. Identification of these three processes helps us to understand why so few girls in this study reject teenzine discourse, although they will, in all likelihood, 'grow out of' teenzine reading. While we might be tempted to understand the rejection of magazines such as *Teen, Seventeen*, and *YM* by older girls simply in terms of their personal/social maturity, here we draw attention to the role of experiential knowledge in textually mediated understandings of Self and of the social. The eventual rejection of teenage magazines can be found in the range of experiences which older readers can deploy in comparing cultural constructions to the extra-discursive world:

Always, every time there's an article, they have to show one of the things that it talks about, like in a picture form so everything's so exaggerated. And they don't even have that much on clothes. Like 'What to never say to a man': how can they tell you what to say? [laughs] And then all these stupid quizzes. I loved them when I was in Grade 8, but I can't imagine how like a thirty-five-year-old woman would sit down and actually do that. 'How good is your judgment?' – You'd think you'd know by then! (Sixteen-year-old Crystal)

It also means that older readers have greater experiential knowledge about gender and gender dynamics:

All the articles seem to be like 'I like him, but he doesn't like me' – like how to get a guy and stupid things like that, you know. Well, I guess it *is* important to know what to do if you like someone, but it just seems kind of like – it's really like too stereotypical teen kind of stuff, what you read in [those] magazines ... Before, when I was younger, I liked these articles a lot, but now that I'm – I guess I've been through more experiences in real life. (Sixteen-year-old Erica, who had indicated in a previous interview that *YM* was her 'favourite magazine')

The fact that girls in this study eventually 'grow out of' teenzine reading does not mean that we should not be worried about commercial media for adolescents. As feminists we need to ask not simply how these texts contribute to young girls' sense of themselves and to naturalization of a patriarchal order. While these questions are indeed important, as sociologists we need to ask why teenzines are among the few discourses available for young girls and how socially organized experiences of young girls make the transition from girlhood to adulthood so difficult for many women. Comments from preadolescent girls[13] suggest that social processes which restrict the range of opportunities available for girls to gain a sense of Self begin very early. Consider these responses to Jennifer's question 'Do you think it's hard to be a girl sometimes?':

Yeah, considering the teachers ... They're kind of sexist because they don't let girls do anything. They think that boys are way stronger so they let them all, let them have all the privileges and everything.
[Interviewer:] What kind of privileges do the boys get?
Like playing hockey. (Ten-year-old)

Some of the guys [at school] are pretty sexist.
[Interviewer:] What do you mean by sexist?
Uhm, like they think that like – 'cause they were playing a soccer game one time and,

like we were all playing and like some of the teachers are actually like that. There're like 'let's split up the boys so that the boys play together and the girls play together.' It was a girl teacher, too! (Twelve-year-old)

No, not unless you're a tomboy or something.
[Interviewer:] What do you mean by that?
Well like if you wear boy clothes and all that stuff, and if you always act like them [boys]. (Eleven-year-old)

There's different groups at school. All the boys hang out together and all the girls, and sometimes friends that are boys that I like to hang out with, they're all with their friends, and sometimes I wish that I was a boy. (Ten-year-old)

Yeah, 'cause guys get lots of stuff.
[Interviewer:] Like what?
Well, school stuff. They get more for sports. They're expected to be way better and they get that ... I think that we should be treated equally. (Twelve-year-old)

While I am not claiming that our culture directs girls toward teenzine reading, it seems reasonable to argue that if the range of venues through which girls exercise Subject-ivity is restricted, magazine reading can become more important in girls' exploration of Self and of the social. As suggested in *Girl Talk*, the structure of everyday life organizes girls' agency around traditionally feminine activities, such as reading, and away from non-traditional activities, including politics and sports. One consequence is that reading – whether magazines, books, or television – can then become one of the few activities through which girls can explore and develop a sense of Self. In this context, teenzine reading is symptomatic of the commodification of gendered time (and space) made possible by the social construction of teenagerhood. For this reason, struggles surrounding adolescent magazines concern more than their content (although we may begin our inquiry there); any meaningful cultural politics must challenge the social processes (in other words, 'social structures') that enable commercial interests to colonize girls' search for socially valued Selfhood.

In summary, readers who do not assign ontological status to discursive constructions occupy a critical distance which allows them to enjoy texts 'for what they are'; they also resemble adult researchers. The important point here is that these readers comprise a minority among the girls in this study. Many more girls are sceptical readers, aware at some level that teenzine messages do not unequivocally advance their interests as women even though these texts resonate with their lived experiences. If sceptical readers reconcile this contradiction by questioning their own experiences or sense of Self, the result can be conflict or anxiety. While this type of finding requires further research, conflict themes are a significant characteristic of interview transcripts in this study. Conflict arises primarily through comparison reading: if readers assign the text ontological status, comparison of Self to the text can result in questioning of Self rather than teenzine constructions. Comparison reading thus blurs the boundaries between the discursive and experiential worlds of adolescence. In our case we limited the experiential world of adolescence to school culture. While other reading contexts require further research, the point of such research is to explore the ways in which society is organized to make the messages of commercial texts relevant to teenagers.

In total, *Girl Talk* moves us away from the treatment of texts as cultural arte-facts to analysis of the text as one element in the process of meaning-making by situated Subjects. Everyday reading draws attention to the ways in which our identities 'as women' both inform and are shaped by social texts addressing female readers. As others have emphasized and as this study shows, reading 'as women' draws on experiences mediated by both the dominant culture and the specificities of our social locations. Because dominant culture is written from the standpoint of the powerful, similar to our everyday social locations of read-ing social texts are organized through relations of ruling based on race, class, age, and so on (see Smith 1987). In our study, both the text and its reading have been shaped by readers' age-specific experiences of being female.[14] While the importance of age makes it tempting to view this identity as a natural rather than cultural construction, one purpose of this study is to show how 'one is not born but becomes a woman.' Becoming a woman is a social process; as such it is shaped by institutions which organize and coordinate individual activities and the discourses through which we attribute shared meaning to these activities. In this study, teenzines are one such institution. As commercial texts, teenzines are part of a more comprehensive discourse through which the publishing industry assigns meaning to social life. While it may be true that texts are open and that editors address issues of interest to their reading audience, the meanings assigned by teenzine texts are not arbitrary or unmotivated. Teenzines have an existence only because they survive as an economic rather than purely cultural institution. As such, the meanings assigned to adolescent feminity are not deter-mined simply by the relations between text and readers. Teenzine messages are a product of the relations among various economic interests that include editors, publishing houses, and advertising agencies and their clients. This aspect of teenzine discourse is made mysterious and hidden from view when social texts are treated as simply cultural artefacts and when the subject is simply 'read off' the text. While individual readers indeed have the power to resist attempts by commercial interests to define the social and construct Subjects along the lines which will serve their interests, in this study the majority of young readers accept the preferred meanings of the text. In the same way that we have understood this effect by looking at the context of teenzine reading, in order to truly treat the text as process we must link teenzine messages to the context of their making. As we shall see in the conclusion, this examination requires a different kind of reading by social analysts from that typically practised by cultural critics.

Towards a Materialist Analysis of Texts: Reading Sociologically

As argued in the introduction, *Girl Talk* maintains an analytical distinction between the cultural and the social realms of adolescent femininity. While the notion of a cultural realm refers to objects and practices which engage girls in meaning-making, 'the social' evokes the lived experiences of teenage girls. *Girl Talk* takes as its problematic the nature of the relationship between the cultural and the social worlds of adolescent identity; in doing so, the study of texts is not a study of culture. Rather, *Girl Talk* adopts the realist epistemology of historical materialism in order to answer sociological questions about social texts. While this epistemology acknowledges that, as power, textual knowledge constitutes objects of social (and political) consciousness, it does not conflate the discursive means (linguistic and conceptual practices) that make representation possible with its object. In MacDonald's words, it does not mistake what is constitutive for what is constituted (1991: 63). While the magazine messages which mediate discourses surrounding femininity (as well as those of women's studies, for that matter) may be said to play a role in constituting the *concept* 'woman,' it is not necessary to then claim that these discursive means constitute women themselves.

As Benton (1984: 194) notes, a commitment to the existence of discursive practices, in itself, is also a commitment to their condition of possibility; that is, to extra-discursive realities on the part of at least some discursive terms. Cultural studies which conflates the cultural and the social represses questions about these conditions of possibility for knowledge. *Girl Talk* is thus a critique of cultural studies which simply reads the social off cultural texts, in isolation of any consideration of what makes these texts and their reading possible. As shown in chapter 7, social texts such as teenzines can never contain 'the entire story.' In fact, we read girls' transcripts as symptomatic of 'something beyond the text.' Gaps and inconsistencies in girls' accounts directed us to disjunctures between femininity as culture and its lived embodiment. By reading girls' reading of magazines against their accounts of school culture, we came to a fuller understanding[1] of how readers' Subject-ivities are mediated by commercial texts. In this chapter, we extend the same critique to sociological texts. Can we read the social off sociological texts? To do so surely is to claim that, while commercial texts constitute objects of consciousness, academic texts reflect knowledge. However obvious the contradictory nature of this claim, it is seldom, if ever, raised in much work which employs a Foucauldian notion of power. Adressing this contradiction, the concluding chapter interrogates the truth status of *Girl Talk*. In Skeggs's words (1995): why does my account of adolescent magazines and their readers matter 'more' than accounts by others, especially those I criticize?

Throughout *Girl Talk* I have argued that by grounding analysis in everyday rather than researcher readings, the current study brings to light aspects of magazine reading which cannot be found within the texts themselves. This answer does not, however, get to the heart of the matter. In this chapter we explore the implications of recognizing sociological knowledge as cultural production. By referring to 'cultural production,' I draw attention to the textual nature of sociological research. Can we read the researched Subject off interview transcripts, for example? I raise such a question because I agree with Skeggs: social research must account for its own production.[2] This question necessarily engages us in epistemological matters as an important point of departure for both the theory and the politics of cultural studies. Here I raise questions of epistemology in order to consider a methodology that allows us to theorize the relationship between the cultural and social study of women. I return to Poovey's claim, raised in chapter 4, that textual analysis must be extended to include the texts produced by cultural critics themselves. In the next section I explore both affinities and discontinuities between Marxist feminist and post-structuralist approaches to sociological inquiry. While I, like others, express difficulty with the way in which political considerations disappear in the post-structural conflation of the cultural and the social, I find its intertextual way of working fruitful. *Girl Talk* thus concludes by reviewing the intertextual nature of its own claims as knowledge and by directing attention to the kind of sociology which this epistemology fosters. In doing so, I do not claim to have identified all the pitfalls, let alone advantages, of integrating discursive methods of analysis into the social sciences. By drawing attention to the potential usefulness of literary theory and ways of working for feminist sociology, I hope to inspire others to take up this project as an empirical, rather than simply theoretical, task.

From the Subject to Subject-ivity: Marxist Encounters with Post-Structuralism

One purpose of the current study is to explore ways in which methodological advances in the humanities can inform sociological analyses of cultural phenomena such as women's magazines. This exploration has been influenced by post-structural theories and ways of working. As MacDonald (1991: 43) notes, 'post-structuralist theorists, Marxists, and feminists have occasionally discovered affinity in their intellectual projects.' She finds this affinity in their common problematization of the Subject.

In contrast to the humanist tradition in sociology, which separates texts and their writing/reading Subject, post-structuralist theories of subjectivity view discursive practices as constitutive of social life. As Easthope and McGowan (1993: 67) point out, these theories reject an epistemology (upon which sociological inquiry is grounded) based on the humanist notion 'I think, therefore I am.' In making this claim, Descartes separated consciousness and being. Assuming that we are the authors of all that we think and speak, he implied that we cannot think a thought without being. In contrast, Derrida asked whether we can think a thought without words. He thus linked consciousness and discursive systems of signification. This connection has led to the view of culture as a 'determinant' rather than 'reflection' of social life. As Weedon notes, by making subjectivity the effect of cultural representation, post-structuralist feminist theory suggests that experience has no inherent meaning because it is given meaning in language, through a range of discursive systems of signification: 'As we acquire language, we learn to give voice – meaning – to our experience and to understanding it according to particular ways of thinking, particular discourses, which pre-date our entry into language. These ways of thinking constitute our consciousness, and the positions with which we identify our sense of ourselves, our subjectivity' (1987: 33). However, feminist post-structuralism goes further by insisting that the individual is always the site of conflicting forms of subjectivity. This means that subjectivity is historically changing along with the various, sometimes competing, discursive fields which constitute our subjectivity. In terms of both a feminist theory and a politics of culture, the goal of textual analysis is to employ theories of language and meaning-making to identify areas and strategies for change.

In terms of these goals, feminist post-structuralism offers an understanding of how our experiences as women have specific meanings, particularly our experiences of oppression. This understanding comes from an examination of cultural venues that feminists have identified as influential sources of patriarchal definitions for womanhood, and as signifying women's oppression in specific ways. The goal of feminist textual analysis has been demystification of the discursive construction of 'Self' and of readers' sense of their location in the social world. This goal suggests that Marxist feminism and post-structuralism share important political agendas. At the same time, however, there are many reasons to believe that Marxism and post-structuralism are, in fact, irreconcilable projects. Foley (1990: 8) maintains that 'the great preponderance of the retheorizing of Marxism going on today under the aegis of post-structuralism constitutes a departure from – indeed, an attack upon – those cardinal principles of Marxism that distinguish it as a science of historical development and a strategy for revolutionary change.' She bases this claim on post-structural critiques of Marxism which advocate a radical pluralism not incompatible with the neo-liberalism of conservative political agendas (also see Hennessy and Ingraham 1997; Stabile 1997). In the place of the meta-theory associated with historical materialism emphasizing the importance of class relations, post-structuralist critics posit 'the supremacy of the contingent over the necessary, the concrete over the abstract, the particular over the general, and eschew the totalizing claims of theory' (Foley 1990: 11). The problem for Foley is that, despite claims to stand outside the ideological imperatives of a master discourse, this position is itself not exempt from hegemonic relations of power: 'the seemingly courageousness of immersing oneself in the contingency and randomness of a history without laws slides easily into acceptance – sometimes cynical, sometimes complacent – of the history that others make for us' (p. 11). She questions whether social groups currently struggling for justice are as ready as elite academic theorists to conflate a master discourse which rationalizes oppression with one that promises emancipation. In the final analysis, although Foley rejects post-structuralism, she maintains that 'there is no doubt that a crisis exists and that Marxism itself must come up with some satisfactory answers if it is widely to regain its credibility as a critical theory and its viability as a revolutionary practice that can shape and transform an oppressive social reality' (p. 9).

One problem in assessing the usefulness of post-structural theory is that it includes a diverse range of work. As Weedon (1987: 19) notes, the term 'post-structuralist' includes, for example, the 'apolitical' deconstructive criticism of U.S. literary critics, the radical writing of some French feminist writers, and the historical analysis of discourse and power by Foucault. While not all forms are necessary productive for feminism,[3] she finds promise in their shared assumptions about language, meaning, and subjectivity. Specifically, post-structuralist theory views language as the place where our sense of Self, as an affective but also coherent Subject, is constructed. Taking as its problematic the constitution of subjects through systems of signification and attendant processes of meaning-making, post-structuralism replaces the humanist Subject with notions of 'subjectivity.' Subjectivity refers to 'the conscious and unconscious thoughts and emotions of the individual, her sense of herself and her ways of understanding her relation to the world' (Weedon 1987: 32). Unlike humanism, which implies a conscious, knowing, unified, and rational Subject, post-structuralism posits subjectivity as a site of disunity and conflict. In short, subjectivity is never fixed: in part, this is due to the inherent nature of meaning-making; in part, it is due to the fact that subjectivity is produced in a whole range of discursive practices, the meanings of which are a constant site of struggle. Because language (and discourse) are sites of struggle over meaning, they are also sites where actual and possible forms of social organization are defined and contested. Thus language and discourse as venues of signification are, ultimately, sites for the operation of power.

A further complication in considering the usefulness of post-structural theories of subjectivity lies in the varying ways in which this term is used by different writers. For example, Weedon includes Althusserian Marxism in her discussion of post-structural theory. Other writers claiming to be post-structuralists appeal, in the last instance, to a rational and self-conscious Subject.[4] As a consequence of these types of difficulties, in this chapter 'post-structuralism' refers to approaches that do not assume the existence of a coherent, stable Subject prior to its signification. In these approaches both Subjects and 'social reality' are constituted, rather than reflected, in systems of signification. In other words, in this chapter 'post-structuralism' refers to the position that all meaning is constituted in language and discourse, and is not guaranteed by the knowing Subject. Obviously, this assumption is a difficult one for sociologists who conventionally view systems of signification (like magazine texts) as the effect and not the cause of human Subjects. From this perspective, post-structuralism and the humanist Marxism characteristic of feminism are irreconcilable. For this reason, I do not consider my own work to be 'post-structuralist,' even though others on occasion have. Rather, I consider the value of *Girl Talk* to lie in its reworking of Marxist feminism through insights from post-structural theories of meaning and its attempt to address questions raised by these theories as sociological ones.

Like MacDonald (1991), in this chapter I distinguish between post-structuralist theories that are based on an analysis of language and a Foucauldian notion of discourse. This distinction reflects my sociological interest in the social organization of meaning through particular discursive fields generated by specific institutions and practices. 'Discursive fields' refers to competing ways of giving meaning to the world and various social practices associated with meaning. Although taking similar phenomena as their subject, different discursive fields offer different subjectivities. As Weedon notes, the concept of a discursive field was first introduced by Foucault as part of his attempt to understand the relationship among language use, social institutions, subjectivity, and power. Unlike many post-structural theories of language, the study of discourse allows an investigation of the social rather than psychic imperatives of behaviour. It is thus more useful for Marxists because, as Smith notes, 'consciousness itself, as Marx and Engels use this term, is not merely something going on in people's heads. Consciousness is produced by people and is 'from the very beginning a social product, and remains so as long as men [sic] exist at all,' (1990: 42). However, although drawing on Foucauldian notions of discourse, I share Smith's (1990) complaint that within Foucault's work both 'power' and 'knowledge' are mystified; his conceptualizations capture something significant about contemporary society that they are incapable of explicating. This is because power has no ontology, no form of existence (p. 70). The central goal of *Girl Talk* is to specify the ontology of power working through social texts such a women's magazines. Like Smith, I locate the observable effects of power in the everyday activities of people. It is these activities, and not the content *per se* of women's magazines, that are the basis for disagreement over the significance of social texts. However diverse in terms of individual expression, these activities are not totally random actions on the part of women going about the business of doing femininity. As members of the social world, women engage in activities that sustain gender difference as integral to social life; the historical persistence of gender difference belies the extra-local coordination of multiple sites of women's actions. However personal our identities 'feel,' as women we act through frames of intelligibility made available through culture. For us, these frames include the social texts of women's magazines. Drawing on the insights of post-structural theory, *Girl Talk* advances a particular reading of the way in which subjectivity, as lived experience, is constituted through the frames of intelligibility surrounding gender. It does so through the notion of Subject-ivity. Subject-ivity allows us to explore what Valverde (1991) calls 'social subjectivity' as a cultural project which engages embodied Subjects. It captures the nature of subjectivity as mediated by social texts while reminding us of the presence of embodied women outside the text.

In the final analysis it is the disappearance of embodied women within post-structuralism which leads me to reject it as an advance for materialist feminism. Implicit in this rejection is the claim that the prime methodologies through which social texts are currently studied as objects are limited when it comes to understanding the effects of texts such as adolescent magazines. However mundane the call for a study of media effects may seem in the 1990s, a politics rather than simply a theory of culture demands that we answer practical questions. It also demands that we move beyond methodologies such as content analysis or interpretative decoding which limit us to descriptions of social texts, however provocative or novel these descriptions may be. As argued throughout this study, to read the social from texts which address women is to mistake embodied women for their cultural representation as 'women,' conflating the cultural and the social. Sociological knowledge must take us beyond the text as 'thing' in order to explore women's everyday encounters with such cultural objects.

In this study, the social texts of femininity were treated as a mediating process through which both the gendered Subject and the social world of heteropatriarchy are reconstituted. While process requires that we study the texts in question, it also demands investigation of their everyday reading by embodied readers. While our investigation of everyday reading found that many of the readers in this study behaved in ways predicted by theoretical readings of texts, this is not to say that readers are determined by the text. Rather, this study brought into focus the importance of the reading context, pointing us to something outside the text. In this study, the 'something' outside the text was explored in terms of school culture, although other processes, such as family dynamics, obviously play an important role in the way in which teenzine meanings will, or will not, be taken up by adolescent readers. Here we saw that a school culture which emphasizes the importance of looks and reinforces the ability of boys to 'define' and label girls gives relevance to textual messages. Moreover, the relevance of teenzines is enhanced by the fact that they provide one of the very few venues where positive values are assigned to teenagerhood and where teenagers' everyday problems are addressed. Apart from feminism – which in my view neglects young women – these problems remain unnamed, hence unspeakable, within the realm dominant culture. Content aside, adolescent magazines should be of interest to feminist researchers because, through their naming, these texts make available a voice for teenage girls. Sociologically speaking, reading draws attention to processes at work which cannot be studied from magazine texts alone, no matter how creatively they are decoded by researchers. These processes are to be found in the lived experiences of readers which account for the relevance of magazine texts; in effect, it is the activities of the embodied readers, not the magazines themselves, that reveal the power of the text. While social texts such as commercial magazines are a form of social power, the secret of their power cannot be found in the immediacy of the text. In other words, we did not conflate agency as meaning-making with the text as a socially significant object.

When the study of social texts is approached in this way, the agency of everyday reading points to 'something' outside the text. As framed in *Girl Talk*, this 'something' evokes 'the social.' Feminist sociologists, for the most part, prefer to access 'the social' through women's experiences because official accounts, historically, have been written from the standpoint of men. Dorothy Smith (1981) argues that a distinctly feminist sociology will begin from women's everyday experiences, because such a point of entry into women's lives reveals new puzzles and sociological questions mystified by a social science written from the standpoint of the dominant academic group – white male scholars. The operative phrase here is 'point of entry,' because, as Smith notes, experience does not give us unmediated access to the 'truth' of women's lives. While experience is raw data for the sociologist, it is always, necessarily, worked over by the cultural, which makes socially constructed, historically specific meanings available. However, we have seen that the lived experiences of adolescent femininity exceed the categories of understanding provided by the femininity of teenzines. The problem is that girls' accounts of their lived experiences, in this case of school culture, are also mediated. Specifically, girls' accounts are mediated or 'worked over' by the research process itself. I would be naive to claim that I can directly access school culture, for example, through girls' accounts. Clearly, I am required to remain faithful to my own critique: that is, I cannot claim to read the social world of adolescent girls off the texts of interview transcripts.[5] Does this mean that we are trapped in an infinite regress of never going beyond the text, of claiming that nothing can exist outside of our reading and writing about it? The position that 'there is nothing except text' suggests that we cannot. Here I want to address the dilemma in a more fruitful way. Positively framed, what can we meaningfully say once we acknowledge that *Girl Talk* is based on researcher readings of girls' readings of texts? While doing *Girl Talk* did not provide me with easy answers to this question, it certainly could not be ignored. The remainder of this chapter explores the way in which I worked through epistemological questions surrounding the sociological analysis of texts. Specifically, it advances an analysis of social texts grounded in a materialist feminism challenged by the current turn to cultural studies for answers to existential questions. At the moment, sociology is open to rewriting, perhaps more so than at any other time since its inception. While feminism is certainly part of this challenge, in my opinion the developments which accompany a growing sociological interest in culture as a system of signification have had far greater impact. In part, this is because they have forced us to think about sociology itself as 'text,' as a method of writing 'the social.'[6] Does this mean that there is no longer a need for the sociostructural analyses of Marxism?

Towards a Materialist Analysis of Textually Mediated Discourse

In effect, the questions raised above require us to assess the postmodern claim that, because of the infinite nature of interpretation, no one interpretation of the social world can be claimed to be more 'truthful' than others, although some interpretations are more valuable because of their effect. Within postmodern reading, value does not lie in the 'methodological rigour' of analysis, but rather in the ability of the reading to generate new interpretations which shock, destabilize, and disrupt established meaning and notions of truth. In the final analysis, because this approach dissolves the distinction between fact and value, there are no grounds for adjudicating competing interpretations. 'Every reading of a text will always be to some extent a misreading, a version that selects certain details, meanings, or structural features at the expense of details which could just as well have figured in the critic's account' (Norris 1982: 129).[7] This denial of a stable, apprehensible truth has led some to claim that postmodernism advocates a new form of relativism; others maintain that it leads to the conclusion that nothing can ever be 'known' because knowledge is nothing except struggle over interpretation. In either case, what is at stake is not certainty, but rather the formulation of interpretations, or readings, which destabilize complacency about the giveness of current knowledge. Rosenau (1992: 117) identifies two postmodern strategies of interpretation which have destabilization of knowledge as their goal: intuitive interpretation and deconstruction.

Rosenau (1992: 118, 119) contrasts postmodern intuitive interpretation to both hermeneutics and conventional forms of interpretation in social sciences. While hermeneutic interpretation seeks to probe the 'silences' of discourse in order to uncover a deeper, hidden meaning, postmodernists claim that there is simply no 'meaning' to discover because all meaning is the effect of inquiry. On the other hand, social sciences typically understand interpretation as careful consideration of 'data,' for the purpose of identifying underlying patterns which reflect some 'truth' about the social world. In contrast, intuitive interpretation is introspective and anti-objectivist, taking the form of individualized understanding. Rosenau claims it is more 'vision' than observation. Intuitive interpretation is thus more difficult to describe than deconstruction, an approach that follows the work of Jacques Derrida.

In a critique of humanist philosophy, Derrida developed a method of 'deconstructive' reading that 'must always aim at the central relationship, unperceived by the writer, between what he commands and what he does not command of the patterns of language he [sic] uses. This relationship is ... a signifying structure that critical reading should produce. ... [A] production [which] attempts to make the not-seen accessible to sight' (1976: 158, 163). Deconstruction, as critical reading, is not about identifying errors through the omission of fact or biases in interpretation. Rather, this method of reading reveals the ways in which the conceptual distinctions upon which the text relies fail on the account of inconsistent usage of these very concepts in the text as a whole. Derrida

Conclusion   293

traces these types of problems to the instability of language itself. He argues that Western philosophers have been able to impose their various systems of thought only by ignoring the disruptive effects of language. One of the founding illusions of Western philosophy is that reason can somehow stand outside language and grasp the world as pure truth. Derrida draws attention to the way in which language undermines the philosopher's project (Sarup 1989: 57).

In exploring the instability of language, Derrida destabilizes Saussure's notion of meaning through (arbitrary) association of signifiers and signified. A Saussurean approach to semiotics analyses meaning as arising from the relations of its elements as a system, for example, through binary oppositions. Rejecting the notion that signifiers have a *necessary correspondence* to their signifieds, Saussure analysed their *association as arbitrary*: meaning is not immanent but rather established through relations of the elements to the whole. Meaning arises through the difference between opposites, such as 'hot' and 'cold,' but also the difference between 'hot,' 'hat,' and 'hit,' and so on. Any element means in relation to what it is not; systems are characterized by relations of differentiation which make meaning present through absence. The major analytic task for semioticians is to identify rules governing these relations. In contrast to Saussure, Derrida maintained that meaning can never be established through pure difference: this would imply a fixity of meaning grounded in a clear distinction between signifier and signified. Instead, Derrida maintained that there is no fixed distinction between signifier and signified. This can be illustrated by looking up a word (signifier) in the dictionary to learn its meaning (signified): all you would find would be more signifiers, whose signifieds you look up, and so on. The process is not only infinite, but circular, because signifieds keep transforming themselves into signifiers, and vice versa. You can never arrive at a signified which is not a signifier itself (Sarup 1989: 35). From this point of view, Derrida argued that meaning arises not simply through difference but also deferral. The word he coined to convey this process is *différance*, according to which meaning is simultaneously the product of differences and subject to deferral. *Différance* implies that meaning can never be fixed in language. Following from this, the Subject cannot be fixed in language but remains dispersed through an infinite chain of signification. Further, meaning cannot be fixed in single texts: just as signs refer only to other signs, texts can refer only to other texts, creating a web of intertextuality in meaning. There is an infinite proliferation of interpretations, and no single interpretation can claim to be the final one.[8] This approach aims instead to provide as many interpretations of any text as possible. For this reason, reading is described as 'productive' and texts which offer multiplicity of interpretation are called 'producerly' because each reading generates new meaning.

The notion of reading freed from normative constraints has been influential in cultural studies. The process of valorizing as many new meanings as possible underscores the celebration of popular culture as an everyday example of productive self-expression. This celebration results from Barthes' (1975) distinction between the readerly and writerly qualities of texts, and the reading strategies which these texts invite. John Fiske (1989b: 103) describes a readerly text as one which invites a passive reader who is receptive to dominant meaning through a 'disciplined' reading method. A readerly text is relatively closed; it is easy to read and is undemanding of its readers. He contrasts this text and the readings it invites to writerly texts: a writerly text challenges the reader to constantly rewrite it, to make sense of it. One way in which this occurs is by drawing attention to textual constructedness and inviting the reader to participate in the construction of meaning. While Barthes applied these distinctions to literary texts, cultural studies writers apply them to popular texts. Fiske maintains that popular culture arises when people select texts/meanings from which they produce new, unintended meanings. He thus argues that a popular text will be producerly: that is, it will contain enough ambiguities and contradictions and will foreground it own constructedness in such a way to invite rewriting. Within cultural studies Madonna is a good example of such a text, giving rise to debates discussed in chapter 1.

It is this focus on the affective rather than objective nature of texts that leads some writers to interpret the pleasures of reading as subversive. Following Barthes (1975), the text becomes important as a source of resistance because of its erotic pleasure and the way that pleasure is linked to desire which can disrupt the social. This resistance to the cultural occurs when reading results in a loss of sense of Self and of the subjectivity that controls and governs Self. Because the Self is socially constructed it is the site of ideological production and reproduction. The loss of Self, such as can happen when the reader is enraptured by the text, losing all sense of space and time, is therefore an evasion of ideology.[9] Barthes likens this effect of reading to *jouissance*: the bliss, ecstasy, or orgasmic pleasure that occurs at the moment of breakdown of culture into nature (Fiske 1989b: 50). *Jouissance* differs from the *plaisir* of reading: while the former arises through transcendence of cultural constructedness, the latter refers to the pleasurable experience of recognizing oneself in a text. Because this recognition arises through a disciplined, social way of reading, it does not escape ideology, but rather reproduces it through ideological reconstitution of the reading Subject. Barthes refers to *jouissance* as 'reading with the body': the body of the reader (rather than mind) responds physically to the body of the text (its physical signifiers rather than its conceptual/ ideological/ connotative signifieds). Because *jouissance* is not a quality of the text, it cannot be identified through analysis. Reading with the body occurs in the body of the reader, at the moment of reading when the text and reader erotically lose their separate identities and become a new, momentarily produced body that defies meaning and escapes ideological discipline (Fiske 1989b: 51). This notion resonates with French feminist 'writing with the body' as a strategy to evade the patriarchal Symbolic Order. In both cases, the body is assumed to offer the potential to disrupt ideological subordination and is thus counterpoised against culture, embracing 'a metaphysics of desire which fails to acknowledge the historical mediation of conceptions of the body and of sexuality by culturally specific systems of signification' (Felski 1989: 37).

The valorization of new meanings as resistance has also been extended to the activities of the cultural critic. In the same way that everyday folks are the heroes of cultural studies through their creative reading and reworking of dominant meaning, academics employ reading strategies to liberate interpretations repressed by methodological disciplining of traditional scholarship. The problem is, however, that cultural critics then claim this manner of reading as characteristic of everyday reading. For our purposes such a claim is problematic: we have seen throughout this study that adolescent girls, for example, do not read like adult researchers. For this reason, I find it necessary to maintain the kinds of distinctions challenged by postmodern critics of the text: distinctions between researcher and everyday reading, between the cultural and the social realms of adolescent femininity. At the same time, however, I acknowledge that sociology, as 'knowledge,' is a form of textual production. Can sociology, as 'text,' escape the kinds of dilemmas that emerge when we acknowledge the constructedness of meaning? What does a sociology which self-consciously recognizes its own textuality look like?

The question for us is whether the postmodern conflation of the social and the cultural is an inevitable consequence of acknowledging that sociological discourse derives meaning from the interrelations among various texts. Answering this question draws attention to the various texts that give meaning to *Girl Talk*, through the ways in which these texts are read against each other. In *Girl Talk* three texts have been read against each other to produce a new system of meaning. These texts include the writings by previous researchers reviewed in chapters 1 and 2, the adolescent magazines that are central to the study, and transcripts as the texts produced through interviews with young readers. As a system of signification *Girl Talk* derives meaning from the way in which I have positioned these texts in relation to each other: I am well aware that another researcher, for example, could (and in all likelihood would) bring these texts together in a much different way. Thus I would never claim that the meaning of *Girl Talk* is inevitable or that it provides the 'Truth' of adolescent magazines. What I am hoping is that it provides a convincing case for new ways of thinking about, and studying, social texts. However, I am also hoping that this new thinking and research will contribute to material changes in the lives of adolescent girls, although at this point it is not clear to me that this will be the case. (In all likelihood, *Girl Talk* will spend most of its days on a library shelf.) While I have already suggested, in chapter 3, that we must pay more attention to our own desire in the text, here I maintain that we carry a burden of proof when we conduct our work in the hope that it will propel social change. On what grounds can we maintain, for example, that our work speaks to the interests of those to whom we claim political commitment? As MacDonald (1991: 44) notes, the recovery of the Subject as central to feminist theory has important political implications which we would do well to recognize. In my view, this type of accountability is in danger of disappearing if our interests are simply other academics or if our way of working erases the social world of embodied women. Given that *Girl Talk* makes claims in the name of young women who have little, if any, opportunity to write 'the social,' I do not treat this burden lightly. In the final analysis, this burden transformed *Girl Talk* from simply a sociological account of teenzine reading into the search for an adequate methodology to study social texts. Like Skeggs (1995), I believe that feminist cultural studies is more than a matter of theoretical speculation because it is about more than simply rewriting women's subordination and resistance through the textual practice of academics. In other words, for feminism there is always 'something' beyond the immediacy of the text. At the same time, however, it seems to me self-evident that we can never 'go beyond' the text. Am I being contradictory?

By acknowledging that experiences of the social are always, and necessarily, mediated by systems of signification, we are also acknowledging that we cannot move beyond the text. Because texts are not only the object of analysis but also the means through which we participate in rewriting (rather than representing) the social, to claim to move beyond the text would be a claim to move beyond established systems of speaking and writing; in other words, beyond language as the given system of communication. This does not mean however that we are hermeneutically locked into an unchanging system of meaning. Clearly, the continual emergence of new, alternative systems of thinking argues against the kind of linguistic determinism which some fear will accompany the self-conscious foregrounding of academic texts as systems of signification. It seems to me that change occurs because of the intertextuality of social thought. While it is tempting at this point to refer to the work of Foucault, I prefer to draw attention to the work of feminists, like Dorothy Smith, who read sociology against the everyday texts of women's lives (see Smith 1980, for example), transforming the way we not only do sociology, but do the social as everyday practice.[10] Thus it seems self-evident to point out that it matters what we say to whom, and for what purpose. It matters how we take meaning from the texts which are the basis for claims we make on behalf of 'the social,' including the claim that there is 'no social' because there is no going beyond the text.

As already noted in chapter 4, in *Girl Talk* texts are treated in two distinct ways. First – whether magazines or interview transcripts – texts are read for their manifest content. Here the appeal to content implies that meaning can be taken at face value. This treatment is not the same as saying that meaning is not a complex or contestable matter. Rather, it simply acknowledges that meaning, especially the meaning of texts which are the basis of a shared culture, can and does have stable, identifiable referents. Texts treated in this manner are seen to provide 'factual' data: here, I use 'factual' to refer to the events and occurrences which interest sociologists who encounter them as the everyday doing of the social. In this study, 'facts' concern which magazines girls read, how frequently, and so on. Although subject to memory loss and other sources of error, these facts provide a description of everyday life for the researcher. Ideally, they provide reliable access to a social world beyond the immediate experience of the researcher. This manner of reading magazines or interview transcripts corresponds to the taken-for-grantedness of 'everyday' conversation. It relies upon consistency in meaning and access to shared understanding. One task for *Girl Talk* is to re-present this type of data in a manner which gives the reader access to (what I deem to be) the taken-for-granted dimensions of teenzine reading. While other researchers may want to challenge the specifics which I present, such as the ubiquity of teenzine reading or the titles which girls prefer, this challenge will likely be premised on the content of my claims, not the assumption that these matters are beyond knowing. This is how I have taken Benton's (1984: 194) claim that a commitment to the existence of discursive practices, in itself, is also a commitment to their condition of possibility. In my view the treatment of data as 'factual' in this way can be ignored only by those who work on existing texts as isolated 'specimens' of analysis. Without 'empirical' research oriented to factual questions – such as 'who reads what, when, and where' – academic work on social texts faces the danger of becoming self-referential.

More to the point, *Girl Talk* employs a second way of reading texts. Described in chapter 3 as symptomatic reading, this second approach reads texts for what is absent, but necessary for shared meaning. Here texts are not read for their content, but for contradictions and 'missing' texts – as symptoms of the difficulties of adequate, or 'full,' representation of the social, these gaps and contradictions direct the analyst to 'something' beyond the immediacy of the text. Symptoms present themselves as gaps, inconsistencies, and 'silences' to be taken up as the analyst's problematic, something in need of explanation. In this study the most interesting symptoms arose from reading girls' accounts of teenzine reading against magazine content. In doing so, I have given primacy to the symptoms in girls' transcripts; specifically, I have read them as pointing to the difficulties of becoming 'a woman' in a patriarchal culture. This manner of reading connects magazine texts to the context which is necessary to give them meaning to everyday readers; as we shall see, it also alerts us to the hidden motivators of the text. This manner of reading symptomatically is not commonly employed in everyday meaning-making; it represents the potential of a sociological analysis of everyday life as 'text.' This is not to say that gaps, inconsistencies, and silences do not present themselves in everyday conversations. Simply, it is to say that they typically do not become a point of introspection or questioning, because taking them up would call the constructedness of the social into question in ways that would continually disrupt social life. In the remainder of this chapter I further explore the intertextuality of *Girl Talk* for purposes of making transparent the methodology of conscious intertextually. As we shall see, recognition of the intertextuality of meaning allows us to read texts as social process rather than as simply cultural artefacts.

Reading Texts as Process

The intertextuality of *Girl Talk* concerns three identifiable texts: previous research on women's magazines, the teenzines which are the subject of this study, and the transcripts of interviews with readers. Reading these texts against each other does not lead to seamless meaning; on the contrary, because intertextual reading draws attention to gaps and inconsistencies in meaning, it leads us through a chain of signification.[11] As argued in previous chapters, the interviews with readers call the research literature into question, for example. In fact, their value lies in their ability to unsettle the received wisdom of feminist cultural studies. In *Girl Talk* their reading drew attention to a disjuncture between the hypothetical readers of cultural theory and embodied readers. This disjuncture points to gaps and inconsistencies in our understanding of precisely how teenzines are taken up by young readers. They are symptoms which direct us to the constructedness of academic knowledge and the kinds of debates which, although missing from the text, make academic knowledge possible. Like Skeggs (1995), the text I find missing from much scholarly readings of texts is methodological discussion of the truth claims made in the name of cultural studies. As Skeggs notes, although academic work is the product of a long process often fraught with difficulties, representations of knowledge typically mask the means of their own production. Her review of feminist research on soap operas, for example, revealed an abundance of ungrounded speculations which led her to question whether cultural theories are 'just a matter of speculation.' It seems ironic to me that a discourse which takes signification as its problematic pays so little attention to its own sources of meaning and claims to knowledge. The discussion in this chapter is thus necessary if my aim is to advance our ways of thinking about the study of social texts. However, in our case methodological questions are not simply a matter of academic interest. Not only academics are interested in what effects (if any) accompany teenzine reading; in my travels, media commentators, clinicians, women's groups, and parents of adolescent girls often express interest in my research.[12] Although the theoretical question addressed in *Girl Talk* is the relationship between the cultural and the social, expressed practically it concerns our ability, as social scientists, to advance practical knowledge about the role of commercial media in young girls' definitions of themselves and the social.

As we have seen, interview transcripts were also read against magazine texts. Again, disjunctures and inconsistencies appear between two stories of 'what it means to be a woman': one put forward by teenzine discourse, the other based on girls' experiential knowledge. In this study, girls' lived experiences exceed the categories and Subject positions available in commercial texts. However, girls' accounts were not simply different; they present what Smith calls 'fault lines' in the reader's consciousness. For Smith, fault lines are important because, as symptoms of the excess of experience, they can draw cultural constructions into question. In our case, however, the experienced importance of good looks, the ability of boys to label girls, and the positive cultural evaluations of Caucasian whiteness lead girls to assign truth value to the text. In other words, by addressing the experiential problems of being a girl in a racist patriarchal culture, teenzine messages resonate with the lived experiences of many girls, naturalizing rather than challenging the femininity idealized by the dominant culture and mirrored in school culture. Despite the ability of adult researchers to 'read against the grain,' in this study teenzine meanings operate to unsettle Self constructions more frequently than they lead to a rejection of the teenzine mandate to look good and to attend to boys' preferences and opinions. From this perspective we took as our problematic the finding that, despite the contradictions posed by dominant definitions of 'being a woman,' the experiences of the young girls in this study did not call the cultural construction of femininity into question.

Other writers and commentators might read the gaps and inconsistencies in girls' accounts of Self against texts which emphasize psychological 'pathologies' of adolescence. However, read sociologically, these gaps and inconsistencies are symptomatic of the societal construction of teenagerhood. As a time 'between' childhood and adulthood, adolescents encounter few societal guidelines or clearly drawn boundaries. Because the most important thing that adolescents 'do' is attend school, it is the milieu within which girls negotiate a sense of adolescent Self. Teenagerhood is often described by adults, and experienced by girls in this study, as a time of uncertainty and social experimentation. Included in this experimentation is the establishment of a social identity distinct from that which accompanies being a 'daughter' or a 'sister' within a family context. The problem is for girls that 'mistakes' can be costly. Within the peer culture of school, girls' behaviours are assessed against dominant, patriarchal definitions of femininity which are, coincidentally, reproduced in teenzine texts. In the final analysis, given the absence of positive definitions of adolescents and other signifiers of belonging, teenzines can take on more significance in readers' lives than seems possible to many adults. This power of the text accompanies its ability to provide a discourse for young girls which addresses them as valued individuals struggling with the existential problems of being a girl in a patriarchal culture.

This ability to define the dominant order extends to magazine definitions of the social. In chapter 7 we explored how teenzines construct the boundaries of 'typical' teenagerhood, giving readers pleasure when their own experiences and everyday problems fall within the bounds of 'normal' teenage life. Despite this pleasure, and perhaps because of it, many readers wished for more diversity in magazine images not only of women, but also of the social. Girls in this study were much more thoughtful and concerned about social problems than implied by the editorial emphasis on beauty, boys, and the female body. As well as identifying boys to be a source of difficulty, girls discussed racism and violence as everyday problems which they would like to see addressed in their magazines:

At our school there's a lot of racial tension. ... You got your normal, your normal white people that don't like Indo-Canadians. And then you got lots of like, white people who don't like the Filippino people and just, it's basically the whites don't like other groups. Like we all get along with everyone. We try to. But there's some people we don't get along with because they don't get along with us. So that's how it is. (Fifteen-year-old Heather)

Like there's so much, like racism and cruelty around places like White Rock. And violence, too. Well I guess, like there's not compared to some schools in Vancouver, but some people – for no reason, like different guys beating up other guys, and everything. (Fifteen-year-old Tiffany)

That's [violence] a big thing in our school. It started – like I had a problem with it when I was about fifteen ... I have really good friend that was stuck in a relationship like that for two years, and she couldn't get out of it. (Sixteen-year-old Michelle)

Within this context, it is interesting to note that Benetton ads, in particular, appealed to many girls. Although the representation in the Benetton ad included for comment in this study was somewhat ambiguous, it evokes poverty in a 'Third World' context. While open to interpretation, many readers (including myself) read it as depicting African refugees in flight. As in the case of other ads which girls found pleasurable, some (but not all) girls claimed this ad portrays 'the real world':

This is like the real world, I think. This one I like too because it's 'real world.' It's something that people actually go through. (Fifteen-year-old Rebecca)

Benetton was applauded by more than one reader for their willingness to 'show the world as it really is':

I could look at this for hours – I like their pictures ... Like, it's showing like, I don't know, I guess the *truth* about what's going on. ... I like it. It's appealing to me. (Fifteen-year-old Kirsten)

I like United Colors of Benetton. They show what's really going on – like in the world, even though it doesn't have anything to do with clothes ... In Africa and stuff like that things like this really do happen. Nobody realizes that. (Sixteen-year-old Melissa)

Benetton ads gave thirteen-year-old Stephanie a sense of belonging:

I love Benetton ... I keep them up there [on her bedroom wall] as a reminder.
[Interviewer:] Reminder of?
That I'm not the only one in this world. Sometimes you get into that frame of thinking that ... Benetton, it does remind you that – it reminds you, uhm somehow it reminds me of 'keeping social' [laughs].

While much more research is needed on adolescent reading of advertising, the findings of this study suggest that editorial reluctance or unwillingness to address social rather than strictly personal problems does not simply create 'gaps' in teenzine discourse. It is possible that the absence of meaningful discussion of the social issues that concern adolescent readers creates a discursive opening for the type of advertising discourse deployed by Benetton (see Goldman and Papson 1996).

In summary, by giving primacy to the symptoms in girls' transcripts, the findings in this study suggest that despite widespread scepticism – among adolescent readers as well as adults – about the social value of commercial texts, the outright rejection of teenzine messages requires the reader to place herself outside magazine constructions of 'typical' and 'normal' teenagerhood, during a period when she needs social acceptance and the approval of peers. While some of the girls in this study certainly did reject teenzines by reading them in this way, an important finding is that such readers are a clear exception. In this study the rejection of dominant definitions of femininity was facilitated by experiences which position girls outside, or on the margins of, mainstream school culture. This finding suggests that if we are seriously interested in addressing the negative effects which cultural representations can have on young women, interventions in the social rather than simply the cultural realm are called for.[13]

Future Research: The Missing Text in *Girl Talk*

As noted in the introduction, my original intention was not only to read girls' transcripts against teenzine texts in order to understand how girls give meaning to these texts, but also to read teenzine texts for symptoms of their relationship, as commodified culture, to the social. As the writing of *Girl Talk* unfolded, it became apparent that this third intertextual reading requires an entirely new effort. In this concluding section I draw attention to the type of reading I have in mind. In part, this discussion is intended to further illustrate the potential of symptomatic, intertextual reading as research. In part, it is intended to encourage others to take up the task of further exploring the relationship between the cultural and the social.

The intertextual reading I have in mind entails the reading of magazine content against interview transcripts (rather than vice versa);[14] we have already seen that girls' lived experiences of adolescent femininity exceed the categories of its textual representation. This led me to question the inconsistencies and missing texts in teenzine discourse. As symptoms, these gaps direct us to another text, absent in teenzines as well as much cultural commentary by academics on social texts. This missing text is found in trade magazines, such as *Advertising Age* and *Mediaweek,* which mediate a discourse among product manufacturers, advertising agencies, research companies, and commercial magazines. These trade journals are interesting because they provide self-descriptions of magazines, such as *Seventeen* and *YM,* written by publishers for 'another' reading audience. In these texts *YM,* for example, is:

The look: A real dazzler! A full inch wider than *Seventeen.* More space, more impact,

for ads and edit. A fashion and beauty showcase ... **The *YM* buy: It beats *Seventeen*!** ...
Better edit-to-ad ratio. Less clutter. Great ad positioning. The new *YM*. Put it on your
list. Finally, a real choice for change. (*Mediaweek*, 1989)

The texts of these trade publications not only describe magazines, however. In
their pitch to advertisers, teenzine publishers also describe their teenaged
readers:

The Target: The Younger Woman! The choice 14-to-20 reader. In college, or prep-
ping to go. Career parents. High HHI. More money to spend. Big buyer of fashion and
beauty. Smarter. More sophisticated. Nobody talks to her better than the new *YM*. *YM*'s
Younger Woman: Your target. (Part of the text quoted above)

Promoters of teenzines are well aware of the contradictions and inconsistencies
in girls' search for Self described in *Girl Talk*. In fact, they view these contradictions as a marketing advantage:

SHE KNOWS THAT LOOKS **AREN'T EVERYTHING.** BUT THEY ARE SOMETHING. She keeps
looking for the perfect dress. She keeps looking for the perfect shoes. *She believes perfect is an abstract idea but then, so are heels.* SHE IS AN **INDIVIDUAL OF STYLE.** She
is an individual who copies looks from models, waitresses, third cousins and friends of
friends of friends she doesn't know very well, but look good. SHE HATES FADS, loathes
fads. *She likes fads that last longer than one week and are then called 'fashion.'* And she
will never mix leather with lace. *Unless it looks really good on her. YM.* 1.9 million in
circulation. Read by 8 million young women from cover to cover, until the covers fall
off. IT'S HER WORLD. WE'RE JUST LIVING IN IT. *YM* **MAGAZINE.** (*Advertising Age*,
November 14, 1994; emphasis original)

While *Seventeen* no longer boasts that their readers are 'born to shop,' their
advertising slogan during 1982 and 1983 claims that 'because she believes in
us, she'll believe in you' (*Advertising Age* 1982 and 1983). While the 'she' of
this text is the hypothetical reader of *Seventeen*, 'you' refers to advertising
agencies acting on behalf of the multibillion-dollar fashion and cosmetic industries. The agency of this hypothetical reader concerns shopping; the *Seventeen*
reader is described as a 'purchasing agent' 'in a class by herself' (ibid.):

Last year 8,500,000 teenage girls spent $7.9 million on their way back to high school
and college. Including $4.4 million on such ready-to-wear items as coats, dresses, and
sportswear. $1 billion on footwear. More than $600 million on accessories. And $1.1 bil-
lion on other purchases, from pens to photography. (*Advertising Age*, February 28, 1983)

The prospective buyer of advertising space is further informed that

> the *Seventeen* reader has terrific brand loyalty. A Yankelovich study shows that 41% of adult women still buy the same brand of mascara they first chose as a teenager. 29% use the same perfume. 26% wear the same brand of bra. *Talk to them in their teens, and they'll be customers for life.* (ibid., emphasis added)

By 1994, Teenage Research Unlimited claimed that teens in the United States spend $57 billion annually of their own money (Whalen 1994: 8). One consequence is the continuing competition among fashion and cosmetic companies for their 'share' of this lucrative market. While much of this battle is waged on the pages of trade magazines, to date I have encountered little, if any, subversive or 'deconstructive readings' of these texts. For our purposes they direct us to another audience which is seldom discussed in cultural studies: advertising agencies. While the writers discussed in chapter 1 provide interesting textual analyses of advertisements, for the most part ads are read from the standpoint of the researcher-reader. One consequence is that the ads themselves, rather than their production, have come to be identified as 'the research problematic.' Whether claiming these texts as harmful or as providing a pleasurable venue for consumption, reading ads in this way reinforces their 'thing-like' status. While reading advertising texts as process includes their reading in the ways described in chapters 1 and 2, it must go further in order to read them symptomatically. Such an undertaking would read advertisements against the texts of magazines such as *Advertising Age* in order to reveal the world of advertising which lies beyond the text.[15] Read in this way, advertising texts connect the cultural and the social dimensions of commercial media because they direct us to the 'hidden' life of social texts: that of their production rather than simply consumption.

While circulation figures are important to teenzine publishers, they do not provide the most important source of revenue for magazine publishers (see Wood 1971). Earnshaw (1984: 411), for example, notes that women's magazines in Britain gain as much as 82 per cent of their revenue from advertisers. As in the case of women's magazines, the primary source of revenue for teenzines results from the sale of advertising space, which itself is based on not simply the 'quantity' of the reading audience but, as suggested above, the 'quality' of this audience. Above we can see that these qualities include purchasing power, brand loyalty, and 'a belief in their magazine.' Agents of advertising companies are well aware of the ability of the text to position readers in specific ways, notably as consumers.[16] For our purposes, it is important to note that these agents include social scientists, often trained in methods of sociological research. Among these agents are Moschis and Churchill, who argue that 'marketers need to understand youthful consumers' behavior and how it is acquired in order to design effective consumer education programs' (1979: 40). Notably, the purpose of this education is to 'create more satisfied customers and reduce government interference with marketers' operations.' Drawing on their research with adolescents, they inform marketers that:

adolescents in higher social classes had significantly greater economic motivations for consumption. Thus, marketing communications stressing the economic or functional aspects of the product may be relatively more effective when directed at adolescents in middle social classes ... [while] message content emphasizing the expressive aspects of consumption may be relatively more appealing to younger, lower-class [sic] and older, middle-class teenagers ... (p. 46)

Because the effectiveness of marketing techniques may differ according to age (with race and gender not yet 'discovered' for their marketing potential), these writers recommend that marketers might benefit by isolating by age group the significant product attributes used in young people's consumer decision-making process and adjusting their product promotion accordingly. Further, because adolescents in 'lower' classes may lack skills to be effective consumers, they many need more 'preparation' for the consumer role (p. 47).

In short, this type of discourse, requiring further research, again directs us to an examination of the ways in which teenage girls are socially as well as culturally positioned as an identifiable 'market.' It also directs us to the ways in which the search for advertisers – as much as young readers – is a motivation of editorial texts, albeit hidden by academic decoding that treats the text as an already-given system of signification.

Because revenues for advertising also depend on the positioning of ads within magazines, a number of researchers draw attention to the influence of advertising on editorial text. Ballaster and colleagues (1991) argue that the financial interests behind magazines as a commodity accounts for similarity among what might at first appear to be a diversity of magazines, as well as their consistency over time. The ability of these interests to shape magazine content is illustrated by the history of *MS*, a feminist alternative to mainstream women's magazines, which espoused a strict policy against the inclusion of sexist or harmful advertising. Despite this stated aim, researchers have pointed out that cigarette and alcohol companies accounted for 30 per cent of ads between 1973 and 1987, while women were frequently depicted as alluring sex objects (Ferguson, Kreshel, and Tinkham 1990). Explaining these types of contradictions, the past editor of *MS*, Gloria Steinem (1990), complained that advertisers require editors to treat their readers as kept women and to provide a context within which concern over fashion and beauty is the norm. Her experiences resonate with claims by researchers that advertising operates as a conservative force in the representation of women. Social historians have noted that this force has transformed women's magazines from the 1920s onwards: '[Features increasingly were devoted to] encouraging women to spend more on beautifying themselves or their homes, or suggesting new leisure time activities or publicizing new entertainments, and increasingly [support for advertisers] came directly, through editorial mentions or recommendations, and the incorporation of advertising matter indistinguishable from editorial content' (White 1970: 68). Doughan (1987) draws attention to the systematic elimination, through advertisers' influence, of references to both feminism and any serious discussion that would limit spending.

As yet, little of this research informs current debates about the social significance of commercial texts. As we have seen, postmodern writers often celebrate the fragmented, discontinuous character of magazine texts as a distinctly 'feminine' cultural genre. Drawing attention to the 'structurelessness' of housework, these writers point out that this character of the text enables women to sequence domestic activities with magazine reading (or television viewing). On this basis, women's consumption of commercial media has been celebrated as resistance to women's servitude within the domestic sphere. Without denying the pleasure that women derive from this type of release from the mundane repetitiveness of housework, I want to draw attention to the social forces which give shape to the gendered cultural genres being reclaimed in the name of feminisim. These forces include the mandate of advertising as the hidden 'motivation' of the text. For example, marketing researchers Norris and Colman (1992) show that the more deeply a magazine reader is involved in articles, the less they remember about accompanying advertisements. In other words, the greater the capacity of texts accompanying magazine ads to engage readers, the less effective are advertising campaigns, the 'real' content of women's magazines. When seen in the context of the advertising imperative of magazine production, the emergence of a distinctly feminine text employing a fragmented, discontinuous format can be read as heralding the 'depoliticization' of commercial media for women.

This depoliticization is important because it directs attention to the way in which commercial media contribute to the 'common sense' notion that we have arrived at a 'post-feminist' era. As mentioned earlier, one component of the current study, not elaborated in *Girl Talk*, is a historical analysis of the emergence and transformation of adolescent magazines. Here, it is significant to note that I was surprised by the amount of 'potentially politicizing text' in adolescent magazines published in earlier years, particularly during the 1970s (see Currie 1994). As a year that coincides with the widespread acceptance of various social movements, during 1971 *Seventeen* contains texts by readers, editors, and advertisers that are an especially rich source of references to women's liberation, racism, and environmentalism. These texts provide extensive commentary on social issues, much of it counter-hegemonic. By 1991, there is a noticeable decrease in political references; this decrease is accompanied by the gradual disappearance of texts (purportedly) authored by teenage readers. Going back to issues of *Seventeen* published shortly after its inception, one can find considerable text attributed to readers. Readers contributed letters, opinion articles, and stories about their lives. Teen reporters regularly interviewed celebrities, including political figures of the time. During 1951, an issue was devoted to 'you the reader,' with the entire content provided by readers. One result is a sense, as a reader of these texts, that teenagers themselves are actively engaged in defining the world of adolescence, often through the construction of a discourse critical of the status quo. By 1991, however, this 'voice' has been replaced by that of primarily adult editors, professionals, and advertisers. Readers' views and responses have been significantly eclipsed, confined to the types of letters and anecdotes analysed in *Girl Talk*. While *Seventeen* has been, since its inception, a commercial enterprise, the point is that reader-identified texts gave the format, as well as content, of *Seventeen* a politicizing potential.

The gradual de-emphasis of reader-identified input gives contemporary *Seventeen* a detached, authoritarian tone, despite the fact that editors adopt the upbeat phraseology used by their young audience. This new tone is also accounted for by an increased amount of factual rather than narrative text. Factual messages often address social issues; it is, therefore, the format, rather than simply the content, that contributes to the depoliticization of *Seventeen*. The earlier reader orientation, found in extensive written text, has been replaced by a visually oriented format consisting of photographic layout, word bites, and boxed information. This fragmented and discontinuous style is characteristic of regular feature columns that update readers on news and noteworthy trends. On the environmental page titled 'Earth Talk,' for example, boxed statistics documenting the amount of trash now in orbit are placed alongside advertorials for products such as earrings made from recycled paper or plastic. This fragmentation and juxtaposition of content thus draws attention away from fashion products as contributing to avoidable environmental waste, as a potentially political message, to the notion of environmentalism through 'informed' consumption, as a depoliticized response to the environmental movement.[17] While this type of analysis requires further research, it seems to support my claim that editorial reluctance or unwillingness to seriously address the social issues that interest young readers does not simply result in a 'gap' in magazine discourse. Rather, it creates a discursive opening for the kinds of responses to advertisers like Benetton, described earlier: claims by young readers that Benetton is 'showing the *truth* of what's really going on' because of its willingness to 'show the world as it really is.' While this type of analysis requires further research, here I draw attention to the way in which the evolution of the format of women's magazines corresponds to 'scientific' advances in marketing research, a powerful force that needs to be addressed in any effort to reclaim commercial media, or women's role in consumption, in the name of women's liberation.[18]

What all this tells us is that, in the final analysis, the necessity for editors to capture specialized groups of women who are identified by market researchers to be potential consumers shapes both the content and the form of women's magazines (see also Leiss, Kline, and Jhally 1985). As a cultural genre, teen-zines (similar to women's magazines) are symptomatic of the relations between the cultural and the social world of adolescence. Clearly, the goal of a *critical* cultural studies is to explicate, rather than mystify, these relations.

Finally, a Conclusion

The complexity of not only meaning, but also social life, means that our work as researchers is never done. As shown in this chapter, reading intertextually necessarily directs the researcher to new, relevant lines of investigation. Throughout *Girl Talk* I have compared researcher readings to the everyday reading of social texts. I have highlighted this comparison, in part, to illustrate why we cannot read 'the social' off cultural artefacts, such as commercial magazines, despite the paradox that, as sociologists, our research is an act of reading. This does not mean that as researchers we cannot make knowledge claims about such artefacts; in this chapter I have attempted to show how researcher reading can advance a political analysis of culture. In order to do so, I have advanced a method of reading texts sociologically.

As for much academic research, institutional demands on my time rather than intellectual considerations brought the current study to a close. However, as I hope to have shown, the never-ending nature of social research does not mean that we can never say anything meaningful along the way. While the current study chose women's magazines as the focus of investigation, commercial texts in general have been argued to be more than simply cultural or textual representations. In this study women's magazines have been explored as a textual form of social power that mediates everyday practices of meaning-making and the 'doing' of gender. I prefer the term 'form' (of power) over other similar but different terms, such as 'expression,' because it moves us from the ideational to the material realm. When conceptualized in this way, the social power of texts can be studied only by treating texts as one moment in a 'process': texts embody both the meanings and the activities of social life organized around commodities, and texts 'work' only when they encounter readers. If we are to understand the social rather than simply cultural significance of women's magazines – we must move beyond the immediacy of the text. It is this move that represents the potential of a sociological rather than literary study of texts.

The insight which we gain by moving beyond the immediacy of the text itself foregrounds what Smith (1987) calls the 'relations of ruling' through which commercial texts, such as teenzines, both come into being and operate as venues of power. Smith defines 'relations of ruling' as 'a concept that grasps power, organization, direction, and regulation as more pervasively structured than can be expressed in traditional concepts provided by the discourses of power [for example, class] ... When I write of 'ruling' in this context I am identifying a complex of organizational practices, including government, law, business and financial management, professional organization, and educational institutions *as well as discourses in texts that interpenetrate the multiple sites of power*' (Smith, 1987: 3; emphasis added). Smith's approach captures the ubiquitous nature of power but moves us beyond the notion that power circulates as part of the 'fabric' of social life. In *Girl Talk* textual power operates in local sites; if readers recognize themselves within the text, they have been positioned, as embodied female Subjects, by patriarchal definitions of both femininity and the social. While this local positioning has been read as symptomatic of the social power of commercial texts, we have not attributed this power to the text, but rather to the ability of commercial texts to colonize social life. While we have studied power in its discursive form, we have not concluded that 'there is nothing outside' teenzine texts and the discourses they mediate. Rather, we have treated social texts as the phenomenal form of power that operates through relations of gender, but also race, class, and generation. While literary methods employed by cultural critics can help us to recognize the symptoms of these relations in their discursive form, these relations do not reside within the text.

In the final analysis, the failure to treat the text as process is to mystify the nature of social relations which make both the text and its reading in specific ways possible. In this way, a 'materialist' analysis is not simply an analysis that treats the magazine as an 'object,' a physical commodity rather than ideational form, although it certainly requires that kind of thinking. A materialist analysis treats women's magazines as a historically specific and culturally significant text which mediates social relations and activities. As Smith notes, as social texts women's magazines mediate discourses of femininity. In *Girl Talk* we have employed the notion of Subject-ivity to investigate empirically texts at work. Subject-ivity is a notion that draws attention to three processes which work through, but lie beyond, the text. The first is *power,* expressed through the re/constitution of dominant interests as both a cultural and a social process; commercial texts are one venue through which we can study the exercise of power. The second process is *agency,* expressed through the making of ourselves as social Subjects; the everyday practices which valorize shared meaning are one venue through which we can study agency as Subject-ivity. Third, the *cultural construction of the social,* expressed through both popular and academic discourse, belies the systems of signification which coordinate the reconstitution of the relations and conditions which make social and cultural life possible. In the current study, we explored how the cultural construction of the social is mediated by adolescent magazines. While the study therefore highlights the importance of meaning-making, it does not imply that the world consists entirely of 'culture.' A study of the text as process directs us to the social institutions which systems of meaning-making both express and bring into being. As Marx might observe, while the young women in this study actively make meanings through which they bring themselves, through Subject-ivity, into being, they do so under conditions that are not their doing. These conditions can become conscious 'objects' of analysis only through cultural study which takes as its task demystification of both the social and cultural world and their making. In *Girl Talk* this task has been accomplished by treating women's magazines as a textual form of knowledge, what Smith (1990b) calls 'objectified knowledge': a form of knowledge that organizes and orchestrates the practices of individuals across time and space from an origin external to the everyday context of their lives. The notion of objectified knowledge is important in this study of social texts for two reasons.

First, the notion of objectified knowledge draws attention to the existence of other forms of knowledge. Alternative forms include the knowledge which arises through our everyday activities and encounters as we go about the business of making sense of the world, of 'doing' social life while sometimes drawing on extra-local official accounts of the 'way things are' and at other times on the wisdom of our experiences as an embodied being who is responded to and acted upon. Importantly, there is the potential that those who are excluded from the making of official, objectified knowledge which does not embody their material interests will encounter disjunctures between official accounts of the social and the way the world 'actually' works. For this reason, feminist knowledge has been posited as distinct from conventional knowledge such as that produced by social scientists in universities or policy makers of the state. Thus women's studies (and, following from this, often feminist theory) has been interpreted to mean the valorization of women's experiences over established knowledge. While the women whom Friedan interviewed, for example, could not 'name' their problem, they gave voice to entirely new meanings to the lives of white, middle-class women in 'middle America.' Included in new meanings was the renaming of the 'privileged' status of suburban housewives as 'oppressive.' However problematic her generalizations of this finding to the condition of all women have subsequently proven to be, Friedan was among the first to question the objectified knowledges of both commercial media and social science from the perspective of the localized, experiential knowledge of the embodied Subjects of these discourses. Here we draw attention to the potential for 'experience' to help us think about agency and resistance in more politically nuanced ways than currently provided by a cultural studies which reads the lives of individuals off texts. I have in mind the tendencies for cultural critics to theorize women's desires by simply reading feminine cultural genres or to interpret every little act on the part of women to symbolically differentiate themselves from oppressive patriarchal norms as 'resistance' (for example, see Arthur 1993). Unless we can understand women's desires and acts of resistance in relation to their consciousness of oppression, 'agency' remains unconnected from feminism as a social form of women's power.

Second, the notion of objectified knowledge provides a way for us to critically interrogate what we do as academics in the name of 'social science.' Feminist critique of patriarchal knowledge is premised on the impossibility of understanding what we do by formulating 'knowledge' as somehow outside ideological constructions because researchers are 'neutral' observers. Along these lines, I think debates raised by postmodernists resonate with feminist inquiry. However, unless we can also account for the processes through which feminist knowledge objectified as 'women's studies' itself is produced, we are simply replacing one outdated author-ization – of knowledge as a 'God's eye view' – with a secular version – of knowledge written by academics who take up the emptied throne. In my view, while most feminist researchers acknowledge the types of difficulties which these types of debates raise, few take the implications far enough. A division has appeared in the scholarly literature between doing empirical research, as the practical work of academic feminism, and theorizing as philosophical practice, unconnected to data collection. This division acts to reinforce the notion that epistemological questions should be treated as entirely theoretical ones. Against this view, *Girl Talk* is an attempt to show that theoretical and philosophical questions about social life are necessarily empirical ones; thus adequate questions about the possibilities for knowledge and their answers will arise *only* through the practice of social research.

Description of Participants
(with pseudonyms)

Thirteen-year-olds

Brittany	Mother a pharmacist; father sells car parts; Euro-Canadian; regular reader of *YM* and *Teen*
Ashley	Mother a adjudicator for Workers' Compensation Board; father manager of autoglass company; Euro-Canadian; regular reader of *YM*, *Vogue*, and *Cosmo*
Jessica	Mother training to be dental receptionist; father a doctor; Indo-Canadian; regular reader of *YM*, *Big Bopper*, *Teen*
Amanda	Mother an accountant; father manages exploration for mining company; Guyanese; regular reader of *YM* and *Teen*
Sarah	Mother cleans houses; father a computer consultant; Euro-Canadian; regular reader of *Seventeen*, *Vogue*, and *Cosmo*
Megan	Mother a student; father a plumber; stepfather a firefighter; Euro-Canadian; occasional reader of *Vogue*, *Seventeen*, and *Teen*
Samantha	Mother manages a restaurant; father an artist; Euro-Canadian; no longer reads *YM* and *Seventeen*
Stephanie	Mother a consultant at Weight Watchers; father works with computers; African-Canadian; avid reader of *Sassy*, *YM*, *Seventeen*, *Essence*, and *Ad Busters*
Caitlin	Mother a housewife; father a longshoreman, Euro-Canadian, regular reader of *YM*

Fourteen-year-olds

Katherine	Mother a cashier; father a firefighter; Euro-Canadian; regular reader of *YM* and *Vogue*
Kayla	Mother a housewife; father a supervisor of university research centre; Euro-Canadian; regular reader of *YM* and *Rolling Stone*

Lauren   Mother a hairdresser; father (absent) a musician; African-Canadian;
              regular reader of *YM*, *Sassy*, and *Seventeen*
Emily   Mother a hairdresser; father a store clerk; Euro-Canadian; occasional
              reader of *Bop, Teen*, and *Sassy*
Jennifer   Mother a teacher; father (absent) a plumber; Euro-Canadian; regular
              reader of *YM*, *Ingenue*, and *Seventeen*
Courtney   Mother a housewife; father a policeman; Euro-Canadian; regular reader
              of *Seventeen*, *YM*, and *Allure*
Rachel   Mother an accountant; father a teacher; Euro-Canadian; regular reader
              of *YM*, *Seventeen*, and *Teen*

Fifteen-year-olds
Nicole   Mother a medical technician; father drafts machine parts; Chinese-
              Canadian; reads *Seventeen* in store or at friends' homes
Elizabeth   Mother a bank investigator; father a bank manager; Euro-Canadian
              (Jewish); regular reader of *YM*, *Seventeen*, and *Teen*
Chelsea   Mother a bank investigator; father a car salesman; Euro-Canadian;
              regular reader of *YM*, *Seventeen*, *Teen*, *Mademoiselle*, and *Cosmo*
Amber   Mother works in meat factory; father a carpenter; East European-
              Canadian (Muslim); regular reader of *YM*, *Seventeen*, *Teen*, and *Vogue*
Rebecca   Mother an accountant; father a draftsman; Euro-Canadian; regular
              reader of *YM*, *Allure*, *Vogue*, *Teen*, and *Mademoiselle*
Christina   Mother a tarot reader; father a reflexologist; Euro-Canadian; regular
              reader of *National Geographic*; used to read *Seventeen*
Tiffany   Mother a nurse; father a pharmacist; Euro-Canadian; regular reader of
              YM and *Seventeen*; browses through 'lots more'
Kirsten   Mother a secretary; father a car salesman; Euro-Canadian; avid reader
              of *YM*, *Seventeen*, and *Vogue*
Heather   Mother a loan supervisor; father a warehouse supervisor; Fijian-
              Canadian; regular reader of *Vogue*; also reads *Chatelaine* and *Seventeen*
              once in a while
Danielle   Mother serves food in a bingo hall; does not know father's occupation;
              Euro-Canadian; regular reader of *Seventeen*, *Sassy*, and *YM*
Hannah   Mother a sales representative; father lives elsewhere; does not know
              father's occupation; very occasionally reads magazines; used to read
              Seventeen and *YM*; currently in foster care

Sixteen-year-olds
Lindsey   Mother a clerk; father a real estate agent; Euro-Canadian; regular reader
              of *Sassy*, *YM*, and *Vogue*

Michelle	Mother owns clothing store; father an auctioneer; Euro-Canadian; regular reader of *Seventeen, YM, People,* and *Soap Opera Digest*
Melissa	Mother an accountant; father a real estate agent; Euro-Canadian; casual reader of *Chatelaine, Elle, Vogue,* and *US*; used to read *Seventeen* and *YM*
Jasmine	Mother a teacher; father an accountant and real estate developer; Ukrainian-Canadian; regular reader of *Seventeen* and *YM*
Erica	Mother a speech therapist and author; father an entrepreneur with employees; Euro-Canadian (Jewish); an avid reader of *YM, Seventeen, Vogue, Mirabella, Elle, Cosmo, Mademoiselle* – 'all fashion magazines'
Kelsey	Mother a college instructor; father 'not in the picture'; Euro-Canadian; regular reader of *Seventeen* and *YM*
Kelly	Mother (lives elsewhere) is homemaker and part-time teacher; father a bus driver; Euro-Canadian; occasionally reads nature and fashion magazines at a friend's house; otherwise does not read magazines
Alicia	Mother a part-time daycare worker; father an engineering consultant; Chinese-Canadian; does not read magazines
Crystal	Mother 'an actress, singer and dancer and social worker'; stepfather owns a construction business; Euro-Canadian; an avid reader of *Rolling Stone, Elle, Vogue, YM, Seventeen, Mirabella, Mademoiselle, People, US, New Yorker,* and *Interview*
Alyssa	Mother a secretary; father out of work; Chinese-Canadian; regular reader of *Shape, YM, Seventeen,* and *Allure*

Seventeen-year-olds

Allison	Mother a housewife who also manages husband's office; father a dentist; Irish-Canadian; avid reader of *Cosmopolitan, Sassy, Vogue, Elle, Seventeen, YM, Time,* and *Maclean's*
Roshni	Mother a housewife; father unemployed and on worker's compensation (worked in wood mill); Indo-Canadian; regular reader of *YM, Elle,* and *Vogue*; used to read *Teen*
Amy	Mother a lab assistant; father an architect; Euro-Canadian; occasional reader of *Elle, Vogue,* and *Chatelaine*
Jamie	Mother works for husband; father an orthodontist; Euro-Canadian; regular reader of *Details, Rolling Stone, Sassy, Seventeen, Vogue,* and *Cosmo*
Laura	Parents divorced; stepmother an office worker; father an architect; Euro-Canadian; an avid reader of *Shape, Vogue, YM, Allure, Mademoiselle, Sassy, Seventeen, People,* and *Harper's Bazaar*
Mary	Mother a receptionist at doctor's office; father head of provincial

government department; Chinese-Canadian; reads *Seventeen*, *Allure*,
and *Mademoiselle* 'religiously every month'

Erin   Mother a practical nurse; father drives courier truck; Fijian-Canadian;
regular reader of *Flare* and *Chatelaine*; used to read *Seventeen* and *YM*

Brianna   Mother an unemployed teacher; father a lawyer; Euro-Canadian
(Jewish); regular reader of *Seventeen* and *YM*

Cassandra   Mother a home-maker; father a fisherman; Mexican-Canadian; regular
reader of *Sassy*, *Seventeen*, *Vogue*; also reads *YM*, *Glamour*, and
Mademoiselle once in a while

Victoria   Mother a baggage handler at airport; father a carpenter; Euro-Canadian;
regular reader of *Seventeen* and *YM*; used to read *Teen*

Alexandra   Mother a secretary; father a geologist; Euro-Canadian; used to read
Elle, *Seventeen*, *Allure*, *Mademoiselle*, *Rolling Stone*, *Interview*, *YM*;
grew out of *Teen*; research assistant describes her as 'breathtakingly
beautiful'

APPENDIX B

'Counting' Meaning

Although previous research provided suggestions about the nature of codes which would be relevant for the current study, all categories for the current work emerged from the texts themselves: no attempt was made to apply categories from previous studies. During the beginning summer months of the study, I read an extensive sample of relevant magazines in order to make early decisions about the nature of coding which would be appropriate to the purposes and goals of the study. The development of categories was informed by an interest in the construction of 'adolescent femininity' as a dominant message through presentation of definitions, goals, and values deemed appropriate for young readers. The coding of content was carried out on two samples of adolescent magazines, one contemporary and one historical. The first sample included all issues of *Seventeen*, *Young and Modern*, *Teen*, and *Sassy* published between June 1993 and May 1994. Because some titles produced double-issues, the contemporary sample consisted of forty-six magazines. This sample covers the year during which interviews were conducted; this data set allows us to chart the content of magazines which the readers were familiar with and referred to during interviews. The purpose of this coding was to identify the dominant meanings of 'preferred reading' – the meanings which would be available to researchers, although not necessarily taken up by readers.

Written texts were emphasized in the contemporary sample. As we shall see, this research strategy proved to resonate with girls' reading preferences. In order to exhaust the potential range of meanings, coding was carried out in three stages by four coders. During the first stage, Nariko summarized texts and developed provisional thematic codes; during the second stage, I coded all texts and refined the categories of coding; in the final stage, Kerri recoded all texts, employing the categories which I had refined but adding any categories which she felt suitable. The final recoding allowed an assessment of interrater reliability for each code, presented in tables B.1, B.2, and B.3. All tables indicate interrater reliability of the categories applied to the sample of *Seventeen* and *Sassy* used in the current study. Because the purpose of coding was to identify dominant

Table B.1: Interrater Reliability, Categories Developed to
Enumerate the Types of Questions on Advice Pages

Category	Seventeen	Sassy
1 Friendship	98.8	98.1
2 Family relationships	95.1	98.1
3 Boys	95.1	96.9
4 Psychological problems	98.8	100.0
5 Health	100.0	98.7
6 Beauty	95.1	97.5
7 Miscellaneous[1]	98.7	89.0
Base N^2	159	82

Each question/answer pair can have more than one theme.

1 Differences here result from the research assistant finding
   more themes. Examples of topics include categories in
   education, career, hobbies, stars/celebrities, and social
   issues. The number of questions/answers falling into these
   categories is too small for separate headings.
2 Taken from all issues published between June 1993 and
   May 1994

themes as well as potential alternative meaning, the coders were trained to develop and
apply codes, but not coached on how to read the texts. Thus the usefulness of interrater
reliability is to exhaust the range of potential meanings and identify dominant meanings
which arise through 'preferred' rather than idiosyncratic reading: themes with both high
interrater reliability and high frequency of occurrence were grouped as 'dominant
themes,' with less frequent themes and/or themes with poor interrater reliability grouped
as 'secondary themes.' In the final analysis, the amount of agreement among coders was
surprisingly high, although this agreement may reflect the fact that we are all feminist
sociologists with academic interests in the texts. As already noted, high rates of reliability do not guarantee validity.

Coding was applied to the contents of six types of texts: advertisements, regular columns, feature articles, advice which appears in 'question and answer' format, readers'
pages, and fiction stories. The units of analysis varied according to type of text: for
example, while the unit of analysis for feature articles and fiction stories corresponds to
the article in its entirety, for 'advice' the unit of analysis is the paired question and
answer, with each advice column, for example, containing from four to eight units. The
unit of analysis is indicated on all tables. Categories were developed which were appropriate to each type of text which identify: subject matter, female and male roles, goals,
and values.[1] Subject matter refers to the topic(s) around which the text is organized and

Table B.2: Interrater Reliability, Categories Developed to Enumerate the Goals Given in the Answers of Advice Pages

Category	Seventeen	Sassy
1 Do what's right for you	84.8	100.0
2 Accept yourself	88.6	90.4
3 Assert your own needs, desires	92.4	93.3
4 Get professional help	96.2	97.1
5 Understand others (not including boys)	89.9	100.0
6 Understand guys better	96.2	92.3
7 Take care of your body	96.2	94.2
8 Get a boy, have a romance	94.9	91.3
9 Improve relationships with family member	98.7	98.1
10 It's not your fault that something happened	96.2	98.1
11 Get rid of problem boys	97.5	98.1
12 Get more education	100.0	100.0
13 Avoid conflict with parents, friends	100.0	99.0
14 Improve communication in relationship	88.6	99.0
15 Make the best of the situation	00.7	96.2
16 Tolerate boys' undesirable behaviours	97.5	96.2
17 Help others in trouble	100.0	99.0
18 Know about the world and your place in it	98.7	97.1
19 Fight an injustice	100.0	99.0
20 Cope with change	100.0	99.0
21 Look better	100.0	84.6
22 Develop a new, practical skill	100.0	97.1
23 Be supportive of someone	98.7	99.0
24 Be patient, wait	98.7	99.0
25 Resist pressure to conform	100.0	100.0
26 Learn from your mistake	98.7	99.0
27 Be open-minded	98.7	97.1
28 Be open, truthful in relationships	96.2	99.0
29 Think of how you affect others	96.2	99.0
30 Make new friends	98.7	99.0
31 Change the behaviour of others	96.2	99.0
32 Question your own behaviour, motives	96.2	96.2
33 Take revenge	100.0	100.0
34 Please boys	97.5	97.1
35 Get a career	96.2	99.0
36 Obey parents	98.7	99.0
37 Change your body	96.2	100.0
38 Challenge someone in a position of authority	100.0	100.0
39 Miscellaneous themes	63.3*	67.3*
Number of units of analysis	79	104

*The differences here result from the research assistant identifying more themes.

Table B.3: Interrater Reliability, Categories Developed to Enumerate the Values Promoted by the Answers of Advice Pages

Category	Seventeen	Sassy
1 Self-esteem	92.4	98.1
2 Heterosexual romance, intimacy	81.0	92.3
3 Independence	98.7	84.6
4 Assertiveness	93.7	100.0
5 Good relationships with parents	87.3	100.0
6 Promotes men's values, points of view	93.7	95.2
7 Physical health	87.3	95.2
8 Tolerance for difference	98.7	92.3
9 Political activism	100.0	100.0
10 Courage	97.5	100.0
11 Physical attractiveness	97.5	95.1
12 Altruism	98.7	100.0
13 Responsibility	92.4	98.1
14 Critical thinking about social institutions, problems	98.7	100.0
15 Self-control, patience, determination	94.9	96.2
16 Anti-racism	100.0	100.0
17 Initiative	100.0	92.3
18 Friendships with same sex	96.2	94.2
19 Multiculturalism	98.7	100.0
20 Sexual equality	93.7	98.1
21 Honesty	96.2	100.0
22 Good relationships with siblings	98.7	99.0
23 Suspicion of boys, men	96.2	100.0
24 Achievement	98.7	98.1
25 Education	97.5	98.1
26 Empathy	96.2	100.0
27 Introspection	92.4	88.5
28 Promotes faith in science	81.0	88.5
29 Miscellaneous themes	91.1	90.4
Number of units of analysis	79	104

are a function of the type of text. For example, six general categories of questions were identified in the 'question and answer' pages, which grouped questions about: relating to boys (such as getting a specific boy to notice or like the reader), dealing with family relationships (such as conflicts with siblings), dealing with relationships with friends (such as competition between girls over a specific boy), psychological problems (such as feeling depressed or afraid), how the body works and/or how to maintain health (such as how to avoid pregnancy or treat acne), and how the body 'looks' (such as fashion and beauty). These six categories exhausted virtually all topics, with very few units of analysis being coded in the residual category of 'miscellaneous' (an example might be questions about dealing with a teacher). Within each general category of questions specific subcategories were developed through thematic analysis; for example, eleven subcategories of 'questions about relating with boys' were developed, seven for 'psychological questions,' twelve for 'how the body works and/or how to maintain health,' and so on. Answers to each question were thematically analysed to identify the goals and values promoted by the editor. A goal refers to an actionable message; because most questions were framed as 'problems,' invariably a goal refers to the adoption of a behaviour or attitude which is presented as a 'solution.' Examples here would be 'get psychiatric help,' 'get rid of a problem boy,' 'try to communicate better with parents,' 'be patient,' 'try to make the best of the situation,' 'think about how your actions are affecting others.' More than one goal could be identified in each unit of analysis. A value refers to the social mores or principle advanced by the aforementioned action. Following the above, examples would be medicalization of interpersonal problems, independence, respect for parents, patience, perseverance, introspection, and so on. Again, more than one category could apply to each unit of analysis; texts varied in complexity and no attempt was made to limit either the number of goals or the number of values identified. Female and male roles refer to both relational and occupational roles in which women and men are situated in the text. Examples include daughter, sister, girlfriend (or 'wanna be' girlfriend), friend, and student. In the final analysis, the coding proved to be much more time-consuming than anticipated. The result was an extensive summary of contents which is too complex to present in its entirety here. The types of texts which proved to be most relevant during interviews are presented in *Girl Talk*; data not presented here will be presented in future publications. A summary of the categories that were developed for the various types of texts appears in the tables accompanying this text. The numerical summary of contents is presented as descriptive findings; as we shall see, these findings were read against interview transcripts in order to analyse how these texts work in a reading context.

Shelley coded the second sample of magazines, which included issues of *Seventeen* published between 1951 and 1991; the purpose of data collection was to chart historical trends and patterns. While the sample was stratified, the issues were not chosen at random since the availability of older issues was limited. In order to avoid seasonal variation, a sample was drawn which included five years (1951, 1961, 1971, 1981, and 1991) matched by months. There is nothing historically significant about ten-year intervals; nor is the regularity of intervals meant to imply that change is 'linear.' The initial intention was to also code the intervening, mid-decade issues after a general overview of fifty years was charted; the scope and complexity of data collection prevented this effort. The number of issues coded for each chosen year varied, according to the type of text and unit of analysis. For example, because the number of fiction stories in each issue is small, all the stories in each issue of each year were coded; because the number of advertisements in each issue is large, advertisements in only six issues of each year were coded. The samples are specified for each table (above).

After a close reading of twenty-four issues of *Seventeen*, I identified the types of texts and categories to be coded in the historical sample. Given the problem of reading out of historical context, coding for the historical sample was limited to an identification of primarily manifest content. A comparative picture was developed through the coding of pictorial content for subject matter; pictures depicting people were coded for: sex, race, categorical age,[2] imputed social relationships,[3] and imputed social role.[4] In order to explore the constructedness of normative femininity, thematic analysis was conducted of advertisements for beauty products and 'problem pages,' the two types of texts where normative femininity dominates meaning-making. Advertisements were coded for both manifest and latent content, identifying three characteristics of beauty advertisements:[5] subject matter, the female characteristics idealized by the ad which are seen to represent the 'sign value' of the product (for example, 'gentle or soft,' 'dramatic or sensational'), and the type of appeal used to promote these values (for example, 'medically proven' or 'ease of application'). The unit of analysis is the individual ad; more than one code could apply for each ad. The problem pages were coded in the manner described above. In summary, content analysis of magazines provided highly reliable, quantitative data which exhaust the range of manifest meanings and provide a systematic and detailed description of the texts used in the study.

Finally, due to my interest in how adolescent magazines mediate readers' understandings of counter-hegemonic social movements, texts with 'potentially politicizing' content were identified in the historical sample. 'Potentially politicizing' messages includes texts which contain explicit references to: sexism, racism, homophobia, feminism (specifically as an expression of the 'women's liberation' movement), (other) social problems (such as environmental degradation), or criticism of the status quo or social institutions (such as criticism of consumerism as a 'lifestyle' or industrial, legal, medical, educational or family systems). While this coding produces a numerical summary which makes comparison possible, the frequency of messages is not used as an indicator of either their significance or their effect. The purpose of this analysis is to identify whether, and how, changing relationships among the institutional sectors which are the origins of magazine content are expressed in preferred messages of these texts. Once again, the complexity of data which resulted from this type of analysis prevents a full discussion in this text; some of the findings of this part of the study appear in Currie (1994, 1997) and Budgeon and Currie (1995).

APPENDIX C

Advertisements Used in *Girl Talk*

Illegal Lengths	*Seventeen*, September 1992; *Cosmopolitan*, December 1993; *Mademoiselle*, December 1993
A Kiss Is Not Just a Kiss	*Elle*, December 1993
Ocean Pacific	*Seventeen*, March 1992
Nothing to Hide	*Seventeen*, April 1992
Beautiful	*Seventeen*, September 1992
Eternity	*Seventeen*, March 1992; *Cosmopolitan*, December 1993; *Elle*, December 1993
Soft & Dri	*Seventeen*, July 1992
Lawman Jeans	*Seventeen*, September, 1993
Jordache	*Seventeen*, December 1993; *Glamour*, November 1993
The Fragrance of Desire	*Cosmopolitan*, December 1993
Saturn	*Cosmopolitan*, December 1993
If This Is Your Dream	*Elle*, 1993
Calvin Klein	*Elle*, December 1993
Diamond Engagement Rings	*Mademoiselle*, December 1993
All You Have to Be Is You	*Seventeen*, December 1993; *Mademoiselle*, December 1993
Guess Footwear	*Glamour*, November 1993
Benetton	*Seventeen*, April 1992
Caboodles	*Seventeen*, September 1992
Fashion	*Seventeen*, March 1992
Prom Nite	*Seventeen*, March 1992

Notes

Introduction: 'Girls Doing Girl Things'

1 For writings which associate 'natural beauty' with white bourgeois femininity see hooks 1992; Hill Collins 1990; and Manning 1986.

2 Also see Coward 1985; Ang 1985; and Wilson 1985 and 1990.

3 A mere 16 per cent of college women in the United States consider themselves feminists (see Friend 1994). I was unable to find comparable data for Canada. Also see, 'Is Feminism Dead?' *Time*, 29 June 1998.

4 As Michèle Barrett notes (1992), although women's studies is premised on a coming-together of disciplines in a way which transcends old boundaries, much women's studies scholarship is marked by the author's disciplinary origins, this work being no exception.

5 However, we will see later that the discourses which have commercial representations of femininity as their common object of analysis also include the statements and claims about the social significance of these texts made by academic researchers and cultural commentators.

6 As Kate Soper notes (1993: 30), the Foucault–feminism connection must not only consider what Foucault brings to feminism, but how feminism prepared some of the discursive space for his emergence.

7 For Foucault, bio-power takes two forms: disciplinary and regulatory. The latter generally refers to the bio-politics of population (see Foucault 1980: 139).

8 See Bordo 1993.

9 For a critique of Foucault's notion of power see Hartsock 1990.

Chapter 1: Just Looking

1 Here it is important to note that while sociology, historically, has neglected the

woman question, early sociologists were interested in the phenomenon of women's fashion, which was analysed in rather negative terms. For example, Veblen (1899) described it as 'conspicuous consumption' which he linked to the subordination of women (also see Tarde 1903).

2 The terms 'mass culture' and 'popular culture' are often used in confusing ways. I explain my usage of 'popular culture' later. Here I point out that the term 'mass culture' refers to printed culture produced through mechanical means of reproduction, and electronic culture produced for the purposes of reaching large, dispersed audiences. Mass culture includes, but is not limited to, commercial media, such as women's magazines, produced for the explicit purpose of economic profit. Thus I use the term 'mass culture' to refer to objectified systems of meanings and representation which have not yet been worked over by consumers, who transform objectified systems of meaning into popular culture. As stated by Raymond Williams (1976: 199), popular culture is 'culture actually made by people for themselves.' The distinction is lost by writers who refer to mass media such as women's magazines, for example, as popular culture.

3 See hooks 1981.

4 For an interesting challenge to Friedan's claims about postwar magazine culture see Meyerowitz 1993.

5 That is to say, white, college-educated married women.

6 Some of the conclusions discussed below were based on research of general media, not specifically women's media.

7 Although this time was one of instability for the magazine industry and many new titles were short-lived.

8 She has in mind the influential Roper Study.

9 For example *Cosmopolitan* became women's answer to *Playboy* because of its centrefolds of nudes; although these photos contributed to its initial success, they were later discontinued.

10 For a contrary view, see Venkatesan and Losco (1975), who claim that the incidences of women portrayed as sex objects have decreased between 1961 and 1971, although those portraying other stereotypes have increased.

11 For an interesting claim that fashion layout constructs the homospectatorial look see Fuss 1992.

12 For a critique of this trend by these models themselves see 'Model Citizens: Black Supermodels Speak Out on Race in the Fashion Industry,' *Paper*, February 1993.

13 While discussing my research I became aware that some people use the term 'teenzines' to include non-commercial publications by adolescents. In the current study, I use the term 'teenzine' to refer to fashion and beauty magazines produced specifically for adolescent readers.

14 Specifically, 'teenager' referred to 'a person who is aged 13 to 19 unless he or she happens to get married' (see Braithwaite and Barrel 1979: 37).

15 See, for example, Cote and Allahar 1994.

16 A description of respondents is included in Appendix A.

Chapter 2: Materialist Feminism

1 For criticisms see Hekman 1990.

2 However, throughout the 1970s and 1980s Marxists still generally believed that texts are capable of representing the 'true' interests of women.

3 Within film theory, see Gledhill 1994.

4 For informative and divergent accounts of the history of the CCCS see Grossberg 1993 and Davies 1995.

5 For an overview of these debates, see Morley and Chen 1996.

6 However, Davies (1995: 37) draws attention to the kinds of issues which were missed or ignored because of this focus.

7 Also see Christian 1984, 1988.

8 See her 'Further Reading,' p. 251.

9 In later work Barthes (1970: 9) argued 'denotation is not the first among meanings, but pretends to be so.' The distinction between connotation and denotation became erased in postmodern writers like Baudrillard (1981).

10 She draws on Freud's notion of dream-work.

11 This exchange can also occur between the viewer and people with whom the viewer would like to be equated, such as Catherine Deneuve, or people enjoying the purported benefits of products. For example, the reader might like to be in the place of a woman perfume user who is surrounded by admiring men.

12 For those drawing on post-structuralist readings of Lacan, the Subject becomes an unstable formation dispersed over the chain of signification, unable to be evoked in the way discussed below.

13 By 'decode' Goldman means analytically dismantling how we read ads.

14 However appealing, his analysis rests on hypothetical readers, a problem explored in chapter 4.

15 A problem discussed later.

16 For example, she notes that Seventeen earned $25.8 million for Triangle Publications in 1982.

17 Within mainstream sociological debate, however, one finds little reference to feminist theory.

18 Also see Sumner 1979.

19 I bracket 'racialized' because, while I believe this to be the case, the reproduction

of racialized domination through women's magazines is not a common theme in the literature which we have reviewed.

20 These comments are about Radway's book, but it is probably fairer to apply them to the tradition from which Radway works.

21 As Nightengale (1989) notes, much of what is called 'ethnographic research' in cultural studies is actually the analysis of tape-recorded interviews (or, in the case of Ang [1988] letters).

22 Although this work was published in 1980, it was first written in 1973 (Moores 1993).

23 As a result, Seaman (1992) complains that the current trend has been to reduce audience research to 'mindless populism' (also see Morris 1998; McGuigan 1992).

24 This view of women being propelled back to romance reading has led some commentators to claim that she sees romance reading as an 'addiction.'

25 Because this complexity arises from the fact that her fieldwork led Radway to topics of investigation she had not anticipated, Moores (1993) cites this study as an example of the value of qualitative research.

26 This does not mean that treating the text simply as a material object will correct for this logic. For example, claims that women's magazines, as commodities, function to reproduce capitalism would exhibit the same problems.

27 Firth (1981) argues that, in capitalist society, people distinguish between work and leisure. While work is a sphere of coercion and necessity, leisure is a sphere of freedom and pleasure; most people work in order to be able to enjoy leisure. Thus, pleasure is premised on the absence of work and is associated with freedom of both time and choice. This freedom is illusory, however, because it also is premised on the 'other,' the necessity of work. Thus, Firth identifies three purposes of leisure in a capitalist society: the reproduction of waged labour physically (through food, rest, relaxation); the reproduction of waged labour ideologically (so that workers willingly consent to capitalist exploitation); and the provision of a market for the consumption of the vast array of goods provided by capitalist production.

Chapter 3: Materialism Revisited

1 For an overview of this work see Livingstone 1990.

2 Here I have in mind Willis et al. 1990.

3 By this I do not mean there is a 'true' account, but point out that narratives based on the 'free play' of meanings may support rather than challenge the social order which it claims to 'refuse,' 'resist,' or 'subvert.'

4 I add this aspect of academic research to Diane Wolf's (1996: 2) identification of the interrelated dimensions of power that work through the construction of academic knowledge.

5 The difficulty of hiring yet-to-be trained sociologists resulted in my hiring Rebecca, an assistant who had, in fact, already completed her MA.

6 A systematic sample of thirty issues of *Seventeen* published between 1951 and 1991 was coded for a historical analysis (findings not appearing in *Girl Talk*) and forty-six issues of the four titles discussed throughout *Girl Talk* published between June 1993 and May 1994 (during time of interviews).

7 This sample includes 10 exploratory interviews with pre-adolescent girls, as well as six pretests. The discrepancy between completed interviews and those analysed for *Girl Talk* reflects, to a large extent, the difficulty of interviewing very young girls, some of whom were rather 'shy.' My initial intention was to complete 100 interviews in order to partition data for quantitative comparisons; however, I judged many of the completed interviews to be of insufficient quality to be included in final analysis.

8 As Barthel (1988) notes, frequency counts of surface contents may produce reliable, but not necessarily valid, measurements. She points out that this problem applies especially to advertisements because the individual ad signifies much more than is apparent in the categorical identification of signs.

9 Barthes (1969) first defined semiotics as the 'scientific study of signs'; however, he did not invoke science in the way it is practised by sociologists, through empirical verification of knowledge.

10 An example is a photograph.

11 An example is smoke used to indicate fire. In advertising 'woman' is often represented indexically by a body part, which is not meant to simply signify the actual body part but her whole being and 'femininity' in general (Dyer 1982: 124).

12 An example is a word or a number. In advertising perfume, for example, red roses might be used as symbols of romantic love. Here the roses do not resemble love (as iconic), nor do they cause love (as indexical signs). While most readers would associate romantic love and red roses, this association is arbitrary and culturally specific (Dyer 1982: 125).

13 It suggests that 'natural' reading groups may be more appropriate for this method of data collection; however, as Frazer (1987) shows, the use of naturally occurring groups of friends does not guarantee readings that will not be mediated by the research setting.

14 This respondent indicated that she was comfortable and enjoyed talking to researchers; she also thought that writing down answers before group discussion would avoid the problem, suggesting that 'truthful' opinions and beliefs are available to researchers.

15 I thank research assistants Jonna and Susan for their library research.

16 All aspects of the study, including interview questions, were subject to approval by the university ethics committee.

17 A plan was formulated, but not followed, to do a similar exercise with written texts; this exercise would require a highly motivated group of older girls.

18 Alissa withdrew from graduate studies, Ann became preoccupied with her academic work, and Rebecca moved away.

19 Subject to errors of recall, telescoping, and so on.

20 In my mind this search for consistency and coherence on the part of research Subjects underlies Frazer's (1987) claim that the girls in her study employed (however unconsciously) differing discourse registers, depending on the immediate context of discussion. While I can never know for sure to what extent the research setting determined how girls talked about magazines in this current study, my analysis focuses on 'shifts' and inconsistencies which occurred within the research context, across different points of the interview.

21 As we shall see, in this study of adolescent readers, it is common for ideology to call lived experience into question; this is an effect of reading repressed within the postmodern celebration of reader agency.

Chapter 4: From Text as Specimen to Text as Process

1 These real agents of deconstruction historically have been excluded from the production of feminist knowledge in the university. As a result, their material as well as discursive absence needs to be challenged through both critical analysis and critical practice.

2 It is significant to note that I made this choice of focus before beginning fieldwork. As we shall see, advertisements are not the focus of girls' attention.

3 It is perhaps ironic that, because advertisements dominate the glossy pictorial texts, the more casual teenzine reading is, the more readers will be exposed to advertising texts.

4 Some of the writing which Pleasance (1991) cites is based on primary research; however, I feel that she might have come to a different conclusion had she employed actual reading by everyday subjects.

5 There was no conscious strategy involved in choosing the ads to be discussed by readers. A series of pictures was taken from a recent issue of *Seventeen*; coincidentally all were advertisements. Pictures were chosen which could easily be reproduced and laminated in order for assistants to carry them to interviews. Retrospectively, I would have preferred to have included more images of working women.

6 This comparison of two ads read by same respondent indicates that differences in responses are not simply differences among respondents. Given that not all respondents were shown the same ads, and that not all readings were suitable for analysis, systematic comparison of readings of the two images by the same respondent was not possible. Only in hindsight – that is, during analysis after the interviews – did the importance of the two images become apparent.

7 While this discussion has been framed in terms of gender stereotypes, it is important to note that other stereotypes were deployed during reading.

8 Clearly, this is a rather fruitless line of inquiry, pursued in social-scientific attempts to link causally such behaviours as magazine reading and eating disorders.

Chapter 5: Teenzine Reading

1 McCracken does not make this equation.

2 As will become apparent, it is not simply that readers vary in age, social class, and ethnicity, however. While these types of differences were taken into consideration in developing the sample, the purpose of analysis is to discover differences in reading rather than in readers. In other words, to assume that girls of differing ethnic backgrounds, for example, read differently would be to impose, a priori, a set of assumptions and analytical categories on the data or to claim differences in the sample as a 'finding' in the data about reading.

3 See Ellen McCraken 1993 and Ballaster et al. 1991.

4 I do not find this suggestion to be supported by their data from discussions with readers, however. In fact, in the main, Ballaster et al. base their argument on their analysis of magazine texts, which they supplement with interview excerpts; in contrast, the current study uses interview data with girls as primary data, supplemented by analysis of magazine text.

5 We will see later that another dominant theme concerns the absence of social issues, especially racism and violence.

6 This comment suggests that the girls have actually looked for magazine fashion when shopping, however. While initial interviews included discussion of shopping for clothes for school, it soon became apparent that, although teenzine reading may be related to shopping, this topic requires a separate study.

7 This approach is one of three identified by McRobbie among feminist commentary on advice columns in women's magazines: realist, feminist, and Foucauldian (1991a: pp. 161–5).

8 Although McRobbie's position arises from her ethnographic research with young readers, her arguments outlined above are based on a discursive analysis (see McRobbie 1991a: ch. 6). Overall, *Feminism and Youth Culture: From Jackie to Just Seventeen* sheds little light on everyday, rather than researcher, reading of adolescent magazines, despite McRobbie's attention to the everyday 'doing' of gender.

Chapter 6: From Pleasure to Knowledge

1 Letters to the editor also take this dialogical form. It is interesting, therefore, to note that they are much less frequently read. Here I suggest that, unlike advice columns,

which are seen to deal with 'real' teenage experiences, letters to the editor are not interesting to readers because they deal with magazine content and perhaps draw too much attention to the constructed nature of teenzine discourse.

2 We also see later that Allison worries a lot about how she looks and what she wears.

3 It would be interesting to learn how boys read these texts. Girls in this study made reference to the fact that, while boys seldom purchase teenzines, they often borrow or steal them to read.

4 At a deeper level, the word 'Mandarin' can be decoded as reference to the ancient Chinese tradition of foot-binding. It is possible that readers who decode this advertorial in this way will be led to a politicized reading of the text.

5 Heterosexual activities include kissing and petting, as well as intercourse.

6 Although not in the ways which opponents to sex education suspect.

7 For her criticisms of Foucault's Subject see MacDonald 1991.

Chapter 7: Doing and Undoing

1 For missing voices see Dolan 1994.

2 It is important to remember that interviews were not conducted for the purpose of exploring the topics discussed here. Rather, the topics discussed here are identified as significant because they emerged in relatively unprompted discussion of the everyday activities of getting ready for school and reading magazines.

3 Most of the first-stage interviews were conducted after school in the respondents' homes, and most of the follow-ups were completed during the summer holidays.

4 Here it may be important to note that Allison attends a private school which requires her to wear a school uniform. Thus, her wardrobe is organized around 'special' occasions, such as going out for dinners or clubbing.

5 Gender domination is less frequently considered.

6 In one interview social grouping by racialized identity was mentioned. In this case a Caucasian respondent described her friendship with girls of colour from minority cultures. Like other respondents, she explained how they shopped together and often dressed the same for school.

7 This raises important methodological questions for future research. Specifically, it points to the importance of ethnographic research in the study of adolescents.

8 For sure, the context of the interview may have biased respondents towards thinking about this question in a specific way. However, these answers are consistent with other findings of this study.

9 Obviously, this is one type of problem which girls attending all-girls schools do not have to face.

10 The other thing she mentions is: 'Now everything is happening to people so young. That we have to deal with a lot more than what our parents had to deal with.'

11 The findings from this chapter reinforce the claim, advanced in chapter 3, that ethnographic research would probably provide the 'best' data on the relevance of teenzines in readers' everyday lives.

Chapter 8: Calling Cultural Constructions into Question

1 A neglected but obviously important dimension of girls' experiences includes their family situation. For this type of discussion, see Pipher 1994.

2 In the final analysis this is also why the opposing views of magazines as either 'liberating' or 'oppressive' are both right and wrong.

3 It is significant that this type of textual format is found primarily in social texts for women: no counterpart exists for a male readership. The importance of self-discovery in teenzines developed later.

4 One exception is Stephanie, who points out that Tina Turner 'does stuff for her community.' The context of the interviews, of course, encouraged specific types of disclosure. It would be interesting to discover whether girls' choices would be different in another research context.

5 The quotations for individual stories have not been edited.

6 Again note the shift here from '*my friends* aren't very well adjusted' to 'we.'

7 While I find Frazer's (1987) observation that girls can, and will, change their discourse orientation according to the social context useful, it cannot account for the kinds of disjunctures that emerge during interviews in this study. In *Girl Talk* these shifts in discursive orientation are treated as disjunctures, read symptomatically for what they tell us about the social construction of 'personal' identity. In the final analysis, I believe that there is much more going on than Frazer suspects.

8 These cases are Samantha, Christina, Kelly, Alicia, Amy, Mary, and Brianna.

9 This description does resonate with slogans from the Soft & Dri ad, discussed in chapter 4.

10 Her case thus suggests that respondents are certainly willing to be frank during interviews; at least Mary did not feel that it was necessary to defend statements which she had made earlier to researchers.

11 This could as be read to suggest that, although she does not currently define herself in terms of teenzine discourse, she understands herself retrospectively according to the stereotypical reader.

12 Here I emphasize that 'alternative' does not include an all-girls school. Whatever the documented evidence of the positive effects of an all-girls school on girls' personal and social development, in this study private girls' schools are associated with articulate criticisms of teenzines accompanied by 'hyper'feminine obsession with clothes and physical attractiveness. This finding requires further study.

13 Exploratory interviews were conducted with ten girls aged ten to twelve years old.

14 Missing in this study, and requiring future research, is the role of adult editors in the construction of teenzine texts.

Conclusion: Towards a Materialist Analysis of Texts

1 I would never claim a 'perfect' understanding.
2 This production involves more than epistemological considerations, however. Although beyond the scope of the current discussion, it includes institutional considerations – who gets to write knowledge, under what conditions, for what purpose, and so on. See Wolf 1996.
3 As Weedon (1987: 13) notes, most of the theorists who have produced post-structuralism are themselves unsympathetic to feminism.
4 I have in mind here Davies and Harré (1990), who claim that people exercise choice in relation to their discursive positioning. They thus claim that, while subjectivity is constituted through discursive practices, a Subject capable of 'choice' exists prior to that constitution within discourse.
5 While I maintain that ethnographic accounts may appear to avoid some of these problems, these data are still a textual account, mediated by the research process. For a good discussion of the epistemological issues of feminist ethnography see Wolf 1996.
6 For a critique of Game, see Currie 1997b.
7 For a critique of this position see Ellis 1989.
8 Sarup (1989: 58) points out that intertextuality has been taken to mean that there is no possibility of truth; Sarup argues that it is more plausible to think of Derrida as trying to avoid assertions about the nature of truth.
9 Writers liken this to the way in which youth 'listen' to music through their bodies. This listening allows them to resist/escape because it transports youth beyond the restrictions of the social (sometimes to the dismay of adults).
10 By this I claim that feminist sociology has contributed to social change. I have in mind social changes which accompany research on violence against women or policy-oriented research on health-care delivery systems.
11 This chain of meaning represents one reason why it was difficult to reach closure on this project.
12 My intention is to produce a text for the latter.
13 While media literacy can also be effective as an individualized skill which I strongly endorse, teaching young women to read the social differently is not the same as changing the world in which they live. Clearly, rewriting the social world is much more difficult than its 'reading,' illustrated by a simple example. During the first-ever strike by faculty at my previous university, one faculty member suggested that we adopt a slogan which tells the world at large that 'we [faculty as opposed to

administration] *are* the university.' In reply, my partner (also a committed materialist) quite aptly quipped: 'If we are the university, then why don't we vote ourselves a raise so that we can all go home.'

14 This is not the same as reading interview transcripts against magazine content, as we did earlier in *Girl Talk*.

15 For a glimpse of this world, see Norris 1990.

16 Pollay (1994) refers to the ability of these commercial texts to construct the 'buyological urge.'

17 For a fuller treatment of the depoliticization of *Seventeen* see Currie 1994.

18 For an exploration of how advertisers attempt to channel key aspects of feminist discourse into the promotion of commodities, see Goldman, Heath, and Smith 1991. As an aside, this force also demonstrates the implication of sociology itself in the production of commercial texts as vehicles for the operation of power.

Appendix B: 'Counting' Meaning

1 As we shall see, the coding for advertisements followed a similar but not identical pattern.

2 Broad categories were children, teenagers, adults, and the elderly.

3 This categorization was assisted by supporting written text and included parent/ child, siblings, same-sexed friends, opposite-sexed friends, teacher/pupil.

4 This categorization was assisted by supporting written text and included an 'occupational' component such as student, parent (mother or father), teacher, model, athlete, celebrity or famous person, as well as a small miscellaneous category of various professionals (often endorsing products) such as scientist and beautician.

5 A 'beauty advertisement' includes all products to be applied to the physical body to enhance its social value, except clothing. Ads for cosmetics, perfumes, and deodorants, and for products for hair care and hair removal, general skin care, dental care, nail care, and body trimming or tanning, were coded.

References

Abercrombie, Nicholas, Stephen Hill, and Bryan S. Turner. 1988. *Dictionary of Sociology*, 2d ed. Harmondsworth: Penguin.

Abrams, M. 1959. *The Teenage Consumer*. London: London Press Exchange.

Althusser, Louis. 1969. *For Marx*. Translated by Ben Brewster. London: Allen Lane.

– 1971. *'Learn and Philosophy' and Other Essays*. London: New Left Books.

– 1976. *Essays in Self-Criticism*. London: New Left Books.

Andersen, Margaret L. 1988. *Thinking about Women: Sociological Perspectives on Sex and Gender*, 2d ed. New York: Macmillan.

Andrew, Gunner. 1978. *Rhetoric and Ideology in Advertising*. Stockholm: LiberForlag.

Ang, Ien. 1985. *Watching Dallas: Soap Opera and the Melodramatic Imagination*. London: Methuen.

– 1988. 'Feminist Desire and Feminist Pleasure: On Janice Radway's *Reading the Romance: Women, Patriarchy and Popular Literature*.' *Camera Obscura* 16: 179–91.

– 1990. 'Melodramatic Identifications: Television Fiction and Women's Fantasy.' In *Television and Women's Culture: The Politics of the Popular*, ed. Mary E. Brown, 75–88. London: Sage.

– 1991. *Desperately Seeking the Audience*. London: Routledge.

Armstrong, Pat, and Hugh Armstrong. 1984. *The Double Ghetto: Canadian Women and Their Segregated Work*. Toronto: McClelland & Stewart.

Arthur, Linda Boynton. 1993. 'Clothing, Control, and Women's Agency: The Mitigation of Patriarchal Power.' In *Negotiating at the Margins: The Gendered Discourses of Power and Resistance*, ed. Sue Fisher and Kathy Davis, 66–86. New Brunswick, NJ: Rutgers University Press.

Baker, Maureen. 1985. *'What Will Tomorrow Bring? ...' A Study of the Aspirations of Adolescent Women*. Ottawa: Canadian Advisory Council on the Status of Women.

Ballaster, Ros, Margaret Beetham, Elizabeth Frazer, and Sandra Hebron. 1991. *Women's Worlds: Ideology, Femininity, and the Woman's Magazine*. London: Macmillan.

Bennett, Tony. 1986. 'Introduction: Popular Culture and "The Turn to Gramsci."' In *Popular Culture and Social Relations*, ed. T. Bennett, C. Mercer, and J. Woollacott, xi–xix. Milton Keynes: Open University Press.

Benton, Ted. 1984. *The Rise and Fall of Structural Marxism: Althusser and His Influence*. London: Macmillan.

Berelson, Bernard. 1952. *Content Analysis in Communication Research*. Glencoe: Free Press.

Berger, John. 1972. *Ways of Seeing*. London: British Broadcasting Corporation; Harmondsworth: Penguin.

Best, Steven, and Douglas Kellner. 1991. *Postmodern Theory: Critical Interrogations*. London: Guilford Press.

Betterton, Rosemary, ed. 1987. *Looking On: Images of Femininity in the Visual Arts and Media*. London: Pandora.

Bibby, Reginald, and Donald Posterski. 1992. *Teen Trends: A Nation in Motion*. Toronto: Stoddart.

Bordo, Susan. 1988. 'Anorexia Nervosa: Psychopathology as the Chrystallization of Culture.' In *Feminism and Foucault: Reflections on Resistance*, ed. I. Diamond and L. Quinby, 87–117. Boston: Northeastern University Press.

– 1990. 'Reading the Slender Body.' In *Body/Politics: Women and the Discourses of Science*, ed. Mary Jacobus, Evelyn Fox Keller, and Sally Shuttleworth, 83–112. New York: Routledge.

– 1991. '"Material Girl": The Effacements of Postmodern Culture.' In *The Female Body: Figures, Styles, Speculations*, ed. L. Goldstein, 106–30. Ann Arbor: University of Michigan Press.

Boskind-White, Marlene. 1985. 'Bulimia: A Sociocultural Perspective.' In *Theory and Treatment of Anorexia Nervosa and Bulimia*, ed. S. Emmett, 113–26. New York: Brunner/Mazel Publishers.

Braithwaite, Brian, and Joan Barrel. 1979. *The Business of Women's Magazines: The Agonies and the Ecstasies*. London: Associated Business Press.

Brown, C. 1993. 'The Continuum: Anorexia, Bulimia and Weight Preoccupation.' In *Consuming Passions: Feminist Approaches to Weight Preoccupation and Eating Disorders*, ed. C. Brown and K. Jasper, 53–68. Toronto: Second Story.

Brown, Mary Ellen, ed. 1990. *Television and Women's Culture: The Politics of the Popular*. Newbury Park, CA: Sage.

Brownmiller, Susan. 1984. *Femininity*. New York: Linden Press / Simon and Schuster.

Brundson, Charlotte, and David Morley. 1978. *Everyday Television: 'Nationwide.'* London: British Film Institute.

Budd, Richard, Robert Thorp, and Lewis Donohew. 1967. *Content Analysis of Communications*. New York: Macmillan.

Budgeon, Shelley. 1993. 'Fashion Magazine Advertising: The Constructions of "Femininity" in *Seventeen.*' Master's thesis, Department of Anthropology and Sociology, University of British Columbia.

Budgeon, Shelley, and Dawn H. Currie. 1995. 'From Feminism to Postfeminism: Women's Liberation in Fashion Magazines.' *Women's Studies International Forum* 18/2: 173–86.

Busby, Linda J. 1975. 'Sex Role Research on the Mass Media.' *Journal of Communication* 25/4: 107–31.

Butler, Judith. 1990a. *Gender Trouble: Feminism and the Subversion of Identity.* New York: Routledge.

– 1990b. 'Gender Trouble, Feminist Theory, and Psychoanalytic Discourse.' In *Feminism/Postmodernism*, ed. Linda J. Nicholson, 324–40. New York: Routledge.

– 1993. *Bodies that Matter: On the Discursive Limits of 'Sex.'* New York: Routledge.

Butler-Flora, Cornelia. 1971. 'The Passive Female: Her Comparative Image by Class and Culture in Women's Magazine Fiction.' *Journal of Marriage and the Family* 33/3 (August): 435–44.

Cancian, Francesca M., and Steven L. Gordon. 1988. 'Changing Emotion Norms in Marriage: Love and Anger in U.S. Women's Magazines since 1900.' *Gender and Society* 2/3: 308–42.

Cash, T.E., and P.E. Henry. 1995. 'Women's Body Images: The Results of a National Survey in the USA.' *Sex Roles* 33 (1/2): 19–28.

Chapkis, Wendy. 1986. *Beauty Secrets: Women and the Politics of Appearance.* Boston: South End Press.

Chodorow, Nancy. 1978. *The Reproduction of Mothering: Psychoanalysis and the Sociology of Gender.* Berkeley: University of California Press.

Christian, Linda K. 1984. 'Becoming a Woman through Romance: Adolescent Novels and the Ideology of Femininity.' Doctoral dissertation, University of Wisconsin-Madison.

Christian-Smith, Linda K. 1988. 'Romancing the Girl: Adolescent Romance Novels and the Construction of Femininity.' In *Becoming Feminine: The Politics of Popular Culture*, ed. L.G. Roman, and L.K. Christian-Smith, 76–101. Philadelphia: Falmer Press.

Connelly, M. Patricia. 1978. *Last Hired, First Fired: Women and the Canadian Work Force.* Toronto: Women's Press.

Cote, James E., and Anton L. Allahar. 1994. *Generation on Hold: Coming of Age in the Late Twentieth Century.* Toronto: Stoddart.

Courtney, Alice, and Sarah Lockeretz. 1970. 'A Woman's Place: An Analysis of the Roles Portrayed by Women in Magazine Advertisements.' *Journal of Marketing Research* 8: 92–5.

Coward, Rosalind. 1985. *Female Desires: How They Are Sought, Bought, and Packaged.* New York: Grove Press.

Culley, James D., and Rex Bennett. 1976. 'Selling Women, Selling Blacks.' *Journal of Communication* 26/4: 160–74.

Currie, Dawn H. 1988. 'Starvation amidst Abundance: Female Adolescents and Anorexia.' In *Sociology of Health Care in Canada*, ed. B. Singh Bolaria and Harley D. Dickinson, 200–15. Toronto: Harcourt Brace Jovanovich.

– 1992. 'Femininity as Popular Discourse: Toward Interdisciplinary Study of Texts.' Presented at Qualitative Analysis Conference, Ottawa, May.

– 1993. 'Unhiding the Hidden: Race, Class, and Gender in the Construction of Knowledge.' *Humanity and Society* 17/1: 3–27.

– 1994. 'Going Green: Mythologies of Consumption in Adolescent Magazines.' *Youth and Society* 26/1: 92–117.

– 1997a. 'Decoding Femininity: Advertisements and Their Teenage Readers.' *Gender and Society* 11/4: 454–78.

– 1997b. In Search of Women's Standpoint: Towards an Epistemology of Experiential Knowledge. Gender Studies Occasional Paper 6. Asian Institute of Technology, Bangkok, September.

Dancyger, Irene. 1978. *A World of Women: An Illustrated History of Women's Magazines*. Dublin: Gill & Macmillan.

Danesi, Marcel. 1994. *Cool: The Signs and Meanings of Adolescence*. Toronto: University of Toronto Press.

Davies, Bronwyn, and Rom Harré. 1990. 'Positioning: The Discursive Production of Selves.' *Journal for the Theory of Social Behaviour* 20/1: 43–63.

Davies, Ioan. 1995. *Cultural Studies and Beyond*. London: Routledge.

Davis, Angela Y. 1981. *Women, Race and Class*. New York: Vintage Books.

de Beauvoir, Simone. 1961. *The Second Sex*. Translated by H.M. Parshley. New York: Bantam.

DeLibero, Linda Benn. 1994. 'This Year's Girl: A Personal/Critical History of Twiggy.' In *On Fashion*, ed. Shari Benstock and Suzanne Ferriss, 41–58. New Brunswick, NJ: Rutgers University Press.

Derrida, Jacques. 1976. *Of Grammatology*. Translated by Gayatri Chakravorty Spivak. Baltimore: Johns Hopkins University Press.

Devereaux, Mary. 1990. 'Oppressive Texts, Resisting Readers, and the Gendered Spectator: The New Aesthetics.' *Journal of Aesthetics and Art Criticism* 48/4: 337–48.

Diamond, Irene, and Lee Quinby, eds. 1988. 'Introduction.' In *Feminism and Foucault: Reflections on Resistance*, ed. I. Diamond and L. Quinby, ix–xx. Boston: Northeastern University Press.

Doane, Mary Ann. 1981. 'Woman's Stake: Filming the Female Body.' *October* 17 (summer): 22–36.

– 1982. 'Film and Masquerade: Theorizing the Female Spectator.' *Screen* 23 (3/4) (September/October): 74–87.

Dolan, Marlena. 1994. *Just Talking about Ourselves: Voices of Our Youth*. Penticton, BC: Theytus.

Donaton, Scott. 1990. 'Teen Titles Grow Up.' *Advertising Age*, 11 June: 41.

Donovan, Josepine. 1985. *Feminist Theory: The Intellectual Traditions of American Feminism*. New York: Frederick Ungar.

Doughan, David T.J. 1987. 'Periodicals By, For, and About Women in Britain.' *Women's Studies International Forum* 10/3: 261–73.

Drotner, Kirsten. 1983. 'Schoolgirls, Madcaps, and Air Aces: English Girls and Their Magazine Reading between the Wars.' *Feminist Studies* 9/1: 33–52.

Dull, Diana, and Candace West. 1991. 'Accounting for Cosmetic Surgery: The Accomplishment of Gender.' *Social Problems* 38/1: 54–70.

Duquin, Mary E. 1989. 'Fashion and Fitness: Images in Women's Magazine Advertisements.' *Arena Review* 13/2: 97–109.

Dyer, Gillian. 1982. *Advertising as Communication*. London: Methuen.

Eagleton, Terry. 1980. 'Ideology, Fiction, Narrative.' *Social Text* 2 (Summer): 62–80.

Earnshaw, Stella. 1984. 'Advertising and the Media: The Case of Women's Magazines.' *Media, Culture and Society* 6: 411–21.

Easthope, Anthony, and Kate McGowan. 1993. *A Critical and Cultural Theory Reader*. Toronto: University of Toronto Press.

Editorial Group. 1978. 'Women's Studies Group: Trying to Do Feminist Intellectual Work.' In *Women Take Issue: Aspects of Women's Subordination*, ed. Women's Studies Group, Centre for Contemporary Cultural Studies, University of Birmingham, 7–17. London: Hutchinson.

Ellis, John. 1989. *Against Deconstruction*. Princeton, NJ: Princeton University Press.

Evans, Ellis D., Judith Rutberg, Carmela Sather, and Charli Turner. 1991. 'Content Analysis of Contemporary Teen Magazines for Adolescent Females.' *Youth and Society* 23/1: 99–120.

Faludi, Susan. 1991. *Backlash: The Undeclared War against American Women*. New York: Crown.

Faust, B. 1980. 'The *Cosmo* Girl: How Did She Succeed?' In *Women, Sex and Pornography: A Controversial Study*, ed. B. Faust, 157–69. New York: Macmillan.

Felski, Rita. 1989. *Beyond Feminist Aesthetics: Feminist Literature and Social Change*. Cambridge, MA: Harvard University Press.

Ferguson, Jill Hicks, Peggy J. Kreshel, and Spencer F. Tinkham. 1990. 'In the Pages of *Ms*: Sex Role Portrayals of Women in Advertising.' *Journal of Advertising* 19/1: 40–51.

Ferguson, Marjorie. 1983. *Forever Feminine: Women's Magazines and the Cult of Femininity*. London: Heinemann.

Firth, Simon. 1981. *Sound Effects: Youth, Leisure and the Politics of Rock*. New York: Panthen.

Fiske, John. 1989a. *Reading Popular Culture*. Boston: Unwin Hyman.

– 1989b. *Understanding Popular Culture*. Boston: Unwin Hyman.

Foley, Barbara. 1990. 'Marxism in the Poststructuralist Moment: Some Notes on the Problem of Revising Marx.' *Cultural Critique* 15/1 (Spring): 5–37.

Ford, James L.C. 1969. *Magazines for Millions*. Carbondale: Southern Illinois University Press.

Foucault, Michel. 1980. *Power/Knowledge: Selected Interviews and Other Writings, 1972–1977*. Selected and translated by C. Gordon. Brighton: Harvester.

Fox, Bonnie. 1990. 'Selling the Mechanized Household: 70 Years of Ads in *Ladies Home Journal*.' *Gender and Society* 4/1: 25–40.

Franklin, Sarah, Celia Lury, and Jackie Stacey. 1991. 'Introduction 1: Feminism and Cultural Studies: Pasts, Presents, Futures.' In *Off-Centre: Feminism and Cultural Studies*, ed. S. Franklin, C. Lury, and J. Stacey, 1–19. London: HarperCollins Academic.

Franzwa, H.H. 1975. 'Female Roles in Women's Magazine Fiction, 1940–1970.' In *Woman: Dependent or Independent Variable*, ed. R.K. Unger and F.L. Denmark, 42–53. New York: Psychological Dimensions.

Fraser, Nancy, and Linda J. Nicholson. 1990. 'Social Criticism without Philosophy: An Encounter between Feminism and Postmodernism.' In *Feminism/Postmodernism*, ed. L.J. Nicholson, 19–38. New York: Routledge.

Frazer, Elizabeth. 1987. 'Teenage Girls Reading Jackie.' *Media, Culture and Society* 9/4: 407–25.

Friedan, Betty. 1963. *The Feminine Mystique*. New York: Norton.

– 1982. *The Second Stage*. London: Michael Joseph.

Friend, Tad. 1994. 'Lock Up Your Sons – the 21st-Century Woman Is in the Building.' *Esquire*, February, 47–56.

Fuss, Diana. 1992. 'Fashion and the Homospectatorial Look.' *Critical Inquiry* 18: 713–37.

Gaines, Jane. 1986. 1986. 'White Privilege and Looking Relations: Race and Gender in Feminist Film Theory.' *Cultural Critique* 4/1 (fall): 59–79.

Game, Ann. 1991. *Undoing the Social: Towards a Deconstructive Sociology*. Milton Keynes: Open University Press.

Garner. D. 1997. 'The 1997 Body Image Survey Results.' *Psych Today* 30/1: 30.

Geise, L. Ann. 1979. 'The Female Role in Middle Class Women's Magazines from 1955 to 1976: A Content Analysis of Nonfiction Selections. *Sex Roles* 5/1: 51–62.

Gerbner, George. 1958. 'The Social Role of the Confession Magazine.' *Social Problems* 6: 29–40.

– 1978. 'The Dynamics of Cultural Resistance.' In *Hearth and Home: Images of Women in the Mass Media*, ed. G. Tuchman, A.K. Daniels, and J. Bennet, 46–50. New York: Oxford University Press.

Giddens, Anthony. 1979. *Central Problems in Sociological Theory: Action, Structure, and Contradiction in Social Analysis.* Berkeley: University of California Press.

– 1983. *A Contemporary Critique of Historical Materialism.* Berkeley: University of California Press.

Glazer, Nona. 1980. 'Overworking the Working Woman: The Double Day in a Mass Magazine.' *Women's Studies International Quarterly* 3: 79–93.

Gledhill, Christine. 1987. 'The Melodramatic Field: An Investigation.' In *Home Is Where the Heart Is: Studies in Melodrama and the Woman's Film*, ed. Christine Gledhill, 5–39. London: British Film Institute.

– 1988. 'Pleasurable Negotiations.' In *Female Spectators: Looking at Film and Television*, ed. E. Deirdre Pribram, 64–89. London: Verso.

– 1994. 'Image and Voice: Approaches to Marxist-Feminist Film Criticism.' In *Multiple Voices in Feminist Film Criticism*, ed. Diane Carson, Linda Dittmar, and Janice R. Welsh, 109–23. Minneapolis: University of Minnesota Press.

Goffman, Erving. 1979. *Gender Advertisements.* Cambridge, MA: Harvard University Press.

Goldman, Robert. 1992. *Reading Ads Socially.* London: Routledge.

Goldman, Robert, Deborah Heath, and Sharon L. Smith. 1991. 'Commodity Feminism.' *Critical Studies in Mass Communication* 8: 333–51.

Goldman, Robert, and Stephen Papson. 1996. *Sign Wars.* New York: Guilford.

Gordon, Colin. 1980. *Michel Foucault: Power/Knowledge.* London: Routledge.

Gramsci, Antonio. 1971. *Selections from the Prison Notebooks.* Translated by Quintin Hoare and Geoffrey Nowell-Smith. London: Lawrence & Wishart.

Gray, Ann. 1987. 'Reading the Audience.' *Screen* 28/3: 24–35.

Grossberg, Lawrence. 1993. 'The Formations of Cultural Studies: An American in Birmingham.' In *Relocating Cultural Studies: Developments in Theory and Research*, ed. Valda Blundell, John Sheperd, and Ian Taylor, 21–66. New York: Routledge.

Grosz, Elizabeth. 1990. *Jacques Lacan: A Feminist Introduction.* London: Routledge.

Hall, Stuart. 1973. 'Encoding and Decoding in the Media Discourse.' *Stencilled Paper* 7. Birmingham: Centre for Contemporary Cultural Studies.

– 1980. 'Cultural Studies: Two Paradigms.' *Media, Culture and Society* 2: 57–72.

– 1982. 'The Rediscovery of "Ideology": Return of the Repressed in Media Studies.' In *Culture, Society and the Media*, ed. M. Gurevitch, T. Bennett, J. Curran, and J. Woollacott, 56–90. London: Methuen.

Hall, Stuart, and Tony Jefferson, eds. 1976. *Resistance through Rituals.* London: Hutchinson.

Hansen, Joseph, and Evelyn Reed, eds. 1986. *Cosmetics, Fashions, and the Exploitation of Women.* New York: Pathfinder.

Hartsock, Nancy. 1990. 'Foucault on Power: A Theory for Women?' In *Feminism/Postmodernism*, ed. Linda J. Nicholson, 157–75. New York: Routledge.

Hebdige, Dick. 1979. *Subculture: The Meaning of Style*. London: Methuen.

Hekman, Susan J. 1990. *Gender and Knowledge: Elements of a Postmodern Feminism*. Boston: Northeastern University Press.

Hennessy, Rosemary. 1993. *Materialist Feminism and the Politics of Discourse*. London: Routledge.

Hennessy, Rosemary, and Chrys Ingraham. 1997. 'Introduction: Reclaiming Anticapitalist Feminism.' In *Materialist Feminism: A Reader in Class, Difference, and Women's Lives*, ed. R. Hennessy, and C. Ingraham, 1–16. New York and London: Routledge.

Henry, Susan. 1984. 'Juggling the Frying Pan and the Fire: The Portrayal of Employment and Family Life in Seven Women's Magazines, 1975–1982.' *The Social Science Journal* 21/4: 87–107.

Hill Collins, Patricia. 1990. *Black Feminist Thought: Knowledge, Consciousness, and the Politics of Empowerment*. London: HarperCollins Academic.

Ho, Mary Louise. 1984. 'Patriarchal Ideology and Agony Columns.' *Studies in Sexual Politics* 1: 3–13.

Hobson, Dorothy. 1982. *'Crossroads': The Drama of Soap Opera*. London: Methuen.

Holland, Janet, Caroline Ramazanoglu, Sue Scott Sharpe, and Rachel Thomson. 1996. '"Don't Die of Ignorance. I Nearly Died of Embarrassment": Condoms in Context.' In *Feminism and Sexuality: A Reader*, ed. Stevi Jackson and Sue Scott, 117–29. New York: Columbia University Press.

Holmes, Janelle, and Elaine Leslau Silverman. 1992. *We're Here, Listen to Us! A Survey of Young Women in Canada*. Ottawa: Canadian Advisory Council on the Status of Women.

Holsti, Ole R. 1969. *Content Analysis for the Social Sciences and Humanities*. Reading, MA: Addison-Wesley.

Honey, Maureen. 1984. 'The Confession Formula and Fantasies of Empowerment.' *Women's Studies* 10: 303–20.

hooks, bell. 1981. *Ain't I a Woman?* Boston: South End Press.

– 1992. *Black Looks: Race and Representation*. Toronto: Between the Lines.

Jaddou, Liliane, and Jon Williams. 1981. 'A Theoretical Contribution to the Struggle against the Dominant Representations of Women.' *Media, Culture and Society* 3: 105–24.

Jhally, Sut. 1990. *The Codes of Advertising: Fetishism and the Political Economy of Meaning in the Consumer Society*. New York: Routledge.

Johnson, Lesley. 1993. *The Modern Girl: Girlhood and Growing Up*. Buckingham: Open University Press.

Kaiser, Kathy. 1979. 'The New Women's Magazines: It's the Same Old Story.' *Frontiers* 4/1: 14–17.

Kaluzynska, Eva. 1980. 'Wiping the Floor with Theory – a Survey of Writings on Housework.' *Feminist Review* 6: 27–54.

Kaplan, Alexandra, and Mary Anne Sedney. 1980. *Psychology and Sex Roles: An Androgynous Perspective*. Boston: Little, Brown.

Kaplan, E. Ann. 1983. *Women and Film: Both Sides of the Camera*. New York: Methuen.

– 1987. *Rocking around the Clock: Music, Televisions, Postmodernism and Consumer Culture*. New York: Methuen.

Keller, Kathryn. 1992. 'Nurture and Work in the Middle Class: Imagery from Women's Magazines.' *International Journal of Politics, Culture, and Society* 5: 577–600.

Kellner, Douglas. 1995. *Media Culture: Cultural Studies, Identity and Politics between the Modern and the Postmodern*. London and New York: Routledge.

Kerin, Roger A., William J. Lundstom, and Donald Sciglimpaglia. 1979. 'Women in Advertisements: Retrospect and Proscept.' *Journal of Advertising* 8/3: 37–42.

King, Alan J.C., and Beverly Coles. 1992. *The Health of Canada's Youth: Views and Behaviours of 11-, 13-, and 15-Year-Olds from 11 Countries*. Ottawa: Minister of National Health and Welfare.

Kolakowski, Leszek. 1978. *Main Currents of Marxism*. Vol. 3. Translated by P.S. Falla. Oxford: Oxford University Press.

Komisar, Lucy. 1971. 'The Image of Woman in Advertising.' In *Women in Sexist Society*, ed. V. Gornick and B. Moran, 304–17. New York: Basic.

Kracauer, S. 1952. 'The Challenge of Qualitative Content Analysis.' *Public Opinion Quarterly* 16/4: 631–42.

Krippendorff, Klaus. 1980. *Content Analysis: An Introduction to Its Methodology*. Beverly Hills, CA: Sage.

Leiss, W., S. Kline, and Sut Jhally. 1985. *Social Communication in Advertising: Person, Products and Images of Well-Being*. Toronto: Methuen.

Lengermann, Patricia Madoo, and Jill Niebrugge-Brantley. 1998. *The Women Founders: Sociology and Social Theory 1830–1930*. Boston: McGraw-Hill.

Lesko, Nancy. 1988. 'The Curriculum of the Body: Lessons from a Catholic High School.' In *Becoming Feminine: The Politics of Popular Culture*, ed. L.G. Roman and L.K. Christian-Smith, 123–42. Philadelphia: Falmer.

Leslie, Deborah Ann. 1995. 'Advertising: Between Economy and Culture.' Doctoral dissertation, Department of Geography, University of British Columbia.

Lingard, Lorelei. 1993. 'Rhetoric and Semiotics in Context: Exploring the Genre of Female-Targeted Advertising.' Master's thesis, Department of English, Simon Fraser University.

Livingstone, Sonia M. 1990. *Making Sense of Television*. New York: Pergamon.

Lorraine, Tamsin E. 1990. *Gender, Identity, and the Production of Meaning*. Boulder: Westview.

Lury, Celia. 1995. 'The Rights and Wrongs of Culture: Issues of Theory and Methodology.' In *Feminist Cultural Theory: Process and Production*, ed. Beverley Skeggs, 33–45. Manchester: Manchester University Press.

MacDonald, Eleanor. 1991. 'The Trouble with Subjects: Feminism, Marxism, and the Questions of Poststructuralism.' *Studies in Political Economy* 35 (Summer): 43–71.

MacGregor, Robert M. 1989. 'The Distorted Mirror: Images of Visible Minority Women in Canadian Print Advertising.' *Atlantis* 15/1: 137–43.

MacLean, Brian D. 1996. 'Crime, Criminology, and Society: A Short But Critical Introduction.' In *Crime and Society: Readings in Critical Criminology*, ed. B.D. MacLean, 1–24. Toronto: Copp Clark.

Manning, Louise. 1986. 'Cosmetics and the Women.' In *Cosmetics, Fashions, and the Exploitation of Women*, ed. J. Hansen and E. Reed, 32–3. New York: Pathfinders.

Massé, M.A., and K. Rosenblum. 1988. 'Male and Female Created Them: The Depiction of Gender in the Advertising of Traditional Women's and Men's Magazines.' *Women's Studies International Forum* 11/2: 127–44.

Mattelart, A., and S. Sigelaub, eds. 1979. *Communication and Class Struggle: An Anthology*. New York: International General Edition, vol. 1.

Mattelart, Michele. 1986. *Women, Media, Crisis: Femininity and Disorder*. London: Comedia.

McCallum, Pamela. 1975. 'World without Conflict: Magazines for Working-Class Women.' *Canadian Forum*, September, 42–4.

McCormack, Thelma. 1982. 'Content Analysis: The Social History of a Method.' *Studies in Communications* 2: 143–78.

McCracken, Ellen. 1993. *Decoding Women's Magazines: From Mademoiselle to Ms.* London: Macmillan.

McDowell, Margaret B. 1997. 'The Children's Feature: A Guide to Editors' Perceptions of Adult Readers of Women's Magazines.' *Midwest Quarterly* 19/1: 36–50.

McGuigan, J. 1992. *Cultural Populism*. London: Routledge.

McMahon, Kathryn. 1990. 'The Cosmopolitan Ideology and the Management of Desire.' *The Journal of Sex Role Research* 27/3: 381–96.

McNay, Lois. 1992. *Foucault and Feminism: Power, Gender, and the Self*. Cambridge: Polity.

McRobbie, Angela. 'Working Class Girls and the Culture of Femininity.' In *Women Take Issue: Aspects of Women's Subordination*, ed. Women's Studies Group, Centre for Contemporary Cultural Studies, University of Birmingham, 96–108. London: Hutchinson.

– 1980. 'Settling Accounts with Subculture: A Feminist Critique.' *Screen Education* 39 (Spring): 37–49.

– 1987. 'Postmodernism and Popular Culture.' *Annali* 28/3: 63–78.

– 1991a. *Feminism and Youth Culture*. London: Macmillan.

- 1991b. 'New Times in Cultural Studies.' *New Formations* 13 (Spring): 1–17.
- 1996. 'Different, Youthful, Subjectivities.' In *The Post-Colonial Question: Common Skies, Divided Horizons*, ed. Iain Chambers and Lidia Curti, 30–46. London: Routledge.

Meyerowitz, Joanne. 1993. 'Beyond the Feminine Mystique: A Reassessment of Postwar Mass Culture, 1946–1958.' *The Journal of American History* 79/3/4: 1455–82.

Michels, James. 1985. 'Roland Barthes on the *Cosmo* Cover Girl.' *Semiotics: Annual Meetings of the Semiotic Society of America*: 195–202.

Millett, Kate. 1970. *Sexual Politics*. New York: Avon.

Millum, Trevor. 1975. *Images of Women: Advertising in Women's Magazines*. London: Chatto & Windus.

Mitchell, John J. 1986. *The Nature of Adolescence*. Calgary: Detselig Enterprises.

Modelski, Tanya. 1982. *Loving with a Vengeance: Mass-Produced Fantasies for Women*. Hamden CT: Archon.

Moores, Shaun. 1993. *Interpreting Audiences: The Ethnography of Media Consumption*. London: Sage.

Morley, David. 1980. *The Nationwide Audience: Structure and Decoding*. London: British Film Institute.

- 1981. 'The Nationwide Audience: A Critical Postscript.' *Screen Education* 39: 3–14.

Morley, David, and Kuan-Hsing Chen, eds. 1966. *Stuart Hall: Critical Dialogues in Cultural Studies*. London and New York: Routledge.

Morris, Meaghan. 1988. 'Banality in Cultural Studies.' *Discourse* 10/2: 3–29.

Moschis, George P., and Gilbert A. Churchill, Jr. 1979. 'An Analysis of the Adolescent Consumer.' *Journal of Marketing* 43 (summer): 40–8.

Mott, Frank Luther. 1957. *A History of American Magazines, 1885–1905*. Cambridge, MA: Belknap Press of Harvard University.

Mouffe, Chantal. 1979. 'Hegemony and Ideology in Gramsci.' In *Culture and Marxist Theory*, ed. Chantal Mouffe, 168–204. London and Boston: Routledge & Kegan Paul.

Mulvey, Laura. 1975. 'Visual Pleasure and Narrative Cinema.' *Screen* 16/3: 6–18.

- 1989. *Visual and Other Pleasures*. London: Macmillan.

Nett, Emily. 1991. 'Is There Life after Fifty?: Images of Middle Age for Women in *Chatelaine* Magazine.' *Journal of Women and Aging* 3: 93–115.

Nichols, Bill. 1981. *Ideology and the Image: Social Representation in the Cinema and Other Media*. Bloomington: Indiana University Press.

Nightengale, Virginia. 1989. 'What's "Ethnographic" about Ethnographic Audience Research?' *Australian Journal of Communication* 16: 50–63.

Norris, Christopher. 1982. *Deconstruction: Theory and Practice*. New York: Methuen.

Norris, Claire E., and Andrew M. Colman. 1992. 'Content Effects on Recall and Recognition of Magazine Advertising.' *Journal of Advertising*, 21/3 (September): 37–46.

Norris, James D. 1990. *Advertising and the Transformation of American Society, 1865–1920*, New York: Greenwood.

Oakley, Ann. 1974. *Housewife*. Harmondsworth: Penguin.

– 1981. *Subject Women: A Powerful Analysis of Women's Experience in Society Today*. Glasgow: Fontana.

O'Brien, Mary. 1984. 'Hegemony and Superstructure: A Feminist Critique of Neo-Marxism.' In *Taking Sex into Account: The Policy Consequences of Sexist Research*, ed. J. Vickers, 85–100. Ottawa: Carelton University Press.

Ortiz, Jeanne A., and Larry P. Ortiz. 1989. 'Do Contemporary Magazines Practice What They Preach?' *Free Inquiry in Creative Sociology* 17/1: 51–5.

Pearce, Lynne. 1995. 'Finding a Place from Which to Write: The Methodology of Feminist Textual Practice.' In *Feminist Cultural Theory: Process and Production*, ed. Beverley Skeggs, 81–96. Manchester: Manchester University Press.

Peirce, Carol Marjorie. 1985. '*Cosmopolitan*: The Democratization of American Beauty Culture.' Doctoral dissertation, Bowling Green State University.

Peirce, Kate. 1990. 'A Feminist Theoretical Perspective on the Socialization of Teenage Girls Through *Seventeen* Magazine.' *Sex Roles* 23 (9/10): 491–501.

Peterson, Theodore. 1964. *Magazines in the Twentieth Century*. Urbana: University of Illinois Press.

Pingree, S., R.B. Hawkins, M. Butler, and W. Paisley. 1976. 'A Scale for Sexism.' *Journal of Communication* 26/4 (fall): 185–92.

Pipher, Mary. 1994. *Reviving Ophelia: Saving the Selves of Adolescent Girls*. New York: Ballantine.

Pleasance, Helen. 1991. 'Open or Closed: Popular Magazines and Dominant Culture.' In *Off-Centre: Feminism and Cultural Studies*, ed. S. Franklin, C. Lury, and J. Stacey, 69–84. London: HarperCollins Academic.

Polan, Dana. 1988. 'Complexity and Contradiction in Mass-Culture Analysis: On Ien Ang "Watching Dallas."' *Camera Obscura* 16: 193–202.

Pollay, Richard W. 1994. 'Thank the Editors for the Buy-ological Urge! American Magazines, Advertising, and the Promotion of the Consumer Culture, 1920–1980.' *Research in Marketing, Supplement* 6: 221–35.

Poovey, Mary. 1988. 'Feminism and Deconstruction.' *Feminist Studies* 14/1: 51–65.

Posner, Judy. 1982. 'From Sex-Role Stereotyping to Sado Masochism.' *Fireweed* 14: 19–39.

Probyn, Elspeth. 1993. *Sexing the Self: Gendered Positions in Cultural Studies*. London: Routledge.

Radway, Janice. 1984/91. *Reading the Romance: Women, Patriarchy, and Polular Literature*. Chappell Hill: University of North Carolina Press.

Ramsdell, Elizabeth A., and Eugene L. Gaier. 1974. 'Identity and Reality Reflected in

Adolescent Fiction: The Early Sixties and the Early Seventies.' *Adolescence* 9/4: 577–93.

Randall, Stephan. 1991. 'Media.' *Playboy*, May, 40.

Reed, Evelyn. 1986. 'The Woman Question and the Marxist Method.' In *Cosmetics, Fashions, and the Exploitation of Women*, ed. J. Hansen and E. Reed, 55–74. New York: Pathfinders.

Reed, Sandra K., and Marilyn Coleman. 1981, 'Female Sex-Role Models in Adolescent Fiction: Changing Over Time?' *Adolescence* 16/63: 581–6.

Reinharz, Shulamit. 1992. *Feminist Methods in Social Research*. New York: Oxford University Press.

Roman, Leslie G., and Linda K. Christian-Smith. 1992. 'Introduction.' In *Becoming Feminine: The Politics of Popular Culture*, ed. L.G. Roman and L.K. Christian-Smith, 1–34. Philadelphia: Falmer.

Rosen, Marjorie, Maria Eftimiades, Sabrina McFarland, Lorenzo Benet, Todd Gold, Kristina Johnson, and Lyndon Stamber. 1992. 'Eating Disorders: A Hollywood History.' *People*, 17 February: 96–8.

Sarup, Madan. 1989. An *Introductory Guide to Post-Structuralism and Postmodernism*. Athens: University of Georgia Press.

Saunders, Carol S., and Bette A. Stead. 1986. 'Women's Adoption of a Business Uniform: A Content Analysis of Magazine Advertisements.' *Sex Roles* 15/3/4: 197–205.

Sawicki, Jana. 1991. *Disciplining Foucault: Feminism, Power, and the Body*. New York: Routledge.

Schwartz, D.M., M.G. Thompson, and C.L. Johnson. 1985. 'Anorexia Nervosa and Bulimia: The Sociocultural Context.' In *Theory and Treatment of Anorexia Nervosa and Bulimia*, ed. S. Emmett, 95–112. New York: Brunner/Mazel.

Schwichtenberg, Cathy. 1993. *The Madonna Connection*. Boulder: Westview.

Seaman, William R. 1992. 'Active Audience Theory: Pointless Populism.' *Media, Culture and Society* 14: 301–11.

Sexton, Donald E., and Phyllis Haberman. 1974. 'Women in Magazine Advertisements.' *Journal of Advertising Research* 14: 41–6.

Sheinin, Rachel. 1990. 'Body Shame: Body Image in a Cultural Context.' *The National Eating Disorder Information Centre Bulletin* 5/5.

Shevelow, Kathryn. 1989. *Women and Print Culture*. London and New York: Routledge.

Skeggs, Beverley, ed. 1995. 'Introduction.' In *Feminist Cultural Theory: Process and Production*, ed. Beverley Skeggs, 1–32. Manchester: Manchester University Press.

Smart, Barry. 1985. *Michel Foucault*. London: Tavistock.

Smith, Dorothy. 1980. 'An Analysis of Ideological Structures and How Women Are Excluded: Considerations for Academic Women.' In *Class, State, Ideology and*

Change: Marxist Perspectives, ed. J.P. Grayson, 252–67. Toronto: Holt, Rinehart and Winston.

– 1981. 'The Experienced World as Problematic: A Feminist Method.' The Twelfth Annual Sorokin Lecture, University of Saskatchewan, Saskatoon, 20 January.

– 1987. *The Everyday World as Problematic: A Feminist Sociology*. Boston: Northeastern University Press.

– 1988. 'Femininity as Discourse.' In *Becoming Feminine: The Politics of Popular Culture*, ed. L. Roman and L.K. Christian-Smith, 37–59. Philadelphia: Falmer.

– 1990a. *Texts, Facts, and Femininity: Exploring the Relations of Ruling*. London: Routledge.

– 1990b. *The Conceptual Practices of Power: A Feminist Sociology of Knowledge*. Toronto: University of Toronto Press.

Soley, Lawrence C., and Leonard N. Reid. 1988. 'Taking It Off: Are Models in Magazines Wearing Less?' *Journalism Quarterly* 65/4: 960–6.

Soper, Kate. 1993. 'Productive Contradictions.' In *Up against Foucault: Explorations of Some Tensions between Foucault and Feminism*, ed. C. Ramazanoglu, 29–50. London: Routledge.

Stabile, Carol A. 1997. 'Feminism and the Ends of Postmodernism.' In *Materialist Feminism: A Reader in Class, Difference, and Women's Lives*, ed. R. Hennessy and C. Ingraham, 395–408. London and New York: Routledge.

Stanger, Greta. 1986. 'The Representations of Family Change in Social Science Journals and Women's Magazines.' Doctoral dissertation, University of Tennessee.

Steinem, Gloria. 1990. 'Sex, Lies, and Advertising.' *MS Magazine*, July/August, 18.

Storey, John. 1993. *An Introductory Guide to Cultural Theory and Popular Culture*. Athens: University of Georgia Press.

Strinati, Dominic. 1995. *An Introduction to Theories of Popular Culture*. London: Routledge.

Sullivan, Gary L., and P.J. O'Connor. 1988. 'Women's Role Portrayals in Magazine Advertising: 1958–1983.' *Sex Roles* 18 (3/4): 181–8.

Sumner, Colin. 1979. *Reading Ideologies: An Investigation into the Marxist Theory of Ideology and Law*. London: Academic.

Taft, William T. 1982. *American Magazines for the 1980s*. New York: Hastings House.

Tarde, Jean Gabriel. 1903. *The Laws of Imitation*. Translated from 2nd French edition by Elsie Clews Parsons, with introduction by Frank H. Giddings. New York: Holt.

Tasker, Yvonne. 1991. 'Having It All: Feminism and the Pleasures of the Popular.' In *Off-Centre: Feminism and Cultural Studies*, ed. Sarah Franklin, Celia Lury, and Jackie Stacey, 85–96. London: HarperCollins Academic.

Thompson, John B. 1984. *Studies in the Theory of Ideology*. Cambridge: Polity.

Tuchman, Gaye. 1979. 'Women's Depiction by the Mass Media.' *Signs: Journal of Women in Culture and Society* 4: 528–37.

Tuchman, Gayle, Arlene Kaplan Daniels, and James Benet, eds. 1978. *Hearth and Home: Images of Women in the Mass Media.* New York: Oxford University Press.

Valverde, Mariana. 1985. 'The Class Struggles of the *Cosmo* Girl and the *Ms.* Woman.' *Heresies* 18: 78–82.

– 1991. 'As If Subjects Existed: Analysing Social Discourses.' *Canadian Review of Sociology and Anthropology* 18/2: 173–87.

Veblen, Thorstein. 1899. *The Theory of the Leisure Class: An Economic Study in the Evolution of Institutions.* New York: Macmillan.

Venkatesan, M., and Jean Losco. 1975. 'Women in Magazine Ads: 1959–71.' *Journal of Advertising Research* 15/5: 49–54.

Waelti-Walters, Jennifer. 1979. 'On Princesses: Fairy Tales, Sex Roles and Loss of Self.' *International Journal of Women's Studies* 2/2: 180–8.

Wagner, Louis G., and Janis B. Banos. 1973. 'Woman's Place: A Follow-up Analysis of the Roles Portrayed by Women in Magazine Advertisements.' *Journal of Marketing Research* 10: 213–14.

Walters, Suzanna Danuta. 1995. *Material Girls: Making Sense of Feminist Cultural Theory.* Berkeley: University of California Press.

Waters, Mary-Alice. 1986. 'Introduction: The Capitalist Ideological Offensive against Women Today.' In *Cosmetics, Fashions, and the Exploitation of Women,* ed. J. Hansen and E. Reed, 3–27. New York: Pathfinders.

Weedon, Chris. 1987. *Feminist Practice and Poststructural Theory.* Oxford: Basil Blackwell.

Weinberger, Marc G., Susan M. Petroshius, and Stuart A. Weston. 1979. 'Twenty Years of Women in Magazine Advertising: An Update.' In *1979 Educators' Conference Proceedings,* ed. N. Beckwith, Michael Houston, Robert Mittelstaedt, Kent B. Monroe, and Scott Ward, 373–7. Chicago: American Marketing Association.

Weinreich, Helen. 1978. 'Sex Role Socialization.' In *The Sex Role System,* ed. Jane Chetwynd and Oonagh Hartnett, 18–27. London: Routledge and Kegan Paul.

Whalen, Jeanne. 1994. 'Retailers Aim Straight at Teens.' *Advertising Age* (September) 5.

White, Cynthia L. 1970. *Women's Magazines, 1693–1968.* London: Michael Joseph.

Williams, Raymond. 1976. *Keywords: A Vocabulary of Culture and Society.* London: Fontana.

Williamson, Judith. 1978. *Decoding Advertisements: Ideology and Meaning in Advertising.* London: Marion Boyars.

Willis, Paul, with Simon Jones, Joyce Canaan, and Geoff Hurd. 1990. *Common Culture: Symbolic Work at Play in the Everyday Cultures of the Young.* Milton Keynes: Open University Press.

Wilson, Elizabeth. 1985. *Adorned in Dreams: Fashion and Modernity.* London: Virago Press.

– 1990. 'The New Components of the Spectacle: Fashion and Postmodernism.' In

Postmodernism and Society, ed. R. Boyne and A. Rattansi, 209–36. London: Macmillan.

– 1992. 'Fashion and the Postmodern Body.' In *Chic Thrills: A Fashion Reader*, ed. Juliet Ash and Elizabeth Wilson, 3–16. Berkeley: University of California Press.

Winship, Janice 1978. 'A Women's World: "Woman" – an Ideology of Femininity.' In *Women Take Issue: Aspects of Women's Subordination*, ed. Women's Studies Group, Centre for Contemporary Cultural Studies, University of Birmingham, 133–54. London: Hutchinson.

– 1981. '"Options – for the Way You Want to Live Now" or a Magazine for a Superwoman.' *Theory, Culture, and Society* 1/3: 44–65.

– 1987. *Inside Women's Magazines*. London: Pandora.

– 1991. 'The Impossibility of *Best*: Enterprise Meets Domesticity in the Practical Women's Magazines of the 1980s.' *Cultural Studies* 5/2: 131–56.

Wolf, Diane L. 1996. 'Situating Feminist Dilemmas in Fieldwork.' In *Feminist Dilemmas in Fieldwork*, ed. D.L. Wolf, 1–55. Boulder: Westview.

Wolf, Naomi. 1991. *The Beauty Myth*. Toronto: Vintage.

Wolseley, Roland E. 1971. *The Black Press*. Ames: Iowa State University Press.

Wood, James Playsted. 1971. *Magazines in the United States*. New York: Ronald Preson.

Wright, Elizabeth. 1984. *Psychoanalytical Criticism: Theory in Practice*. London: Methuen.

Young, Iris Marion. 1990. *Throwing Like a Girl and Other Essays in Feminist Philosophy and Social Theory*. Bloomington and Indianapolis: Indiana University Press.

Author Index

Subject Index

interviews as data, 109–11, 127–8, 146,
330 n. 20, 331 n. 4
interviewing girls, 106–7

Jackie, 62, 65, 87
jeans, importance of, 211–12
jouissance, 294–5

knowledge as meaning, 140–5

labelling as an aspect of school culture,
216–18, 224–8, 229–37
language role in consciousness, 286–8,
293–4
letters to the editor, 331–2 n. 1
literary methods as employed by sociologists, 10, 91–4, 119, 309. *See also* textual analysis
looks, importance of to girls, 230–4

Mademoiselle, 42
Madonna as a role model, 8, 35, 262
make-up use, 3, 177–81, 248, 266. *See
also* 'doing' the Subject
male approval: magazine appeals to, 189,
205–7; at school, 234–7
male authority, appeals to, 186–7,
188–90, 199–200, 205
male gaze, 32–3
market segmentation, 37–8, 40–2, 75
marketing research, 305
Marxist feminist analysis of magazines,
56–79, 97, 286–98, 309; issues in,
96–7
mass culture, 65, 85–6, 326 n. 2
materialist analysis: of ideology, 142–5;
of texts, 96–7, 117–18, 288–311
modes of objectification, 15
moralism in feminist debates, 34–5
MS, 305–6

mythology, 70–1

'naming' experience, importance of, 209,
247
'natural beauty,' appeals to, 123
negotiation of identity, 4
negotiation of meaning as a theoretical
construct, 128; analysis of, 128–45,
204–7, 254–68
'new traditionalism,' 30

objectified knowledge, 12–13, 140–5,
310–11
overdetermination, 59

peers, importance of, 211–37
performance theory, 5
personal problems as focus of magazine
advice, 27; appeal of, 163–8. *See also*
individualism
plaisir of reading, 294
pleasure: as an analytical theme, 62,
66–9, 77–8, 84–6, 125–6, 154–5, 164,
166–71, 300; rejection of, 158–9, as
resistance, 86
pleasures: of consumption, 5–7, 29, 35,
53; of femininity, 34–5; of reading,
66–7, 171–3, 250–3, 277, 294–5
popular culture: definition of, 58, 65–6,
219, 326 n. 2; relevance to feminist
cultural studies, 66
positioning of the reader, 85, 116, 138–9,
154, 169–71, 189–202, 204–7, 252–3,
327 n. 11
post-feminism, 30, 306; as a magazine
message, 30, 136–9
post-structuralism, usefulness for sociology, 92, 286–91
power, 15–16, 18, 141–5; competing
feminist views, 53; how power works